ASIA REBORN

BY

MARGUERITE HARRISON

Harper & Brothers Publishers

New York and London

1928

CONTENTS

BY WAY OF EXPLANATION

SHALL we ever see a United States of Asia? Will an Asiatic League of Nations be the final crystallization of the revolt of East against West? Is European civilization doomed to go down before that of Asia? Are the Yellow races to dominate the world instead of the White? What is the ferment that is stirring Asia to its foundations, and has it succeeded in putting the fear of God and of the Future into the peoples of the West?

Not long ago such questions would have been regarded by most of us as purely speculative, and far too "deep" for discussion in the daily press or current magazines, but our attitude has undergone a radical change since the World War. Actual happenings have made live news of abstract problems. We can no longer shudder agreeably and impersonally over a highly colored but purely imaginative picture of a world that has ceased to be "white." We realize that the complexion of international affairs has altered, that it is no longer possible for us to ignore the significance of recent events in Asia, which have made it apparent that something is stirring in that great continent— something which we must understand. Instead of the vague uneasiness created in our minds by the highly sensational literature of exponents of the so-called "racialism"—too often merely race prejudice—there has come a genuine desire to know "what is really going on in Asia."

To answer this question by any general statements is obviously impossible. The movements and tendencies that are influencing present-day developments in Asia are too complex to be dealt with empirically. They must be interpreted in the light of actual happenings since the World War—happenings of which most of us have only a fragmentary knowledge.

The average person, for example, has a very vague idea of the important territorial changes that have taken place in Asia since the World War. He cannot accurately define the actual inter-

national boundaries. He has no clear notion as to which countries are racially homogeneous or which have a heterogeneous
population. He knows practically nothing of the form of government in the independent Asiatic countries, little of the extent
to which the new movements have percolated among the masses
of the people. He has no conception of the fact that there are
millions of nomads still living under some form of tribal organization in Asia or of the social conditions among the agricultural and urban populations. He knows nothing of economic
situations as they affect internal affairs in the various countries.
He has the vaguest possible conception of the religious and racial
feuds and antagonisms. It would probably be news to most
people to hear of the wars that have been waged in Asia since
the world peace. The revolt of Kemalist Turkey, its war with
Greece and the establishment of the Turkish Republic, have
had a most profound influence on all of Asia. The creation of
the Mandate System and its administration is of vast importance.
The steady growth of Russian imperialism is realized by few
people.

There was no country in Asia, however remote, that did not
react to President Wilson's doctrine of self-determination. There
was no region, however isolated, that escaped the shock of the
great cataclysm in Soviet Russia. There are no peoples to-day
among Asia's teeming millions who have not responded more
or less to the call of nationalism and the challenge of "white"
superiority.

Consequently, any writer who attempts to outline the trend of
events in Asia must give his readers a succinct account of the
post-war history of Asiatic countries, singly and in relation to
the racial groups to which they belong. He must also outline
social economic and psychological conditions and Asia's reactions
to world movements in the light of historical happenings.

That is the task I have set myself to accomplish in this book,
based largely on my own observations in various Asiatic countries, where I have spent much time since 1919.

It has not been easy to condense all that has happened in Asia
since the Armistice into a single volume, particularly as it was
essential to preface the account with a short historical survey.

Many important happenings have necessarily been touched upon briefly and there are many unavoidable omissions.   But I have tried to throw into relief the important facts which may serve as a background for the appraisement of daily news dispatches from Asiatic countries, by the busy every-day individual who has no time or inclination for a profound study of history or political economy.

MARGUERITE HARRISON.

RABAT, MOROCCO, August 1, 1927.

ASIA REBORN

Chapter One

THE ASIATIC DRIFT

THE vital significance of recent developments in Asia to the world at large is a fact so universally accepted as to need no restatement. Since the World War we have all begun to realize that the popular catchword of the "unchanging East" stands for an amiable fiction. The boasted supremacy of the West, racial, cultural, and political, has been challenged, not to say imperiled, by actual happenings during the past few years—happenings that have occupied front pages in our newspapers and have affected, in various instances, our lives as well as our pocketbooks. They have awakened in many of us a genuine desire to understand the causes underlying the great movement sometimes called the Asiatic Renascence, which has brought about such radical changes in relations between Europe and Asia.

It is usual to attribute the present ferment in Asia to reactions produced by contacts with Europe, but we must go further back than the beginning of "Europeanization" for the fundamental impulse—back almost to the beginnings of a continually changing, rather than *un*changing, East.

The history of Asia has been largely determined by two factors which we do not always take into account—climate and geography. Look at the map and you will understand what I mean. The first thing you will notice is that one-third of the entire continent is occupied by Siberia, which has a population of less than twenty millions.

Why?

Because, although it is enormously rich in natural resources, it possesses a climate extremely rigorous and forbidding to all but the hardiest races.

Another large area on the map comprises the arid tablelands and mountain ranges of Central Asia—the roof of the world, where, for hundreds of miles on end, the lowest elevation is five thousand feet above sea-level and the average nearer ten thousand; where few crops will grow, few domestic animals can thrive, and life is a continual struggle to wrest bare means of subsistence from an ungrateful soil. This area includes most of Mongolia, Chinese Turkestan, and Tibet, parts of Afghanistan, and the central portion of Persia.

The Arabian Peninsula at the western gate of Asia, is more than half desert. Asia Minor and Syria are the only large areas in the Near East with sufficient rainfall in certain parts to produce substantial crops without extensive irrigation, and the rainfall all the way across the vast plateau of Central Asia is far below normal.

In contrast with these countries, where the population is sparse and living conditions are so difficult, are the overpopulated lands of China, India, and the Japanese Archipelago—overpopulated because it is in these regions that the most favorable conditions exist for human life and its development. China and India, since before the dawn of history, were the goal of successive migrations of tribes from the north in search of a milder climate and all-the-year-round pasturage. Undoubtedly at one time the climate of Central Asia was milder, the rainfall was more abundant than now, and the struggle for existence was not nearly so acute, but when men first began to preserve the traditions and records which constitute the beginnings of history, the forced migrations had already begun.

It is impossible to determine with any accuracy the reasons which prompted the earlier migrants from Central Asia to take certain roads. All we know is that the tide of humanity which moved steadily southward for many centuries gravitated toward three centres: the valley of the Yangtze-kiang river, the heart of modern China; the subcontinent of India beyond the Himalayas; and the valley of the Tigris and the Euphrates now known as Mesopotamia. The first invaders, who built up distinctive civilizations when they had reached their respective Canaans, corresponded to the three great divisions of the human family which we call roughly, the Mongol, the Aryan, and the Semitic.

The precise origin of these three great families is shrouded in the mist that still envelopes the prehistory of the human race. It is thought, however, that the Aryans originated in Europe somewhere near the present countries of Latvia and Lithuania. Certain it is that they form the basic stock from which all European peoples are descended. Some of them wandered into Asia, becoming the forbears of the Aryan inhabitants of the Asiatic continent—the Persians, Afghans, and Indians. The beginnings of the Semitic and Mongol races were on Asiatic soil. The Arab peoples, together with the Jews and Armenians, are commonly considered to constitute the Semitic family. The Mongol stock was split in very early times into two distinct branches, the eastern branch forming what we know as the Yellow races and the western offshoot developing into the Mongol-Tartar and Turanian groups comprising the Turks and many of the inhabitants of Central Asia.

The Aryans became the dominant race in India, absorbing or pushing farther south the original inhabitants; some of whom wandered as far east as Malaysia to escape the invaders. They were, in their turn, subjected to other invasions from the north at intervals, down to modern times, and it was only at the beginning of the last century that the Mogul dynasty, imposed on India by a Mongol-Tartar invasion three hundred years before, finally passed into oblivion.

The Mongols, who had taken possession of China, developed a very distinctive type, producing a remarkable civilization which had nothing whatever in common with the original Mongol stock. They were the people who overflowed into Korea and Japan, where they quickly differentiated themselves from the Mongols who had taken roots in the Yangtze Valley. The Chinese, who soon succeeded in building up a powerful state, regarded the Mongols of the north as barbarians, and several centuries before the birth of Christ the Great Wall of China was built to form a barrier between them and their northern kinsmen. The Chinese Empire withstood the southward pressure for many centuries, and its existence served to divert part of the tide of migrations westward rather than south.

The result was a series of invasions from the east, lasting for over a thousand years, which submerged the Roman Empire, plunged Europe into barbarism, and at one time created a vast Mongol-Tartar Empire which stretched from the shores of the Pacific to the gates of Vienna. These mass migrations westward only ceased in the middle of the fifteenth century, when the Russians in the north, and the Ottoman Turks farther south, had established powerful buffer-empires between Europe and Central Asia.

Semitic civilization, which produced series of great kingdoms in the valley of the Tigris and Euphrates, while it is supposed to have been founded by migrants from the east, received its distinctive character as well as its name, from the people who pressed into the fertile "Land between the Rivers" from the huge desert regions of Arabia. It survived many invasions. The Aryan Persians who had not followed the great mass of their people into India conquered and partly assimilated Mesopotamia. The Greeks and Romans coming from Europe reduced it to subjection. The genius of Mohammed produced a renascence among the Semitic peoples of Arabia. Inspired by the faith which bears his name, his successors, the Khalifs, became temporal as well as spiritual rulers of a Moslem Empire of which Baghdad was long the capital. The Mongol-Tartars halted their march toward Europe to take possession of and lay waste the Empire of the Baghdad Khalifs, but the Semites subjected to continual pressure, nevertheless grew and expanded with the remarkable vitality so characteristic of their race, until diffusion brought weakness. The Saracen Empire that extended across North Africa and through Southern Spain to Europe, became too widespread to have very deep roots in Asia.

Mesopotamia, owing to climatic changes and the destruction of its wonderful irrigation system, by the earlier Semitic invaders, became less desirable. The Arab countries which had been centres of Semitic civilization were eventually absorbed by the Turanian Turks as part of the Ottoman Empire. Finally, they took possession of the Khalifate, thus becoming the champions and defenders of Islam, the great religion which owes its origin to Semitic genius.

Thus the shifting of population which had taken place during a period extending over many thousand years had resulted in a more or less stable condition by the end of the sixteenth century. The struggle for existence in Central Asia had brought about such a thinning and deterioration of its peoples that mass migrations were no longer to be feared from the Asiatic plateau. Such incursions as took place spent their force on Persia, which underwent many changes, now dominating or being dominated by her Turanian neighbors; but few of these readjustments were felt beyond the limits of Central Asia.

India was held together more or less, politically speaking, by her Mogul conquerors, but she was less a nation than a continent. Her people were divided by barriers of religion and caste more powerful than deserts, seas, or mountains. She was apparently set for ever in a many-partitioned and rigid mould!

The Chinese Empire was self-contained behind the impenetrable wall of its ancient civilization, and the internal struggles for power within it, had scarcely any repercussions in the rest of Asia. Few people had even heard of the thickly populated islands of the Japanese Archipelago. They had scarcely come within the range of Asiatic, much less Western vision.

It was during this period of relative quiet, a very short interval in world-history, that the Europeans who had begun to engage in trade and commerce with Asia, thanks to the discovery of sea routes to India and the Far East and the comparative safety of the land routes since the cessation of the Western migrations, began to speak of the Unchanging East. They could not realize that the natural forces making for flux and change were only temporarily inactive. However, to the rest of the world Asia was an inert mass, presenting a more and more inviting field for European exploitation for more than three centuries.

By the middle of the eighteenth century the increasing rivalry between France and England, the principal competitors for the trade of India, had brought about territorial aggressions. Control of certain markets necessitated political control, and the struggle for the possession of India ending in the victory of the British, laid the foundations for the era of Western Imperialism in Asia. All the influences which were bringing about social and political changes seemed to be exerted from without, until at the close of the last century it became apparent that the age-old agencies of climate and geography still played an important part in the destinies of the Asiatic continent.

India and China once more became subject to pressure from the north. Central Asia was the gateway for penetration both of India and of China as in the days of the mass-migrations, but instead of the hordes of barbarians who formerly stormed the mountain-gates to India and the man-built barriers of the Great Chinese Wall, the approaches to the south were being steadily undermined by the political, diplomatic, and military manœuvres of another great Power, driven, though in a different form, by the same instinct of self-preservation.

Russia, originally the buffer Empire between Asia and Europe, had grown almost to incredible proportions. Situated as she was between two continents, with a population part European, part Asiatic, Russia for a long time lingered at the crossroads. With the consolidation of the Empire had come development of foreign trade and commerce, which necessitated an outlet to the sea. Russia was a landlocked country. The great rivers which served as internal arteries for trade were useless as long as their mouths could be blocked by hostile Powers. The Black Sea afforded no exit to the Mediterranean as long as the Ottoman Empire held the Dardanelles. There was the Baltic to the north, but access to it was blocked by Sweden. To the east were the vast steppes of Siberia, the plateaux of Central Asia, and beyond both, to the south, were the treasure-houses of the Orient, the goals of world-commerce,—China and India.

It was not long before Russia realized that, being shut off from the sea routes, she must develop land routes of trade. After several hundred years of expansion she had, by the beginning of the eighteenth century, secured a precarious exit to the Baltic Sea through harbors often blocked with ice, and the road thence by sea to the Indies was long and perilous. The Turks still shut off the entrance to the Mediterranean and the overland-carry to the Gulf of Persia which, until the opening of the Suez Canal almost in our own day, was the shortest route from Europe to India.

There remained to Russia the development of the land routes to the Orient, which was enjoined on the Russian people in the famous document popularly supposed to be the last will and testament of Peter the Great. Penetration of Central Asia was systematized through the formulation of a definite policy by Russia in the middle of the nineteenth century.

Meanwhile circumstances had brought about the colonization of Siberia, and the Russians found themselves possessors of a huge Asiatic Empire continuous with their dominions in Europe, but equally devoid of sea outlets except a few Pacific ports that were icebound for nearly half the year. The impulse to push south in the Far East became just as imperative as the impulse towards India. What had happened thousands of years before was happening again. Race instinct was driving Russia south, just as it had driven the Mongols and the Tartars!

But conditions at the beginning of the twentieth century were very different from those which prevailed during the great migrations. Economic and commercial needs quite as imperative, had caused Great Britain to penetrate by sea routes into Asia as Russia was seeking to penetrate by land, and the conflict between the two Powers, of which the end is not yet in sight, has obscured the elemental significance of Russia's southward march. It is just as well to remember that if Great Britain had no stake in India, and if Russia were still a monarchical instead of a Soviet Empire, she would have an eye on the Punjab and on the Yangtze Valley just the same.

There is another phase of the problem of Asia which springs from causes just as fundamental as Russia's southward advance: it is the Japanese question. Japan, whose existence was scarcely noticed for several centuries after contacts had begun between Europe and Asia, emerged from the mists of the Pacific as a full-fledged nation with an expansionist policy, almost overnight. From a medieval hermit-kingdom she developed into a world Power within less than half a century. Her imperialism, which soon made itself felt, came from more than mere lust of conquest. It was the result of the industrialization of a great part of her population, which had become so large that it could no longer be supported on the land. The need for markets and raw materials has been driving her ever further afield, and this need is being supplemented by another which promises to become just as imperative.

Japan will not be able to keep her teeming millions very much longer within the limits of her archipelago—even the acquisition of the Philippines if that were possible would only temporarily satisfy her future necessities. The natural way for her to go is over the route by which her people came; westward across the Japan Sea, through Korea and Manchuria, to China. She must sooner or later come into collision with Russia, by all the laws that have influenced race movements and race conflicts since the beginning of the world.

If we keep these facts in mind they will help us to understand many things in connection with Asiatic politics. The great movements which are stirring Asia to its foundations cannot be dissociated from them. Whatever may be the political, cultural, and social developments of the future in the countries composing the Asiatic continent, however the balance of power may shift, and whatever international combinations may be formed, they will always be influenced by the drift of all Asiatic peoples towards certain centres, of which the valley of the Yangtze-kiang and India are the most important. They are the pivots around which revolves the future of Asia.

Chapter Two

THE COURSE OF EMPIRE

WHILE climate and geography have had a profound influence in shaping the course of events in Asia, they are slow-moving forces and their effects are not apparent, unless viewed in long perspective down the vista of centuries. But we do not need perspective to perceive the changes brought about in Asiatic countries as the result of contacts with the West. The Europeanization of Asia, as it has been called, has been accomplished within a comparatively short space of time, and it is responsible in large measure for the awakening of the East and its revolt against the West.

The contacts which produced this state of affairs were the outgrowth of certain natural causes such as have turned the course of empire towards the East more than once during the history of the world. The penetration of Western Asia by the Greeks, who colonized Asia Minor and at one time reached Northern India, was the inevitable consequence of their rise to power and their need for expansion, and the Romans followed in their footsteps; the check to Arab dominion administered through the Crusades in the Middle Ages was in response not only to religious fervor, but also to an instinct of self-preservation on the part of Europe.

In modern times, the possession of sea-power and the development of a superior material and mechanical civilization, enabled the peoples of the congested and largely industrialized countries of the West to expand in all directions in search of new outlets for population, new trade channels, and new sources of supply for raw materials. Rivalries between the great Powers and efforts to secure a monopoly of the benefits from expansion, gave birth to an Imperialism which sought not only commercial but political domination, even in countries where there was no attempt at colonization. This was particularly true in Asia.

9

Europeanization was one of the instruments in the imperial policy of penetration and domination, and so persuaded were Western statesmen of its efficacy that it would have been difficult to convince the Empire-builders of the nineteenth century that it would act as a boomerang against them. But, as a French missionary in India the Abbé Roussillon, recently remarked of Orientals: "Having taught them to make plates we need scarcely be surprised to find that they have also learned to break them over our heads." Imperialism, however, was a very gradual growth, less the goal than the means to an end in the beginning of the contacts between Asia and Europe.

Asia with its immense wealth and natural resources, was the nearest, the most promising, and consequently the first portion of the known world to engage the attention of our European forbears, before they learned that there was a new world to the west. There was trade between the Mediterranean countries and Asia long before the Greeks established their first colonies in Asia Minor. All through the Dark Ages and during medieval times, whenever the migrations from the East receded or were pushed back, trade grew up spontaneously. Christianity came from Asia and took root in Europe, to be carried back in the seventh century by the first Nestorian missionaries, who penetrated as far as China, and some people even think to Japan itself.

The adventurous early traders took all the ancient highways from Europe to Asia. Foremost among them were the Venetians and Genoese who went with native caravans across Asia Minor to Persia and thence to India; from Syria to Damascus and Baghdad, then the seat of an Arab Khalifate, and to India through the Persian Gulf; or from Constantinople through the Black Sea to Central Asia. Others embarked from Egypt for the journey to the Orient through the Red Sea, and a few hardy souls, like Marco Polo, traveled overland to China across Central Asia from the Mediterranean, while Russian traders began to come down the Volga to the Caspian Sea, and down the valley of the Oxus to Khiva, Bokhara and Samarkand.

Many of these routes were closed after the rise of the Ottoman Empire, which was almost continually at war with one or more European countries, in an effort to expand its dominions in the

West. But with the discovery of the new sea routes to India and the East via the Cape of Good Hope by Vasco da Gama in 1498, and of the passage through the Straits between South America and Terra del Fuego by Magellan a few years later, not only new trade-channels but also new roads to conquest in Asia were opened to the nations of Europe. If it had not been for the discovery of the two Americas and later of the Australian continent and New Zealand, the "Return to Asia" might have assumed the proportions of a European invasion.

As it was, however, the flood of colonial expansion was diverted in several directions and of all the European Powers the only ones that acquired possessions of any consequence on the Asiatic mainland during the era of expansion, were Great Britain, France, and Russia. The Portuguese, once the foremost maritime nation of the world, declined after the sixteenth century, and within a comparatively short space of time had nothing to show for their efforts at expansion in Asia but a few scattered trading posts in India, the Malay States, and China. Their failing energies were concentrated on the newly discovered Western Hemisphere, where they disputed with Spain the right to an overseas Empire. The Spanish had no Asiatic possessions and never went far beyond the Philippines, where they ousted the Japanese who had penetrated into Luzon and several other islands, in the early part of the sixteenth century.

It would be far beyond the limits of a book like this to describe the gradual process by which European expansion crystallized into Imperialism. The concessions and privileges wrested from weak rulers and states torn by internal dissensions, for the purpose of trade or as strategic points in the long line of communications between Europe and Asia, grew gradually in political importance, until finally competition for Asiatic trade brought about a mad scramble for territorial footholds and spheres of influence, in the last half of the nineteenth century. A brief survey of the character and extent of European penetration of Asia up to the beginning of the present century, when the tide of Imperialism touched the high-water mark, is sufficient to show by what means Europe laid the foundations for the Asiatic renascence.

It was inevitable that the countries which had always proved the magnets for Asiatic races, should also draw the attention of the European nations seeking markets and trade in Asia. Consequently India and China became centres of attraction.

The English were the first to take root in India, and the British East India Company, which received its charter from Queen Elizabeth in 1600, soon captured the major portion of the India trade. Undoubtedly the East India Company's object in the beginning was merely to obtain commercial privileges from the Mogul Emperors; but such was the unsettled state of the country that, as its interests grew larger, it was obliged to institute a certain amount of administrative control in and around its trading-posts. The supremacy of the Company did not long go unchallenged, however. By the end of the seventeenth century it had a formidable rival in the French East India Company.

Competition between the two companies led to endless intriguing and scheming, each trying to acquire paramount influence with the decadent Mogul rulers and the native princes. Finally the Seven Years' War in Europe, in which France and England were opposed, afforded an opportunity for a show-down. The Continental battle fields were extended to the colonies, and within ten years the French had lost Canada and India, and Great Britain had laid the foundations for a Dominion and an Empire. Nevertheless, it was not until nearly a hundred years later that India became an integral part of the British Empire.

The East India Company continued to administer affairs in India. British troops under Clive had been sent out to defend the Company's possessions during the war with France, which resulted in securing its undisputed right to expansion in India, but the British government for a long time confined itself to the exercise of a certain amount of control over the Company's actions. The Government of India Act, passed in 1784, provided for the appointment of a Governor General by the Crown, and for the creation of a Council, both responsible to the British Parliament.

Meanwhile the Company's territorial possessions had grown to formidable size. Bombay was a gift from King Charles II, who had received it as a part of the dowry of his Portuguese wife. Large slices of Southern India were ceded by the French; Calcutta, the nucleus of the present province of Bengal, was a land grant from the Mogul Emperors; other lands were acquired by purchase from native rulers. From time to time the sovereigns of small states sought the Company's protection and became its vassals in return for aid against their more aggressive neighbors.

All this while there had been no definite program for the consolidation of British power in India. The assumption of authority was so gradual, and so much the result of circumstance rather than design, that British policy was constantly changing. Occasionally it became necessary for England to engage in campaigns against the rulers of native states, particularly after the collapse of Mogul sovereignty, when but for the British, there would have been complete anarchy in India; but on the whole the first century of British rule in India was mainly an effort to maintain the East India Company's trade monopoly through the least possible extension of administrative control. This state of affairs resulted in a division of India which has continued down to the present day. A large portion of the country known as British India, fell under direct British administration, and the rest remained in the hands of native rulers, who one by one became vassals of the Crown, but retained their power to greater or lesser degree.

Two hundred and fifty years of more or less uninterrupted control by the East India Company brought about many changes in British India. Millions of Indians came under the influence of Western civilization, exerted by administrators good, bad, and indifferent. There were periods of corruption and periods of exceedingly honest administration. Men like Warren Hastings advocated reforms which were neglected or carried out several generations later. Western education had been introduced, but in haphazard manner; European customs, manners, and religion, had reacted on, but had not been assimilated by, the Indians. The result of the clash of the two opposing civilizations was the great Indian Mutiny, which ended in the liquidation of the East India Company and the assumption by the Crown of full control over British India. Queen Victoria was proclaimed Empress of India in 1877, becoming the ruler of a subcontinent, with over three hundred million inhabitants, speaking more languages, professing more religions, divided by more social barriers, than any other peoples occupying territory of the same extent anywhere in the whole world.

By this time the imperialistic policy of Great Britain had been definitely formulated. India was to be a link in the great Empire on which the sun would never set. Europeanization was to bring about her complete acquiescence in the Pax Britannica. With the understanding of Western ideals she would appreciate all the more the inestimable benefits of British rule. We shall see how subsequent developments entirely upset these calculations; the Empire builders in India, from Lord Dalhousie to Lord Curzon, who has been sometimes described as the last of the great Proconsuls, did not foresee all the pitfalls of Europeanization.

The old causes of discontent were largely removed among the more intelligent classes, but in their place was the new ferment of Nationalism largely inspired by European events such as the unification of Italy and the consolidation of the German Empire. By 1885 the Nationalist movement had become so well organized that it was consolidated in the Indian National Congress, which thereafter played an important part in Indian politics.

India's pivotal position as well as its immense resources, made it of vital importance in the imperial scheme. It was the halfway point between Europe and the Far East. Gibraltar, Suez, Egypt, South Africa, India, Singapore, all under British control, were so many stages from England towards the valley of the Yangtze-kiang, the center of the coveted "China trade."

Burma, strategically most important as affording a land approach to China, was the next country to come under direct British administration. By 1900 only the little independent kingdom of Siam and the small states composing Indo-China prevented the extension of British influence across all of Southern Asia from the Persian Gulf to the Pacific. Even France, which had acquired a protectorate over Indo-China, was neatly shut off from Singapore and the Malacca Straits, which controlled the entrance from the Pacific to the Indian Ocean. Within her small limits, however, Indo-China was a French India undergoing very much the same process of Europeanization as her huge neighbor.

While Great Britain had been consolidating her Indian Empire, and France had found consolation for exclusion from India in Indo-China, Russia had been extending her Asiatic dominions. In beginning a discussion of Russian expansion in Asia, it is important for us to bear in mind that it has always been an open question whether Russia is an Asiatic or a European Power. Certainly, if we maintain that Russia belongs to Europe, she is the only Western Power which has colonized on the Asiatic continent. When all is said and done, this fact places Russia on a different footing from the other great Powers in Asia. The colonization of Siberia has given her an inalienable right to a voice in Asiatic affairs. Perhaps the recognition of this right, apart from their racial and moral kinship, makes the Asiatics less antagonistic to the Russians than to any other foreign people.

Russian imperialism, as far as Siberia was concerned, did not involve the crushing or subjection of an ancient culture or an ancient civilization. At no period in history, until after its exploration and colonization by Russia, was there any central government in Siberia. Its various tribes never at any time formed a federation or looked up to one overlord, except for a very shadowy claim of the Manchu Emperors of China to overlordship in Eastern Siberia. The Russians found nothing,—therefore they could destroy nothing. What little they did was constructive, and Siberia to this day, with its immense undeveloped resources, is still to Russia what the Great West was a generation ago to the United States—a pioneer country on which the Russian people have a prior claim.

The first Russian traders began to buy furs from the Siberian tribespeople in the Urals, during the relatively quiet intervals between westward migrations of the Mongols and Tartars which swept over Russia until the middle of the fifteenth century, but it was not until the invasions from the East had ceased, that penetration of Siberia really began. The indomitable restless Cossacks were the first settlers. Sometimes they went of their own free will, sometimes whole communities were deported, by order of the Czar, in consequence of some outbreak or rebellion. They were followed by other political refugees and a steady stream of pioneers and adventurers. The first capital of the new province was Siber, which gave the country its name.

By the middle of the seventeenth century, Russia had extended the boundaries of her Empire to Lake Baikal, four thousand miles from Moscow—and this in an area where the only transportation was by rivers frozen for a good part of the year and on roads that were little more than trails in the wilderness.

The colonization of Siberia thus far had been no easy task. It was a country subject to terrible extremes of heat and cold, icy winds, torrential rains, fierce snow storms, and its land communications were across vast steppes and interminable stretches of wild desolate country inhabited by nomad and semi-sedentary tribes.

Notwithstanding these difficulties the Russians pressed steadily eastward, obeying the instinct that bade them seek sea-outlets for their huge inland empire. Eventually they obtained from China all of Eastern Siberia to the seaboard, principally through a series of treaties of which the first, the treaty of Nerchinsk signed in 1689, was the first ever concluded between China and a European Power.

The Chinese Emperors who thus signed away their claims to Eastern Siberia doubtless attached little importance to the resignation of titular sovereignty of such wild and barren territory which did not invite settlement, and whose trade was negligible. In the main their relations with Russia were friendly, and the Russians were the first Europeans to receive permission to send a permanent mission to Peking in the days of Catherine the Great.

During the latter half of the nineteenth century the port of Vladivostok was opened, affording Russia access to the Japan Sea, and the opening wedge for penetration farther south was driven into Manchuria. Moscow was joined with the Pacific by the Trans-Siberian Railway, and the Russians not only secured permission to construct the last lap of it across Manchuria, part of the Chinese Empire, but also obtained a leasehold of a commercial port Dalny, and a naval base Port Arthur, on the Yellow Sea.

It was not difficult for Russia to consolidate her power in her Siberian possessions. As we have said before, there had never been any central government in Siberia, and the Russians found the inhabitants very amenable to their authority. Besides the Cossacks, who belonged in a class by themselves, there were other distinct communities and innumerable tribes, mostly of Mongol-Tartar origin; some of these, such as the inhabitants of Yakutsk, had well defined forms of self-government and prosperous towns and settlements; others like the Buriats, lived in villages during the winter and took to their tents in summer; still others, like the Kirghiz who roamed the vast steppes of southwestern Siberia, were genuine nomads.

The Russians, being partly Asiatic themselves, thoroughly understood how to handle these people. Wherever it was possible they were permitted to exercise local self-government, being required only to pay taxes, to recognize the sovereignty of the Czar, and not to molest the Russian colonists. The latter fell into two classes: the farmers, who almost invariably had title to the land they worked, either through purchase or through a grant from the Russian government, and the inhabitants of the new towns, which had grown up around trading-posts. They acted as middlemen for the sale and barter of skins, wool, hides, grain.

Besides the colonists there was a third class of what might be called involuntary immigrants—the enormous numbers of political exiles and prisoners. The practice of deporting rebellious subjects and political malcontents to Siberia, begun in the reign of Ivan the Terrible, grew apace with the centuries, and a very terrible thing it was. Soon exile became one of the most frequent forms of punishment under the penal code, and in 1823 the famous Bureau of Exile was formed. It was this Bureau, which had representatives in each of the Siberian provinces, that was responsible for the condemnation of thousands of human beings to a living death, in the penal settlements scattered throughout the country, where conditions were simply appalling.

Many of the political prisoners and virtually all the criminals were employed in building roads and working in the mines which were constantly being prospected and opened on the slopes of the Urals, and along the Amur river, the great artery of Eastern Siberia. The penal settlements of Shilka and Nerchinsk where the prisoners worked in lead and quicksilver mines, dying slow deaths from poisoning, will go down in the annals of history with the Black Hole of Calcutta and the torture-chambers of the Inquisition. Here and there were settlements of political exiles which later grew into flourishing towns, and it was not an uncommon thing for the criminals who survived their terms of imprisonment to settle down to prospecting, farming, or trapping in Siberia. In time these various elements formed a sturdy independent population, too much occupied with the business of wresting a living from unwilling Nature to bother consciously about expansion. The southward pressure came from the foreign office in St. Petersburg.

With Siberia as an immediate base, however, Russian penetration of Manchuria continued apace. Russian settlements were built up along the Chinese Eastern Railway connecting the Trans-Siberian system with China and the Pacific. Russian influence was paramount in Peking, and the way was gradually being paved for the extension of the Russian sphere of influence in the direction of the Yangtze-kiang Valley—all of which was scarcely less displeasing to Great Britain than the Russian advance in Central Asia which was threatening the Empire of India.

Russia's course of action in this part of Asia was very different from that which she had followed in Siberia, being governed by totally dissimilar conditions. Peopled by descendants of the Mongol-Tartar hordes who once claimed the Dukes of Moscow as vassals, the Moslem kingdoms of Central Asia still retained for several centuries the traditions of pomp and power and the remains of an ancient culture, in spite of Russian penetration.

This penetration was purely peaceful in character till the middle of the nineteenth century, when Russia began to sense the danger of British influence which was expanding from India through Afghanistan and Southern Persia, and reaching out towards the region east of the Caspian and north of Afghanistan. By a series of brilliant military campaigns accompanied by a frenzied activity in railway construction, she succeeded in subduing or securing the allegiance of the two Emirs of Khiva and Bokhara, and in virtually annexing Turkestan and the Trans-Caspian province as part of the Russian Empire.

Still earlier she had pushed down through the Caucasus to the narrow strip of country which separates the Black Sea from the Caspian Sea. She had subdued the small independent states of which it was composed, including the kingdom of Georgia, and adding portions of Armenia and Azerbaijan from Turkey and Persia respectively, had annexed them all together as the province of Trans-Caucasia.

In all this territory the Russians were supreme politically and commercially, but they never made any attempt at real colonization. They had no need for outlets, for a surplus population— the Russian Empire was much underpopulated. What they needed were warm-water ports and the products of warm countries. Central Asia was a halting place in the march to India, and possession of the Caucasus was a move towards Constantinople, the coveted exit to the Mediterranean. It was in an effort to checkmate this last move that the British, until shortly before the World War, were frequently on the side of the Turks in any dispute between Russia and the Ottoman Empire.

The conquered provinces were administered by Imperial governors who left native institutions very much as they were, confining their activities to collecting taxes and tributes and to protecting the interests of their countrymen. Turkestan, where an important cotton industry existed at the beginning of the present century, was the only region to which Russians emigrated in any great numbers. Notwithstanding the fact that the Russians did infinitely less for the inhabitants of Central Asia than the British did in India, and were often despotic and frequently brutal, they never aroused the same antagonism and hatred. "Scratch a Russian and you will find a Tartar," used as a term of disparagement in the West, was an open-sesame east of the Caspian. Different as they were on the surface, there were elements in common between Russian and Asiatic culture.

The opening of sea routes to Asia neutralized the importance of the Ottoman Empire as a buffer between East and West. The Turks had found a ready-made civilization and a ready-made commercial system among the Greeks and Armenians of Asia Minor, and they had not bestirred themselves to learn to administer and govern. Consequently they were constantly losing through revolts and rebellions the territory which they had won by conquest, and their Empire was held together only by strict observance of the "divide and rule" principle.

By the end of the last century they had lost control of Egypt and of the Red Sea; Turkey in Europe, which at one time had extended nearly to the gates of Vienna, had been gradually reduced by the amputation of Greece and the Balkan States until it included only Thrace and Macedonia. Turkey in Asia consisted of Asia Minor and Syria, both seething with racial and religious hatreds, and Arabia, restive and rebellious. Only the spiritual prestige of the Khalifate and the tradition of temporal power attached to the office of Khalif, which was vested in the Ottoman sovereigns, held the Empire together. Moreover, none of the European Powers wished to see the actual dismemberment of Turkey. The problem of its partition was far too delicate a one to be precipitated. Besides Great Britain, the Mediterranean powers and the Balkan States, each of which would expect to gain a share of the Ottoman spoils, there was Germany, who coming into the imperial race rather late in the day, had chosen the Near East as her especial field, and had her own designs on India through Turkey and Mesopotamia.

For all these reasons and also because Turkey and the Arab countries were without the commercial lure of China and the Indies, there were very few attempts at foreign penetration. The only infringements of Turkey's sovereignty had been the granting of certain privileges known as "capitulations" to European governments for the benefit of their nationals residing within the Ottoman Empire. By the capitulations they acquired a special status so that they were not subject to Moslem or Ottoman law but came under the legal jurisdiction of their respective countries. However, there were relatively few foreigners in Turkey; and Europeanization had not made much progress within the Ottoman Empire.

In spite of the important rôle she had played in the history of Asia up to the end of the seventeenth century, Persia was of very little importance as a nation during the period of European expansion. Her trade and commerce were stagnating and her internal development at a standstill. Nevertheless, there were certain contacts between her and the West that were destined later to bring forth fruit. Nasr-ed-Din Shah, who ruled Persia during the last quarter of the nineteenth century, was the first Persian sovereign to go to Europe. He travelled extensively abroad and

THE COURSE OF EMPIRE

brought back many European ideas and expensive tastes. Partly to gratify these and partly from a genuine desire to improve conditions among his subjects, he granted many important concessions to foreign firms which were the first steps towards the influx of new ideas that later led to real reforms.

As far as the rest of the world was concerned, Persia, with Afghanistan and Tibet, constituted a sort of political No Man's Land over which Great Britain and Russia were fighting a titanic battle for supremacy.

China was one of the first countries to feel, and one of the last to succumb to, the pressure of Europeanization. Always the goal of Western traders, Cathay with its wonders dominated the imagination of venturesome spirits in Europe from before the days of Marco Polo. The opening of the sea route to China by the Portuguese was followed by a tremendous growth of the China trade, which was eventually largely monopolized by the British East India Company; but for two hundred and fifty years foreign intercourse with China was conducted through a single centre, the port of Macao, the only place where foreigners were allowed to live. True, occasional travellers penetrated into the interior, but they were not allowed to stay. Peking had been visited by occasional missions, but none had ever been permitted to remain permanently except, as we have seen, a semi-diplomatic Russian mission.

After a while, foreign merchants were permitted to go to Canton during the trading season, but all intercourse between foreign representatives and the Chinese government was carried on through the intermediary of an association of merchants known as the Co-Hong.

Whether there was any foreign trade or not was a matter of supreme indifference to the central government, and indeed to the overwhelming majority of the inhabitants of the Celestial Empire. While they had a despotic and actually an alien government, since the ruling race of Manchus represented only a small minority, the Chinese State itself, above all dynastic and internal changes, was unchanging and immutable, the symbol of the oldest continuous civilization on earth. Self-contained economically, socially, and intellectually, the Chinese could not conceive of the need for outside intercourse with peoples whom they felt to be immeasurably inferior to themselves in culture and civilization. They never doubted the permanence and immutability of their institutions.

Unfortunately, too, there was little in their first contacts with the West to encourage the Chinese to abandon their policy of exclusion. The strangers were vulgar, noisy and pushing, arrogant and self-assertive in Chinese eyes—often unscrupulous, not considering it necessary to observe European standards in dealing with Chinese merchants; Peking continued to ignore them, notwithstanding the fact that foreign trade, particularly British trade with China, continued to grow by leaps and bounds.

Finally, attempts by the Chinese officials to suppress the traffic in opium, largely carried on from India in British bottoms, resulted in a war between Great Britain and China ostensibly over this issue but really to force the opening of China to outside commerce.

Vigorous bombardments of Chinese ports, which the Chinese were utterly unable to counter because of their lack of modern military equipment, finally forced the government to sign the treaty of Nanking which opened China to foreign trade through five seaports; recognized the equal rights of foreigners with natives in China; ceded the island of Hongkong at the mouth of the Yangtze-kiang to the British.

But the treaty of Nanking was forced from the Chinese, and they never accepted it except as a disagreeable necessity. On the other hand, British penetration of China proceeded inexorably and methodically till the inevitable friction brought matters to a head. The French, who had acquired important commercial interests in Southern China, joined the British in a demand that their governments should be respected and the interests of their nationals safeguarded, and another war which ended in 1860, with the capture of Peking by Allied Forces, marked the virtual capitulation of the old China to the West.

After that, the imperial authorities were powerless to stop European invasion. Little by little a large part of the natural resources of China fell into Western hands. By the various treaties and agreements forced on the Empire following the

Allied occupation of their capital, the Chinese were gradually obliged to open the valley of the Yangtze-kiang, the key to the Empire and the goal of many nations, to international trade. In addition a whole chain of treaty ports was added to those already in existence along the seaboard; foreigners and their officials and consular representatives were given the right to travel in the interior; the ministers of foreign Powers were allowed to live in Peking and to negotiate on terms of equality with the imperial officials. It was not long before foreign advisers were included among these same officials—the Customs service in particular becoming a British-administered department, under the famous Sir Robert Hart who held the post for nearly fifty years.

The period between 1860 and 1900 was a period of dissolution for China. The whole theory on which the unity of the Empire was based—the immutability of the Chinese State and the inviolability of the Imperial House—had been shaken to its foundations when the Allies first entered Peking. There remained only the sacredness of the family. With the prestige of the throne destroyed, the Chinese began to revive their ancient hatred of the alien Manchu dynasty which had seized the power three hundred years before. The eighteen provinces of China, each quite distinct, with individual differences of manners, customs, languages, and even of races, had begun to sense the slackening of the bonds that held them together. One after another the dependencies of the Empire passed under alien influences—Tibet, Mongolia, Siam, Tonkin, Burma, either fell into the hands of other powers or maintained a divided allegiance. Rebellions became chronic all over the Celestial Kingdom.

The central government at Peking came more and more under foreign influence. Extraterritoriality, which included the immunity of foreigners from the jurisdiction of Chinese courts and their right to be tried by a foreign judiciary for all offenses committed on Chinese soil, had been established in the treaty ports in the early days when the contemptuous superiority of the Chinese gladly conceded to the despised foreigners the right to settle their own disputes in their limited concessions. But the new treaties opening up the interior of the country to foreigners carried with them the extension of these privileges, and their abuse was one of the chief reasons for the intense hatred of Europeans which succeeded the old scornful indifference. Extraterritoriality had come to be regarded as a menace to China's sovereignty, which indeed it was. By 1900, practically every European Power enjoyed and incidentally abused its privileges.

Even more serious than this danger were the constant efforts of the Powers to obtain territorial footholds in China. The era of the "Unequal Treaties," begun by endeavors of foreign states to secure trade rights and protection for their Nationals, developed into a race among the treaty Powers for predominant influence in China.

The number of treaty ports, leased territories, and foreign-controlled concessions, continued to grow apace until the ancient Empire of China was like a well-worn blanket dotted with tiny moth-holes. Rarely if ever were the concessions to foreign interests reciprocated by any real equivalents to China. The Imperial government in spite of sporadic efforts at reforms was hopelessly hidebound; its officials and provincial governors were hopelessly corrupt. European influence had undermined all that was stable in China without as yet giving her anything in place of the old institutions, but Western education was nevertheless making headway. Everywhere missionaries were encouraged and supported by their governments as adjuncts to commercial penetration. It was believed that Europeanization through Christian teachings would create an atmosphere favorable to the West, by encouraging the Chinese to overthrow their reactionary government. We shall see how the new knowledge later proved a double-edged sword.

Great Britain and Russia, until the close of the nineteenth century, led in the race for spheres of influence in China, and Great Britain scored first in obtaining control of the coveted Yangtze-kiang Valley, through her ownership of Hongkong and concessions in all the principal river ports. Russia virtually controlled Manchuria and the North China trade. Germany, which had come late into the imperial race in Asia, had a long lease-hold of the Shantung peninsula, with the best harbor north of Hongkong, at Tsingtao. France had her leased territories at Kwang-chow in South China and was building a railway system up into the southern provinces from her own protectorate of Indo-China, and all the lesser Powers shared lesser spoils. America was the only great nation with no leaseholds and no imperialistic designs on China's territorial integrity, and she confined her efforts to the maintenance of the "Open Door," so called, or the equal right of all nations to share in the China trade.

Such was the state of affairs in the late nineties when close observers of Far Eastern politics began to perceive the existence of a new current in the surging flood of Imperialism—a cross current from the East. Japan's phenomenal growth was beginning to excite the attention of the Powers with interests in China, particularly Russia.

The main outlines of Japan's evolution from a medieval to a modern country are well known, and it is scarcely necessary to repeat them here. We need only recall that Japan was virtually closed to the outside world until the opening of the first treaty port by an American naval officer, Commodore Perry, in 1854; that it was governed by feudal barons until 1869, when the authority of the Emperor, under a constitutional monarchy, took the place of the feudal oligarchy; that until well within the last quarter of the nineteenth century there were no railways, no telegraphs, no modern cities, no modern administrative apparatus for conducting the affairs of the nation, and no foreign entanglements to disturb the isolation of the Nipponese.

Japan proved extraordinarily susceptible to modern ideas once they were introduced. With their naturally quick intuition the Japanese realized that their national survival in an era in which power was measured in terms of machine-made civilization depended on their adopting the methods of the West. And at the same time they felt practical necessity of expansion because their population was growing too large for their small islands. In this respect the Japanese at the beginning of the twentieth century were very much in the same position as Great Britain at the beginning of her era of colonial expansion, only with this difference—that when England began to colonize the world was full of empty places, and when Japan began the vast majority of these empty spaces had already been pre-empted by other nations.

Consequently, the pursuance of a foreign policy which would further not only economic but also territorial expansion was the first aim of Japanese statesmen. Their initial efforts were concentrated on the building up of a strong army and navy and a sound fiscal system. By 1894 Japan, shrewdly gauging the general demoralization and the weakness of the Peking government to be in her favor, felt herself strong enough to engage in a war with China, for the purpose of obtaining a foothold on the mainland. Her pretext was the alleged violation of an agreement with China to keep "hands off" in Korea.

Japan had long had her eye on the peninsula of Chosen governed by the decadent Korean Emperors over whom China claimed a vague sovereignty and the result of her victory over China, in due course, was the recognition of Korean independence, which meant the preponderance of Japanese influence, and the acquisition of the Liaotung peninsula in Manchuria, as well as the island of Formosa. The latter, with the Kurile Islands lying far to the north, almost completed the Nipponese chain which barred the approach to the Asiatic mainland from the Pacific, from Kamchatka to the mouth of the Japan Sea. There was only one missing link, the island of Sakhalin.

Japan's expansion in Manchuria was temporarily curbed by Russia, who, asserting her great friendship for China, forced the Japanese to surrender their right to the Liaotung peninsula, in return for a cash indemnity. As a matter of fact, most of the disputed territory was shortly afterwards acquired by the Russians as the site of their naval and commercial bases of Dalny and Port Arthur. A railway line through South Manchuria connected the peninsula with the Chinese Eastern Railway, the last link in the Trans-Siberian system, which crossed Northern Manchuria to Vladivostok. Thus Russia at last secured the coveted warm-water outlet on the Pacific. The Chinese Eastern was built principally on bonds floated by the Russian government through the Russo-Chinese, later the Russo-Asiatic, Bank. Its management was by mutual agreement vested in a Russo-Chinese board of directors with a Russian chairman, and the Chinese government was to be given the privilege of buying out the

Russian interest in the road after a certain number of years. Needless to say, this concession assured to Russia a preponderant interest in Manchuria and cut the ground from under the Japanese. They never forgot how they had been "done" by Russia, and bided their time to get even.

Meanwhile, Japanese aspirations were encouraged by certain Powers, particularly England, which regarded them as an excellent antidote to Russian ambitions; but Japan's strength was only imperfectly estimated by the Western nations, for her foreign policy was based on a remarkably sound and intelligent internal administration. Her navy was not built up at the expense of a merchant fleet, nor her army at the expense of commercial and industrial development. Education was regarded as of first importance, and the creation of a modern judicial system left no possible grounds for protest against the abolishment of the capitulations, which were done away with by a succession of "equal" treaties with the Powers. Added to this, the Japanese had preserved as the heritage of their age of chivalry a strong sense of clan loyalty which became fused with a powerful sentiment of national loyalty and patriotism. They were beginning to feel that they had an important rôle to play in the Far East.

At the same time neither they nor any other Asiatic people had openly questioned the supremacy of European Imperialism in Asia, though in many places there was a sullen undercurrent of revolt which now and then broke out in anti-foreign demonstrations. The most serious of these was the Boxer Rebellion in China. Originally a mere Chinese movement against the unpopular Manchu dynasty, the secret organization of the Boxers was turned into an uprising against all foreigners, partly by the skilful diplomacy of the "Old Buddha" the Dowager Empress of China, and partly through the universal popular indignation against the series of foreign aggressions that marked the last years of the nineteenth century in China.

We all know how the foreign legations in Peking were besieged by the Boxers for many weeks; how a wave of hatred against Europeans swept the country; how finally Allied warships landed detachments of sailors and marines who fought their way to the beleaguered legations; how the Dowager Empress fled from Peking, and was finally forced to sue for a peace bought at the price of economic slavery to Europe.

But the Boxer movement at the time seemed merely an ineffectual protest—in reality it was a warning. New forces were undermining European influence, forces which Europeans had themselves unloosed; the changes taking place in Asia for the moment were not so much political as social, and the East was learning from the West many new conceptions of society, among them the idea of race-prejudice, or the essential superiority of one racial group over another.

As we have seen, the history of the Asiatic Continent, as well as the rest of the world, has been largely the history of conflicts between races or the members of one racial family. For centuries, a struggle immortalized in the epics of Persian and Hindu poets as the fight between Iran and Turan, raged between the Mongol and Aryan peoples. In our own day, the memory of this traditional enmity was still sufficiently vivid to serve as one of the causes which contributed to keep the Persians, Afghans, and Moslem Indians, all largely Aryan peoples, on the side of the Allies in the World War, as against the Turanian Turks. There was always a certain amount of antagonism among the various Mongol peoples. It was very marked between the Chinese and the dominant Manchus, of the same original stock, not to mention the mutual dislike of the Chinese for the Japanese and of the Koreans for both.

Religious differences, such as those between Hindus and Moslems, in India had roused bitter feuds; hatred for the conqueror had always existed among the conquered; peoples possessing a greater degree of civilization had always looked down on the less advanced peoples. But now a new bitterness was injected into the resentment of the Asiatic against Western Imperialism by the assumption of superiority by Europeans based on color. The White, or European, races were divinely appointed to world dominion; the colored races, including all Asiatics indiscriminately, even those of Aryan stock to whom Europe owed its origin, were essentially inferior!

It is difficult to trace the beginning of the thin dividing line of color which has widened until it has made the race issue a problem involving the future of all civilization. We shall try to do this later in discussing the conflict of ideals between Europe and Asia.

At the close of the last century, it was less apparent in Asia than in some other countries, but it had created irreconcilable differences between the British and a large section of the educated classes in India, who had learned the bitter lesson that an Oxford degree did not bring social equality, and that education could not overcome the handicap of color in British eyes. Recognition of this fact had brought about the reactionary, and at the same time revolutionary, movement headed by Tilak which taught that the only road to freedom was through the destruction of all Western institutions and a return to primitive conditions. More sober minds did not agree with him, but even among the Indians most loyal to British Empire there was a subtle change of mental attitude, almost a challenge. It was reflected in the Indian National Congress, which since its foundation in 1885 had based all its hopes of reform on co-operation with the British government. Among the great masses of India the blind confidence in the power of the British was shaken by a succession of famines and an outbreak of bubonic plague, with which the authorities were unable to cope.

In the Far East, the color feeling was not as strong as in India, partly because European domination was less directly exercised, and partly because of the race-exclusiveness of the Yellow Peoples, who did not seek the contacts that had been eagerly sought from the first by the sensitive, highly intellectual, and receptive Indians. Western education was welcomed first by the Japanese and then by the Chinese as a means of defending their own institutions. So self-contained was their culture that it did not dawn on them for some time that the foreign barbarians actually believed themselves superior.

Wherever Asiatics had come under the commercial or political domination of the West, color feeling had begun to influence their attitude towards Europeans; but so complete was the ascendancy of the White Man physically and materially, in spite of sporadic outbreaks against his authority, that it would have taken a miracle to shake their belief in his invincibility.   But miracles sometimes happen.   The miracle that turned the course of empire in Asia was the Russo-Japanese War.

Chapter Three

A MIRACLE AND ITS CONSEQUENCES

MIRACLES, if we use the word in a broader sense than its ordinary scriptural meaning, are the results of the operation of natural laws, which appear supernatural only because we fail to understand them. Such was the miracle wrought by the Russo-Japanese War, which destroyed the legend of the superiority of the White over the Colored races, at least in Asiatic eyes. Curiously enough, it was precipitated by the very power whose Empire was most seriously menaced by its ultimate consequences —Great Britain.

At the beginning of the present century Russia was the ever-present preoccupation of British statesmen. Her penetration in Central Asia was threatening India. In Manchuria she was pushing slowly but steadily southward towards Great Britain's sphere of activity, the Valley of the Yangtze-kiang in China, beyond which there was still another road to India through Burma. She had reached an understanding with Germany and France which gave her a clear field in the Extreme Orient as far as those two Powers were concerned, and looking about for a counter-agent to Russian Imperialism in Manchuria, she found it in Japan.

We have already seen how Japan had begun her expansion on the Asiatic mainland by a war with China through which she obtained a territorial foothold in Manchuria and the island of Formosa. A Continental combination, consisting of Russia and France aided and abetted by Germany for her own ends, had forced the Japanese to part with most of the fruits of their victory over the Chinese in Manchuria, and Russia had later obtained leaseholds of the Liaotung peninsula, which Japan had been compelled to return to China. Moreover the Boxer Rebellion had served as an admirable justification for the Russian occupation of Manchuria, which was continued under one pretext or another, long after the necessity for it had ceased.

Despite the fact that the pacts following the war between China and Japan which guaranteed the independence of Korea had been agreed to by Russia, the latter Power had not hesitated to meddle in the affairs of the weak Korean Empire. Neither had Japan, for that matter, regarding Korea as practically if not officially within her sphere of influence, and the rivalry between the two Powers for the control of the "Land of Morning Calm"—rather, the Land of Continual Discord—added to the bitterness in Japan over the loss of Dalny and Port Arthur, where the Russian naval and commercial bases were a continual reminder of what was regarded as a colossal injustice.

At the same time, while Japan resented the inroads of Russia she showed no disposition to become the champion of the East against the West. On the contrary, she aligned herself with a Western power by concluding an alliance with Great Britain in 1902. In the light of subsequent events the Alliance with Japan, which was courted by Great Britain at the time, was fraught with consequences which proved to be far more of a menace to the British Empire than the Russian advance.

Its immediate result was to give the Japanese a feeling of security in the event of war with Russia, for a reciprocal pact concluded with Great Britain and concurred in by the United States, guaranteed them England's support in case any third Power went to Russia's assistance. The Anglo-Japanese Alliance also left the British free to concentrate on counteracting Russian influence in Central Asia, and it was in 1904, while Russian attention was diverted to the Far East that Sir Francis Younghusband undertook his famous expedition to Tibet, which penetrated as far as the forbidden city of Lhasa to secure recognition of England's right to a special interest in that country. During the same period the British also extended their hold on South Persia.

Relieved of the fear of a possible European combination against her, Japan deliberately and consciously prepared for the inevitable war with Russia. To the Japanese it was to be no ordinary war. Revenge and the instinct of self-preservation are two of the strongest motives for human action, and every citizen of Japan, from the Emperor down to the humblest soldier in the ranks, was animated by both. In less than fifty years Japan had completed her transition from medievalism to modernism, even keeping pace with Western industrial development. She had built up the third largest navy in the world in her own yards at Nagasaki and Yokohama, and the Japanese army was up to date in every particular; the resources of the country, however, were very limited in comparison with the almost inexhaustible supplies of men and materials in Russia, and when Tokyo finally took the aggressive, breaking off negotiations with Russia on the subject of Korea and giving the order to the fleet to attack the Russian fleet at Chemulpo and Port Arthur in February, 1904, it seemed incredible that, as one well-known writer has put it "the young Asiatic David could smite down the European Goliath."

Nevertheless, certain factors were in Japan's favor. The Russians were separated from their fighting front by six thousand miles of railway across Siberia. The very remoteness of the scene of war made it unpopular in Russia, where the average citizen could not see the advantage of fighting for a timber concession on the Yalu River, or the right to tell the Korean Emperors what they should do. Besides, there was a real and very menacing revolutionary movement going on inside the country itself, and the bureaucracy against whom it was largely directed, was thoroughly corrupt and incompetent.

Eventually, no doubt, the cumbersome Russian fighting machinery would have acquired momentum sufficient to crush Japan, which could not have held out either in men or in money during a long drawn out conflict; but the Japanese struck quickly!

It has often been asserted that their surprise attack on the Russian navy was made to block an attempt by King Edward of England to stop the war at the last moment, because with his remarkable political insight he realized, what his ministers failed to grasp—that if Russia should be defeated by Japan, an impetus would be given to German Imperialism, then just beginning to penetrate along the "Berlin to Baghdad" route, which no less than that of Central Asia, led to India. It was also said that the influence of Australia, which feared Japanese immigration and competition, and which would have liked to see the power of

Japan curbed by Russia, fortified the Japanese in their decision
to steal a march on the Russians. However that may be, Russia
was undoubtedly unprepared at the moment; the Japanese naval
victories were followed up by a land campaign culminating in a
great battle at Mukden in March, 1905, where the Japanese gained
a decisive victory under General Nogi, and a few weeks later,
Admiral Togo intercepted and annihilated the Russian Baltic
fleet, which had been sent out to reinforce the remains of the
Pacific fleet, in the Straits of Tsushima.

Notwithstanding these terrible reverses, the resources and fighting strength of Russia were far from exhausted; but she was
beginning to feel the demoralizing effects of the social unrest
within her European dominions. Great Britain, to tell the truth,
was a bit appalled at the prowess of her Eastern ally; she began
to foresee that a too complete triumph by Japan might have unexpected consequences. The United States shared much the same
feeling. The Japanese themselves had paid dearly for their victories in man-power and they were finding it more and more difficult to finance the tremendously expensive military and naval
operations. Consequently, both adversaries gladly accepted President Roosevelt's offer of mediation, and the peace treaty signed
between Japan and Russia at Portsmouth as a result of America's
good offices, brought about at least a temporary clarification of the
Far Eastern situation.

Russia ceded to Japan the southern half of the island of Sakhalin, with Port Arthur, Dalny (rechristened Dairen), and the
Liaotung peninsula. Japan also obtained the right to operate
the South Manchurian Railway with recognition of her special
interests in South Manchuria and extraterritorial privileges within
the railway zone, despite the fact that American interests had
favored the internationalization of the Manchurian railways.
Russia retained joint control with the Chinese, of the Chinese
Eastern Railway which connected with her trans-Siberian system
and resigned all pretensions to Korea, which was forthwith made
a Japanese protectorate. Subsequent agreements settled all matters at issue between Japan and Russia. China was saved from
the danger of Russian penetration and her territorial integrity
was guaranteed.

The changes effected by the Portsmouth treaty were of little importance in comparison with the change in Asiatic mentality brought about by the Russo-Japanese War. The defeat of Russia was the defeat of Europe in Asiatic eyes. It marked the destruction of the myth of European invincibility and the birth of new hopes. "Asia for Asiatics" was the slogan of the new movement which swept the continent from one end to the other. Japan had risen almost by magic, it seemed, from an obscure little ally of England, to the status of a world Power, with pretensions to become the dominant Power in the Pacific. A miracle had indeed been wrought, or so it seemed to the masses who celebrated the victory of Tsushima in China, Siam, Tonkin, India. Even the Philippines and the East Indies began to look towards the Empire of the Rising Sun as the champion of the oppressed peoples of the East.

But the leaders of the growing national movement in many Asiatic countries perceived the natural causes underlying the miracle. Japan's defeat of Russia was due to her rapid assimilation of Western civilization and her adoption of European methods and equipment in industry and commerce, as well as in military and naval matters. She was able to fight the West with its own weapons. All at once they began to realize how they too might profit by the educational advantages that had been offered them through the missionaries and teachers, whom they had previously regarded, especially in China, as merely the vanguards of Imperialism. The thirst for Western education and Western training spread to every country in Asia. Asiatics began to see in it the instrument of their liberation—the vehicle of the renascence.

While all Asia was profoundly stirred by the Japanese victories, it was moved to concrete action by the social upheaval which was one of the indirect consequences of Russia's reverses. The revolutionary movement in Russia had been smouldering for some time, but it burst into flame at the close of the war with Japan, which, it was felt, had been lost largely because of the incompetency and corruption of the bureaucracy. Although it was eventually subdued, the Revolution of 1905 was nevertheless instrumental in bringing about many radical reforms that struck a body-blow at autocratic government. Coming as it did at a time when Asia's contacts had become international, and on the heels of the first military victory of an Asiatic over an European Power, the Russian Revolution gave a tremendous impetus to the new movements that were beginning to make their appearance —a revolt against all despotism, a vague groping for a new social order, and a dawning perception of national or race solidarity.

The new ferment was not by any means confined to countries under the sway of European Imperialism. It brought about radical changes in three independent states. In Turkey it produced the Union and Progress party, which made a bloodless revolution in 1908, deposed the reactionary Sultan Abdul Hamid, put in his place another, a more liberal monarch, and gave Turkey a Parliament and a constitution. The Union and Progress movement was not so much a liberal as a racial movement, however. The Young Turks, as the members of the party were called, believed that the regeneration of the Ottoman Empire could be brought about only through the absorption or extermination of all its non-Turkish elements. All racial and religious minorities were relentlessly pursued and persecuted, and the non-Turkish groups within the Empire—Arabs, Greeks, Kurds, Armenians, Syrians, and others—developed under this pressure a unity such as they had never before possessed. Racial and religious hatreds grew apace, and national movements aiming at autonomy or independence were formed in Armenia, Mesopotamia, Syria and among the states of the Arabian peninsula. They did not make much headway—organization, funds, and above all the essentially European quality we call teamwork, were lacking among them—and the Young Turks ruled with an iron hand.

In Persia, events were no less influenced by the Russian Revolution though they followed a different course. The movement to establish a constitutional government was inaugurated by a small Nationalist faction which hoped thereby to prevent the country from falling into foreign hands. During the preceding quarter-century Persia had been almost mortgaged to Great Britain and Russia through the greed of the Imperial government, which had contracted loans to obtain revenue, without a thought for Persia's interests, invariably giving in return some concession which tightened the hold of one or the other of the two rival

Powers.   The Russian Revolution, besides inspiring the small truly liberal element in Persia, roused hopes in the Nationalists as well.   Temporarily, at least, Russia was occupied with her own affairs and the British, for reasons of their own, were not averse to the constitutional movement.

By 1906 the popular pressure for constitutional reform had become so strong that the Shah, realizing the drift of affairs, voluntarily issued a firman (an Imperial edict) ordering the drafting of a constitution by a National Convention to be elected by the three estates—the nobility, the clergy, and the tradesmen. This Assembly, known as the Medjliss, duly drew up a constitution providing for a limited monarchy.

The real governing power was to be vested in the new Medjliss or Parliament, composed of two houses, an assembly and a senate.   The cabinet was to be responsible to the Medjliss.   Nevertheless, the Nationalist program was not carried out at once. There was a reaction during which the absolute monarchists were supported by the Russians and then a coup d'état engineered by the Bakhtiari chief, Samsun Saltanneh, supported by his tribespeople, which restored the power of the Medjliss.

Unfortunately for Persia, however, Russia's defeat in the East and her consequent difficulties at home had made her more than ready to reach an understanding with Great Britain.   The Anglo-Russian agreement of 1907 which divided the country into British and Russian spheres of influence, with the government subject to crossfire from both sides, made it most difficult for the few Nationalist leaders with vision to accomplish anything towards the establishment of a really representative national government in Persia.   All attempts to escape from the leading-strings of Russia or Great Britain, such as the appointment of W. Morgan Shuster an American, as financial adviser to the Persian government, were unsuccessful; nevertheless, the example set by Japan was not lost.   There was a change of attitude in Persia as elsewhere. She was merely biding her time.   Meanwhile, the thirst for Western education was spreading like wild-fire among the better classes.

China was slower than Persia or Turkey to react to the new influences.   She felt them profoundly, notwithstanding.   The

Japanese victories had been a revelation no less to the court of
Peking than to the Chinese people. The old Dowager Empress,
who had fled before the Allies when they entered Peking in 1900,
at last realized as well as any of her younger statesmen the necessity of welcoming Europeanization as a means of self-preservation, and she entrusted the institution of a series of far-reaching
reforms to Yuan Shih-kai, Viceroy of Chihli, the province in
which Peking is situated. The throne even went so far as to sanction the creation of elective provincial councils. But it was too
late. Opposition to the Manchu bureaucracy, from which the
governors of the provinces had been drawn since the Manchu
conquest of China, rendered such measures ineffective.

The men who were fitted to carry out any widespread reforms
were unanimously against the Manchu dynasty. Many of them,
banished during the reactionary era immediately preceding and
following the Boxer Rebellion, had been educated abroad, mostly
in the United States, or in foreign educational institutions in
China. Their leaders were chiefly drawn from the southern
provinces, whose inhabitants had never really accepted Manchu
rule, and where there had been sporadic revolts against Peking
ever since the conquest. They could not believe in the sincerity of
the dynastic reforms, and moreover their European education
had made them unwilling to accept anything short of revolutionary changes. Their contacts were international. They had been
deeply influenced by the Russian Revolution and the development
of Marxist political philosophy. Their first aim was to rid the
country of the Manchus, root and branch; their second, the establishment of a republic in China.

Canton became the headquarters of the revolutionary party,
the Kuomintang, founded in 1900 by Sun Yat-sen, of whom we
shall hear more later. It had world-wide affiliations. Wherever
there were Chinese colonies, in Singapore, the East Indies, Man-
ila, San Francisco, it had its followers and adherents—out of
touch with the China, they wished to transform into a modern
country overnight by the pronouncement of the magic formulas
of revolution.

Meanwhile complications in China's relations with foreign
Powers had not been lacking. Japan had replaced Russia in

Manchuria, while in spite of the many important-sounding agreements between her and the other treaty Powers guaranteeing the integrity of China, in spite of her understanding with the United States that she would support the open-door policy ratified by the Root-Takahira agreement of 1908, she was steadily scheming to acquire greater influence in China.

The Imperial government was becoming more and more deeply involved in debt. Besides the indemnities to which it had been forced to agree after the Boxer Rebellion, it had incurred obligations extending over a number of years in the form of loans from the great Powers for administrative and constructive purposes. The interest on these loans had been guaranteed by turning over to the Powers certain revenues, such as the Maritime Customs and the Salt Tax. All these loans, which should have strengthened the internal position of the government, only served to weaken it and give force to the propaganda of the revolutionaries, because they were usually dissipated by the corrupt bureaucracy without benefit to the country at large.

The old Empress died in 1908 without realizing the force of the gathering storm. With her death the government passed into the hands of the reactionaries, who dismissed Yuan Shih-kai and governed through a regency in the name of a baby emperor only three years old, while the Kuomintang kept up a steady agitation against the Manchu dynasty and bureaucrats—lock, stock, and barrel.

Finally the long feared revolution broke out in the valley of the Yangtze, soon involving all South China. The Regent, terrified, placed himself in the hands of Yuan Shih-kai, who proceeded to play his own game. First convincing the Regent that nothing but a republic would satisfy the people, he forced the abdication of the little Emperor on February 12, 1912; then outwitting the Kuomintang, which had elected Sun Yat-sen provisional President, and seizing the power by a clever coup d'état, he had himself made President of the new Chinese Republic.

With the passing of the Empire the Chinese state in the old sense ceased to exist. The division between North and South made a sharp line of cleavage in Chinese politics. Yuan Shih-kai became the dictator of the Republic, but he could not succeed in restoring the unity of the Empire. Soon North and South split into many factions, forming endless combinations like the colors in a kaleidoscope. The one stable element in the situation was the new attitude towards the West, which China shared with other Asiatic countries after 1905.

While the influence of the Russo-Japanese War was momentous in determining the trend of events in Asia, there were no very startling developments in the mutual relationships of the great Powers with territorial or commercial interests in Asia during the decade between the Japanese victories and the Great War. But it marked the beginning of a new era in the relations of imperialistic Powers with Asiatic countries. From that time on the rivalries of nations contending for spheres of influence were complicated by the necessity for combating loss of prestige, and the new social and political movements which were so rapidly gaining force in Asiatic countries. While Imperialism had received a body-blow, nevertheless it was not by any means prepared to admit defeat. There were in fact two new combatants in the imperial arena, Japan and Germany.

We have already reviewed, though in merest outline, the rise of Japan from an obscure insular kingdom to a first-class modern Power with the successful termination of her war against Russia and the renewal of her alliance with Great Britain in 1905. The years between the signing of the Portsmouth treaty and the Great War were comparatively uneventful as regards the external relations of Japan.

The outstanding events of this period were her annexation of Korea in 1910, a series of clashes with the United States over commercial differences, and the immigration question. The Japanese protectorate over Korea was inaugurated in 1905, after the signing of the Portsmouth treaty which established it as part of Japan's legitimate sphere of influence. The rapid commercial expansion of Japan in Korea necessitated the establishment of a stable government which its effete and degenerate rulers were utterly unable to supply. Japanese political, military, and economic interests were paramount in Korea; ostensibly to protect these interests, in 1905 the Japanese installed a Resident-General, the famous Marquis Ito, at Seoul the capital, to administer the government nominally in co-operation with the Korean administration.

Little by little the entire control passed into the hands of the military or imperialistic party in Japan, which had grown steadily since the war with Russia and, believing that the only possible instrument for expansion was military imperialism, it was constantly demanding the annexation of Korea.

The assassination of the liberal Marquis Ito by a misguided Korean fanatic removed the last obstacle to the abolition of the protectorate. The Emperor of Korea, who had long been sovereign only in name, was forced to abdicate and sign an agreement for full annexation of Korea by Japan.

The new military nationalism of Japan took no account of the existence of any nationalism in Korea, and a deliberate campaign was inaugurated for forcible assimilation of the Koreans. Viscount Terauchi, the first Governor-General under the new administration, was personally kind and broad-minded, but he was nevertheless under the influence of the militaristic and bureaucratic spirit that prevailed in Japan. A host of petty Japanese officials, arrogant, supercilious, and assuming airs of infinite superiority towards the gentle backward Koreans, filled every important position in the government.

Many improvements were inaugurated from the material point of view. Conditions were stabilized through the peninsula. Law and order were established; all administrative departments put on a sound basis; railways, modern public buildings, public works, a modern sanitary system, and an efficient though purely Japanese education system transformed the country as far as externals were concerned. But the process of assimilation had made little headway up to the beginning of 1914.

It was evident, however, that the Japanese were acting under the pressure of necessity and none except sentimentalists could have denied the urgency of the reasons which impelled them to take over Korea. Its possession gave them an undeniably strong strategic hold on the Asiatic mainland, as did also the bases which they had acquired after the Russo-Japanese War in Manchuria, where their commercial and economic hold constituted a virtual monopoly. To all this Great Britain acquiesced for the time.

Japan was valuable as a counter-irritant to Russia and she did not tread seriously on England's toes because British interests were concentrated in the Yangtze region, much farther south.

The steady growth of Japanese influence in Manchuria was conceded by all the Powers, and even to America, which was definitely committed to the open-door policy, Japan gave no opportunity for complaint. Whatever violations of international agreements she may have committed there, with regard to further encroachments in China, were in spirit rather than in letter, and her increasing commercial rivalry with the United States was not serious.

The immigration question, however, was a different matter. Japanese emigration to America had begun shortly after the middle of the nineteenth century, and in the late eighties the presence of Japanese in California began to be resented by the Californians. This antagonism was purely local, however. It was not until after 1900 that there was any serious agitation for the exclusion of Japanese immigrants from the United States. The Asiatic Exclusion League, formed in 1905, as a result of this agitation, inspired the anti-Japanese legislation subsequently passed, first by the state of California where most of the Japanese coming to the United States had settled, and later by Congress, which in 1907 put through a Japanese Exclusion Act. In the same year a presidential proclamation forbade the entrance of Japanese laborers into the United States from Hawaii, Mexico, and Canada. Such a storm of indignation was aroused in Japan by this action that President Roosevelt intervened personally to keep the peace and concluded a so-called "Gentleman's Agreement" by which Japan pledged herself to prevent the emigration of Japanese laborers to the United States.

The controversy with America over the immigration question served still further to enhance the prestige of Japan. Even if she had not been successful Japan had come forward as the sponsor of the claims of the Asiatic to racial equality, for the true nature of the agitation in the United States was plain. The economic menace of Japan to American interests in California and the fear of Japanese imperialism were grossly exaggerated to account for what was, at bottom, race prejudice. Other Asiatics had felt it without being able to protest against it. The Chinese, who had been excluded from America in express violation of early treaties, and the Indians, who smarted under the disabilities inflicted on them in the English colonies, particularly South Africa, regarded the Japanese as their spokesmen, and their protests made articulate the universal resentment of the Colored races against the White.

The attitude of the West in general and of America in particular had an important influence on Japan's foreign policy. Faced with the necessity for emigration, she was obliged to find an outlet for her surplus population. The hostility of the two Americas, the handicap of distance, difficulty of transportation, and the necessity of creating a giant navy to safeguard a programme of expansion on the other side of the Pacific, with the added probability of war with the United States should she press such a policy, contributed to the development of a Japanese Imperialism with the Asiatic mainland as its objective, and the domination of all the Yellow races as its ultimate aim.

Germany first appeared as a factor in the Asiatic situation in the last quarter of the nineteenth century, when economic pressure —the search for new markets and new sources of supply for raw materials—began to force the German people, who had only just achieved national unity, into a career of colonial expansion. Territorially speaking, Germany up to 1914, had been able to acquire no foothold in Asia except her leasehold of the province of Shantung, which she had wrung from the feeble Peking government as compensation for the opportune murder of several German citizens in 1895. Russia, Great Britain, and Japan were in a position to block any possible territorial acquisitions, but the Emperor William II and his advisers had planned to offset this with a scheme almost unparalleled in world history. Germany's aim in the years preceding the World War was the hegemony of the Near and Middle East; her ultimate goal, like that of Russia, penetration to India and the domination of world trade with Asia. The "Drag nach Osten" was in some respects a recrudescence of the dreams of Alexander and Napoleon. The German process of penetration proceeded logically and with characteristic Teutonic thoroughness. Military aggression was not part of the immediate programme. First came the establishment of bases for the eastward advance in Europe—the Austro-German alliance, then the spread of German influence in the Balkan States, its extension to Constantinople and the rest of the Ottoman Empire.

The Kaiser's visit to the Sultan Abdul Hamid of Turkey, in 1900, was one of the outstanding events of that year. There was something fantastic, almost ludicrous, in his announcement that he had been converted to the Moslem faith and his espousal of the doctrines of Pan-Islamism, but it was effective.

Today the traveller to Syria will see in a French museum the bronze tablet recording his visit to the ruins of Baalbek. Visitors to the British High Commissioner in Palestine may still see in the chapel of the Residency, which was built for a German hospice, heroic-size figures of the Kaiser and Kaiserin done in mosaic.

The visit of Kaiser William did much to expedite the carrying out of a great German scheme which had been begun some twelve years before when a group of German business men had received a concession to build a railway line across Anatolia from a point on the Bosphorus opposite Constantinople to Konia. It was planned eventually to extend the main line which ran south to Konia, with branches east to Angora, and still farther south to Syria, and Baghdad in Mesopotamia. The Turkish government guaranteed 125,000 francs per mile and Germany retained the majority control. The lines to Angora and Konia were completed by 1896, but meanwhile the German Foreign Office had become interested in the Baghdad Railway project and diplomatic pressure was exerted on Turkey to secure the concession for the extension of the existing line to Aleppo in Northern Syria, Mosul, and Baghdad, thence to Basra at the top of the Persian Gulf where German commerce was already beginning to penetrate, Koweit a little farther down, and Khanikin on the Persian border. To carry out this colossal project a new company was formed, called the Société des Chemins de Fer de Baghdad, in which the Germans, however, still retained a controlling interest despite British, French, and Russian protest. It was financed principally by the Deutsche Bank group and backed in every possible way by the German government.

Germans managed to secure the vast majority of concessions in

Anatolia for public works and the development of natural resources. Soon the bulk of the commerce of the Levant was in German hands and German educational institutions were established everywhere throughout Asia Minor.

German influence in Constantinople was greatly increased by the successful coup d'état of the Union and Progress party. Its leaders were nearly all pro-German and convinced that only close alliance with Germany could assure the Ottoman Empire against the aggressions of the Russians. Indeed, their "Turkification" programme aimed at nothing short of a federation of all Turanian peoples, including those under Russian dominion in Central Asia. Its execution, if it could ever have been accomplished, would have necessitated their taking the offensive against Russia.

The German advance in the Near East was viewed with considerable alarm by both Great Britain and France. France had important commercial interests in Syria as well as a moral and spiritual ascendancy. Since the days of the Crusades she had been the historic champion of the Christian peoples of the Near East. She controlled the existing railway system in Syria and enjoyed special commercial privileges secured from former Sultans.

Great Britain was not at all inclined to see without protest the creation of a strategic line of communication by land that would have partly destroyed the effectiveness of her command of the sea route to India through the Suez Canal.

Russia also was not entirely pleased by the spread of German influence in Asia Minor and Constantinople, but her aims for the moment were concentrated on the Balkans and Central Asia, and on regaining the ground lost in the Far East.

For a time there was a race between Germany on the one hand and France and Great Britain on the other, for concessions and spheres of influence. France finally got the concession to build a railway from the interior of Anatolia to the Black Sea, and schemed for the control of the Hedjaz railway which had been built by Sultan Abdul Hamid to carry Moslem pilgrims from Damascus to Medina. Great Britain obtained a commercial foothold in Smyrna, a concession to build a railway connecting

Smyrna with the interior, as well as rights of navigation on the Tigris and Euphrates rivers in Mesopotamia.

The struggle went on until, shortly before the outbreak of the war, there came a lull in the conflict brought about by the conclusion of agreements between all the Powers concerned as to their respective rights, privileges, and spheres of influence, in all of which Turkey was at the mercy of Europe partly because the country had been systematically exploited by the Ottoman rulers and was still being exploited no less by the unscrupulous and ambitious Young Turkish group.

After all these agreements recognizing Great Britain's rights and France's interests, the Germans still held the whip-hand up to the outbreak of the World War, in the control of the Baghdad Railway, which was rapidly approaching completion. If the World War had come two years later the railway would have been completed and the Germans would perhaps have been able to strike their contemplated death-blow at British supremacy in India.

The German Foreign Office had been active in other directions as well. Besides supporting the Union and Progress party, which brought about the revolution of 1908, it adroitly fostered the Pan-Turanian and Pan-Islamic movements of which the Young Turks in Constantinople were the protagonists. Germany was to sponsor a great spiritual and political revival of Islam, and the Ottoman Turks were to dominate a great Islamic federation with Germany as their ally.

There was no doubt that most of the Turkish leaders were completely taken in by German promises and looked to Germany as the only European Power whose interests in Asia coincided with their own. Thus Germany possessed in Asia an influence that could not be measured by the extent of her territorial and commercial possessions, due to the Russo-Japanese War, which with its indirect results had contributed to the weakening of Russia's Asiatic policy.

Meanwhile, Russia, France, and Great Britain, the three Powers which had first acquired territorial possessions in Asia, had other preoccupations than their increasing interest in the progress made by Japanese and German penetration. As we have intimated before, they were chiefly occupied with bracing the foundations of the Imperial structure against the new forces let loose in Asia. Probably the least concerned of the three was France. Her interests and those of the other Powers did not conflict except in the Near East. Her control of the Indo-Chinese peninsula, acquired little by little since the middle of the nineteenth century and conceded by Great Britain, gave her a territorial foothold quite sufficient for the advancement of her commerce in the Pacific. She had long since given up the struggle for power in the Far East and her main energies were bent on extending and consolidating her African colonial empire, which was of much more importance to French interests than far-away Asia.

Great Britain and Russia had compounded their differences and declared a truce through the Anglo-Russian Convention of 1907 with regard to Persia, Tibet, and Afghanistan.

Russia had much lost ground to regain in the Far East, and an Empire to consolidate in Central Asia. But in a few years she had again begun her southward advance towards China, this time through Mongolia, the vast buffer state between Siberia and China. Mongolia was the legacy of the once all-powerful Mongol conquerors to the Empire of China, but was sparsely inhabited by a primitive people pastoral and semi-nomad. Thanks to its rigorous climate and the vast stretches of the Great Gobi Desert separating its more fertile southern portion from the mountain ranges and rolling steppes of the north, Mongolia as left to stagnate for centuries. Nominally part of the Chinese Empire, it was administered by colonial governors sent from Peking, who interfered little with the local form of government beyond collecting taxes. Mongolia was a theocracy, ruled by a priest-sovereign called the Living Buddha, and its religion was a corrupt form of Lamaism. In spite of their backward social development, the Mongolians always resented Chinese sovereignty. When the first traders from Russia began to establish caravan routes across Mongolia from Siberia to China they were welcomed by the natives, who soon began to look to Russia for protection against the Chinese. A systematic cultivation of the friendship of the Mongolians was from its inception part of the Imperial policy. All Mongolia's contacts with the West were through Russia, and

Russian statesmen were not slow to recognize and take advantage of the ancient enmity between the Chinese and Mongolians.

When the Chinese revolution broke out it was with Russian aid that the Mongolians demanded and obtained autonomy from the new republic for all the territory known as Outer Mongolia, including the Great Gobi Desert and the high table-lands and mountainous regions between it and Siberia to the north. Actually this so-called autonomy resulted in an increase of Russian influence in Outer Mongolia which almost amounted to a protectorate.

In her Central Asiatic possessions and dependencies Russia had remained stationary for some years, and the agreement with England tended to stabilize conditions still further. A certain amount of colonization went on in Turkestan, and as we have seen, Russian influence was exerted within its prescribed sphere, in Northern Persia. The Moslem peoples under Russian rule remained temporarily quiet. Such unrest as there was, found expression in the spread of Pan-Islamism, which, however, produced no results politically.

Constitutionalism, nationalism, and the social ferment which had begun to make themselves felt even in near-by Persia, had not yet penetrated to the heart of Central Asia.

In the Caucasus, never entirely subdued, nationalism was perennially simmering underneath the surface, and the policy of the Imperial Russian Foreign Office did not tend to create peaceful conditions. The Russian programme for penetration to the Mediterranean depended for its execution on the eventual dismemberment of the Ottoman Empire, and one of the chief weapons of the Slav diplomacy was the fomenting of internal disorders in Asia Minor.

Turkey's friendship with Germany and the reforms of the Young Turks were both unfavorable to Russia's aspirations. Consequently Russian propaganda among the Armenians, which had been responsible in large measure for the unrest culminating in the massacres that gave rise to the catch phrases about the "unspeakable" and the "terrible" Turk, was renewed, in support of a growing Nationalist movement centering in the largely Armenian provinces bordering on the Caucasus.

Russia's recovery from the disaster which had overtaken her in the East and from the shock of domestic disorders was on the whole remarkable as far as her influence in Asia was concerned. Much more directly interested, much less altruistic in her attitude towards her dependents, she lost less prestige than Great Britain. There were many reasons for this, but the fundamental one was the close kinship between the Slav and the Asiatic, and the former's utter lack of race prejudice.

In spite of the fact that Great Britain was the ally of Japan and had furnished her the moral support and assurance of security from outside interference which had helped to win the war with Russia, the reaction to the Japanese victories was damaging to British prestige, particularly in India.

The immediate advantage of the removal of the bugbear of a Russian invasion was as nothing compared with the difficulties in which England found herself involved in India, after the treaty of Portsmouth.

To the Indian Nationalists, who had contracted an undying hatred for the British bureaucracy from whose ranks they were so rigidly excluded, the revolution in Russia following the Eastern fiasco, even though it was unsuccessful, was in the nature of a highly edifying example. Western revolutionary doctrines were part of the European education they had acquired in the English institutions that had pampered their love of the abstract and philosophical and fed them on theories instead of training them for the Civil Service, the Army, and the technical professions. The Russian revolution had suggested methods of applying these doctrines.

The destruction of the myth of White invincibility had wrought a miracle. The bulk of intelligent Indian opinion, which only a few years before would have been content with a very modest measure of autonomy, now demanded nothing less than Dominion status for India.

Unfortunately for Great Britain, just at this critical moment when Indian sentiment should have been handled with kid gloves, Lord Curzon was viceroy. Curzon, as Sir Valentine Chirol has put it, was a graduate of "the latest school of Victorian Imperialism." He might have added, "the last," for British Imperialism of the brand perfected by Lord Curzon received at Mukden and Tsushima a blow from which it never recovered. A great autocrat, a great administrator, to quote Chirol once more, "Lord Curzon seldom if ever showed himself possessed of the spiritual vision which is the essence of real statesmanship." To him, India was an integral part of the British Empire, to be administered paternally, benevolently, but none the less despotically, and the Indian, a creature of another stripe to the Briton, belonging to the essentially "inferior" Asiatic races, whom it was England's mission to govern.

His reforms, many of them wise and beneficial, were all nullified by his advocacy of an appallingly impolitic measure, the partition of the Province of Bengal into two separate provinces. From the administrative point of view it would have been a wise step. Bengal, both in size and in population, was unwieldy to manage as a unit. But the Bengalis were very proud of themselves and their province, which came nearer to forming the nucleus for a modern nation than any other part of India. They had led the way in European education, in the Congress movement, and they had a strong sense of unity and local patriotism; the proposed partition of Bengal dealt a heavy blow to their national pride. Moreover, it would have separated the Mohammedan from the Hindu element and have given the former an importance which the majority of Bengalis who were Hindus would have deeply resented. The proposed measure, although never enforced, gave birth to an era of violence, the like of which had not been seen in India before, to which the Japanese victories gave still further impetus. Gone was the old feeling of almost superstitious awe before the power of the White man!

The Indian National Congress was an utterly insufficient outlet for the ever increasing nationalism. The extremists led by Tilak, profiting by the example of the Russian Nihilists, began openly to advocate violence. The boycott of all British-made goods and the substituting of "Swadesh," or Indian-made products, and a series of bomb outrages, were the outcome of the development of the revolutionary movement. Repression only served to drive in terrorism, with the inevitable result—a vast ramification of secret revolutionary societies.

The Indian Councils Act, passed in 1909, providing for the addition of elected members to the provincial legislative councils, was almost without effect even on the more moderate Nationalists. One of the most curious features of the revolutionary movement was that while its most ardent sponsors were men who had been educated in Western institutions, they had reverted to the ancient Hindu faith with all its manifold gods and goddesses. It was a symbol of the racial gulf between them and the English.

The policy of the government of the United States with regard to the Philippine Islands after the Spanish-American War in 1898 had done much to widen the breach. With the establishment of civil government in the Islands under Governor-General William H. Taft, who later became President of the United States, a completely new vehicle of propaganda was furnished to the Indian extremists. There was a lot of sentimental talk in the United States about the "little brown brothers" of the American people and high-sounding phrases about preparing them for self-government. It was supplemented by the installation of a system of popular education and by a policy which favored the employment of native officials wherever and whenever possible—often to the detriment of the people at large. All these things were duly noted and magnified in India.

It was several years before the government succeeded in creating a better atmosphere. A series of reforms inaugurated under Curzon's successors, notably the transfer of the capital of British India from Calcutta to Delhi, the admission of Indians to the Viceroy's Council and the Council of the Secretary of State for India in England, and a new settlement of the Bengal question, did much to quiet the unrest, which for the moment had exhausted itself. But it was quite evident to those with eyes to see, that the old conception of the Empire and the old submissive attitude were gone, never to return.

Elsewhere in Asia Great Britain's expansion was commercial and economic rather than territorial, during the period following the Russo-Japanese War. Beyond an extension of her influence in Tibet, her policy was rather defensive than offensive.

She had, however, acquired a peculiar interest in Persia, safeguarded in part by her agreement with Russia, through a conces-

sion for the development of the immensely rich oil fields of
Southern Persia, obtained in 1901 by a British concern, the Anglo-
Persian Oil Company. Petroleum, one of the basic raw materials
in the modern economic scheme of things, was just beginning to
be adopted as a fuel for the navies of the world. It was the race
for petroleum which partly inspired the German penetration of
the Near East, and it was one of the principal contributory causes
of the World War.

In China, British commercial and financial interests were growing rapidly in spite of disturbed conditions. Japan, though dis-
quietingly self-assertive, was a loyal ally and a good customer.
Singapore, Suez, and Gibraltar still guarded the communications
between Great Britain and the uttermost parts of her Empire.
On the whole, conditions just before the beginning of the World
War were not such as to excite grave apprehension for the immediate future in the minds of the men who were administering
the interests of the Imperial Powers in Asia. Farseeing statesmen and publicists realized that European supremacy, morally and
intellectually, was a thing of the past and they foresaw the ultimate political possibilities of an Awakened Asia, but for the
moment they were concerned rather with the part Asia would play
in the war which, it was seen, was then imminent in Europe.

Chapter Four

ASIA AND ARMAGEDDON

WHEN Russia declared war on Germany on August 2, 1914, and France followed suit, the Germans retaliated by the invasion of Belgium; and from that moment British participation in the war was inevitable. From the first, the vital concern of France and Great Britain was to stem the tide of German invasion on the Flanders front while Russia concentrated her armies on the invasion of East Prussia to effect a diversion in favor of the Allies. For the first few weeks the World War was confined to Europe only, but it was obvious that it would eventually involve practically all of Asia.

Undoubtedly one of the objects of the Germans would be to strike at Great Britain through her overseas empire in India, and for a short time there was considerable uneasiness as to the attitude of British India and the native states, but it soon became evident that India would remain loyal to the Empire in spite of the fact that the Nationalist movement had attained very formidable proportions. It is true that a reaction was about due after the era of bomb-throwing and violence which had lasted for several years, caused by the ill-advised attempts of Lord Curzon to partition Bengal. In addition most of the Nationalist leaders in India were wise enough to discern a far greater menace in autocratic German Imperialism than in the milder constitutional brand of Great Britain.

Lord Hardinge, who was Viceroy at the time, was personally popular and known to be in sympathy up to a certain point with Indian National aims, and a large number of Nationalist leaders expected, or were led to expect, that India would be accorded Dominion status as a reward for her co-operation in the war. Utterances of cabinet ministers like Mr. Asquith and of other responsible persons in the British government, whether intentional or not, were accepted as virtual promises by all but a few extremists among the Nationalists. Even the best informed of Anglo-Indian officials, however, were amazed at the remarkable unanimity with which the population of India espoused the British cause.

The supreme test of Indian loyalty came when the Ottoman Empire declared war against the Allies. All the efforts of the German-inspired Pan-Islamists to draw Mohammedan India into a holy war proved unsuccessful, and the Indian Moslems remained as unshaken in their loyalty as the Hindus who composed the majority of the population. India contributed £200,000,000 to the war exchequer, nearly a million men to the Imperial armies, and her native expeditionary forces performed valiant services in Mesopotamia and German East Africa. There were only a few Indian revolutionists in the pay of the German Foreign Office, who kept up the anti-British agitation, and they had but scant following. Indian troops fought on practically every front, and the loyalty of the Mohammedan soldiers withstood the test of fighting against the Khalif, for the Sultan of Turkey was also the spiritual head of the Moslem world.

The Germans had counted on Islamic solidarity to help them in the war, but they failed to reckon with Nationalism—the concrete expression of concrete aims of the subject Moslem peoples, very different from the abstract Pan-Islamic movement which had been fostered by Abdul Hamid to bolster up the waning prestige of the Khalifate and the Ottoman Empire.

It was not until the third year of the war that signs of serious political unrest began to appear once more in India. The promises of Mr. Asquith that "henceforth Indian questions would have to be approached from a different angle of vision" had as yet borne no fruit—nor had the Allies triumphed over Germany as the Indians expected. On the contrary the reverses of the Allies on the Russian front, the slow progress of the British in Mesopotamia, and the failure of the Gallipoli campaign, had still further diminished British prestige, which had received its first setback through the Boer War and a second far more serious blow at the time of the Japanese victory over Russia.

Agitation for Swaraj, home rule, was taken up once more by Tilak and the extremists, and the increasing disorder finally forced the British Parliament to consider Indian affairs despite its absorption in war problems. Mr. Edwin Montagu, Secretary of State for India, went out to conduct an inquiry on the spot in co-operation with the Viceroy Lord Chelmsford, and the result of his investigations was the laying before Parliament of an elaborate scheme for reform which contemplated eventual Home Rule. The story of the so-called Montagu-Chelmsford Reforms belongs rather to the post-war than the war period, and we shall discuss it later. The internal situation, serious as it was, did not prevent Indian co-operation until the very end of the War.

Indo-China, Burma, the Malay States, and Siam, constituting the southeastern corner of Asia, all came definitely within the Allied sphere. France controlled the destinies of the Annamese and Tonkinese, who contributed countless labor battalions of poor little yellow men who shivered and plodded through the cold rains and bottomless mud of Northern France. Burma was part of India and added her share to the splendid Indian effort in Asia and Europe. The Malay States were unimportant—only Singapore counted and it was secured by British mastery of the seas. Siam, the only independent country in the southeastern group, which owed its independence to a ten-year-old agreement of France and Great Britain to maintain a buffer state between the French and the British East Indies, was officially one of the Allies and sent a detachment of troops to France besides contributing towards the war exchequer.

The attitude of the three largest independent Asiatic Powers—Japan, China, and the Ottoman Empire—was still to be determined at the outset of the war. Eventually all were drawn into the world conflict, but for the sake of clarity we shall deal first with the rôle played by Japan.

Officially of course there could be no doubt as to the attitude of Japan. The Anglo-Japanese Alliance was still in force and Japan was virtually pledged in the event of war to support Britain as her ally. But public opinion in Japan was by no means unanimous on the subject. The Japanese had a most profound respect for German organization, efficiency, and military discipline. Many people felt that Germany was bound to win the war and that the interests of Japan would best be served by siding with the presumptive victor. But there were other features of the situation that determined Japan to stand by her treaty obligations.

The Japanese had not forgotten that Germany had backed Russia twenty years before in her demand for the retrocession of Port Arthur after the Sino-Japanese War; moreover, it had become known to the Japanese Foreign Office that Germany was endeavoring to secure the neutrality of China by an agreement to abandon the Shantung peninsula. Japan also had her eye on the many German islands scattered through the Pacific. While her military forces as well as her fleet were in first-class condition there was the chance to widen the wedge of Japanese penetration on the Asiatic mainland by the seizure of the German leaseholds in China. Count Okuma, who was then prime minister, determined to stand by the Allies, and an ultimatum was sent to Germany on August 15th, followed by a declaration of war.

The first aggressive act of the Japanese was to occupy such island possessions of the Germans in the Pacific as the Marshall and Caroline groups practically without opposition, their fleet co-operating with the Australian squadron in the Pacific. Their next was to capture Tsingtao, Kiaochow, and the whole of the Shantung peninsula where German interests had formerly reigned supreme. These acts, until Japan in 1918 participated in the Allied expeditionary occupation of Siberia, constituted Japan's only direct military participation in the World War, although her fleet rendered valuable assistance to the Allies by patrolling trade routes and forwarding stores and munitions to Russia.

In the latter part of 1915, Japan was a party to the Pact of London entered into by the Allies for the purpose of defining the part that each was to play in the conduct of the war. It was definitely settled that Japan should continue the occupation of the German colonies in the Pacific and should contribute to the Allies' supply of munitions but should not send any armed contingents to the Western front. In the following year a second agreement was entered into by Japan, this time with Russia, by which she agreed not to embark during the war on any continental Asiatic policy against the interests of Russia.

Nevertheless, from the first the Japanese had taken advantage of the World War to pursue a policy of their own with regard to

China, which had remained neutral. In January, 1915, they presented and forced on the Chinese government the ultimatum known as the Twenty-one Demands, divided into five groups, of which the first group only dealt with the Japanese occupation of Shantung. It exacted the assent of the Chinese to any agreement which might be made thereafter by Japan with the German government in relation to the province of Shantung. It forbade the ceding or leasing of any part of Shantung to a third Power, granted the Japanese the right to build a new railway within the province, and provided for the opening of commercial ports under Japanese direction.

The second group of demands sought the acknowledgment of Japan's special interests in South Manchuria and eastern Inner Mongolia, and not only guaranteed to the Japanese special commercial privileges and prior rights to railway and mining development, but also placed in their hands the virtual political control of the territory in question.

The third group put all the Han-Yeh-Ping mines under Japanese control. The fourth group engaged China not to cede any bay or harbor along its coast to any other Power. The fifth provided for the employment of Japanese advisers to the central government, accorded the right to own property in the interior of China to Japanese subjects, provided for the joint policing of "important places" by Japanese and Chinese, pledged the Chinese government to the purchase of a fixed amount of munitions of war from Japan, and to the employment of Japanese technical experts to supervise her munition industries.

China was not to borrow foreign capital without consulting Japan. She was to accord Japan exclusive rights for the construction of two railways in Central China, and Japanese subjects were given the right to make missionary propaganda in China.

At this period the military party was in power and its policies were undoubtedly supported by the great mass of the Japanese people. Japan was taking advantage of the fact that the other interested Powers had their hands full in Europe, to establish a firm territorial foothold in China proper. It was a definite expression of Japan's ambition, born of necessity and fostered by circumstances, to become the acknowledged leader of a vast Far

Eastern Federation which should embrace all of the Yellow peoples. Although her methods have radically changed since 1915, this is still the goal of Japan's foreign policy and I shall discuss it further, when dealing with post-war developments in Asia.

After their first participation the Japanese sat back and watched the progress of the World War with somewhat mixed feelings. They fulfilled their engagements with respect to munitions and other matters to the letter, meanwhile extending their foreign trade by leaps and bounds, especially in regions formerly almost monopolized by British interests.

There was no government at this time able to restrain the high-handed proceedings of the Japanese in China. Even the United States, which had always taken the stand that the territorial integrity of China must be preserved at any cost, was placed in an awkward position, for to precipitate a crisis over Shantung might have seriously handicapped the Allies in their conduct of the war, and the administration of President Wilson while pursuing the "too proud to fight" policy for unavoidable reasons which cannot be discussed here, nevertheless was somewhat more than benevolently neutral.

In 1917, when the United States entered the World War, the administration felt that it was necessary to cement the lukewarm loyalty of Japan and considerations of expediency led to what was known as the Lansing-Ishii agreement in the month of November, by which the United States virtually recognized the validity of the Shantung demands. In the meantime the Germans had made surprising progress on the Western front.

Shortly after the United States declared war on April 6, 1917, the German armies, for a second time since the beginning of the war, advanced almost to the gates of Paris. On the Eastern European line they pushed forward into Russia, occupying Minsk and Kiev, advancing almost without opposition after the revolution in March, 1917, had brought about the collapse of the Russian armies. All this had a tremendous moral effect on Japan, which was one of the reasons that caused the Allied War Council to consider sending an expeditionary force to Siberia; the other was the state of affairs in Russia.

In January, 1918, the Allies were faced with the possible defection of Russia owing to the rising flood of Bolshevism. But the situation was as yet by no means hopeless. The first Russian Revolution, in March, 1917, which overthrew the monarchy by a revolt of the democratic and socialist parties, headed by Kerensky, had failed, largely owing to the incompetence of its leaders. The Communist or Bolshevist element under the leadership of Lenin and Trotzy, who had returned from exile in Europe through German connivance, had brought about a second revolution in November, 1917. The newly formed Soviet government which their party had organized after the November Revolution was, however, actually in control of only the central portion of Russia.

The demoralized Imperial army was still maintaining a show of resistance against the Germans on the Western front and opinion was still divided even among the Bolshevist leaders as to the advisability of making a separate peace with Germany. The remnants of the Imperial forces in the Ukraine, the Crimea, and the Caucasus, were holding out against the Bolshevists.

Siberia, while revolutionary, was not Bolshevist by any means. In some portions the monarchists still held control, in others the local government was administered by democratic Zemtsvo councils; a provisional democratic government known as the Ufa Directorate was operating in Western Siberia; there was a strong possibility that with proper support a force could be organized in Siberia which would advance and overthrow the Bolshevist dictatorship at Moscow, reach the demoralized but not entirely disintegrated army on the western front, and keep up at least a defensive line against Germany.

While possible intervention in Russia from this quarter was being discussed, an entirely new turn was given to events by the signing of the Treaty of Brest-Litovsk between Russia and Germany in June, 1918, which of course put an end to any hope of resistance against the Germans on the Eastern front. But at the same time it created a new situation which made it imperative for the Allied Powers to take some action in Siberia.

Since the beginning of the war, Siberia and Central Asia had been used by the Russians as a sort of huge internment camp for German prisoners of war, and the thousands of Austrians taken during the campaign on the Galician front in 1916. Among the latter were numbers of Czecho-Slovaks who had been conscripted by the Austrian government against their will, and whose sympathies had from the first been with the Allies and were still further enlisted by President Wilson's pronouncements about the "rights of the little peoples." There had long been a strong nationalist movement among the Czechs and the Slovaks, both Slavic peoples, who had never been really assimilated any more than the Hungarians, as part of the Austro-Hungarian Empire.

Taking advantage of the demoralized conditions in Russia following the Revolution, large bodies of these prisoners interned in the Volga basin and the Urals, had united under the leadership of their own officers, forming a well-organized military force. They had managed to seize enough munitions to arm themselves quite efficiently during the confusion attendant on the first days of the Revolution, and they announced their intention of fighting on the side of the Allies. For a short time the Kerensky government and later the Soviet government, planned to use them against the Germans, but after the peace of Brest-Litovsk they refused to lay down their arms and declared that they would fight their way out, if need be through Siberia, to join the Allies. In the Ural Mountain regions where they were concentrated, the Bolshevists had not yet obtained control and the weak Siberian Directorate had no force to oppose anything they might wish to do.

An appeal was sent by the Czecho-Slovaks to the Allied Powers to recognize them and to assist them in getting out of the country. Meanwhile they began to make preparations for moving eastward, seizing trains and locomotives and requisitioning supplies. Partly with the object of assisting them in their eastward march and partly in the hope of being able to utilize them as part of an anti-Bolshevist force to be organized in Siberia, the Allies determined to send an expeditionary force to Vladivostok.

It was agreed that each of the Allied Powers should send a detachment of not more than 8,000 troops, whose avowed object would be to maintain communications along the line of the Trans-Siberian Railway—then menaced by so-called partisan bands "red" and "white," who were really little more than brigands and local military leaders who had set up temporary governments of their own, mostly reactionary—so as to permit the undisturbed exit of the Czecho-Slovak divisions, forty thousand strong.

The real object of the expedition, however, at first carefully concealed—for the Allied statesmen had no desire for an open break with Soviet Russia—was to supply munitions to the loyal Russian forces via the Trans-Siberian Railway and to use the Czecho-Slovaks as part of the anti-Bolshevist armies which were being organized in Western Siberia. On August 3, 1918, the first Allied detachments were landed at Vladivostok and soon a mixed expeditionary force, composed mainly of French, British, American, and Japanese troops, was patrolling the Trans-Siberian Railway from Vladivostok to beyond Omsk and helping to maintain order in the far eastern provinces.

It was with many misgivings that the European Powers watched the participation of the Japanese in the Siberian adventure. Only a few months before, in the spring of 1918, when the Germans had advanced perilously near to Paris on the Western front and the Peace of Brest-Litovsk was imminent, a scheme is said to have been actually outlined in Japanese military circles and not without powerful support in certain governmental quarters, to force the government to renounce allegiance to the Allied cause. The former German and Austrian prisoners of war, of whom there were many thousands in Siberia, were to be organized and armed—a comparatively easy task owing to the demoralization brought about by the Revolution. This combined force of Germans and Japanese was to advance from the East, take Moscow and effect a juncture with the Germans, who had advanced in Russia to a point beyond Minsk and only a few hundred miles west of Moscow. The conclusion of peace between Russia and Germany naturally precluded the carrying out of this scheme, if indeed it was ever seriously contemplated.

However, whether or not Japanese loyalty was open to question, there was not a doubt that Japan would use any opportunity to obtain a foothold in Eastern Siberia as well as further control in Manchuria, where, as we have seen, her interests were already extensive. It was partly for this reason that an agreement was reached between the Allies limiting the number of troops which each country should contribute to the expeditionary forces. But from the very first, Japan was out of hand; alleging the necessity for protecting the interests of her nationals, she dispatched more than her quota to Siberia, and on one pretext or another it was later increased from time to time until it far exceeded that of any other of the Allies. When the armistice was declared therefore, the Japanese had obtained a foothold in Siberia which was obviously the prelude to an attempt at military penetration with a view to economic and commercial penetration and eventual political control of Eastern Siberia.

China's part in the Great War was not determined for nearly three years. She was far too absorbed in her own affairs and her relations with her neighbor Japan to give much heed to the world conflict.

At the beginning of 1914, international conditions in China gave promise of greater stability than had existed for some time. Yuan Shih-kai, after his coup d'état, was securely installed as President of the Republic. The military governors of the provinces whose insubordination and vast power were a constant menace to internal tranquillity were at peace with each other and the central government. The chronic deficit in the budget was smaller than usual; the interest on foreign obligations had been met; domestic loans were floated with success, negotiations with European bankers for new foreign loans were progressing and China seemed to be on the road to something like real national prosperity.

The Great War put a stop to all European co-operation in projects for the rehabilitation of Chinese finances, and the virtual dictatorship of Yuan Shih-kai received a severe blow when the administration finally accepted, though under compulsion, Japan's Twenty-one Demands. The President was blamed bitterly for his subserviency to the Japanese, and a national Day of Shame was inaugurated, to be kept forever in memory of China's humiliation. As a matter of fact, he could scarcely have done anything else. The success of the central government he was trying to build up in Peking depended very largely on his ability to secure loans for administrative purposes and for maintaining his own army to counteract the influence of the powerful provincial bureaucracy. With Japan's aid he could at least finance his administration—with her enmity he could not even oppose a vigorous defense against internal foes, and he had no outside backing. Even the United States failed to take any action to prevent Japan's coercive action.

Besides, it is highly probable that the President was anxious to temporize until he had realized his long-cherished ambition— a restoration of the monarchy with himself as Emperor. He allied himself with the Anfu party, a reactionary group which later adopted a pro-Japanese policy. A cleverly manipulated referendum apparently revealed a desire for a return to monarchical government, and Yuan Shih-kai was made Emperor by the Chinese Parliament. Just as the new regime was about to be inaugurated, however, revolts broke out in various parts of the Empire, and nearly two hundred members of the original National Assembly which had proclaimed the Republic, joined by the Southern radicals, met at Nanking and demanded the immediate restoration of the Republic.

Yuan was hesitating as to what course he should take when Fate solved the problem for him. He died very suddenly in June, 1916. Whatever his faults, he was an able administrator and a forceful leader. If he had lived he might perhaps have been able to weld China into something like unity. But there was no one who could take his place. No central government had a chance of permanence except as a dictatorship. China was too formless for representative government.

During the period following the death of Yuan Shih-kai, the Chinese had little interest in the world conflict, being too much engrossed with the internal situation. Gradually control of public affairs passed into the hands of the Anfu party, which began quite openly to show Japanese leanings, in spite of the popular boycott of Japan since the seizure of Shantung and the Twenty-one Demands.

Among individuals in China, sympathies were divided between the Allies and the Central Powers; though resentment of Japan's rôle in the war had caused a strong current of feeling in favor of Germany, officially the country remained neutral.

In the early part of 1917, however, when it became evident that the United States would shortly be drawn into the war, the advantage of having China on the side of the Allies was obvious, America needed to feel secure in the Pacific if she was to concentrate her efforts on sending a huge expeditionary force to Europe, and when President Wilson issued a proclamation to all neutral countries urging them to break off relations with Germany as a protest against submarine warfare, strong pressure was brought on China to induce her to abandon her neutrality. After considerable bargaining between the Allies and the new President of China, Li Yuan-hung, China finally declared war against Germany in August, 1917.

The bargain driven with China involved certain promises on the part of the Allies, failure to keep which is one of the reasons for the present crisis in the relations between China and the other Powers, particularly Great Britain.

The terms of the Allies' agreement with China are so important in view of recent happenings that, in order not to confuse our minds with an enumeration of the various political dissensions and manœuvrings that took place in China during 1917, we will pass them and recall some of the promises made by the Allies.

The portion of the Boxer indemnity due to Germany was to be cancelled. Payments on the same to the Allies were to be suspended. The customs tariff which had been arbitrarily fixed by the treaty Powers to insure the payment of the interest on their loans to the Chinese government and the promotion of their own commercial interests by absence of a tariff wall, was to be revised immediately. The Chinese government was to have a direct loan in place of loans administered through an Allied consortium; it had been proposed and it was hoped by many Chinese that as a reward for their country's participation in the war they would obtain during the peace negotiations the return of Shantung, then still occupied by the Japanese.

This idea was certainly encouraged by the Allies, who needed Chinese co-operation in many indirect but nevertheless vital matters. China as a neutral country was a base for the German agents who were stirring up trouble in Central Asia, Thibet, Afghanistan, and Turkestan with a view to striking a blow at India. The German Asiatic Bank in China supplied these agents with the sinews of war. The German ships interned in China waters would be of great assistance to the Allies, who needed merchant ships for transportation, and Chinese ports would afford valuable supply bases. Also a certain amount of trade could be carried on since the Australian and British fleets had eliminated German naval strength in the Pacific.

But it was not until November that the Chinese began to suspect that they had been bribed with false promises, when the text of the Lansing-Ishii agreement made with the United States by Japan was published. It showed that the United States had no intention of crossing Japan's designs in Shantung. The Anfu party twisted the incident to serve its own ends. It was argued that after all Japan and China possessed certain interests in common, that if the United States, considered China's best friend among the Western nations, had seen fit to abandon her, a rapprochement with Japan was the only course left open to the Republic. The Anfu leaders, backed by Japanese intrigue, were so powerful that they were able to put over a secret military agreement with Japan by which the latter, through what was known as the War Participation Bureau, obtained control of the finances, the army, and all the national resources of China, and until after the Armistice the government was completely under control of the Anfu leaders.

It was the latter who consented to the military control by the Japanese of the portion of the Trans-Siberian Railway running through Manchuria, the Chinese Eastern Railway, under pretext of protecting Manchuria from the Bolshevists, which as we shall see later came near precipitating a crisis that was only averted by the Washington Conference.

China's participation in the Great War was negative rather than positive. She never put an army into the field, though Chinese detachments were used as labor battalions. But late as it was, her indirect assistance was invaluable to the Allies.

Meanwhile, the opposition to the Anfu government had resulted in the defection of the large group of Southern leaders headed by Sun Yat-sen, who established a rival government at Canton. The South Chinese government was partly a protest against Japanese domination, partly an expression of the rising Nationalist sentiment, which included hatred of the Manchu domination with antagonism to the foreigners. Consequently China, at the moment of the Armistice, was seething with unrest from without and within.

From the beginning of the war the position of the Ottoman Empire left little room for doubt. At that time, as we have seen, the hopes for the regeneration of Turkey which had seemed so bright in 1908, after the deposition of Abdul Hamid, had faded into the dim and distant background. The so-called constitutional government was a mockery. The Union and Progress faction constituted a virtual dictatorship; the entire country was depleted from a series of wars of which the last, the Turco-Bulgarian War, had terminated only a short time before the beginning of the Great War, and Turkey had very nearly lost Constantinople to the Bulgarians.

There had been a series of uprisings in Asia Minor, due to the aggressive programme of the Young Turks for the forcible assimilation of all non-Turkish elements within the Empire. The Armenian National movement, encouraged by the Russians, had been ruthlessly crushed, and the Young Turks had completed the alienation of the Arab portions of the Empire by meddling with the Islamic faith, the one tie which bound them to Turkey. Their proposal that all prayers in the Mosques should be conducted in Turkish instead of Arabic, the traditional tongue of the Faith and of the Koran, aroused the most bitter antagonism. The temporal authority of the Sultan-Khalif was more honored in the breach than in the observance throughout the Arabian peninsula outside of certain centres where Turkish governors and Turkish garrisons kept relative law and order, though nominally he was still the overlord of the small Arabian principalities as well as of Egypt, which had been "temporarily" occupied by Great Britain for nearly forty years.

In August, 1914, while the Sultan and the majority of his cabinet were in favor of strict neutrality, the Young Turk leaders were pro-German and, by a series of adroit moves carried out by Enver Pasha, then Minister of War, Turkey was placed in a position of aggressor against Russia. The Union and Progress party was ardently pro-German, as was the Turkish army, which had long been trained under German officers and steeped in German military ideas.

The Germans had made munificent promises to Turkey to secure her participation in the war on the side of the Central Powers, guaranteeing the return of Cyprus and other islands in the Aegean Sea which she had lost to Great Britain and Italy, and the extension of Turkey's territories and spheres of influence in Asia; full Turkish sovereignty was to be re-established in Egypt, and Turkey was to have the entire region of the Caucasus then under Russian control, with its valuable oil wells and its two ports of Baku and Batum, one on the Caspian and the other on the Black Sea.

While a number of Turks did not altogether trust these promises, they actually believed they could utilize Germany and also the idea of Pan-Islamic solidarity, to pave the way for a renascence of the Turanian race of which the Ottoman Turks were a part. Enver Pasha in particular dreamed of the establishment of a vast Pan-Turanian federation which would embrace all the Mongol-Tartar peoples of Asia from the desert steppes of Mongolia to the shores of the Aegean and the Mediterranean.

Added to this, was the consideration duly emphasized by German agents that finally determined Turkey to cast in her lot with the Central Powers—the fear and hatred of Russia. For this, as we have seen, there was much justification. While the attitude of the Ottoman government towards its Christian minorities, particularly during the nineteenth century, was indefensible on many grounds, the Armenian massacres that appalled the world in Mr. Gladstone's day and later were not entirely due to the "unspeakable" Turk. As a matter of fact, the average Turk, when left to himself and not inflamed by propaganda or fanaticism to outbreaks of racial hatred, is an exceedingly kindly, even lovable individual.

From the beginning of the nineteenth century, as early as the reign of Paul I, the successor of Catherine the Great, Russian agents with their eyes on the Caucasus had stimulated the antagonism between Turk and Armenian by every possible manner of provocation. Much of the moral responsibility of the Armenian massacres rests on the Russian Foreign Office.

From the beginning of the war it was an open secret that Russia was to have Constantinople and the Dardanelles, and the reported agreement between Russia and Great Britain to this effect was used as propaganda material by the Turks to stir up feeling against the Allies. However, formal declaration of war was delayed until the month of September, 1914.

Turkish participation complicated matters considerably for Great Britain. She was obliged not only to defend her long line of communications with various parts of her Empire, but also to conduct simultaneous offensive campaigns in Arabia and Mesopotamia to prevent the Turco-German forces from taking Egypt and the Suez Canal on the one hand, thereby cutting off the route to India, and on the other to block their advance through the valley of the Tigris and Euphrates to the Persian Gulf, one of her most vulnerable spots on account of its proximity to India and to her principal source of supply for petroleum in Southwest Persia.

Consequently it became necessary for Great Britain to organize immediately two expeditionary forces. One, with Egypt as its base, under General Allenby, was to defend the Suez Canal and advance through Hedjaz and Syria, the capture of the railway line to Damascus being its immediate objective. Once this was safely in British hands, Egypt would be secure, as the Central Powers were not in a position to make an attack on Egypt from the sea.

The second expedition, under General Maude, was to operate from the Persian Gulf with India as its base, its object being the control of the strategic approach to the Persian Gulf from Turkey by way of Mosul, Baghdad, and Basra. It was this force that was almost entirely manned, equipped, and maintained by Great Britain's loyal subjects in India.

In addition to these two forces, the British War Office undertook the ill-advised expedition to the Dardanelles, and the Gallipoli campaign, with its shocking mismanagement, was a severe tax on the resources of the Empire and an appalling waste of splendid human material. Unsuccessful as it was, however, the Gallipoli campaign had one redeeming feature from the Allied point of view. By creating another fighting front it effected a diversion and prevented the Turks from making a vigorous offensive that might have endangered Egypt and the Suez Canal.

From the outset, Turkey was in a particularly disadvantageous position with regard to her own fronts. There was no other country among those that participated in the World War which had an equal number to defend simultaneously. There was the Caucasus, where the Russian forces threatened Armenia, which was seething with nationalism and disaffection. There was Constantinople itself, where only the disgraceful Allied mismanagement of the Gallipoli campaign proved the salvation of the Turk. There was the Balkan campaign, in which the Turks and their late enemies the Bulgarians were made cat's-paws by General von Mackensen against the Serbians.

General von Falkenhayn directed the operations in Asiatic Turkey and Arabia, conducted by two armies, one with Damascus as its base operating against Allenby's forces; the other with Baghdad as its headquarters. From the first, the Turco-German forces were handicapped by the fact that they were operating in countries where the native inhabitants were far from loyal. The Syrian campaign was fought in a country largely peopled with non-Turkish nationalities. The districts of Aleppo and Damascus were Arab. Lebanon, with the important port of Beirut as its capital, was inhabited by a Christian majority. Palestine was predominantly Arab, with a sprinkling of Jews and Christians and a few Turks, and along the line of the Hedjaz railway as far as Medina were Arab tribes mostly under the rule of Hussein the Sherif of Mecca, himself the descendant of the Prophet with aspirations towards the Khalifate and no love for Turkey.

The valley of the Tigris and Euphrates with the exception of the districts centring in Mosul, where there were numbers of Turks and Kurds, was inhabited by Arabs, the majority of whom were a pastoral, or semi-nomad population. With the exception of the inhabitants of the three cities of Baghdad, Mosul, and Basra, which were pro-Turkish, the tribes were disaffected. Outside the cities already mentioned, there were few large centres in Mesopotamia except the so-called Holy Cities of the Shiah Moslems, largely Persian in their affiliations and traditions, and not

particularly predisposed to sympathize with either group of
participants in the World War.

The remainder of the country was thinly populated by nomadic
Bedouin tribes without any sense of national or even racial cohe-
sion or solidarity. While they were utilized to a certain extent by
both the British and Turco-German forces the Mesopotamian
campaign was in the main a strategic issue between the two
armies. The British gained possession of Basra at the mouth
of the Tigris River early in the war, thereby blocking any attempt
of the enemy to attack the Anglo-Persian Oil Company's port of
Abadan near the mouth of the Tigris. The campaign as a whole
progressed slowly. The Mesopotamian expeditionary forces had
no nearer supply base than India. The character of the country
and the climate constituted in themselves formidable difficulties.
At one time, a detachment of British forces was trapped on a
narrow peninsula which formed an elbow in the river Tigris at
Kut el Amara and some 8,000 British with their leader, General
Townsend, were taken prisoners by the Turks, after a prolonged siege.

It was not until the spring of 1917 that the British took Baghdad, and Mosul the last stronghold of the Turks in Mesopotamian territory surrendered only on November 8, 1918, three
days before the general armistice ended the World War, and a
week after the separate armistice signed by Turkey at Mudros.

In Syria, matters were different. There the Turks had to contend with the large disaffected Christian population of the
Lebanon and the strong Arab national movement which had
begun to spread before the World War.

There had been no feeling of solidarity among the Arab peoples
after the Ottoman conquest in the fifteenth century. In the latter
part of the nineteenth century the perennial discontent against the
Turkish régime showed signs of developing into a genuine Nationalist movement, but at that time the Pan-Islamic policy of
Sultan Abdul Hamid was sufficiently strong to counteract this
tendency. The Pan-Islamic movement, however, was merely a
stage in the evolution of the Asiatic peoples; its influence in the
Ottoman Empire was given a severe blow by the Young Turks
with their programme of forcible Ottomanization.

When the war broke out, Arab National Committees had already been formed throughout Arabia proper, in opposition to the Committee of Union and Progress. In Syria and Damascus the Turks were able to suppress Arab manifestations and to a certain extent to dominate the Hedjaz through their control of the railway to Medina. The small principality of Yemen had long been a Turkish penal colony and was therefore strongly occupied by Turkish troops, but the other states of the Arabian peninsula paid only nominal allegiance to the Sultan of Turkey, and from the beginning of the war they were neutral when not actually hostile. The British, from their control of the Persian Gulf, exercised a predominating influence on the east coast of the peninsula, and the remaining rulers of Central Arabia were hardly more than patriarchal chiefs of tribal groups or units.

While among these people there was no intellectual movement corresponding to the Arab movement in the more advanced provinces of the Ottoman Empire, there still existed a strong racial antagonism to the Turks and a genuine spirit of independence. Obviously here was the raw material for resistance to the Turco-German plans to unite the Moslem world in a Jehad, or Holy War, as well as for the more immediate purpose of assisting the British expeditionary force in its Syrian campaign. The British were not slow to take advantage of this state of affairs and by judicious promises and propaganda succeeded in inciting an Arab revolt against Turkish rule.

The man chosen by them to head the nationalist revolt was Hussein, the Sherif of Mecca, who had for several years been secretly dreaming of a restoration of an Arab empire with himself as leader. At first, however, he was uncertain as to whether or not he and his sons Ali, Feisal, Abdullah, and Zaid should throw in their lot with the Allies.

The failure of the Dardanelles campaign did not enhance Allied prestige and beyond the capture of the Sinai peninsula controlling the Suez Canal, the British had made no progress. It was the Turks who precipitated the decision of Hussein to join forces with the Allies. Djemal Pasha, who was commander of the Turkish forces in Syria, instituted a veritable reign of terror there against the Arab Nationalist leaders, based on incriminating documents found in the closed Allied consulates.

As a result, negotiations were begun between the Sherif of Mecca and the British High Commissioner in Egypt, which resulted in the making of certain promises to Hussein by the British on behalf of the Allies. Although no formal agreements were signed, they were sufficient to constitute the basis for claims of breach of faith later made against the British by the Arabs and they have been responsible for a number of complications which have produced conditions in the Arabian peninsula that still constitute a menace to political stability in the Near East.

The correspondence between Hussein and the British government lasted for nearly a year. The British government in reply to a letter from Hussein asking for recognition of the future independence of Syria, Mesopotamia, and the entire Arabian peninsula, and the recognition of an Arab Khalifate in return for military support and special privileges and concessions from the Sherifian government, gave assurance that "Great Britain has no intention of concluding any peace in which the freedom of the Arab peoples from German and Turkish domination does not form the central condition." A communication from the British High Commissioner in Egypt went even further:

Excepting the districts of Mersina and Alexandretta, which were predominately Turkish, and the Syrian Littoral, which was principally Christian [the High Commissioner wrote]—with the above modification and without prejudice to our existing treaties with Arab Chiefs, we accept these limits and boundaries; and in regard to those portions of territories in which Great Britain is free to act without detriment of her Ally, France, I am empowered in the name of the Government of Great Britain to give the following assurances and make the following reply to your letter: Subject to the above modifications Great Britain is prepared to recognize and support the independence of the Arabs within the territories included in the limits and boundaries proposed by the Sherif of Mecca.

The letter further stipulated that the prospective Arab kingdom should be under the advice and guidance of Great Britain and that the Arabs would recognize the special interests of the British in Mesopotamia. No formal treaty was signed and no more definite conclusions reached so far as we know, but subsequent events made it quite clear that while the future relations between Arabs and Allied Powers were not settled, the Arabs firmly believed that the great Powers were pledged to accord them independence in return for their co-operation.

As a matter of fact, however, at the very time these negotiations were proceeding, the Allies themselves had entered into a series of agreements for the partitioning of the Ottoman Empire beginning with the accord between Russia, France, and Great Britain, in the spring of 1915, in which the Russians' claim on Constantinople was recognized. Further negotiations culminated in an agreement according Russia parts of Armenia and Kurdistan, and France portions of Anatolia, Cilicia, and the Syrian littoral. Later on, claims of Italy to a share of the spoils were recognized, and she obtained, on paper, the right to Adana and Smyrna in Asia Minor. British interests were to be served by the acquisition of southern Mesopotamia and the ports of Haifa and Acre on the coast of Syria.

A supplementary document, known as the Sykes-Picot agreement between France and Great Britain, divided the entire Arab area in which the British had by correspondence with Hussein definitely recognized Arab rights, into five zones, including red and blue zones of British and French administration, corresponding zones of British and French influence, and an international brown zone corresponding with Palestine.

These agreements were kept secret from Hussein and were not known to the world at large until they were made public by the Bolshevists at the end of 1917.

Hussein, ignorant of all this, still had faith in British promises; moreover, in the spring of 1916, it became clear that the Turks and Germans were planning to use Arabia as a base for operations in the Red Sea and on the coast of Africa. Hussein realized that such action would mean direct Turkish control and this decided him to throw in his lot with the Allies.

With the assistance of a number of British officers sent from Egypt, among whom was the now famous Colonel Lawrence, an Arab revolt was organized which resulted in the formation of an irregular army under the leadership of the Emir Feisal, Hussein's second son, co-operating with General Allenby's forces.

By the end of 1916, all the isolated Turkish garrisons in the Hedjaz had been swept away, Medina was invested, and the long line of railway between Medina and Jerusalem was the point on which their offensive was centred. As the British expeditionary force advanced, the Arab auxiliaries, chiefly composed of light cavalry, constantly harassed the Turks on both flanks, and Arab propaganda, skilfully directed by Lawrence and his associates, won over tribe after tribe among the Arabs in the invaded territory.

Jerusalem was taken in the autumn of 1917, its capture being followed by an intensive political campaign among the Arabs. During the final offensive in the autumn of 1918, ending in the capture of Damascus a month before the Armistice, the Arab forces played an important part and their military assistance was undoubtedly of great value, though their greatest help was political. The espousal of the British cause by the Sherif of Mecca served to concentrate all Arab disaffection.

From Damascus may be dated the downfall of the old Ottoman Empire. At the close of the war the greater portion of what had once been Turkey in Asia was classed as occupied enemy territory—Syria, Palestine, Hedjaz, Mesopotamia, the purely Turkish province of Cilicia, even portions of Anatolia; and a little later Constantinople, came under the Allied occupation.

Having outlined the part played by Asiatic countries which actively participated in the World War, we still have to consider the so-called neutral countries. Of these there were only two in Western Asia—Persia and Afghanistan. At the beginning of the war, Persia was torn with conflicting impulses and as far as practical action was concerned was quite helpless. Her official neutrality did not prevent her from becoming one of the lesser battle grounds of the world conflict, and as a matter of fact the losses of Persia in the Great War were greater than those of China or Japan, both belligerents.

In 1914, as we have seen, Persia was politically divided as far as her external relations went between two spheres of influence, Russian and British. Her western frontier, touching that of Turkey, naturally made her the objective of the German agents, whose aim it was to stir up revolts against Russia in Central Asia and to strike at Great Britain through Persia and Afghanistan.

Consequently, soon after the opening of hostilities, the Russians moved troops into northern Persia from the Caucasus so as to attack the Turks from that quarter, and to stir up the Assyrian Christians, who lived in eastern Kurdistan on both sides of the Turco-Persian frontier, to revolt against Turkish dominion. They were assisted in this territory by a small force of British.

There is no time here to tell the full story of the little Assyrian nation which has been described as our smallest ally. It is one of the most tragic episodes of the World War. The Assyrians claim to be the descendants of the founders of Nineveh, the warlike people who under Sennacherib came against the kingdom of Judah "like the wolf on the fold." Within modern times, however, they have been known as one of the oldest Christian peoples of the East, their religion being a form of Nestorian Christianity. Under the Ottoman Empire they enjoyed almost complete autonomy. Their organization was in family groups and they were ruled over by a king-patriarch called Lord Simon—Mar Shimun. The majority of the Assyrians shared the eastern portion of Turkish Kurdistan with the Kurds although considerable numbers of them were settled across the Persian border in the district around Lake Urumia.

The Russians, seeing in them a possible aid on their Caucasus front, persuaded them to join the cause of the Allies and formed them into irregular battalions with Russian officers. These battalions after the Russian retreat kept up a guerrilla warfare against the Turks under Russian direction, until the final dissolution of the Russian army in 1917. Even then, they still held out against the Turkish Kurds, and subsequently they retreated into Persian territory, where they were attacked until they were force to flee *en masse* to avoid extermination.

Their patriarch was killed by a Kurdish chief. His successor was only a little boy, but under the leadership of Surma Hanum, the sister of the murdered patriarch, 70,000 of them undertook a march to Hamadan near the Mesopotamian frontier, then under

British control. They were nearly all the way under fire from the Turks and Kurds, and their number during the forced march was reduced by two-thirds, thousands being massacred in the headlong flight. The remnants of the nation were finally assembled in a camp on the borders of Mesopotamia in what is now the kingdom of Iraq.

During the early part of the War the British occupied several positions along the Gulf of Persia to facilitate troop movements in the Mesopotamian campaign and to defend the Anglo-Persian oil fields. As far as the central government was concerned, they contented themselves at first with countering the moves of the German intriguers at the court of Teheran; but the British, equally with the Russians, had been guilty of so many attempts to infringe on Persian sovereignty, that the Turco-German party was able to exert considerable influence.

By 1916, German influence was predominant at court and German agents, in particular one Wassmuss, whose name became a household word among the tribespeople, had created such a strong current of sentiment that it seemed inevitable that Persia should join the Central Powers; being perilously near the Caucasus frontier and the Caspian Sea, and with Russian forces already in Northern Persia, it was evident that if Persia did throw in her lot with Germany, Teheran would almost certainly be occupied. It was planned to move the government to Isfahan, the old capital of Persia, and on December 14th, when the Shah was about to flee from Teheran under the escort of military units controlled by the Turco-German agents, the British and Russian Ministers drove to the palace and persuaded the young Shah Ahmed not to take this decisive step.

During this period, Great Britain had not let matters drift in her own special sphere of influence in South Persia, where besides the oil fields there were other important interests. Sir Percy Sykes was sent to Persia with a small detachment of Indian troops to restore order and open trade routes. By November, he had entered Shiraz, the metropolis of southern Persia, and he had organized a body of troops known as the South Persian Rifles which patrolled the roads, kept order in the cities, and generally put the fear of God and of the British into the easy-going unmilitary Persians of the south.

The only difficulties he encountered were with the migratory tribespeople of the western Persian mountains, who were virtually independent of the central government, with ancient feudal systems of their own which had remained intact for many centuries. Some were won by promises, others by display of force. Communications were vastly improved by repairing existing trade routes and by the opening of a new caravan road known as the Lynch Road from Isfahan to Bushire.

In March, 1917, Sir Percy Sykes was officially recognized by the Teheran government as head of the Persian gendarmerie for the south and central sections. He soon had an efficient force of military police composed of some 11,000 Persians, 5,000 tribespeople and a small number of Indians all under British officers.

Actually this constituted an occupation of Persia in obvious violation of Persia's neutrality, but the fact that had they not done so the Turco-German forces would have taken similar action, seemed to the British sufficient moral justification for what in principle was a gross violation of international law.

From that day there was never any question of Persia's participation in the war. Nevertheless, at the time of the armistice when the nations of the world began to take stock of profits and losses, the Persians found themselves in a most unfortunate position. After the collapse of the Russia Imperial armies on the Caucasus front following the Revolution, the Russian forces, it was true, had been withdrawn or rather had melted away in northwestern Persia; they had done much damage, living off the country, requisitioning without payment, and creating unsettled conditions throughout the entire area.

The Kurdish and Turcoman tribes of the northwest, who were virtually independent of the central government, had caused no end of trouble by their depredations. When the Russians had withdrawn, the Assyrians, abandoned by their Allies and hard pressed by the Turks and Kurds, had swarmed over the Persian frontier in the neighborhood of Lake Urumia. They were a military people, they were desperate and starving, and they were not always particular as to how they obtained their supplies. They helped themselves from the countryside and the Persians retaliated by sending mixed detachment of regulars and gendarmerie against them. There were several engagements in which the Persians sometimes had the worst of it.

The British were in absolute control of the country as far north as Isfahan and in the western provinces adjoining Mesopotamia.

The new Bolshevist propaganda was active in the northern part of the country where conditions were chaotic. After the capture of Baghdad, detachments were sent from British expeditionary forces into northwestern Persia to block possible Turco-German penetration following the Russian collapse. They, too, more or less lived off the country, though they helped to preserve order, but the Russian and Turkish troops who had advanced into the same territory during the war had plundered and pillaged all along their line of march.

As a result of all these disturbances and the consequent interruption to agriculture in the most fertile parts of the country, Persia suffered from a terrible famine during 1917, and 1918. There are no reliable statistics as to the actual number of deaths, but the suffering was widespread and acute, particularly in northern Persia. At the close of the War Persia appeared neither as one of the victors nor as one of the vanquished, yet her territory had been overrun; her people had starved and fought and died in vain. England for the moment was virtually occupying the country, and its destinies seemed to be in British hands.

Afghanistan had fared much better during the war. Shortly after the declaration of war on the Allies by Turkey, a German-Turkish military expedition arrived in Kabul, the capital, and every effort was made to force Afghanistan into the war on the side of the Central Powers. It was hoped that the Afghan Moslems would join the Jehad or Holy War to be proclaimed by the Khalif, who was also Sultan of Turkey. But there were several reasons that held the Afghans on the side of the Allies.

In the first place, there is in Afghanistan a strong infusion of Aryan blood as opposed to the Mongol-Tartar strain that is predominant in Central Asia. As in Persia, this fundamental racial difference had proved a stumbling block to Pan-Turanian

aspirations more than once in history. The old antagonism between Iran and Turan at the time of the Great War was still
strong enough to help divide the sympathies of both Persians
and Afghans. Habibullah Khan, the Amir of Afghanistan,
was strongly pro-British and he had been for many years receiving an annual subsidy from Great Britain, whose special sphere
of influence in Afghanistan had been recognized by Russia. Besides which, Russia, Afghanistan's nearest neighbor, was also
the ally of Great Britain.

Failing either to penetrate Persia through Turkey or to rouse
the Afghans to revolt and invade India, the emissaries of the
Central Powers had to content themselves with stirring up small
disturbances along the borders of Afghanistan and India.

But their agents used it as a route of penetration to the Far
East, and all through the war there was a steady infiltration of
intrepid German spies. Now they were among the tribes along
the approaches to the Khyber pass leading into India through
Kashmir, now crossing the Pamir into Chinese Turkestan and
the western provinces, now on the Tibetan marches, making
propaganda in Bhutan, Nepal, and Ladak, even pushing their
insidious influence into the Forbidden Country itself. Everywhere
they went they fanned the embers of race and religious antagonism, of anti-foreign feeling, of rebellion and revolt whenever they
could be turned to the advantage of the Central Powers or the
detriment of the Allies. There are many thrilling chapters of war
history yet to be written concerning German espionage and Allied
counter-espionage in High Asia. While directly the Central
Asiatic countries played no part in the world conflict, nevertheless,
they, like the rest of Asia, felt the influence of the closer contacts
with Europe.

All the ideas and ideals that were setting Europe on fire had
their reactions in Asia. The Asiatics who fought on European
fronts brought them back to be disseminated at home, together
with more or less uncomplimentary comments on Western manners and morals. They had seen Europe's "feet of clay." Increased
facility of communications in many parts of Asia and the growth
of industrialism largely due to war conditions had created new

problems and stimulated new movements common to both continents. The East and the West had been brought together whether they would or no.

There were broad-minded statesmen in Europe who realized the momentous possibilities of the readjustment period following the Armistice, but they were few. The Europeanization of Asia produced a fallow field on Asiatic soil for planting seeds of peace or seeds of future discord. We shall see how the Allies albeit unintentionally took the latter course and sowed the dragon's teeth which have been producing armed harvests ever since.

Chapter Five

NOR WAR, NOR PEACE

WHEN Trotsky and Lenin in March, 1918, met the German plenipotentiaries with whom they were to sign a treaty of peace in the little Polish town of Brest-Litovsk, Trotsky, who was opposed to making peace with Germany, is said to have scribbled on the wall of the room in which the delegates of the two countries met, "Nor War, Nor Peace" (Ne Voina ne Mir). What he meant of course, was that as long as the capitalistic nations of the world remained as such, there could be no real peace between them and proletarian Russia. But his words were in another sense curiously prophetic and they might truthfully have been written by the representative of any one of the great Powers on the walls of the throne-room at Versailles.

Ever since that day in June, 1919, when Count Brockdorf-Rantzau signed the treaty of peace for Germany with such ill grace there has been no World Peace, and nearly as many lives have been lost through conflicts in Europe and Asia as in the four terrible years between 1914 and 1918. The reason is not far to seek. The Allies, having won the war largely through their espousal of the doctrine of self-determination and the rights of small nations, proceeded to make peace on the old imperialistic basis. The Peace deliberations throughout were dominated by the selfish interests of the Allied Powers. Small wonder that the peoples who at one time saw the dawn of the millennium in the Wilsonian ideals, subsequently put their faith in revolt and revolution.

Although the publication of many of the secret treaties and agreements between the Allied Powers had shaken the belief of Asia in Allied justice, there were high hopes in the breasts of many of the delegations from Asiatic countries which attended the opening of the peace deliberations at the French Foreign Office, on the Quai d'Orsay, in Paris early in 1919. Practically every country in the length and breadth of the Asiatic continent was represented with the exception of vanquished Turkey.

China, Japan, and Siam, all sovereign Allied states, sent their ministers plenipotentiary. India was represented by Mr. Montagu, British Secretary of State for India, and two native delegates. Persia and Afghanistan sent representatives to watch over their interests, and in addition to the official delegates, innumerable representatives of national groups were sent to ask a hearing before the Allied Supreme Council. The Arabs sent the Emir Feisal to represent King Hussein of the Hedjaz, who was to plead the cause of an Arab federation. The Armenians presented the case for an Armenian Republic. The Syrians sent delegates to ask for an independent Syrian State. The Assyrians, who as we have seen were almost annihilated during the war, put in their plea for autonomy and there were numberless delegates representing other groups of whom the world had never heard as separate peoples, demanding recognition, independence, autonomy and asking for new territories or reclaiming old ones long since lost.

Amid the babel of tongues and the multiplicity of demands at the Peace Conference, the Supreme Council was obliged to face not only the task of settling the actual peace terms with the Central Powers, but also reconstituting the boundaries of considerable portions of both Europe and Asia; of settling indemnities and satisfying not only the larger but the smaller Powers that had fought on the side of the Allies.

The Supreme Council itself, composed of representatives of the great Powers that had brought the war to a successful conclusion, was torn and divided on many important points and above all, was faced with the problem of reconciling past diplomatic traditions with the new aspirations born of the war, and first made articulate by President Wilson. America's participation in the war though at the eleventh hour had been a decisive factor in the conflict, and the strong personality of President Wilson backed by this obvious fact had for the time being more or less imposed his doctrines on the world at large.

The idea of a League of Nations which should prevent all future wars by uniting the nations of the world as members of a great human family, had an immense popular appeal for the war-weary peoples. It was espoused by many shrewd European statesmen as a new vehicle for acquiring power, and by the smaller nations as a means of securing protection and justice. In the first post-war reaction there was a genuine and spontaneous movement of enthusiasm in its favor throughout Europe and Asia. Even the conquered peoples looked to the League of Nations as their one hope of salvation, while the doctrine of self-determination which was accepted by all small nations of the world as the corollary of the League principle, was stirring Asia to its foundations. The right of every people to self-government within its own ethnic boundaries was a fundamental principle of the new creed, altruistic no doubt, but utterly impossible of fulfilment as the world has since found out to its cost.

Asiatic problems were necessarily brought up at the beginning of the Versailles conference, for one of the first questions to be considered was the disposal of the German possessions in the Far East. President Wilson had proposed, as part of his League of Nations scheme, that the colonies of the Central Powers, together with such portions of their dominions as were inhabited by subject peoples of different race or religion, should be considered as wards of the League of Nations under a guardianship or Mandate administered by the "Advanced Nations." This system was theoretically a tremendous step forward in international politics. In practice, however, it hid a maze of pitfalls into which the unwary world was precipitated when, because of President Wilson's insistence, the Covenant of the League of Nations was made an integral part of the Peace Treaty.

The partitioning of the German possessions in the Pacific was accomplished after considerable discussion, between Japan, the United States, and Great Britain. The United States was not at all anxious to see the Japanese Empire extended to within a short distance of the Philippines. Great Britain was not disposed to run counter to the claims of Japan who was still her ally. Australia, where there was strong anti-Japanese feeling, did not desire the proximity of Japan any more than did the United States.

It was finally agreed that Australia should have the Mandate for the islands south of the equator, and Japan for all north of that line, including the tiny island of Yap, important as a strategic base and as a centre of the trans-Pacific cable system.

The question of the former German holdings in China was not settled so easily. Japan was still occupying the province of Shantung and while she disclaimed any intention of keeping it permanently, she insisted that the question was one which she would settle by a separate agreement with China, which had already acceded to her occupation by accepting the Twenty-one Demands.

President Wilson was convinced of the justice of the Chinese claims but he was finally forced to yield in the matter to Japan, supported by Great Britain, for as the Conference wore on differences had developed among the Allies which were imperilling the League of Nations Covenant, and he did not dare to run the risk of having Japan withdraw from the Conference. He was forced to desert China by pressure exerted by France, Italy, and Great Britain, all of whom sided with Japan.

Feeling in America at that time was strongly pro-Chinese and the President's failure to resist the pressure brought to bear on him with regard to Shantung was partly responsible for the crystallization of the latent hostility to the League of Nations Covenant which had already begun to show itself in America. In spite of the President's weakness with regard to Shantung, he succeeded curiously enough in antagonizing not only the Chinese whom he had failed to protect, but also the Japanese whom he had sought to propitiate as well as the other Asiatic countries in general, by defeating a Japanese resolution establishing the principle of racial equality.

In the eyes of the Asiatic this was the climax of a series of injustices. It caused discontent even among the Japanese who had profited so obviously in a territorial sense, by their participation in the war. It rankled in the breasts of the Chinese even more than the military occupation of Shantung. Had not China been willing to do her bit in the war to aid the Allies, and had not they been more than willing to accept her help at the crucial moment? It brought an added bitterness into the situation in India, where the people, tragically disillusioned in their hopes for Home Rule as a reward for their great services in the war were, under Gandhi espousing the boycott and non-cooperation movements. It intensified everywhere racial, group, and national solidarity.

Moreover, in Asia many of the decisions reached at Versailles seemed inconclusive and impermanent in view of the fact that Russia had no share in the peace deliberations. As we have seen, she had made her own peace terms with Germany following the Bolshevik Revolution and seven months before the Armistice. During the Versailles Conference the Allies still clung to the delusion that the existence of the Soviet government in Russia was a matter of weeks or months only. They recognized the anti-Bolshevik government set up in Siberia by Admiral Kolchak but half-heartedly, never going so far as to pretend that it was an all-Russian government. Permanent settlement of questions in which Russia had an interest was postponed indefinitely.

Meanwhile, Japan, under the pretext of maintaining order on the outskirts of the Russian Empire was policing the former Russia concessions in Manchuria and calmly taking possession of the eastern portion of Siberia. China had taken advantage of Russian demoralization to reassert her sovereignty over Mongolia and send an army to support her pretensions. The Bolsheviks were beginning to impose their authority in Central Asia, and the anarchy and chaos which prevailed from the Caspian to the Pacific inspired little confidence in World Peace.

No one knew just then when or how Russia would make her reappearance in the field of international politics, but it was a foregone conclusion that she would sooner or later have much to say with regard to Asiatic affairs which might not be in accord with the dictates of the Peace Conference.

More than seven months elapsed between the conclusion of the Armistice with Germany and the signature of the Treaty of Versailles—months during which the Allies argued, wrangled, and intrigued among themselves, to the great detriment of their prestige in Asiatic eyes. Meanwhile they had done virtually nothing towards settling one of the most serious problems of reconstruction in Asia,—the determination of the status of the countries composing the former Ottoman Empire.

The participation of Turkey in the Great War had been ended by the separate armistice signed between the Turks and the Allies at Mudros eleven days before the conclusion of the general armistice. By the terms of the Mudros armistice all of Arabia, Syria, and Mesopotamia, with portions of Asia Minor, became what was officially known as Occupied Enemy Territory.

Early in 1919 the occupation was organized. Each of the Allied Powers sent a High Commissioner with a detachment of troops to Constantinople. The French took over Syria and the Turkish province of Cilicia within the zones fixed by various agreements with England, and British Occupationary Forces were confined to Mesopotamia and Palestine. Italy was given possession of Adalia, portions of Southern Anatolia and several of the Aegean Islands including Rhodes, while the Greeks were permitted to occupy Smyrna. The Versailles Peace Conference did not directly affect any of these arrangements; the whole question of the disposal of the former possessions of the Ottoman Empire being dealt with in the Treaty of Sèvres between the Allies and Turkey, which was not signed until August, 1920. Indirectly, however, it made the application of the mandatory system obligatory in the Near East, as it was embodied in the League of Nations Covenant, which had been accepted as an integral part of the Treaty of Versailles, by all the Powers except the United States.

While there were some ardent nationalists who would have been satisfied with nothing less than complete independence among the liberated peoples of the Near East, the majority recognized the necessity for some sort of guardianship until they were able to stand on their own feet. The mandatory plan would have been welcomed in Syria and Arabia had it not been evident from the first that the Mandates were to be made to serve the ends of the Powers with special interests in those countries.

France and Great Britain, having settled upon their respective zones of occupation and influence, proceeded to organize the administration of these zones without so much as a "By your leave" to anybody, and along lines suited to their own political aspirations. It took them nearly two years to reach mutual agreement as to the boundaries of the areas for which they ultimately obtained mandates from the Supreme Allied Council.

When Great Britain was finally assigned the Mandates for

Palestine and Mesopotamia, and France received a mandate for Syria, no serious attempt had been made to ascertain the wishes of the inhabitants. The Palestine Mandate, obtained by England for the purpose of fulfilling her war-time pledges to the Jews to aid in the establishment of a National Jewish Homeland, outraged the sensibilities of the Arab majority in Palestine. The Christian population of Syria claimed that France had violated her promises to further the creation of a Syrian State. The Arab leaders who had supported Great Britain during the Syrian campaign expected to have her assistance in the upbuilding of an Arab confederation, and they felt that they had been betrayed by their ally. No one was satisfied, and the high hopes of the Arab peoples had ended in bitterness and disillusionment.

The partitionment of the Occupied Territory was what might have been expected from the old theories of international relations, but it was not what the inhabitants had been led to expect from the declarations of President Wilson embodying the principle of self-determination as the basis of the Great Peace.

The Sèvres Treaty, dealing with the parts of the Ottoman Empire still under Turkish control, was no less disillusioning. It forced the Turks not only to recognize the dispositions already made of the occupied regions, but also to consent to what was virtually a dismemberment of Asia Minor itself. The treaty, which was drawn up by the Allied Powers without the participation of any of the peoples concerned, was from the very first a mere scrap of paper. The Turks, the Greeks, the Armenians, the Arabs, and the Christian minorities, all of whom were affected by its provisions, were not permitted to take part in the negotiations. No attempt was made to enforce its provisions, but no treaty ever written was more completely disregarded. Few have had more momentous consequences.

The peace that was to settle the Turkish question forever, brought about open war in the Near East, war by proxy between two of the Allied Powers, the birth of a new Turkey, the signing of a new treaty reversing the rôles of conquerors and conquered in Asia Minor, and the formation of a possible nucleus for an Asiatic League of Nations.

It had taken nearly two years for the Allies to reach these totally unsatisfactory arrangements with regard to the Near East, and during that time all Asia had been treated to a series of highly unedifying revelations of Western diplomatic methods.

All the secret agreements regarding the partitionment of the Ottoman Empire were in direct contravention of promises to the Near Eastern peoples. Innumerable differences, jealousies, hatreds, and dissensions had been aired from the very beginning of the post-war period, and all these things were known and understood as never before in Asia. War-time exigencies had drawn Europe and Asia closer together physically than ever before.

The process of Europeanization already well under way was hastened by a sort of artificial forcing system. With knowledge of European methods came understanding of European motives and the familiarity that sometimes breeds contempt. If the Allies had acted promptly and co-operated wholeheartedly, the future course of events in Asia might have been very different, but the East had discovered the vulnerable heel of the European Achilles. Western diplomacy was no longer formidable. The Persian delegates who were refused seats at the Versailles Conference owing to the intrigues of England, learned enough in the lobby to block the designs of Lord Curzon in their own country. The Turks who were shut out at Sèvres, took the floor at Lausanne and held it. The Chinese who were refused in Paris what seemed to them, common justice, have retaliated since in the Nanking outrages; Japan, denied equality with the European Powers in the West, began to pave the way for the assertion of her superiority in the East.

To understand something of the new mentality of Asia, we shall have to put together the happenings of the last seven years in Asiatic countries. As it is necessary to follow some plan, let us begin in Western Asia, where the surface changes have perhaps been greatest.

Chapter Six

THE GROWTH OF THE MOSLEM BLOC

THE story of happenings in the Near East since the close of the Great War is a story of plots and counterplots, rivalries, intrigues, of many mistakes, of incredible blunders on the part of the great Powers. It is a story of wars, rebellions, and insurrections, of Nationalism pitted against Imperialism, of reaction against progress, of race against race, and religion against religion, staged amidst the débris of the former Ottoman Empire. The result of all this ferment has been a series of changes, so complete and so far-reaching that the world at large has as yet scarce begun to realize their significance.

Perhaps the best concrete evidence of the political changes since 1918, was the conclusion of a mutual security pact between the sovereign states of Turkey, Persia, and Afghanistan in the autumn of 1926, just eight years after the Mudros Armistice which ended the war in the Near East, with Turkey crushed and all but dismembered, Persia on the verge of becoming a British protectorate, and Afghanistan a vassal to Great Britain.

These three Powers at that time not only concluded a series of mutual agreements but also united in an alliance with Russia as the first step towards creation of a Western Asiatic Federation. For we must never forget that the Federation of Soviet Republics includes all of the Caucasus, the bridge between Europe and Western Asia, Russia, and the Central Asiatic Republics comprising the former states of Khiva, Bokhara, and Turkestan, whose peoples are closely allied by blood and religion to the Turks, Afghans, and, to a lesser extent, the Persians. Consequently the conclusion of this pact marks the formation of a solid bloc in Western Asia.

Its importance will depend largely on the success or the failure of the programme of modernization instituted in the participating countries, but more particularly on the success or failure of the Turkish Republic. Indeed, it may not be too much to say that the fate of a large portion of Asia is dependent on the ability of the Turks to make good in their experiment in self-government.

TURKEY

There are few episodes in all history as romantic as the rise of the Turkish Republic. Mustapha Kemal Pasha, the liberator and today the president of Turkey, enjoys a fame and prestige that spread far beyond the limits of his own country. Wherever you go in Moslem lands, wherever there is a Moslem population, Mustapha Kemal Pasha is known and revered. You will find his picture in the Souks of Tunisia, Algeria, and Morocco, in the bazaars of Cairo, and Isfahan, Calcutta, Bombay, and Delhi. You will find it among the Moros in the Philippines, among the Moslems of China, in the market towns of Central Asia, and yet this Mustapha Kemal Pasha who is so revered by Moslems the world over, a few years ago abolished the most ancient and the most sacred office of Islam, that of Khalif, which for more than three hundred years had been vested in the Sultans of Turkey. He has curbed the power of the Moslem hierarchy in Turkey, cut down its revenues, abolished its schools, done away with its Koranic law and placed many restrictions on its priesthood. Notwithstanding all this, he commands the whole-souled devotion of all but the most reactionary elements in Moslem countries. The reason is not far to seek. It is because he is the embodiment of the Nationalism which has inspired the subject races and peoples of Asia with new hopes of freedom, new ideals, and new faith in the future.

The other portions of the Near East, classed broadly as the Arab countries, have not been as fortunate as the Turkish group. At the crucial moment, the Arabs found no such leader as Mustapha Kemal Pasha. Their political, social, and geographic conditions were against solidarity and as a result from the Arab National movement, so far nothing concrete has developed except the extraordinary rise of a Moslem Cromwell, the puritanical Ibn Saoud, Sultan of Nejd, who has extended his power over a broad belt through Central Arabia from the Persian Gulf to the Red Sea, including Mecca, the Moslem Holy of Holies, where thousands of Pilgrims assemble every year to worship at the Prophet's tomb.

The remainder of the Arab territory which once formed part of the Ottoman Empire, is divided into small states under mandates from the League of Nations administered by France and Great Britain, or enjoying a precarious quasi-independence.

For the present at least, the amazing development of Turkey and its possible consequences are the most significant events that have yet taken place in the Near East. It may be that Turkey's war of independence will prove a turning point in the history of Asia fully as vital as the Russo-Japanese War.

Shortly after the humiliating armistice at Mudros on October 30, 1918, the strictly Turkish portion of the former Ottoman Empire, comprising what we know as Asia Minor, and Thrace, had been virtually partitioned between the victorious Powers. The collapse of Czardom had naturally precluded the fulfilment of the promise to turn Constantinople over to Russia made by the British at the beginning of the war, but by a series of agreements, many of them secret, Turkey was divided up into areas of influence.

It would be wearisome to enumerate the many pacts, agreements, and conventions, in which Turkey was parcelled out between 1918 and 1920. That the Turkish people might have something to say about the dismemberment of their country seemed never to have occurred to the Allies, and indeed it seemed scarcely possible that they could be capable of offering any resistance. It was sheer exhaustion that induced the Turks to sign the Mudros armistice. The man-power of the country had been depleted by virtually six years of war, for the World War had followed closely on the conflict between Turkey and Bulgaria which ended only a little over a year before the outbreak of new hostilities.

Turkish troops, ill equipped and half starved, had fought on many fronts with an appalling loss of life. The cost of living in Constantinople was fabulous. The lower classes were starving. In Anatolia the Germans during the war had carried off all the food they could lay their hands on to feed their own troops. As

a result of the chauvinism of the Young Turkish party which had
been in power since 1918 the Ottoman government had to contend
with the active or passive disloyalty of its racial or religious
minorities, comprising two million Armenians and as many
Greeks, three million or so Kurds, and several hundred thousand
Assyrian Christians besides even smaller tribal groups. At the
time of the Armistice most of them were vociferously demanding
autonomy or independence, spurred on by President Wilson's
enunciation of the doctrine of self-determination.

The government was quite powerless to prevent the occupation
of Constantinople by a mixed force of British, French, and Italian
troops, or the assigning of various areas to the three Powers.
Cilicia was occupied first by the British, later by the French. The
Italians stationed troops in Southern Anatolia. In March, 1919,
the Allies permitted Greek troops to occupy the port of Smyrna
and the surrounding area, under the pretext that protection was
necessary for the Greek minorities. All this was acquiesced in by
the helpless cabinet in Constantinople. In Anatolia it was a
different matter.

The occupation of Smyrna by the Greeks was the match that
was needed to set flame to the smouldering embers of resentment
against the Allies. The Greeks were the hereditary enemies of the
Turks. They were descendants of the Byzantines whom the
Turks had conquered nearly five hundred years before, and whom
they had never assimilated. In Asia Minor the Greeks had
always remained as political and religious minorities. The Turks,
who retained much of their primitive tribal instinct and were good
fighters but poor business men, had always depended on them to
do their business. Banking and commerce were almost entirely
in Greek hands, as were the manufactures of carpets and the fig
exportation industry. The small Turkish farmers of Western
Anatolia sold their figs and raisins to sharp Greek middlemen for
a song. The Greeks were exempt from military service. During
many wars they had stayed at home and grown richer and richer,
while the Turks had fought the battles of the Empire and grown
poorer and poorer.

Despite these facts, however, the Greeks had on the whole lived
on fairly good terms with the Turks, the occasional massacres that

had taken place having been usually the result of deliberate incitement to racial and religious hatred on the part of the central government, which believed in the "divide and rule" principle in the administration of the Empire. But during and immediately after the war, nationalist feeling had spread among the Greeks as among the other small nations the world over and the Hellenic Greeks had begun to recall the fact that the Greeks of Asia Minor were their brothers in faith and blood. They had already annexed portions of Western Thrace and were claiming all of Turkey in Europe, including Constantinople. Although they had done next to nothing for the Allied cause during the war they demanded their share of the spoils, and it suited Great Britain, which wished to counterbalance the French influence in the Near East, without opposing French claims directly, to support the pretensions of the Greeks.

To the insistence of David Lloyd George, then prime minister of England, that Greece be permitted to occupy Smyrna, may be attributed the rise of the Nationalist movement which ended in the emancipation of Turkey. From the first it was bitterly resented, and atrocities committed by Greek soldiers in the outlying districts near Smyrna were the signal for a series of uprisings all over Anatolia culminating in the revolt at Samsun, in May, 1919, of the Third Army Corps, which defied the Allies and the central government. A young officer, Mustapha Kemal Pasha, who had distinguished himself in the Dardanelles campaign was sent out from Constantinople to put an end to the revolt. Instead, he joined with the rebels and called on the Turkish people to rise in a united movement against foreign domination. His slogan was "Turkey for the Turks!"

The first step taken by Mustapha Kemal and his associates, among whom were Raouf Bey, (the Turkish admiral who had signed the Mudros Armistice,) and Ismet Pasha, who has since achieved world fame as the negotiator of the Lausanne Treaty, was to organize revolutionary groups known as Committees for National Defense. On July 10, 1919, these groups met at Erzerum and seven weeks later, at a much larger conference held in Sivas, they proclaimed the National War of Liberation and proceeded to elect Deputies to a National Assembly which met at

Angora in April, 1920. The new Parliament immediately passed the Turkish Declaration of Independence known as the Missak Millié, the first draft of which had been completed at Erzerum and adopted in principle by the moribund Ottoman Parliament, which received its death blow when the Kemalists held their elections in Anatolia.

The proclamation of the Kemalists was a challenge to the Allies and their answer was the impossible Treaty of Sèvres which the Sultan's Ministers in Constantinople were forced to sign under British pressure.

The Sèvres Treaty outraged every one of the principles laid down in the National Pact, which demanded first and foremost that the integrity of Turkish territory should be respected. It would have deprived Turkey in Europe of Eastern Thrace with Adrianople the ancient capital of the Ottomans. Turkey would have been left only Constantinople and a few miles of surrounding territory. The administration of the Straits Zone would have passed out of Turkish hands. The recognition of an Armenian republic and the cession to Greece of sovereign rights over the district of Smyrna, would have reduced the Turkish State to a small area in Asia Minor, not as large as the old Anatolia.

When the terms of the treaty became known, the smouldering embers of revolt burst into flame all over Anatolia, and were reflected throughout the Moslem world as friends began to rally on all sides to the Kemalist cause. In the three years during which Mustapha Kemal Pasha maintained his struggle for Turkish independence, the foundations were laid for a close union of the Moslem countries of Western Asia. Afghanistan, Persia, and Bokhara, concluded treaties with the new government of Angora. The Moslems and Hindus united in India to demand the independence of the Khalifate; the revolt of the Moplahs in Malabar, of the Bedouins in Mesopotamia under the leadership of Sheikh el Senussi, who came all the way from Africa to place his sword at the disposition of Mustapha Kemal, were a protest against the humiliation imposed upon Islam through the Sèvres Treaty. Angora became the hope of every true believer.

At this juncture another ally came to the assistance of the Turkish Nationalists—Soviet Russia—despite the fact that Rus-

POLITICAL MAP OF

ASIA

1914

Scale of Miles
0   200   400   600   800   1000

Russian Empire
Russian Sphere of Influence
British Empire
British Protectorates
British Sphere of Influence
Japanese Empire
Chinese Republic
French Possessions
Ottoman Empire

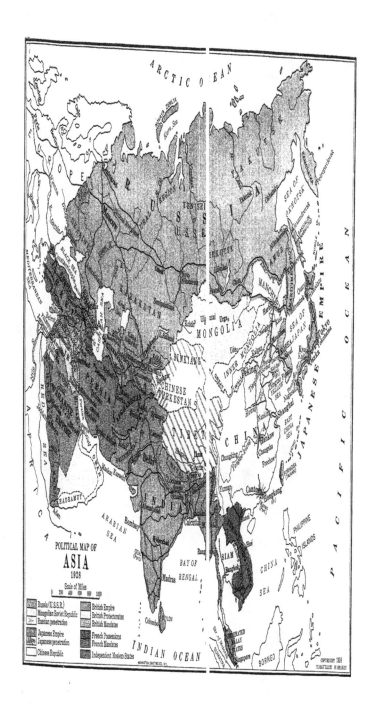

POLITICAL MAP OF
ASIA
1928

Scale of Miles
200 400 600 800 1000

Russia (U.S.S.R.)
Mongolian Soviet Republic
Russian penetration
Japanese Empire
Japanese penetration
Chinese Republic
British Empire
British Protectorates
British Mandates
French Possessions
French Mandates
Independent Moslem States

sia and Turkey for centuries had been hereditary enemies. The aims of both nations at the moment were virtually the same. The Soviet Government wished nothing more than to bring about a revolt of all Moslem peoples against the colonial powers, particularly Great Britain, and negotiations were opened which led to a treaty between Angora and Moscow signed on March 16, 1921. Meanwhile the two Powers in co-operation had made short work of Armenia, whose independence had been recognized in principle by the Allies. The British, who had occupied Batum and Baku since 1918, abandoned Trans-Caucasia in the early part of 1920, notwithstanding the fact which they must have realized, that the Kemalists, and the Bolsheviks, who were gradually pushing down towards the Caucasus, would eventually settle the fate of Armenia. Within a few months after the British evacuation the Turks and Russians had overrun Armenia and divided it between them. By a treaty ratified at Kars in September, 1921, the Turks obtained that city and the Russians the district of Erivan out of which they created an Armenian Soviet Republic.

The rest of the Armenian population of Asia Minor did not fare so well as that of the Caucasus; thousands of Armenians were massacred during the early days of the rebellion, thousands more perished in a headlong flight from the scene of revolt, and still more died on the long forced marches while being deported en masse, by order of the Turkish authorities. In Cilicia, where there was a large Armenian population, the French, who were then occupying the country, were powerless to prevent massacres or to stem the tide of refugees that steadily flowed down towards the Syrian border. Their efforts to bring about order resulted in a popular uprising which became identified with the Kemalist movement and with which they found it both difficult and expensive to cope.

Meanwhile, the Allies, realizing that something had to be done and that none of them were prepared to force the execution of the Sèvres treaty on the Turks, held a conference at London in March, 1921, and drafted a revision of the treaty. It would have given to the Turks sovereignty over an autonomous district of Smyrna and the chairmanship of the International Commission which was to control the Dardanelles, together with other concessions to

Turkish National sentiment; but neither the Turks nor the Greeks had been consulted, and both refused to accept the proposed revision.

At that time, undoubtedly the sympathies of Great Britain as well as those of most of Europe were with the Greeks. Greece, which had come into the World War at the last moment on the side of the Allies and had played such a small part, had been made to assume the rôle of protector of Christendom in the Near East. All the old hatred of the "unspeakable Turk" of Mr. Gladstone's day had been revived in the heat of war propaganda and the romantic ideal of a restoration of the old Byzantine Empire dazzled many sentimental enthusiasts in England and Europe. There was to be a pan-Hellenic revival and a new Golden Age was to dawn in the land of Pericles and Alexander the Great.

The spokesman of the new Hellenic Imperialism was Venizelos, the remarkable Prime Minister who became dictator, and started the movement for expansion. Besides, as has already been stated, the fostering of this idea was exactly in line with the politics of Lloyd George, who feared nothing so much as the opposition of France, for the latter had always felt that the control by Great Britain of Palestine and Trans-Jordania, which, according to French ideas, should have been included in the Syrian mandate, was inimical to her interests. Foreseeing that he could not successfully oppose the French openly, Lloyd George had undertaken to support the Greeks, who were committed to Great Britain and could be used to counterbalance French influence in the Near East.

It is possible that he did not foresee the danger in a Russo-Kemalist alliance or that he did not believe that the French would conclude a separate peace with Turkey, but it must be assumed that he privately gave a certain amount of encouragement to the Greeks in their refusal to consider the proposed revision of the Sèvres Treaty. All this time, while the Allies were wrangling and debating, and Lloyd George and Poincaré were holding innumerable fruitless "conversations," the Kemalists were organizing a national army.

The guerrilla warfare which they had maintained against the Greeks since 1920, developed into a genuine military campaign to oppose the Greek offensive which was launched in earnest in the month of July 1921. Thanks to their alliance with Russia, the Kemalists had at their disposal all the troops that had been used to suppress the Armenian revolt, as well as arms and ammunition furnished them by their new allies.

The Greeks, who were better equipped and furnished with tanks and gas bombs by the British army, swept across Anatolia to the banks of the Sakharia River within striking distance of Angora, where they were held in check, and shortly afterwards were forced to retreat. If the Greeks had been wise, they would have negotiated a peace after this decisive setback.

The French meanwhile had definitely refused to countenance Greek aims. They had evacuated Cilicia and had concluded on their own account a preliminary understanding with the Turks which culminated in the signing of a treaty at Angora by M. Franklin-Bouillon in October, 1921. By this treaty the Turks obtained possession of all Cilicia, and the Turco-Syrian frontier was established virtually as it is today. After the signature of the treaty the relations between France and Great Britain became critical. For six months the Greeks, spurred on by England, and the Kemalists, aided by France with money and ammunition, prepared for the final show-down.

Lloyd George in the summer of 1922 went so far as to order the Greeks to march on Constantinople, which they would have been able to take through the co-operation of General Harrington, the British High Commissioner in Constantinople. They were only held in check by the fact that the French High Commissioner General Pellé himself undertook the defense of the city. The war had become a thinly disguised conflict between France and England, and if the Greeks had not been intimidated by the prompt and vigorous action of Pellé, another European war might have been precipitated. Besides, the Greeks were hard pressed in Anatolia, where they felt the loss of the three divisions sent on the wild goose chase to Constantinople; the morale of their troops was bad, and at this juncture Ismet Pasha, commanding the sector from which the troops had been withdrawn, started an offensive which took the Greeks by surprise and swept all before it. They began a headlong retreat to Smyrna. Their demoralization was complete. As they retreated they burned and pillaged wantonly, and Greek excesses committed at that time can parallel any similar accounts of Turkish atrocities during the Armenian flight from Asia Minor.

The Turks took Smyrna on September 9th, and during the street fighting that ensued, the city was burned with appalling loss of life notwithstanding the assistance rendered by America, France, and Great Britain, which sent all their ships available in Eastern waters to carry off the panic-stricken refugees.

Responsibility for the Smyrna disaster has never been satisfactorily determined, and it is said that the findings of the Allied Commission which conducted an investigation were not made public in their entirety.

Both the Greeks and the Turks categorically denied having been responsible, and according to the most reliable evidence it seems most likely that the city was fired by the Armenians. Certainly the Turks who had taken Smyrna had no reason to destroy it—the Greeks were scarcely likely to have committed an act which would materially hamper their own retreat in the face of the enemy, depriving them of the means of leaving the city and causing additional loss of life among the civilian population, as well as among the retreating troops. The Armenians, on the other hand, had taken no part in the actual fighting. They would not have been evacuated with the Greek army, and they were about to be delivered into the hands of their bitterest enemies.

The capture of Smyrna was followed by a series of happenings that threw all Europe into a state of tense excitement. It caused the overthrow of King Constantine of Greece, who was forced to abdicate after the failure of his militarist programme, as well as the resignation of Lloyd George. The victorious Kemalist troops promptly occupied the Neutral Zone around the Dardanelles provided for in the revision of the Sèvres Treaty. It was a direct challenge to the Allies. Only the fact that the Allied governments for the first time since the beginning of the Near Eastern complications acted with some degree of unanimity, made it possible to avert a war which might have involved the entire Moslem world. At that moment Mustapha Kemal was the true "Defender of the Faithful," and the prestige of the Khalif was as nothing compared with his.

Great Britain sent a formidable naval squadron to the Dardanelles and France dispatched a smaller force but made it clear that she would not take part in any war against Turkey. Italy, Yugoslavia and Rumania took the same attitude, and, though it was a bitter blow to her prestige, England was compelled to fall in line with the other Powers and agree to an armistice which was signed at Mudania on October 9th. Mustapha Kemal Pasha agreed to evacuate the Neutral Zone and to take steps for the protection of the Greek and other Christian Minorities in Anatolia, and in return he received the assurance that Turkey would recover Eastern Thrace, the last remains of the European possessions of the Ottoman Empire, and that all of Anatolia including Smyrna should be restored unequivocally to the Angora government.

The Mudania Armistice also provided for the calling of a General Peace Conference at Lausanne within a month at which every Power interested in the Near Eastern questions would be represented.

The Lausanne Conference opened on November 20th, Ismet Pasha, who had conducted the victorious campaign against the Greeks, representing Turkey. Great Britain, France, Japan, Italy, Rumania, Yugoslavia, and Greece, had seats at the Conference. Of all the interested Powers the only one refused a seat was Russia, whose delegation participated only in the supplementary agreement to the Treaty known as the Straits Convention which established Constantinople as a free port and opened the Dardanelles to merchant and naval ships of all nations. The exclusion of Russia caused Chicherin, Soviet Russia's Foreign Minister, to send a protest to the Powers. After recalling the fact that Russia had been the first to recognize Turkey's rights to Constantinople and to undisputed possession of all strictly Turkish territory in Asia and Europe, as well as her advocacy of the freedom of the Dardanelles under the supervision of the Powers bordering on the Black Sea states, Chicherin stated that the Russian Government must protest in the most categorical fashion against this usurpation by the Western Powers of the rights of Russia and her allied republics.

"Russia, with her allies, the Ukraine and Georgia, is, after

Turkey, the Power which occupies the first place among those who are interested in the freedom of the Straits. The Russian Government renews its former declaration that Russia will not recognize any decision taken without her participation and without consulting her interests." An ominous statement for those who closely follow world affairs. One of the most interesting features of it is that Russia, in alluding to "Western Powers," places herself by inference among the Oriental nations. We shall later see throughout the tangled web of Asiatic affairs the development of this policy. Some call it Soviet Imperialism. "Russia's Eurasian policy" is perhaps a better term.

It would take much too long to record all the debates and bickerings which led to the breakdown of the Conference in February, and its resumption some ten weeks later, finally culminating in the signature of the Treaty on July 24, 1923. The Lausanne Treaty restored Anatolia and Eastern Thrace unconditionally to Turkey. The European boundary of the new republic was fixed along the valley of the Maritza river. The boundary between Turkey and Syria was unaltered from that provided for in the treaty with France. That between Anatolia and Iraq was to be left to the League of Nations with the British still in possession of the disputed district of Mosul, claimed by them as part of their Mandate for Mesopotamia. No mention whatever was made of the Armenian question and in fact, as far as Turkey was concerned, it had been disposed of by the creation of Russian Armenia and the mass evacuation of Armenian refugees during the terrible years between 1914 and the signing of the Treaty. Constantinople was to be evacuated and the Dardanelles opened to the merchant vessels and warships of all nations. Turkey's pre-war debt was to be subdivided among the territories composing the former Ottoman Empire.

Turkey agreed to protect and afford full liberty to all religious and racial minorities, and a compulsory exchange of populations between Turkey and Greece was to make Anatolia purely Turkish, and Greece Hellenic to the core—at least on paper. Turkey was free. Freer than she had been for many centuries. There were no more "capitulations" no more "protectorates" for Christian minorities, no "war indemnities."

Ismet Pasha, the head of the Turkish delegation, displayed astuteness amounting almost to genius throughout the negotiations; never stressing Turkey's needs, he played upon the rivalries and jealousies between the Powers until he got substantially everything he wanted. He bargained, argued, bullied, and wheedled until he frequently carried his point by exhausting his adversaries, and the Treaty in its final form was a brilliant triumph for Turkish diplomacy.

Its significance, however, was far deeper than the superficial facts it established. It marked a definite step in the development of relations between East and West. European prestige had received a blow as decisive as that given it by the Russo-Japanese War. France, it is true, had profited to the extent of gaining some economic advantages by her early peace with Turkey, but at the loss of considerable moral prestige. Great Britain had suffered irreparably as we shall see later, not only directly through her unsuccessful efforts to back the Greeks and bully the Turks, but indirectly in Afghanistan, Persia, Arabia, Egypt, and her own Empire. The Lausanne Treaty was the first step towards the emancipation of the East.

Perhaps it was a realization of this fact that made the evacuation of Constantinople by the Allied troops a particularly impressive occasion. Certainly it was the first ocular demonstration to the Turkish people that they had once more come into their own. I happened to be in Constantinople at the time. On the eve of the evacuation the city was swarming with British, French, and Italian troops and the Bosphorus was filled with the warships of all three nations.

Early the next morning, I went down to the square in front of Dolma Bagtche, the Sultan's Palace facing the Bosphorus, where the Allied generals were to greet the incoming Turkish commander and take their leave for ever of Constantinople. The approaches to the little square were packed with dense masses of people, all very orderly and silent. The Turks are not noisy and excitable like their fellow Moslems, the Arabs. Grave and courteous gendarmes made a way for our party consisting of members of the American High Commission, till we reached a point where we could get a good view of everything. Three sides of the square was occupied by detachments of Allied soldiers. Facing the Bosphorus were the British Tommies. The French Poilus were on one side of them, and the "Macaronis," as the French used to call their Italian Allies, on the other. The fourth side, skirting the quay, was quite empty. Beyond it were the waters of the Bosphorus shining in the sun, and, in the distance, the shores of Turkey-in-Asia.

There was a hush over the entire assembly—every one was waiting. Suddenly, in the distance, we heard an unfamiliar bugle call, then music, a harsh strident rhythm and the sound of tramping feet.

A few seconds later, the first detachment of Turks wheeled into the quadrangle and, spreading out, closed in the vacant space. They looked like veterans, these Turkish troops, sun-browned, rugged, hard-bitten. Their uniforms were not spick and span, like those of the Allied soldiers, but stained with the blood and mud of past campaigns!

No sooner had they taken their places than there was an exchange of salutes and courtesies between the Turkish and Allied generals, and then the British moved forward and their colors dipped as they passed through the Turkish ranks towards the quays at the water's edge, where launches were awaiting to carry them to their transports lying at anchor in midstream. The French and the Italians followed suit and the Turks, still silent, watched them leave. There was not a cheer or a shout, and the silence was more eloquent than any demonstration. The evacuation proceeded rapidly and by the early afternoon the entire Allied squadron led by the great "Iron Duke," the British battleship, steamed slowly out of the Bosphorus headed for the Dardanelles and the open sea. Three days later, the main body of Turks crossed the Bosphorus at Scutari. Then there were rejoicings and celebrations from Sirkedji near the Old Seraglio where they landed, all the way to the Harbié barracks in Pera as they ended their triumphal march. The whole town was gay with bunting and with flags, bands were playing, people cheering, and on the famous Galata bridge hapless woolly sheep were sacrificed in front of the incoming army. It was a day never to be forgotten!

The Lausanne Treaty was shortly ratified by England, France, and Japan, and not long after by Italy. The United States having never been in a state of war with Turkey did not sign it.

Therefore America was the only world Power which did not recognize in principle the abolition of the Capitulations and Turkey's changed status. Unfortunately, although America has recently concluded a working accord with Turkey re-establishing diplomatic and consular relations and a commercial agreement, all purely provisional, she has not yet concluded a treaty embodying the features of the Lausanne Treaty. While the political consequences of this attitude on the part of the United States have been unimportant, its moral effect has been bad, not only in Turkey but throughout Asia. It has helped to widen the breach between East and West created by racial and religious prejudice.

Peace had now been secured in the Near East, though at a heavy cost to Europe, but there were several features of the pact that created grave misgivings in the minds of many thoughtful observers. In the first place, Russia had had no voice in any of the deliberations at Lausanne except those relating to the status of the Dardanelles. She was in no way bound by any of its provisions. Secondly, the Allies had not kept their promise to Bulgaria to secure her a port on the Aegean Sea. They had failed in the adjustment of the boundary between the old Turkey and her former Arab domains, and they had sanctioned the compulsory exchange of populations between Turkey and Greece, which meant a shifting of peoples more extensive than had ever taken place since the great migrations from Central Asia.

But the Turks were much too busy to worry about these uncertainties. Having secured their external position they at once began to put their house in order, and it was a colossal task!

Before we attempt to review what Mustapha Kemal Pasha and his associates have accomplished since 1922, it would be just as well to try to visualize the raw material they had to work on. For the first time in many centuries, the Turkish government was called upon to govern a people almost exclusively Turkish. All the alien portions of the former Ottoman Empire had been cut loose from it. The great masses of the non-Turkish population of Asia Minor had been deported or had fled to avoid the massacres in which so many thousands of their fellows had per-

ished. The remainder were soon to leave under the Compulsory
Exchange agreement with Greece. The Turkish people had been
almost continuously at war for twelve years, and the war of independence from 1919 to 1922 had been carried on in the midst of
an internal revolution; its leaders were outlawed and were rebels
against their Sultan.

The Turkish army had been sacrificed relentlessly during the
World War by the Germans, who had drained Anatolia of all the
supplies they could lay their hands on, and the Kemalist army was
poorly armed, miserably equipped, and half starved. The full
story of the heroic struggles to create the national army and to
keep it in the field will probably never be written. There were no
enterprising war correspondents at the front with the Kemalist
troops in Anatolia! Every Turk who could bear arms joined the
Nationalist forces. Fathers and sons fought side by side, sometimes mothers with their sons as well, boys who were still children
shouldered rifles and put on cartridge belts. The women of the
peasantry organized supply battalions and where there were not
enough draft-animals they themselves dragged the heavy *kanis,*
wagons containing ammunition, to the troops in the front trenches.
When there was no ammunition, they manufactured it.

Two years after the war, when I was visiting a small village in
the Taurus Mountains, my host, a fine old Turkish peasant who
had fought the battles of Turkey in at least three wars, showed
me how he and his wife had made bullets at their own fireside and
had manufactured bombs from empty petrol-tins, to arm the company of irregulars which he had organized and commanded during the guerrilla warfare against the French.

Naturally this supreme effort on the part of the Turkish people
left Anatolia poorer than ever. A large section comprising one
of the most fertile areas in Asia Minor from Eski-Shehir, where
the Baghdad Railway connects with the road to Angora, all the
way to Smyrna on the Aegean Sea, was swept absolutely bare.
There was scarcely a village or a house left standing, or a single
draft animal to do the spring ploughing, after peace had come.
The southern part of Anatolia, comprising Cilicia, and the fertile
Aintab region had been only a little less devastated. Along the
Black Sea where the fruit and tobacco crops are exceptionally fine,

there had been no men to plant or harvest for a number of years; the eastern part of Turkey had been invaded by the Russians in the early part of the war, and fought over later during the Armenian rebellion, while the Kurds, who under the old Sultans had been semi-independent, living in their own tribal communities in the Zagros Mountains, had contributed little or nothing towards the support of the Nationalist cause. The high arid plateau whereon Angora is situated is almost desert. The peasants of that region even in prosperous times would have fared badly except for their wonderful goats and sheep, which produce the beautiful Angora wool.

As regards its social and material development Turkey was practically still a medieval country and the Turks themselves were a race of peasants and soldiers with a few great families but no hereditary aristocracy, a small middle and official class, and village community life very little removed from the tribal existence of their nomad ancestors.

At least three-fourths of the population were illiterate, communications had remained almost as they were in the Middle Ages, there were only two railways of any length in Asiatic Turkey—the Baghdad Railway, with its branches to Smyrna and Angora, and a short line connecting Erzerum with Trans-Caucasia. The roads throughout Anatolia were poor, better fitted for mules and horses than for carriages, the peasants still spoke of automobiles as "Satan's Arabas" and there were only a few cities in Asia Minor with any modern improvements.

When I was in Konia in 1923, the municipal electric light plant was not working because the Swiss company operating it had not been able to collect its bills. In Smyrna all public utilities were temporarily put out of commission. In Angora, the capital, there was neither electric light nor water, no sewage system, no modern hotel, and the population, which increased almost overnight from twenty to nearly fifty thousand, was undergoing an acute housing crisis. Deputies to the National Assembly slept three and four in a room, in tumble-down houses of hard-baked mud. Throughout Anatolia the provincial administration was still in the hands of old officials trained under the corrupt régime of the monarchy, their salaries were inadequate, and they were often not above supplementing their meagre incomes by bribery and extortion.

Constantinople was a modern city it was true; in it as well as in numbers of provincial cities, there were small groups of young Turks, alert, progressive, imbued with intense Nationalism and convinced that Westernization and the adoption of democratic ideas were the only means by which the Turkish nation could reassert itself and carry out its destiny of becoming the leader of the Turanian peoples. But these men and women—for there were some women among them like Halidé Edib, who helped to organize the Ministry of Public Instruction under the Republic, and Nakié Hanoum, who took her degree in medicine at the University of Vienna—were mostly drawn from the upper-class families.

The bankers, merchants, artisans, and skilled workmen were almost exclusively Greeks or Armenians; even among the administrative classes there were large numbers of Greek and Armenian functionaries. The only field they had not invaded was that of military activity, and in all the wars Turkey had fought, the Greeks and Armenians had been exempt from military service. The Turks had come as conquerors into Asia Minor, and had remained as conquerors, utilizing the ready-made commercial and economic system of the Byzantines to supply their material needs while they continued to rule and make war and till the land very much as they had done when they followed their leader Othman westward from the steppes of Central Asia.

Consequently Mustapha Kemal and his associates found a very small class from which to draw men and women who were to help build up the new Turkey. It is impossible to estimate or properly gauge the progress they have made unless we realize this fact; it is as yet even too early to judge whether they have, as a race, any genius for administration.

At the close of 1922, the first problem before the Turkish leaders was to established a legal form of government. The Grand National Assembly constituted the actual Government of Turkey, but the Sultan Mehmet VI was still de jure the head of the Turkish State. The Kemalists had proceeded with great caution in regard to the Sultan, leaving the whole question in abeyance because the Sovereign of Turkey was also Khalif of

Islam, the Spiritual and Temporal Head of the Moslem world. In their struggle for independence they needed the support of other Moslem countries. If they had deposed the Sultan in the beginning, they would have run the risk of losing the sympathy and assistance of Moslems in Egypt, India, Afghanistan, and Persia, where the growing Nationalism had not yet supplanted the old ideal of the temporal power of the Khalif and the political unity of Islam; but during the three years of the Nationalist struggle in Turkey there had been a growing sentiment of solidarity among Asiatic peoples.

Mustapha Kemal Pasha had become the champion of all the Moslem countries—he symbolized their ultimate triumph over Western Imperialism. After the defeat of Greece he could have done anything he liked and he knew it.

On November 1st, the National Assembly of Angora passed an act suppressing the Sultanate, thereby taking over the political power. The office of Khalif was to be retained, however, the Khalif being elected by the National Assembly. Eighteen days later the last Sultan, Mehmet VI, took refuge on a British warship which carried him to Malta. The next day his cousin and heir apparent, Abdul Medjid, was proclaimed Khalif by the National Assembly. So great was the prestige of Mustapha Kemal Pasha throughout all Islam that the abolition of the Sultanate excited almost no opposition and merely passing comment. The Sultan became an obscure political exile, one of the many half-forgotten deposed monarchs of Europe, and the news of his death last year at San Remo excited only mild interest in Moslem communities.

Less than a year after the deposition of the Sultan, on October 29, 1923, Mustapha Kemal Pasha was unanimously elected President of the new Republic of Turkey.

Actually he was less President than Dictator, for there was but one recognized political party in Turkey—the so-called Popular party of which the Pasha was himself the head. The monarchist element would not have dared to organize an opposition, and it was too small to have made an impression; the republican leaders, however much they might differ in some respects with Mustapha Kemal and his associates who formed a small clique, realized

that the only chance for the infant republic lay in unity of action.
There could be no question of creating a large independent and
intelligent electorate in a country which had been so long under
an Oriental despotism, and where the vast majority did not even
know the meaning of the word "republic." The Grand National
Assembly prior to the adoption of the Constitution presented the
extraordinary spectacle of a parliament which sat one day as a
party caucus, and the next as a legislative assembly. By the spring
of 1924, however, this curiously constituted parliament had drawn
up and adopted a Constitution.

The new Constitution of Turkey is not an elaborate document.
The people of Turkey are its sovereigns and the Grand National
Assembly elected by them exercises both legislative and executive
power. The President of Turkey is elected by the Assembly for
a term of four years and has the right to choose his own cabinet.
The judiciary functions are exercised in the name of the Assembly
by independent tribunals. All citizens over eighteen years of age
are entitled to the franchise, and it is interesting to note: "The
name Turk as political term shall be understood to include all
citizens of the Turkish Republic without distinction of, or refer-
ence to, race or religion. Every child born in Turkey or in a
foreign land of a Turkish father; any person whose father is a
foreigner established in Turkey and who chooses upon attaining
the age of twenty to become a Turkish subject; and any individual
who acquires Turkish Nationality by naturalization in conformity
with the Law, is a Turk" (Article 88).

The problem of minorities is solved, theoretically at least, by
the clause just cited, with Article 75, which provides: "No one
may be molested on account of his religion, his sect, his ritual, or
his philosophic convictions. All religious observances shall be
free on condition that they do not disturb the public peace, or
shock public decency, or exist in violation of social conventions,
or the Law."

Meanwhile, in consequence of the compulsory exchange of populations, the Turks were in a fair way to eliminate their minorities. From the close of 1923 until the beginning of 1925, the
extraordinary bargain driven between Turkey and Greece at the
instigation of Dr. Nansen the great Arctic explorer and inter-

national philanthropist and sponsored by M. Venizelos was being carried out. It was an effort to solve once and for all one of the most serious problems of the Near East, where approximately half a million people had been expatriated either forcibly or otherwise during the troubled period between 1913 and the Mudros Armistice.

After the taking of Smyrna in September, 1922, over 800,000 Greeks and Armenians sought refuge in Greece from Anatolia, and over 200,000 from Eastern Thrace. Consequently, nearly 2,000,000 persons had been expatriated in Turkey, Bulgaria, and Greece during a period of ten years; the impossibility of repatriating all these families, whose homes in many instances had been laid waste and taken possession of by others, as well as the desire of Turkey and Greece to have a homogeneous population, prompted the conclusion of the exchange agreement.

The number of persons subject to exchange after the Smyrna disaster was relatively small. Exclusive of the Greeks in Constantinople who were subject to a special arrangement, there were roughly speaking 50,000 Greeks to be deported from Anatolia, and 350,000 Moslems to be sent from Greece, under the auspices of the mixed commission of eleven members comprised of representatives of both of the interested Powers and two neutral countries.

The exchange was carried out with remarkable efficiency. It is noteworthy that during its operation there were more births than deaths, and no epidemics. The number of persons actually exchanged, including those from Thrace and various islands in the Aegean which had changed hands, amounted to 354,000 Turks and 177,000 Greeks. Certain relief organizations, notably the International Red Cross, the American Near East Relief, and the Turkish Red Crescent, did valuable work in assisting the refugees temporarily, but the real brunt of the work had to be borne by the two governments.

It is not within the scope of this book to tell how the Greeks, whose population had been increased by more than two million people in less than ten years, handled their refugee settlement problems, but it may be said that while they had to face the difficulties of overpopulation, the Turkish problem was rather the reverse.

Anatolia was underpopulated; the population of the Turkish Republic was estimated at a little over 13 millions, whereas economic experts had stated that it could accommodate 80 millions of inhabitants. Transportation facilities were so crude as to make it very difficult to distribute the Turkish immigrants properly over Anatolia; most of them were farmers, chiefly growers of fine tobacco, but they had no tools, no farm implements, no live stock—much of the country which it was most desirable to repopulate had been so completely devastated during the Greek retreat that there were no farm houses, no shelter even, and nothing but the burned and blackened remains of villages over miles and miles of what had once been fertile territory.

The Turkish government created a special ministry, which was later merged with the Ministry of the Interior, to handle the settlement question, and the Assembly voted an appropriation to build temporary homes and supply tools, seeds, and live stock to the immigrants. Every vilayet, or province, had a local representative of the Department of Immigration and the settlers assigned to any district at once applied to the local bureau. Theoretically they were entitled to receive property equivalent to one-fifth, and land equalling one-half of their former holdings in Greece, Thrace or Macedonia. If they had documentary proof of ownership their claims were filed with the Mixed Commission, to be paid, if ever, after many years, for the adjustment of all the claims filed on both sides as a result of the exchange of populations bids fair to consume more time than the proverbial English suits in Chancery. Meanwhile the settlers were to pay the Turkish government in semi-annual instalments extending over ten years, for whatever had been supplied them by the Department of Immigration.

When I was last in Turkey in the summer of 1925 the Department was disbursing a budget of 5,000,000 Turkish lire a year (about $2,500,000) and had received in addition a special appropriation of 1,500,000 lire, for the construction of new homes for the immigrants.

I visited many of the areas around Smyrna and Brusa where nearly a hundred thousand immigrants had been settled. Some were still living in tents and barracks, but the majority had been installed either in old villages abandoned by the Greeks, or in new communities.   The little houses put up by the government were exceedingly practical and comfortable, and while they were still terribly short of live stock and farm implements, nearly all the settlers had managed to plant at least a crop of tobacco and a few vegetables.

The Turkish government with the limited funds at its disposal had done wonders, but it was evident that there would nevertheless be much poverty and suffering among the newcomers before they finally took root on Turkish soil.   It was also rather appalling to note the economic waste caused by the wholesale transplantation.   There were whole villages that had been devoted to the silkworm industry, others surrounded by vineyards that had once been flourishing, still others where all the inhabitants had been rug-weavers.   These had gone to ruin—the trees were dying, the vines were untrimmed and unproductive, the looms idle. Skilled workmen were scarce, for nearly all the artisans in Anatolia had been Greeks or Armenians.   This lack had made itself felt everywhere in Turkey.   In Cilicia, after the wholesale evacuation there were scarcely any artisans left, and the landlady of my pension in Adana was unable to get a coffee-grinder mended because all the Armenian tinsmiths had gone.

The immigrants who had come from Macedonia and Thrace, were, on the whole, far superior in education and intelligence to the native Turkish peasants.   They had been more prosperous, their standards of living were much higher.   Racially, many of them looked to me purely Hellenic, just as many of the so-called Greek refuges from Asia Minor were obviously of the same blood as the Turks, for the exchange was based on religion, not on race. Since its completion most Turks insist that it has made Turkey a homogeneous state, and so it has from the standpoint of religion; but the leaven from across the Bosphorus introduced new elements that may eventually have a profound effect on the country.   There is a certain spirit of sturdy independence among the Balkan Turks, which is lacking among the Anatolians.

Politically and economically, the exchange policy has created certain difficulties for the new Turkish Republic.   It will take some time to replace the skilled workmen, and certain industries like rug-making, have passed over to Greece, possibly forever, but it has gained an infusion of new blood that will stimulate the lethargic peasantry of Antolia. For example, in several of the new villages I visited near Brusa, the settlers had built their own schoolhouses and were paying their own teachers. The exchange is the logical working out of the movement begun by the Young Turks under Abdul Hamid, to expel all Christians from Asia Minor; it may create a greater degree of international stability in the Near East, but it has thrown Turkey definitely back into Asia, whereas had the Allied policy been different in the period immediately following the armistice, she might have been utilized as a link between East and West.

Turkey's future lies East. That she has ceased to concern herself with Europe was shown by the relative indifference with which the Turkish delegation at Lausanne consented to permit all Greeks and Armenians who had been established permanently at Constantinople prior to the armistice, to remain there. Consequently there is still a Greek population of more than 100,000 in Constantinople. The future of the Imperial city of Constantine forms a fascinating subject for speculation. It is obvious that the new Turkish government is doing everything possible to minimize its commercial importance, developing Smyrna and the Black Sea ports at its expense. No longer a centre of trade or politics Constantinople is fast becoming a city of historic monuments, petty traders, and former Imperial functionaries. It is not impossible that some day it may be made the subject of a bargain between Turkey and Russia or fall under the joint jurisdiction of all the Powers bordering on the Aegean and the Black Sea, by virtue of some future pact between Turkey and the interested countries. This trend is shown by the selection of Angora as the capital of the Turkish Republic and by Turkey's evident tendency to extend her influence in the Balkans, not by territorial acquisitions, but assuming an attitude of friendly co-operation with the small Powers who have not found all the security they had hoped for, under the aegis of the League of Nations. If she ever again encroaches on Europe it will not be by conquest, but through political combinations.

Thus the foreign relations of the new republic at the present time are most satisfactory and her position in the Near East is unassailable, because of an extraordinary combination of circumstances; the pact with Russia and the two Moslem states of Persia and Afghanistan, the conclusion of treaties with Iraq and Syria, the establishment of a modus vivendi with Bulgaria and Greece have combined to strengthen her position so well grounded by the Lausanne Treaty.

The most serious problems confronting the leaders of the Turkish State since the signing of the treaty of Lausanne, have been purely domestic. When the National Assembly proclaimed itself the sovereign power in Turkey and deposed the Sultan, it also declared Islam the religion of the State and proclaimed the right of electing the Khalif. This arrangement, while all very well in theory, did not prove satisfactory in practice. The new Khalif Abdul Medjid prior to his accession had never taken any part in public affairs; nevertheless after his election to the Khalifate he was not content to be merely a figurehead in ecclesiastical matters, although there is no evidence that he was disloyal to the Angora government. However, he did protest vainly against the very apparent efforts of the National Assembly to curtail the powers and authority of his office.

For some months Abdul Medjid continued to live in his splendid palace of Dolma Bagtche, where he received visits and occupied himself with his painting. Once a week he attended the weekly ceremony of the Selamlik, or public prayer, but otherwise he was a nonentity. This state of affairs aroused considerable indignation not only among the more devout of the Turks, who as a people are less religious than most other Moslems, but particularly among the Moslems of India. They, like the Moslems in the remaining Islamic countries, had been inclined to accept, even to endorse the abolition of the Sultanate because they believed it would further the liberation of Turkey, and therefore of the Khalifate, from Western domination, but they did not view with favor the interference of Angora with the purely spiritual functions and physical freedom of the Khalif.

A letter of protest on this subject endorsed by practically all the Indian Moslems was dispatched to the Angora Government by their representative, the Aga Khan, well known in Europe as an owner of race horses and the frequenter of the smartest establishments in Paris, and on the Riviera. It seems paradoxical that he should be regarded as the champion of a spiritual movement, but such is actually the case. To millions of Moslems in India he is an almost sacred being and he is revered by the sect of Ismaelites in Syria as the descendant of one of the Imams, the immediate successors of the Prophet.

Fortunately or unfortunately, the Aga Khan's letter sent during the month of January, 1924, was published in several Turkish newspapers before it was received at Angora. As a result, the government, alarmed for its own stability, took severe repressive measures. A so-called Tribunal of Independence was created in Constantinople. By order of this tribunal numerous arrests were made, and the prosecution of 800 individuals was undertaken. Among them were the editors of five Turkish newspapers, one of whom received a sentence of three years in prison, later commuted. Others were exiled or fined.

The prosecution brought to light, or so it was asserted, a number of intrigues and plots with the object of restoring the Sultanate, and while it was never claimed that Abdul Medjid had any hand in these movements, the government, now thoroughly roused, resolved on a drastic step—the removal of the Khalif.

Immediately after the passage of the edict for his deposition he and all the members of the Royal family, together with his entourage, were ordered to leave the country within twenty-four hours. He was escorted in a special train to the frontier before even he and his family had had time to collect their personal belongings.

The departure of the Royal party was effected so quietly that very few in Constantinople knew what had happened until it was all over and the Khalif was installed at Territet in Switzerland, where he has lived ever since. Thus the Angora government had taken another momentous step in its process of national housecleaning. Since then Church and State have been entirely separate in Turkey; all cults are accorded equal protection, and all the special privileges of the Moslem clergy have been abolished. The system of Evkav, the pious foundation of the Moslem church, was placed under the control of the Ministry of Cults, and the old Code of Moslem Law, the Shariat, was done away with by the passage of the new Civil Code. Today theological students are wards of the government just the same as the students in the military academies. They no longer wear robes and turbans, but dress like everybody else.

It was not so much anticlericalism as fear of the reactionary intrigues woven around the Khalif which prompted the Angora government to take these steps. The Dervish orders in particular were centres of disaffection, notably the Mevlevi or Dancing Dervishes, whose chief, the Chelebi, had always had the right to gird the sword of Osman the Conqueror on the Khalif at his accession.

Besides the clergy there were a few old families and a few conservative communities that remained faithful to the idea of a Sultan-Khalif but on the whole the abolition of the Khalifate excited much more controversy outside of Turkey than within the country; even so it did not have the effect of a thunderbolt upon the Islamic world, as many people unfamiliar with the history of the Khalifate or the new tendencies in Islam had predicted, but this we will discuss later. It is sufficient here for us to realize that it had no profound effect in Turkey.

More important, however, was the controversy between the Turks and the British over the Mosul boundary question, which had been referred to the League of Nations for settlement by the terms of the Lausanne Treaty. The League had sent a Commission to Iraq to examine the disputed territory. After an exhaustive inquiry the Commission decided that the Mosul area should be included in Iraq, provided that Great Britain would agree to retain the Mandate in Iraq for twenty five years. The British accepted this verdict, which was reinforced by a decision of the Hague Tribunal that the award of the League of Nations should be obligatory. Turkey declined to accept its decision. For some months negotiations were at a standstill. Great Britain and Turkey both made gestures calculated to reinforce their claims, the former concluding a pact with Italy for assistance in case of war, the latter effecting an even closer rapprochement with Russia. The matter was not finally settled until June 5, 1926, when Turkey, Great Britain, and Iraq signed a treaty accepting the boundary line fixed by the Council of the League of Nations with one or two minor corrections. All Turks living in Iraq were to have the right to choose whether they would become citizens of Iraq or Turkey, and the Turks secured certain financial advantages, notably an agreement that they were to receive ten per cent of the Iraq Government's revenues from the Mosul oil fields, and a guarantee of security along their southern frontier.

Meanwhile the Turkish government had had to deal with a revolt in Kurdistan during the period when it looked as though there might possibly be war between Turkey and Great Britain over Iraq. It was claimed quite openly by the Turkish government that the British had a hand in the matter during the bitter discussions that preceded the decision with regard to Iraq. The Kurds, who number about three million, are the only considerable non-Turkish element in the Republic today. Of a race conceded by most ethnologists to be of Aryan origin, and perhaps descended from the ancient Medes and Persians, the Kurds were never assimilated by the Turks. Shut in by the mountain ranges of the Zagros, they continued to occupy their own territory in the southeastern portion of Asia Minor adjoining Mesopotamia and Persia. Maintaining their warlike spirit and their tribal organization, they succeeded in securing for themselves a special status under the Ottoman Empire. They were "Ashiret," that is to say, they enjoyed complete local autonomy. The Ottoman Sultans, often faced by intrigue and rebellion among their own subjects, found it convenient to maintain this status, as the Kurds could be counted on when necessary to support the dynasty. Under the Sultan Abdul Hamid they were organized into bands of irregular cavalry known as the Hamidiés and maintained as mercenaries very like the Cossacks in Russia, in the old days of the Czars.

Under the Republic their status was changed. They were invited to share the rights of other Turkish citizens in a government which they did not in the least comprehend or appreciate. They greatly preferred the special status they had enjoyed under the Sultans, which left them free to live with their own ancient feudal system in tribal communities. They, like all the minorities in all the countries of the globe, had heard of and been impressed by the doctrine of self-determination, and they had promptly started a "movement" (confined, however, to a few leaders) for an "independent" Kurdistan.

There had been a similar rebellion among the Kurds in Persia, just across the border from their Turkish brothers, and many disturbances among the half a million Kurds who were included in the territory of Iraq, the truth being that they resented the establishment of any strong national governments which were disposed to impose the duties as well as confer the privileges of citizenship. Formerly they had known no national boundaries. One-third of their tribes were migratory, following the pasture with the seasons, and their wanderings often took them back and forth over the Persian border, which they had disregarded just as they did the new Iraq frontier. The immediate cause of the revolt was furnished by Sheikh Said, the Kurdish leader, who sought to gain adherents by proclaiming himself the champion of the Khalifate and urging a Holy War for its restoration. He did not succeed in this but he did raise a rebellion which it took three army corps and months of fighting to put down, and which was a severe drain on the resources of the Republic.

The spectacle of a people under Turkish rule in revolt, was a moral help to Great Britain in her fight to obtain Mosul for Iraq, as was the fact that the Turks had handled the Assyrian Christians living on the border with great cruelty during the rebellion, though probably not without provocation.

Until after the signing of the Lausanne Treaty the dictatorship of the Popular party was supreme. It carried on the traditions of the Union and Progress party which had brought about the first revolution in 1908. In the National Assembly, just as in the former Turkish Parliament, there was no organized opposition; it was not until the Republic was secured from outside attacks that certain differences of opinion began to appear among the members of the party. For some time these differences were confined to criticisms of the cabinet, but finally after the general elections the Assembly in 1925 split into three sections. The Popular party continued to favor the absolute dictatorship of Mustapha Kemal and his associates; a Republican party was formed including among its members Raouf Bey the signer of the Mudros armistice, Refet Pasha, who took Smyrna, as well as many former adherents of the Union and Progress party; a third element held aloof. In addition there was considerable secret agitation among the conservatives, who were shocked and offended beyond measure at what they considered the anticlerical policy of the government, and at the ruthless sweeping away of old customs and traditions.

The opposition which continued to grow in the National Assembly had no reflection in the nation, however. The vast majority of the Turkish people had not the faintest conception of the potential power of a nation with a representative form of government, just as they had no idea of what was meant by the word "republic." When I was in Anatolia during the winter of 1923-24, shortly after its proclamation, I was often asked by peasants who was this "Jumhouriet Effendi" (Mr. Republic) of whom there was so much talk, and whether he was Vizier to Mustapha Kemal.

The government was in the hands of a few, and so was the opposition. The party struggles were waged between those who supported unequivocally the dictatorship as instituted by Mustapha Kemal, and those who favored extending the oligarchy. It was a war of cliques, rather than parties, which culminated in an ill-advised plot to assassinate the President, engineered by some of the former members of the Union and Progress party, resulting in the condemnation and execution of thirteen prominent Turks in July, 1926. All the members of the opposition figured more or less in the prosecutions by the Tribunal of Independence which followed the discovery of the plot, including innumerable deputies and former ministers and six generals, among whom was Kiazim Kara Bekir Pasha, who had put down the Armenian revolt. Some of the accused prudently left for Europe before the storm broke.

By this summary action the opposition was "liquidated," to use a favorite expression of the Turks, but in the early part of this year, its reconciliation with the government was so complete that Kiazim Kara Bekir Pasha was elected President of the National Assembly and the Tribunal of Independence was dissolved, though the government still retained an emergency measure of National Defense similar to the "Dora" act in Great Britain during the World War.

While these party disputes gave the government considerable concern, they were not nearly as serious as they appeared. Actually there has never been any real danger of the overthrow of the Dictatorship, and there never will be as long as Mustapha Kemal Pasha is alive. The Turkish people may be bewildered and confused by the reforms imposed by the government, they may be offended and shocked by its attitude towards the church and its disregard of time-honored customs and manners, but in the final analysis any disaffection they may feel is overbalanced by their overwhelming personal devotion to Mustapha Kemal. No opposition party could take any action leading to the overthrow of the President without risking its own existence and perhaps that of the Republic. It will be some time before representative government will be understood at all in Turkey. Indeed there seems to be some doubt as to whether Parliamentarianism will ever really supersede a benevolent despotism. Even in Europe, at the present time the increasing number of dictatorships constitutes a challenge to political democracy.

Internal reconstruction has been the vital preoccupation of the Angora government during the last five years and notwithstanding many failures and mistakes the amount accomplished has been colossal. People in Western countries have been too prone to overlook this and to stress only the superficial changes brought about by government edicts which are often sensational, frequently amusing, and sometimes intensely annoying.

No government order ever caused more excitement in any country than that abolishing the fez as the national headgear, which produced riots in many places and an unprecedented run on the hat-shops in Constantinople and other large cities. It took other edicts to do away with the time-wasting custom of serving coffee at all hours in government offices, to compel state functionaries to wear European costumes, and to force them to adopt surnames instead of the confusing given name and patronymic.

Women under the new constitution have been allowed equal **rights** with men, and women in government employment have

been forced to abandon the veil, while every effort is being made
to induce all the women of the country to follow their example—
a difficult matter in the conservative provinces. Not long ago
the municipal council of Trebizond passed a regulation rendering
the abandonment of the "harem" trousers compulsory for women.
It almost caused the disruption of the city administration . . .
the ladies of Trebizond still wear trousers! On the other hand, in
Constantinople and other modern cities the women are exceedingly progressive. I shall never forget my amazement on wit-
nessing, in the summer of 1925, a contest, held publicly for
charity, to determine the possessor of the prettiest pair of feminine
legs in Constantinople!

The National Assembly abolished the old Moslem Calendar,
adopting the Gregorian, and provided that the beginning of
Ramadan, the month of fasting observed by all Moslems, should
be fixed by the astronomical observatory instead of by watchers
from the minarets of the mosques who announce it on the first
sight of the new moon.

Together with a number of admirable regulations for quarantine, the extermination of malaria, and other matters affecting
the public health, the Assembly passed a rule requiring that after
the prescribed medical examination of all persons about to be married, the examining physician should affix a seal on the left wrist
of each of the contracting parties!

No effort was spared to stimulate the national revival.
The Turkish language was made obligatory in all business operations and preachers were required to deliver their sermons in
Turkish. Foreign firms were considerably handicapped at first
by the requirement that the majority of their clerical staff should
be Turkish, and all foreign schools and educational institutions
were required to include Turkish in their curriculum. Occasionally controversies arose over the last-named dictum, resulting in
the closing of some of the foreign institutions. The Jewish
schools were at one time not a little embarrassed by an order
forbidding them to use the French language as a means of instruction, and requiring Hebrew instead, which was rather difficult
because aside from the Rabbis there were almost no Jews in Constantinople who spoke colloquial Hebrew!

Tourists landing at Constantinople were compelled to make use of the official guides furnished by the government, and an American friend of mine who lived in Constantinople was arrested for acting as guide without a license, while she was showing the sights to some friends who had just arrived on one of the Mediterranean cruise parties.

More serious were the government's restrictions on trade, and its attitude as regards concessions, which was conservative to the verge of retrogression. This came from two causes: first, the exaggerated idea of their own importance and their own capabilities, which the Kemalist leaders had acquired as a result of their extraordinary success in carrying out the programme of liberation and revolution; and secondly, the fear lest foreign assistance should lead to political intrigue and renewed efforts at foreign domination.

Consequently, the Assembly built up tariff walls which made the importation of many foreign-manufactured goods almost prohibitive, and the tariff regulations were constantly and arbitrarily changed. At one time the shipping in the port of Constantinople was held up because the authorities had decided that all the pilots must be Turkish citizens. There was hardly a Turk qualified to take out a pilot's license! Agricultural machinery was the crying need of the country, for Turkey must depend for a long time upon agricultural production to increase her national wealth, but the rural credit banks just organized did not have enough capital to grant extensive credits, and the government hesitated to contract large foreign loans, fearing the introduction of foreign capital.

For the same reason, comparatively few concessions have been granted to foreign firms for municipal improvements and developments of railway systems and national resources. A concession to the Ottoman-American Development Company on the basis of one made informally to the American Admiral Chester by the Sultan Abdul Hamid many years before, was signed by the Angora government at the close of 1922. A group of Canadian-American capitalists agreed to build a network of railways to cover Anatolia from the Black Sea to the Gulf of Alexandretta, on the Mediterranean; with the railway construction rights went many rights to mining development and oil concessions. But a dispute arose between the American and Canadian groups interested in the venture, the work was not begun within the specified time, and the concession was declared forfeited.

Following this fiasco, Angora displayed more caution than ever. It was announced that the government would itself exercise an old option to purchase the famous Baghdad Railway, with its Anatolian branch line connecting Constantinople with Angora, and that Turkey's railway system would be developed under exclusively Turkish direction. Since then the government has deviated somewhat from this policy; important contracts for railway and harbor construction have been granted to Swedish and Belgian firms, and Turkish foreign trade last year showed a slight improvement, while a loan from American bankers of $20,000,000 for railway construction has been agreed on in principle.

Financially, while Turkey is considerably impoverished, her situation is sound. The gold standard was maintained even through the post-war period, and the amount of paper money outstanding against the new republic was not more than 70 million dollars. The internal war debt has been settled; the pre-war external debt of the Ottoman Empire has been apportioned by the Lausanne Treaty so that Turkey is only required to bear 60 per cent of the total, and the government is still haggling with the foreign holders of the debt, principally French, in the hope of being able to secure a settlement on the basis of the depreciated exchange.

The educational programme inaugurated under the Republic contemplated the establishment of universal popular education, in spite of the lack of trained teachers and the exceedingly small budget allowed the Ministry of Public Instruction. It has already accomplished wonders considering its handicaps. At present, a Turkish Commission abroad is studying European educational systems, and a Belgian expert has been employed as adviser to the Ministry of Public Instruction.

That the Turks might have progressed more rapidly if they had been willing to employ more European assistance is undoubtedly true, and to the Western observer there is something rather naïve in the know-it-all attitude of the Angora Government; but this very egotism has been a protection. Perhaps it was just as well that Turkey should endure her poverty and consolidate her internal position; it is certainly just as well that the liberal constitution is administered by a benevolent dictator. Internal stability is more important for Turkey than money, or railroads, or industries, for upon the ability of the leaders of Angora to Westernize their country without sacrificing its national individuality, depends not only the future of Turkey but that of the entire Asiatic Bloc with which she has associated herself.

The West commonly assumes that Asiatics as a whole are deficient in administrative genius. Turkey has set herself to prove the contrary on behalf of Asia—nothing could be more foolish than a sweeping assertion, or denial, of her ability to do so. The world can only wait and see, but any unprejudiced observer must admit that the Turks have made a good beginning, that they bid fair to become the leaders of the Moslem Bloc.

PERSIA

At the close of the World War, Persia, as we have seen, occupied virtually the position of a conquered nation. There seemed to be nothing in the way of the aspirations of Lord Curzon to create a Persian Protectorate which would have extended the frontiers of the British Empire to Mount Ararat and the Caucasus. British troops were in control of all of Northern Persia with detachments in the Trans-Caspian region beyond the frontier, and the South Persian Rifles under British officers kept order in the South. Ahmed Shah, was a weak, pleasure-loving boy, quite unfit for the responsibility of directing affairs of state. There was much misery among the people, for agriculture and commerce had suffered greatly as a result of war conditions. The Persian Parliament and the leading statesmen were hopelessly divided; chaos and corruption reigned in all governmental departments, and there was not enough strong national sentiment to create an overwhelmingly popular movement against foreign domination, as in Turkey.

It is highly probable that if Great Britain had pushed the matter at the Peace Conference at Versailles some agreement would have been reached by which she would have obtained a League of Nations Mandate for the country; but the imperialistic designs of Lord Curzon did not brook any interference. Instead, the Persian delegation to the Conference was refused a hearing at British instigation and Sir Percy Cox, acting on behalf of Great Britain, drew up in Teheran an agreement known as the Anglo-Persian Convention, which was actually signed by the Prime Minister, Vossuq-ed-Dowleh, Prince Firuz, the Minister for Foreign Affairs, and Saram-ed-Dowleh. The day after the signing of the Convention the three ministers received over half a million dollars which was divided between them.

This was too much even for the easy-going Persians, whose traditional indifference to foreign domination had been shaken by the impulse towards national self-assertion which had swept the world after the Armistice. Moreover, such a flagrant attempt to absorb Persia as part of the British Empire could not go unchallenged. It raised a storm of protest in the outside world and called forth a sharp note to Great Britain from the United States. From the standpoint of British diplomacy it was almost as great a blunder as the espousal of the Greek cause in Asia Minor, and as in Turkey, though in a lesser degree, it had the effect of stimulating a genuine national movement.

There was tremendous popular sympathy for the Nationalists who, in danger of arrest by the British, fled to the Holy Cities of Iraq; sporadic outbreaks here and there, particularly the insurrection in the Northwest provinces under Mirza Kuchik Khan, a sort of Persian Robin Hood, and leader of the bands known as "Jangalis" (Foresters) testified to the universal unrest.

Beneath the surface, even in the early part of 1920, Bolshevist propaganda was very active, and there were certain Persians who were already visualizing the possibility of playing Russia off against England. The British had begun to lose prestige, when, at the close of 1919, they withdrew their troops from Baku and Batum in Trans-Caucasia, which was taken as a sign of weakness in the Middle East. As we have seen, the immediate result of their action, in Turkey, was to liquidate the question of Armenia and to hasten an understanding between the Kemalists and Moscow.

The Persian statesmen of that time might have been poor administrators, but they were clever diplomatists and farseeing. While Great Britain was concentrating all her anti-Bolshevik activities on assistance to the Poles and the Russian monarchists who were making war on Moscow, the Soviet Foreign Office was laying the foundations for an Asiatic Empire.

In the summer of 1920, emissaries from Russia were already making overtures to the Persian government; unofficial Persian envoys were in Moscow.   The Soviet press was hailing Mirza Kuchik Khan as the liberator of his country, and in June a Soviet force was sent out to Enzeli, on the Persian shore of the Caspian, ostensibly to protect the fisheries which had been in Russian hands under an old concession, but actually to war against the Anglophile government.   The British forces in North Persia withdrew to Resht, as the first step towards eventual withdrawal, which had already been decided on in London after the plans of the Foreign Office to support the buffer states in Trans-Caucasia had been abandoned; but their action, which was taken as an evidence of weakness, had a strong influence in hastening the rapprochement with Russia.

During all this period British diplomacy never relaxed its pressure on the cabinet at Teheran.   The subsidies which had been paid to the Persian government for more than two years were suddenly cut off in the summer of 1920, and at the same time the Anglo-Persian Oil Company obtained a monopoly of the Persian oil fields under circumstances that roused indignation in the breasts of the Nationalists.

For the last quarter-century or more, the smell of petroleum has clung to many of the political manœuvrings of the great Powers, particularly Great Britain, in the East, and we have seen how the strategic position of the Persian fields was one of the factors which impelled the British to undertake the Mesopotamian campaign during the war, and the guardianship of Iraq afterwards.   The story of the struggle for petroleum in Asia would be a whole volume in itself, but as the Anglo-Persian Oil Company has played, and still plays, a supremely important rôle in the affairs of Persia, a short account of it here may help in an understanding of Persian politics.

The first concession to exploit the Persian oil fields was pro-
cured in 1901, by a farseeing Englishman, William d'Arcy, who
foresaw the day when petroleum would to a large extent supplant
coal as fuel. By 1908, when the enterprise was incorporated as
the Anglo-Persian Oil Company, the probability had become a
certainty; and a few years later, when the British navy began
to replace coal with oil-burning engines on the ships of its fleet,
the government itself put considerable sums of money into the
"A.P." and in return acquired a large block of the stock.

In August, 1921, according to a report made by Sir Austen
Chamberlain to the House of Commons, the British government
owned two-thirds of the common and over one-tenth of the company's preferred stock, with two votes for every share of the
former, and one for every five shares of the latter. Under the concession, which does not expire until 1960, the Persian government
was to receive 16 per cent of the net profits as royalties. Other
royalties were also stipulated for, to be paid to the Bakhtiari
princes, owners of the land in Khuzistan, on which the deposits
were located. Some idea of the magnitude of the "Anglo-Persian," may be gleaned from a report made to the directors at the
annual meeting of the Company in November, 1924, by Sir
Charles Greenway, the chairman, who has since retired.

At that time, the "A.P." owned 700 miles of pipe-lines, 9
refineries, 164 miles of railway, and 330 steamships. It had distributed £9,500,000, in dividends, and divided up £19,000,000 of
profits since 1914. Its production for 1924 was 3,714,216 tons,
and it employed a personnel of more than 50,000.

On the Persian Gulf the Company possessed two ports:
Mohammerah, where its main offices were located, and where it
had built a superb modern administrative centre; and Abadan,
where its tank steamers were loaded and all the pipe-lines from
the interior discharged their contents. The steamers navigating
the Karun River, the only navigable stream in Persia, which
empties into the Gulf at Mohammerah and provides the easiest
access to the oil fields, are all operated by the Company. Its
settlements in the interior are completely self-sustaining, with
their own militia and municipal control.

It is a marvellous organization—a fact in itself sufficient to make it an object of suspicion to any weak government, the more because the Bakhtiari territory in which it is located is even at the present time, none too securely attached to the central administration.

The Bakhtiari, most of whom are migratory, divided into tribes under two princes known as the Il-Khani and Il-Begi respectively, who are elected from the ruling family, were virtually independent although they acknowledged the suzerainty of the Shah. By standing in with the "Khavanin" (the Princes) the British had always been able to get exactly what they wanted without the formality of asking leave of Teheran. The same was true of the Sheikh of Mohammerah, the absolute ruler of the territory in which their offices were situated.

But since the war, a new situation had arisen with regard to "Oil." The existence of fields in Khorassan, a northeastern province of Persia, probably fully as rich as those of the Bakhtiari region had been known for some time, and before the war the concession had been awarded to Russian interests. This claim, known as the Koustaria Concession, was sold to the Anglo-Persian, and when the Company applied to the Medjliss for its ratification the storm of Nationalist sentiment that burst over the capital caused the downfall of the Anglophile cabinet. Vossuq-ed-Dowleh had seen it coming and had gone to Europe; other members of his cabinet were less fortunate and were put into prison on account of their lack of perspicacity.

A coalition cabinet which came into power in June, 1920, had tried to play both ends against the middle and had been negotiating a treaty with Russia while promising the British to bring the Anglo-Persian convention before the newly elected Medjliss. British policy had become hopelessly involved. Northern Persia had been abandoned to the Bolshevists, possibly with a view to exercising pressure on the Teheran government, possibly because of the change of policy in London with regard to Trans-Caucasia, but the Persians, instead of imploring the aid of England, had displayed an unexpected activity. A campaign against the Russians conducted by Persian troops commanded by a former Czarist officer had resulted in the retirement of the Bolshevist forces from the province of Mazanderan which they had overrun, and in the defeat of Mirza Kuchik Khan, who had become the protégé of the Reds.

A Persian offensive against the Soviet Republic of Azerbaijan had not ended so happily. An armistice was concluded with Soviet Russia, and the reorganization of the Cossack division of the army, a military gendarmerie corresponding somewhat to the Canadian Mounted Police, which had done most of the fighting, was undertaken by a group of young officers among whom was Reza Khan, a junior colonel. They set themselves resolutely in opposition to the appointment of British officers to train the Persian army, and they began to acquire a large following.

Meanwhile it had become evident to the British that their Middle Eastern policy would have to undergo a radical reformation. It was obvious that the treaty could not be forced on the Persian people.

The Bolshevist menace had no terrors for the astute Persian diplomatists who had seen how their neighbors the Kemalists were utilizing Russia in their struggle against the Sèvres Treaty, and particularly against England. They had also witnessed the edifying spectacle of a war between Afghanistan and England in 1919, in which, notwithstanding their military victories, the British had sustained a moral defeat, being forced by their domestic situation to accept the Emir as an equal and as an ally, for England, no less than the other countries of Europe, was suffering from the demoralizing effect of post-war readjustment.

The year 1920, marked the crest of the wave of discontent and unrest consequent upon the demobilization of the army and the reconstruction of British industry on a peace footing. Economic distress and social agitation always go hand in hand. The Communists and Independent Laborites found ready listeners to their diatribes against the government. Had it not been for the sops offered to Labor by Lloyd George in the form of the unemployment dole and other legislation, and his withdrawal of direct support to the forces that were seeking to overthrow the Bolshevist regime in Russia, it is not improbable that there might have been a revolution or an attempted revolution in England. In addition to having to face the consequences of earlier mistakes, Great Britain was being forced to a complete readjustment of her whole policy in Asia. Under the circumstances it was quite wonderful that she eventually succeeded in salvaging so much of her lost prestige in Persia.

Young Ahmed Shah, who had returned in June, 1920, from a journey to England where he had a very fine time and was received by King George as a fellow-sovereign, must have had in his suite some shrewd and not entirely supine observers who grasped the state of affairs. Certain it is that Sir Percy Cox was forced by public sentiment to leave Persia, and his successor Mr. Norman succeeded no more than his predecessor in frightening the Persians with the bogy of Bolshevism. The announcement that all British troops would be withdrawn from Persia in the spring of 1921, was received with equanimity.

The Sepahdar-Azam, one of the great feudal princes of the north who headed the cabinet, was laying the foundations for an understanding with Persia's neighbors, Turkey and Afghanistan; he was carrying on negotiations with Russia and was plainly playing for time, when the army took a hand in the proceedings.

Reza Khan and his fellow officers, who had first been concerned merely with reforms in the Cossack division of the army, finding that the government was too weak or too corrupt to back their efforts, had gradually been drawn into a group of Nationalists at the head of which was Seyid Zia-ed-Din, editor of the liberal newspaper "Raad" in Teheran. On February 21, 1921, a detachment of the Cossack division in command of Reza Khan, stationed under General Ironside at Kazvin, marched on Teheran unopposed, overthrew the cabinet and placed Zia-ed-Din at the head of the government, Reza Khan himself becoming commander-in-chief of the army with the title of "Sardar Sepah."

It was not long before it became apparent that Reza Khan was the real ruler of Persia! For the first two years of his dictatorship he left the government ostensibly in the hands of a succession of Prime Ministers whom he removed at will; as Minister of War, he devoted himself to the building up of an army and to the suppression of the various powerful feudal chiefs controlling tribal communities, who had taken advantage of governmental chaos to rebel against the central authority. By October, 1923, he had sufficiently consolidated his power to proclaim himself

Prime Minister, and when two months later the Shah left for Damascus en route for Europe with his suite and his personal fortune packed in ten automobiles, everyone realized that his departure was merely a camouflaged flight.

During the period between the coup d'état and Reza Khan's assumption of the premiership, events moved rapidly in Persia. The government of Zia-ed-Din did not last long. He alienated the rich landowners by inaugurating a new system of taxation affecting their properties; he was suspected of pro-British tendencies; and he soon became involved, to his own undoing, in disputes with the military group which lost him the support of Reza Khan.

Besides subduing the rebellious tribespeople, Reza Khan had many delicate problems of international administration to deal with. The first and most crying need in Persia was the reorganization of the finances. The Treasury was empty, the fiscal system was chaotic, and never since the beginning of history had there been a Persian budget. Certain departments of the government had been assigned the revenue from certain taxes and other sources of income, and these had been spent either without any accounting, or with such corrupt and makeshift systems of bookkeeping, that it was impossible to fix the responsibility for the huge sums that completely disappeared without anyone being the wiser.

Reza Khan had imperative need of money to maintain his army, and the Amnieh, the militia whose duty it was to patrol the roads. The fundamental condition for the reconstruction of Persia was, at the moment, the re-establishment of internal order. Therefore Reza Khan's first act was to appropriate the right to collect and spend all the indirect taxes of every kind from the province of Teheran, for the country at large. Then he began to look about for foreign fiscal experts to reorganize the finances of the country. Such a reorganization had been contemplated in the Anglo-Persian Convention, and British interests in Persia were sufficient to have made the appointment of a financial mission almost inevitable, had England been more cautious or more tactful in her demands on Persia.

British interests were by far the greatest in the country. Besides the holdings of the Anglo-Persian groups they included the greater part of the export and import trade through the Persian Gulf, the Imperial Bank of Persia with twenty branches, the Imperial Ottoman Bank, the Indo-European Telegraph system, and a host of other enterprises. In addition, the British had a lien on the customs revenues of Southern Persia, as security for loans made to the Persian Government, and other claims more vague—but with some foundation—for large sums advanced to the administration during the period of British domination.

As in 1911, when she had obtained the services of W. Morgan Shuster for a similar purpose, Persia turned to America; upon the recommendation of the American Department of State, Reza Khan's emissary, Mirza Hossein Khan Ali, secured the services of Dr. A. C. Millspaugh, formerly economic adviser to the Department, with a staff of his own choosing, for the financial reorganization of Persia.   Dr. Millspaugh's contract with the Government was for a period of three years and it cannot be denied that when he and his staff arrived in 1922, to take up their duties, few people thought that they would remain until the expiration of their contract.   Both British and Russian interests were presumably hostile to them, as were many other groups in Persia; they had to create order out of chaos, and produce substance out of what was virtually a void—by no means an easy task.

That they succeeded, was due not only to the ability, disinterestedness, and absolutely unpolitical attitude of all the members of the Mission, but also to the determination and farsightedness of Reza Khan.   It must be remembered that Dr. Millspaugh and his staff were not advisory as is sometimes thought, nor did they constitute a mission in the real sense of the word.   They were not in any way connected officially with the American Department of State; they all received their salaries direct from the Persian Government, and they had to obtain authority from the Minister of Finance, or the Parliament, for all their actions.

Dr. Millspaugh's first step was to acquire control of the government's revenues. It took a whole year to unite and centralize financial control. This was finally accomplished with the exception of the revenues allotted to the Ministry of War, which were fixed at the lump sum of $750,000 a month; up to quite recently, all Dr. Millspaugh's efforts to obtain a strict accounting of

military expenditures had been unavailing. It is possible that a
difference with the government on this subject may yet prove his
undoing.

As regards other departments he was more successful, and
Persia's first budget, drawn up tentatively in 1923, showed a
deficit of only 5 per cent. At the close of the year 1925-26, there
was a surplus! This amazing state of affairs for Persia was
brought about not by any radical reforms in the fiscal system,
but by efficient supervision of revenue and expenditure.

A Civil Service Administration controlling the personnel of the
Ministry of Finance was able to diminish considerably, although
it could not stamp out, the widespread corruption among officials;
the insistence of Dr. Millspaugh that all the outstanding claims
against the Persian government be met, resulted not only in the
prosecution of individuals such as many of the great landowners,
but also in military expeditions against certain of the feudal chiefs
who refused to pay their own taxes, or allow the government to
collect taxes in their domains.

Reza Khan never failed to back up such demands with force;
thanks to his newly organized army he was usually successful.
As a matter of fact, the last step towards his complete assumption
of the Dictatorship was facilitated by an incident provoked by the
American Financial Administration. Among the most powerful
feudal chiefs in the Shah's dominions was the Sheikh of Mohammerah, who was, as we have seen, a protégé of the British. The
headquarters of the Anglo-Persian Oil Company were built on his
territory, and part of his enormous fortune had been accumulated
through British subsidies. In the early days of the war, when
Basra was the object of the British Expeditionary Forces, he had
been deemed sufficiently powerful to be threatened, bribed, and
cajoled in turn.

When I was in Mohammerah in the early part of 1924, relations between the Sheikh and the central government were exceedingly strained owing to the fact that he had refused to pay arrears
of taxes amounting to something like $12,000,000, demanded
from him by the American Financial Administration. By the
autumn he had persuaded the powerful Bakhtiari and their

neighbors the Kashgai tribes, to join with him in defying the central government.

Reza Khan took quick and decided action. With over 20,000 men of his well trained army of 40,000 he advanced to the edges of the Bakhtiari country, making such a formidable demonstration that the Bakhtiari voluntarily laid down their arms, and the Sheikh of Mohammerah telegraphed his submission to Reza at Shiraz. But this was not enough: Reza Khan got on a gunboat and proceeded up the Persian Gulf to the Sheikh's capital, where he not only received the submission of his unruly vassal, but sent him and one of his sons back to Teheran as security for their promises!

Between 1924, and the close of 1925, the new Dictator of Persia had succeeded in bringing about internal order. He had stabilized the fiscal system, built up a strong army, an excellent gendarmerie, and had brought back a considerable measure of material prosperity to Persia. Small wonder that he had dreamed of establishing his power on a firm constitutional basis! His first attempts along this line had been made through Parliament in 1923 and 1924, when his adherents acting under his orders had endeavored to put through resolutions abolishing the monarchy and proclaiming a republic; but these efforts had not been successful. The people of Persia were not yet ready for a democratic form of government.

Everyone knew that the return of the Shah was out of the question, but the priests, who were still enormously powerful, to whom the Shah was spiritual as well as temporal Lord, were against the abolition of the monarchy. No one seems to have thought of replacing Ahmed Shah with his brother, who was acting as regent in his absence, and it was not until a show of force had been exerted, that the military party, backed by the prestige of Reza Khan, was able to force a declaration through the Medjliss deposing Ahmed Shah, and to appoint Reza Khan as Provisional Ruler of Persia.

A Constituent Assembly was called together, and promptly voted as it had been told to do, for the retention of a monarchical form of government with Reza as Shah. On April 25, 1926, Reza Khan became Reza Shah, adopting as the appellation of the new dynasty the ancient name for the Persian language, Pahlevi,

which he had taken as Minister of War when he had been instrumental in having passed a law abolishing all titles, and replacing
them with family names. Of Reza Khan's own people this much
may be said with certainty—they possessed neither name nor
titles. While little is known about his origin, most accounts agree
that he came of a respectable family of small farmers in Maz-
andaran, one of the northwest provinces of Persia. He was employed as a guard at a Foreign Legation in Teheran, and served
for a number of years in the Cossack gendarmerie, where he first
came into notice.

When I met him in the summer of 1924, I was struck by a
quality in him which is not often found in the Orient. He was,
as they say in America, "hard-boiled." One felt that he had few
scruples, no illusions. Boundless ambition, great determination,
and a certain dogged persistence coupled with keen insight and
an exceedingly practical, unemotional, but none the less consistent form of patriotism are his chief characteristics. Whether
or not he will succumb to the pitfalls of greatness remains to be
seen. At least he has made Persia an independent nation and put
her in a position to reassert her historic importance.

Persia, from its situation at the apex of the crossroads between
Europe and Asia, is a natural fortress. It is in the main, a high
plateau, almost completely encircled by high mountain ranges
intersected by long valleys running parallel to its frontiers and
broken here and there by rugged easily defended passes. Only in
the south towards Baluchistan, and in the north towards the
Caspian Sea, does the land slope easily down to sea level. It has
about eleven million inhabitants, of whom the majority are illiterate and still, socially, little better than serfs. They are part Aryan
and part of the same stock as the Turks, with a small mixture of
Arab blood. Until recently two-thirds of them have been living
under feudal chiefs.

Most of the cities of Persia are situated in or on the edges
of the central plateau. None of them is large as cities go, and
while many have electric light and Teheran boasts a tram service,
there is not one with a modern sewage system, factories, or an
adequate school system. Though many railroads are projected,
there is yet only one of any consequence in all Persia, twenty-two

miles in length, running between Tabriz and Julfa on the Russian frontier.   Until the war there was only one automobile road connecting Teheran with the outside world, built by Russians, to Enzeli on the Caspian through Kazvin.   Travelling was by diligences drawn by three or four horses, by carriage, or on horseback.

The British had built a commercial caravan road from Bushire on the Gulf to Isfahan, which was completed in the early part of the war, and during the occupation they constructed a complete road system for military purposes from Southern Persia to Teheran, and from Kazvin to the Mesopotamian border, where a spur of the Baghdad Railway joined it with the capital of Iraq.

The natural resources of Persia have never been properly developed.   With the exception of her oil wells, her mineral deposits, said to be quite extensive, have never been scratched.   Copper, coal, lead, manganese, and nickel are known to exist, but no one knows in what quantity.   In this respect Persia belongs to the many "forgotten" countries, whose mines were exploited in antiquity with primitive methods, lost sight of to a large extent during the period of barbarian invasions, and ignored when the discovery of the Americas had apparently opened up an inexhaustible El Dorado.   Later still South Africa and Siberia revealed other fields for mining enterprise, and until very recently no extensive efforts were made to gauge the wealth of the old mines in Asia Minor and Central Asia.   At any rate, there can be no question of extensive mining operations in Persia until there are railroads.

Before the introduction of machine-made articles, the Persian handicraftsmen were among the finest in the East, but within the past decade Western importations made terrible inroads on native arts and crafts and the Great War completed the ruin of the silk-weaving industry.   The lack of extensive irrigation systems has kept the cultivable land in Persia down to a minimum, but there are enormous desert areas which could be made productive.   Of late many of the great landowners have adopted modern machinery; only last year more than three hundred tractors were sold in Persia, but most farming is still done by primitive methods. Among the nomads sheep-raising is practised in a most haphazard fashion and even the carpet industry, one of Persia's chief sources of wealth, could be better organized. Nevertheless, the country is self-supporting and if proper communications were assured it would have a much larger export trade than at present.

There is a great deal of wealth in Persia, but it is in the hands of a few, as is education. The educated classes have a background of culture extending over many centuries. It was they who preserved and carried on the traditions of the Greek philosophers during the Dark Ages, when all Europe was engulfed by the barbarians, through the Sufi mystics and metaphysicians, keeping alive free thought and philosophy even under the relentless yoke of Islam.

Persian literature became the model for all Arab and Turkish writers, and Persian art was long supreme in the Middle East. Persia's culture was so profound, so vital, and so distinctive, that it always impressed itself deeply on the peoples with whom it came in contact. The Persians have always been intellectually free.

This is the explanation of the comparative apathy with which the Persians in times past, and more recently, have submitted to a certain amount of foreign control and influence. They have been so conscious of this intellectual ascendancy that they have not concerned themselves about material supremacy. They let themselves be conquered, and then absorbed their conquerors.

But there are evidences that this old psychology is rapidly disappearing. Persia has been inoculated with the fever of unrest from which the whole world has been suffering since the war. The masses are stirred by it without grasping its meaning, and by it the classes have been roused to a complete revision of old ideals and old standards.

There is a tremendous thirst for education in Persia. Even the nomads and the peasants are beginning to learn to read and write. Reza Khan, who is scarcely literate, is sponsoring the adoption of a universal system of education. The missionary schools and colleges are crowded as never before. There is a native university in Teheran and the government is sending hundreds of young students to other countries.

After the example of Turkey, Persia is thirsting for Westernization as a means of furthering her national aims and her new race patriotism.

During all the period which we have been discussing, Persia's foreign relations underwent a no less amazing evolution than her internal affairs. It was only a few weeks after the coup d'état in 1921, that the Ministry of Zia-ed-Din announced the conclusion of a treaty with Soviet Russia, which as we have seen was already being tentatively discussed while there was a nominal state of war between the Soviet Republic of Azerbaijan and Persia.

By the treaty with Persia the Russians gave up all claims to the old Russian concessions, with the exception of the fisheries in the Caspian Sea, which were to be the subject of further negotiations, and offered to compensate the government for the loss incurred by the Bolshevist invasion in Northern Persia. A short time later, in June, when the Shah opened Parliament, he was able not only to denounce the treaty of 1919 with England, but also to announce in addition to the Soviet treaty, the conclusion of accords with Kemalist Turkey and Afghanistan. The three Moslem Powers constituted a Middle Eastern Triple Alliance, which has assumed an even greater significance since the definite triumph of Turkey in her war with the West, and the conclusion of the Lausanne Treaty.

It might have been assumed that under these circumstances Great Britain would have seen fit to abandon the field in Persia, but such was not the case. By the close of 1926, British interests were securely intrenched and British prestige, while not by any means what it was, had been in a large measure restored. This was due to a series of remarkably astute moves on the part of England.

When it became evident that the Anglo-British Convention was dead, Sir Percy Cox, who had negotiated the agreement, was withdrawn, and Mr. Norman sent to take his place in Persia. Within a short space of time he in turn was superseded by Sir Percy Loraine. Lord Curzon, at this time Foreign Minister, having been thwarted in his original plans for Persia, withdrew all British participation in the affairs of the country. Diplomatic relations were perfunctorily observed, British commercial interests were protected, and Great Britain bided her time. One thing was certain—whenever the government became sufficiently strong to carry out any policy of reconstruction it would be obliged to seek the co-operation of the British.

Sir Percy Loraine observed the turn of affairs, and never overstepped the bounds of discretion. For a time he supported the Sheikh of Mohammerah in his opposition to the government, but when in the summer of 1925 it became evident that Reza Khan's position was secure beyond question, Sir Percy became one of his warmest friends and personal advisers. This friendship has continued, notwithstanding certain important matters still in abeyance, such as the northern oil claims.

At one time it looked as if the Sinclair Oil Company of America would obtain the northern concessions in co-operation with the Russian government. Then the Standard Oil Company of New Jersey, backed by the Anglo-Persian, entered the field and up to the spring of 1927, neither group had obtained a decisive victory.

One of the reasons for the sudden growth of British prestige in Persia has been the need for an antidote to the increasing influence of Russia. After all the upheavals of the post-war period, the relations of the two rival Powers to each other and to Persia seem to be drifting into even deeper waters than prior to the Anglo-Russian agreement of 1907.

Russia still has preponderant interest in Northern Persia. Practically all the foreign merchandise supplied to Teheran and the cities of the north comes through Russia. The importance of the Russians in the economic system of Persia was shown by the resignation of the Persian cabinet in the spring of this year, forced by Parliament because it had not published its correspondence with the Anglo-Persian Oil Company regarding the proposed concessions in Northern Persia, and because it had failed to conclude a commercial treaty with Russia. An embargo placed on Persian imports into Russia which has existed since 1925, instituted as a reprisal for Persia's failure to conclude this treaty, has caused much suffering in North Persia.

British interests reign supreme in Southern Persia, however, and this state of affairs has its advantages. Whenever either

Great Britain or Russia becomes too domineering or too exacting, one can be played off against the other.

Politically, Bolshevism and communist doctrines have gained but little hold on the Persian people. While the development of political parties dates from the granting of the Constitution in 1906, it has not proceeded very rapidly. Nearly one-half of the population of Persia consists of migratory, pastoral tribespeople, who are not yet beyond the feudal stage of government. An almost equally large number are rayats, or peasant farmers. There is a small middle class in the cities, with a sprinkling of intellectuals, a still powerful aristocracy, and a fanatical and equally powerful priesthood.

The political parties are almost entirely made up from the last three elements. The Conservatives compose the majority. The electorate which they control is made up of parasites, hangers-on, and feudal dependents. The Moderates are composed of the intellectuals, frequently men of high social position. The Democrats are the most numerous of the liberal parties, but they are not well organized and are still powerless against the priests and the aristocracy. The Socialists, usually confined to the larger cities, are chiefly drawn from the students and the lower middle classes. They represent the same tendencies and movements as in other countries, running the gamut from Laborites to Communists. All the radical parties are conducted with a vast amount of intrigue by secret committees with thrilling names: "The Committee of Chastisement," of the "Black Hand," or "Iron," or "Steel"!

Parliament itself is divided into only two factions: the majority and the opposition. When a ministry is overthrown it is always by a combination or coalition of the opposing parties. Any minister who is forced to resign, automatically ceases to be a member of Parliament.

Whatever they may lack in political training, however, the Persians make up in diplomacy! Up to the present they have had two weapons with which to counterbalance any undue outside influence—one the American Financial Administration, which has always served as a buffer in economic disputes, and the other their friendship with their neighbors the Turks and the Afghans. United, the three countries control all the crossroads joining the

Mediterranean countries with farther Asia; even the route to
India via Iraq and the Persian Gulf would be insecure if threatened by Turkey and Persia. Afghanistan commands another
key to India from Russia and Central Asia. Until recently,
religious differences have been the greatest bar to a complete
understanding between the three countries, but with the growing
tendency throughout Islam to place a more liberal interpretation
on the teachings of the Prophet, these differences are becoming
less important.

Turkey, Afghanistan, and Persia have certain racial and cultural affinities. In each country there is a very strong infusion
of Mongol-Tartar blood. Persia has for centuries exerted a profound influence on the culture of both Afghanistan and Turkey.
Each has, through different means, secured hard-won independence, and each has developed a sturdy nationalism. Together
they may become a force in Asiatic politics, and so far they constitute the only group sufficiently homogeneous to form a bloc.
In the final analysis all their interests would attach them to
Russia rather than to any other Power. In spite of her imperialistic designs, scarcely camouflaged under the red banner of internationalism, they have seen her true face. They know that the
Great Empire of the Soviets is not part of Europe. It has only
brought part of Asia into Europe. . . . When all is said and
done they understand one another.

AFGHANISTAN

Afghanistan is a small country, so small that most of us, I
fancy, would have difficulty in describing its exact position on the
map of Asia; even then we would be likely to overlook its political
importance unless we happened to remember that it forms the
third state in the Asiatic Triple Alliance including Turkey and
Persia, the significance of which has already been emphasized.
It is almost the apex of the Islamic wedge which extends from the
Mediterranean to China.

By its very nature it seems to have been created to be a buffer
state, shut off from India by the ranges of the Hindu Kush and
from Chinese Turkestan by the mighty peaks of the Chinese

Pamirs, with other and lower mountain ranges separating it from Baluchistan and Persia. The country is split into a succession of deep valleys, mostly running parallel from east to west, that form a series of barriers, not only to would-be invaders but also to communications between its own inhabitants. Into these valleys various races have drifted in times past, and for the great part they remain there almost strangers to, and frequently enemies of, their next-door neighbors.

Most of the Afghans are of Aryan origin; some are Semites, claiming descent from Afghana the grandson of Saul, who still call themselves "Children of Israel." Among them are also tribes of Turanian stock: Turcomans, Uzbegs, and Tajiks, first cousins to the Moslems of Asiatic Russia and the Turks.

Five passes through the mountains give access to India, one of which, the celebrated Khyber Pass, is known the world over for the many scenes of horror it has witnessed. Through Afghanistan the river Oxus flows from Turkestan and it was down this river, called the Amu Daria, that Alexander the Great led his armies to the conquest of India.

Nearly every one of the peoples of Central Asia has in turn dominated Afghanistan. It was the birthplace of the great Mogul dynasty which conquered India in the sixteenth century. At one time it was under the sovereignty of Persia, but for the last two hundred years it has been ruled by a native dynasty. For a long time, because its position was well isolated and fortified by nature, few Europeans penetrated to Afghanistan, with the exception of occasional intrepid travellers and explorers. The only European country to establish any contact with Afghanistan before the nineteenth century, was Russia, which sent two missions to Balkh and Kabul during the seventeenth century. After that for many generations there was no official intercourse between Russia and Afghanistan.

It was not until the Russian expansionist policy in Central Asia made the friendship of Afghanistan desirable, that the Imperial Foreign Office considered it advisable to send a permanent mission. General Stoletov, who established himself at Kabul in 1878, became a warm friend of the Amir Shere Ali Khan. That friendship cost the latter his throne, for the British, alarmed for their prestige in Afghanistan, invaded the country, defeated the Amir's forces, and compelled him to flee to his mountain tribes-people, among whom he died, a fugitive.

The British had had several similar encounters with the Afghans since the early part of the nineteenth century, when it became apparent that peace and security along the northern frontier of India were dependent on drawing Afghanistan within the British sphere of influence. It had not been two hundred years since Southern Afghanistan had formed part of the Mogul Empire of India, and the Afghans still considered that they had a proprietary interest in Northern India. It would be wearisome to recount all the wars, negotiations, intrigues, and schemes, by which Afghanistan was coerced, coaxed, bullied, and bribed into submitting to a British protectorate. The number of lives lost, the energy expended, the mistakes made, and the money spent on maintaining British influence in turbulent Afghanistan, constitute one of the most costly and tragic pages in the history of the British Empire.

The designs of Russia, focused on securing a short overland route to India, embraced Afghanistan, and the rivalry between her and Great Britain soon reached an acute stage. "Hands off" agreements in 1886, and 1895, only partly solved the problem. For a while the struggle for spheres of influence was centred in Persia, and the whole question was finally settled, apparently for all time, by the celebrated Anglo-Russian Agreement drawn up by Lord Grey and the great Russian foreign minister Isvolsky in 1907, to which we have frequently had occasion to refer. It recognized Afghanistan and Tibet as spheres of British influence and settled all issues between Russia and Britain in Central Asia by the creation of these two buffers, and the partitioning of spheres of influence in Persia.

We have seen that this agreement held in the main, up to the close of the World War and the subsequent upheavals which entirely altered conditions in Central Asia.

When Amanullah Khan came to the throne in 1919, after the assassination of his father, Habibullah (it was suspected on account of his pro-British sympathies), conditions were most favorable for the assertion of complete independence which had long been the dream of the large anti-British faction in Afghanistan. Great Britain had, to use a vulgar expression, bitten off almost more than she could chew in Asia. British occupationary forces were in Syria, Mesopotamia, Palestine, Constantinople, Persia, Trans-Caspia, and the Caucasus, and British military missions had penetrated as far as Turkestan.

England was pledged to the task of pacifying and administering Mesopotamia and Palestine; she was compelled to take some steps towards fulfilling her promises to the Arabs who had helped her in the Syrian campaign against the Turks. India was seething with discontent which threatened at any moment to break out into open rebellion, and British taxpayers at home were clamoring for reduction of the army budget, the recall of all overseas forces, and concentration on domestic problems, which were sufficiently pressing. Russia was still in the throes of civil war and was not to be feared at the moment.

Amanullah was quick to grasp the situation. One of his first acts was to engage in a short but bitter war with the government of India. It did not have the result he had anticipated. The Mohammedans of the northern provinces did not rise, as he had hoped, after his proclamation of a Holy War—partly because their leaders had been arrested in time by the British—and the Afghan forces were pushed back from the Khyber Pass and the approaches through Baluchistan to India. To have undertaken a campaign in Afghan territory would have been a far more serious matter for the British however, and they were quite willing to conclude a temporary peace and send a mission to Kabul to negotiate a treaty after four months of fighting.

Meanwhile Amanullah had very shrewdly agreed to receive a Soviet Mission, but neither the Bolsheviks nor the British succeeded for the time being in negotiating a treaty with the wily sovereign of Afghanistan, who trusted neither the one nor the other. He proceeded first to form alliances with the Kemalist government of Turkey and his neighbor Persia.

Treaties with these Powers were signed in 1921, and before the end of the year Sir Henry Dobbs, acting for his Majesty's Government, had signed a pact at Kabul by which Great Britain recognized Afghanistan as a sovereign state. The new treaty provided for the establishment of diplomatic relations between the two countries on a footing of perfect equality.

Almost at the same time the Afghan government ratified an accord concluded in September, 1920, with Moscow, according mutual recognition and providing for exchange of diplomatic representatives. The Russo-Afghan treaty was without particular significance at the time it was made except as a weapon to secure better terms from Great Britain and as a precautionary measure against possible eventualities; with the reconquest of Trans-Caucasia, most of Turkestan, and the establishment of Soviet republics in the Moslem states of Khiva and Bokhara, the Bolsheviks had immeasurably improved their position in Central Asia and it seemed just as well for Afghanistan to establish friendly relations with the increasingly powerful Soviets. On the other hand Amanullah did not intend to commit himself irrevocably until he saw which way "the cat was going to jump."

The Russo-Afghan Treaty specifically pledged Afghanistan to recognize whatever form of government might exist in Khiva and Bokhara, but this did not prevent Amanullah from secretly supporting a reactionary movement in Turkestan and Bokhara known as the Basmatch Revolt, fostered by a group of Pan-Turanian enthusiasts, among whom was the notorious Enver Pasha who had been one of the leaders of the Union and Progress party in Turkey before the war. At one time relations between Russia and Afghanistan became so strained as the result of widespread sympathy with the Basmatchis that an attack was made on the powerful Russian wireless station which had been established at Kabul, and the Russian Ambassador Soritz left the country. When Amanullah saw that the Basmatch movement was doomed to failure, he discreetly changed his policy and friendly relations were restored. A few years ago, after a flight of Russian aviators from Tashkent to Kabul, the Afghan government ordered a number of Russian airplanes and decided to employ Soviet instructors to create an Afghan air force.

Commercial relations between Russia and Afghanistan are distinctly friendly at the present time, but it is difficult to estimate the true significance of the alliance between the two countries. There is no question that Russia would like to see the "Sovietization" of Afghanistan, and there are certain factors which would seem to favor her aims in this direction.

Russia is the normal outlet for Afghan trade. The Oxus River, which skirts the entire boundary-line, forms a natural highway. All the principal cities of Afghanistan, with the exception of Kabul, are near the Russian border on the northern slopes of the mountain ranges which divide this part of the country—known as Afghan-Turkestan—from Afghanistan proper. Through each of these centres of Afghan-Turkestan a vast amount of merchandise, consisting chiefly of rugs, hides, wool, silks, and dried fruits, passes into Russia. Into them comes also a steady stream of Russian imports consisting of petrol, sugar, tools, agricultural implements, and manufactured goods.

Moreover, the population of this part of Afghanistan is ethnically the same as that of near-by Russian Turkestan, so that naturally the inhabitants are pro-Russian. They are also much more peaceable and less independent than the Afghans of Kabul. The latter are intensely nationalistic, not to say imperialistic, and if they have aspirations outside the maintenance of their independence, they hope to regain Baluchistan, over which Afghanistan once exercised sovereignty, with the port of Karachi, and to combine with the Moslems of Northern India to re-establish the glories of the Mogul Era.

Amanullah has dallied with this idea, which in its more ambitious phases embraces a Western Asiatic federation, and he has more than once asserted his claim to the Khalifate; but wisely enough he has devoted most of his efforts to the modernization of his country. He has succeeded in doing away to a large extent with the feudal system which did much to keep Afghanistan in the medieval stage of development. Tribal chiefs are gradually being superseded by orderly regional governments. A cabinet of ten Ministers and a Council of one hundred members composed of representatives from various districts provided the nucleus for the establishment of a modern constitutional monarchy.

The Amir, applying his new principles to his own office, last year abolished his ancient title and took that of King of Afghanistan. He has had an excellent English education and he is deeply interested in establishing a school system for the country. Also, since his accession hundreds of young Afghans have been sent to study abroad, in England, France, and Japan. There is a modern university and a technical school in Kabul, and education has been extended to the villages and even to a certain extent among the nomad tribespeople in the mountains. Among the fifty or more schools founded by the Amir, three are for girls; these are under the protection of the Queen Mother and are directed by the wife of the Minister of Foreign Affairs, who made a visit to France to study French schools for girls.

Not long ago a weekly paper for women, published in Kabul, was added to the eight newspapers already in existence in Afghanistan. It was called the "Power of Women." A normal school has been established to provide teachers for the new educational system, and a committee of lawyers appointed to draw up a Civil Code for Afghanistan. The King has made every effort to encourage Afghan industries, and while he has adopted European dress and made it the official court costume, his "English tweeds" and broadcloths are woven, cut, and made in Afghanistan.

Kabul has begun to take on the appearance of a European city. The official quarter is laid out in Anglo-Indian style, with wide avenues, public gardens, and palaces; the various Ministries are lodged in modern buildings with lifts and electric lights. Numbers of foreign advisers are employed in various departments, and missionaries have been given permission, for the first time, to settle in the country. The army has been put on a modern footing, principally by Russian and Turkish instructors. It has a peace-time strength of between 50,000 and 60,000 and a potential strength of more than 100,000. Not long ago a French scientific society received permission to conduct archaeological research-work in Afghanistan.

Afghanistan, like Turkey and Persia, is undergoing a forcing-house process of modernization. She is very much in the position of Japan in 1868, when she had just abolished feudalism. Some of the new government regulations throw most interesting sidelights on the country and people. Those governing the administration of the Customs, drawn up by the King himself, form a fascinating and curious document. Throughout, it reflects his

puritanism and intransigent Moslem prejudices, combined with a
real perception of the country's needs.

It begins with a denunciation of merchants who seek to evade
the tariff impositions, and ends with advice to Customs officials,
admonishing them never to forget that Allah is ever present, and
to discharge their duties with due regard to the instructions of
their Sovereign, the grandeur of Islam, and their own personal
honesty.

In order to discourage the importation of luxuries which the
King considered would weaken the morale of his people, heavy
duties were imposed on all articles falling under this category in
the King's estimation, as well as on articles which could be manufactured in Afghanistan : tobacco, playing-cards, cheese, milk, and
butter were taxed 200 per cent ; artificial flowers, cosmetics, European carpets, mirrors, combs, toys, artificial pearls, candies, neck-
ties, silk lingerie, and articles for the bath, 100 per cent ; cloth,
50 per cent ; sheet metals, 5 per cent ; foreign exchange, one-half
per cent ; while Korans and commentaries, arms and ammunition
were exempt from all duties.

Thus Afghanistan like the rest of Asia stands on the threshold
of a new era.   Its 250,000 square miles of rugged territory and
its 10,000,000 inhabitants, proud, energetic, sober, and independent, are capable of exerting considerable influence, and recognition
of this fact by the other Powers of Central Asia has made Kabul
one of the most important centres of Oriental politics.

In Kabul many of the issues between Lenin and Mohammed
will perhaps be brought to a head, for King Amanullah may be
considered to dispute with Ibn Saoud of Nejd today the right to
appear as the champion of conservative Islam.

Economically, Afghanistan may prove of great importance in
the future.   While no comprehensive geological survey has been
made of the country, it possesses deposits of lead, coal, copper, and
there are gold-bearing sands in its rivers, signs of oil in many localities, and many deposits of precious stones.   It has important
forests and orchards and a well-developed industry in hides, furs,
camel's hair, wool, silk, and carpets.   Afghans are excellent traders and they wander far afield.   Today they are to be found in
Australia, New Zealand, South Africa, and many other places,

besides Burma and India, where there are large numbers of prosperous Afghan merchants.

If the Asiatic Triple Alliance holds together, and is able to preserve its individuality in spite of the all leveling influence of Soviet propaganda, and the tendency always present in Asiatic politics to follow individual leaders rather than ideas, it may play an important part in the formation of an Asiatic League of Nations.

Chapter Seven

CROSS CURRENTS IN ARAB LANDS

SYRIA

THE chapter of world history dealing with post-war happenings in Arab countries is not a pleasant one. Nowhere have the fallacies and weaknesses of the Wilsonian doctrines been so painfully apparent, nowhere did the Peace that brought no peace create more confusion or leave more problems unsolved than in the portion of the Arabian peninsula known after the Armistice as Occupied Enemy Territory.

As we have seen, the Versailles Treaty evaded all the issues involved in the settlement of this portion of the former Ottoman Empire, by applying the Mandate system incorporated in the Covenant of the League of Nations. After the ratification of the Versailles Treaty in January, 1920, the Mandates were allocated to France and Great Britain. The three Mandates in the Arabian peninsula came into the class known as "A" Mandates; that is, they were supposed to be exercised by the mandatories only for a limited period, in order to assist in establishing stable governments in the various mandated areas. And according to the last sentence in Article 22 of the League Covenant, the selection of the mandatory Power was to be based on the wishes of the various communities. This provision was never carried out; although in Syria an American Commission went through the form of conducting an investigation to ascertain the wishes of the inhabitants, its findings could not be regarded as conclusive. Agitation, propaganda, and the mad contagion of the idea of self-determination made it impossible for the investigating Commission to reach any conclusion except that the Christians of the Lebanon wanted complete independence, which was obviously out of the question. The San Remo Conference at which the Allied Council assigned the Mandates, merely carried out the decisions reached in a series of diplomatic "conversations," most of them secret, which had been going on for three years between Great Britain and France. Great Britain accepted Mandates for Mesopotamia and Palestine, and France for Syria and the Lebanon. At the same time Great Britain and France reached an agreement with regard to the petroleum deposits of Mesopotamia by which the French were promised 25 per cent of the future output of these oil fields in return for the surrender of any claims to influence in North Mesopotamia. We shall see later how this agreement had an important bearing on the controversy between Turkey and Great Britain for the political control of the territory of Mosul, in which the fields are located. Broadly speaking Great Britain attained her principal object, which was to secure direct control over Mesopotamia and Palestine.

Mesopotamia not only constituted an important link in the chain of British protectorates guarding the land approach to India, in which it was hoped to include Persia and Afghanistan as well, but also commanded the access to the Persian oil fields which supplied most of the oil for the British navy. With the Mosul district which she hoped later to include within the Mesopotamian mandated state, Great Britain would have obtained control of the entire valley of the Tigris and the Euphrates up to the Zagros Mountains, which formed a natural boundary and strategic defense.

Palestine was vital to England for two reasons. She was pledged by the Balfour Declaration of 1917 to aid in the creation of a Jewish National homeland. The Zionist elements within the Empire were far too powerful to permit the government to repudiate this pledge, as it had repudiated its promises to the Arabs; besides, in the event of the partial or complete abandonment of Great Britain's hold on Egypt, Palestine was a valuable base from which to defend the entrance to the Suez Canal.

France's reasons for insisting on the protectorate over Syria were partly sentimental, for ever since the period of the Crusades, when the French founded the short-lived Christian Empire of Jerusalem and the principalities of Tripoli and Antioch, French influence had been strong in Syria. The predominantly Christian population of the Lebanon, though officially part of the Ottoman

Empire, enjoyed local autonomy under French protection almost continuously from the middle of the seventeenth century till the outbreak of the World War, and the many French schools and missions had strongly impressed Gallic culture and mentality on the country at large. It was no secret in certain French circles that France regarded Palestine as part of her rightful sphere of influence, but many considerations had influenced her in giving up these pretensions, one of which was the San Remo Oil Agreement and another the recognition by Great Britain of her right to include in her sphere of influence the Turkish province of Cilicia for which Northern Syria is the natural outlet.

Subsequent agreements between the French and the British resulted in certain modifications of the frontiers of the Syrian and Mesopotamian Mandates; the intermediate zones between the two areas were wiped out after political developments which we shall later discuss, and today the French Mandate for Syria includes the four districts of Aleppo, Damascus, Lebanon, and the Alaouites. Cilicia was restored to Turkey under the terms of the Franco-Turkish Treaty in 1921. Mesopotamia, now known as Iraq, has had its frontiers definitely established by the conclusion of a treaty with Turkey, which surrendered the coveted Mosul Era. Palestine has remained the same, but with the possible exception of Iraq it cannot be said that the Mandates have proved satisfactory in operation. Admirable in intention, they were instituted under artificial conditions. With the best will in the world the mandatory Powers could never have succeeded in bringing contentment or stability.

In order to understand why the Mandates have proved so difficult to administer, we must try to picture the hopes, aspirations, and disillusionments, as well as the racial and religious differences, among the inhabitants since the Armistice. The delegations sent to the Peace Conference by all the minorities as well as by the Arabs themselves, received scant consideration, as we have seen. Despite the Anglo-French Declaration of November, 1918, in favor of the establishment of "National Governments and Administrations drawing their authority from the initiative and free choice of native populations," it was only too apparent that

Great Britain neither could, nor would keep her promise to aid in the establishment of an Arab state.

Relations between the French and British had become exceedingly strained soon after the Armistice, because of the efforts of English statesmen to steer a middle course and reconcile their war-time pledges to Hussein, Sherif of Mecca and his sons, with the various agreements Great Britain had made with her ally France. All that the Emir Feisal obtained in the way of support from the British was their assistance in his project, shortly afterwards realized, of establishing himself as sovereign of the so-called kingdom of Damascus, including all of the Syrian hinterland. Such a state of affairs obviously could not last. It would have restricted the French occupation to the Lebanon and a narrow strip of land along the coast, and when in July, 1920, the tension between the French and Feisal's government at Damascus reached a state where French intervention became necessary, the British stood aside, permitting their protégé to be ousted from Damascus by a force under General Gouraud. France was at last in possession of an area identical to that for which a Mandate had been allotted to her by the Supreme Council at San Remo.

General Gouraud was appointed Military Governor, and the French proceeded to embark on a series of administrative experiments, most of them highly unfortunate, of which the end is apparently not yet in sight, and which have not yet resulted in assuring any degree of political stability to the area under their protection. Their troubles had begun immediately after the Armistice when the Christian communities of the Lebanon began to agitate through the Syrian National Committee for the establishment of a republic. The Arabs of Northern Syria and Damascus had hoped for inclusion in the promised Arab Confederation. The tribespeople of the mountainous regions were emphatic in demanding local autonomy. There were wide differences not only in social and cultural development but also in race and religion among the various elements, which under the Turkish régime no one had ever dreamed of trying to assimilate, and the French were called upon to make them into a nation by a purely artificial process.

They were wise enough to see that any centralized government

was out of the question. Under General Gouraud five autonomous states were created for the purposes of administration—
Great Lebanon with Beirut as a capital, Damascus, Aleppo, the
Territory of the Alaouites and the Hauran which included the
country of the Druses extending through the region lying south of
Damascus and touching the Palestinian border. In each of the
new divisions local officials were set up, supervised by French advisers, and a year later General Gouraud had elaborated a plan for
a Syrian Federation, composed of states identical with the original
divisions. The Hauran and the Great Lebanon were to be autonomous. Damascus, Aleppo, and the Alaouite territory had their
separate Councils of State and native Governors assisted by French
advisers.

Each state was to be represented in a Federal Council. This,
however, was only a paper scheme, the Christian Lebanon and the
pagan Druse country refusing to take part in the Syrian Federation.

Meanwhile the state of internal affairs in Syria was not such
as to aid the French in their efforts to set up a stable government.
During the war, the people of Syria had suffered indescribably.
When the Allied forces had first occupied Syria they had found
a most appalling state of affairs. Thousands had already died,
and thousands more were dying of famine in Beirut. The country
had been bled white during the terrible four years when Djemal
Pasha, commander of the Turkish forces had maintained a reign
of terror in Syria. There was no security anywhere—brigandage
was rife, civil officials had fled or were powerless to exercise their
functions, commerce was dead, agriculture had sunk to its lowest
depths, and the country was facing ruin. The only profession
which flourished was that of political agitation, which thrives on
misery.

While the French military authorities took immediate steps to
restore order, and facilitated the work of famine-relief carried
on by government and private agencies, among them the American Near East Relief, their attitude from the first was resented
by many of the more intelligent Syrians.

General Gouraud was primarily a soldier, as were the men
under him who were called on to act as administrators of the

Mandate. Privately they thought very little of what must have seemed to them the slushy sentimentality of the Mandate declarations in the League Covenant. Syria was to them an occupied country, to be completely subdued and governed. They cared nothing for the susceptibilities of the inhabitants. The energetic but ignorant officers who were sent to administer outlying districts failed to realize that Syria was a country with an ancient civilization. They treated the Syrians exactly as they might have treated the natives in the Soudan or the Congo.

Ignoring the fact that the Christians constituted only a little over one-fourth of the entire population, General Gouraud, in fulfilment of France's traditional policy of favoring the Christian minorities, gave them in the Lebanon a state that was disproportionately large, and which completely cut off Damascus, the most important city in Syria, for which Beirut was merely the outlet to the sea.

By including the port of Tripoli in the state of the Alaouites, he also deprived Aleppo of a seaport. Almost simultaneously, the home government decided on the evacuation of Cilicia, followed by a peace which restored it to Turkey. Aleppo, which had been the market for a large portion of southern Turkey, lost the trade which in pre-war days had made her one of the most prosperous cities in the Ottoman Empire. Not one of the states artificially created by Gouraud for the purpose of administration had the resources to enable it to become self-sustaining.

In 1923, General Gouraud was succeeded by General Weygand, a man of most liberal views. He instituted a policy of reconciliation and tried to satisfy the Arab element by the creation of a republican state of Syria composed of the former states of Aleppo and Damascus, subject only to the French High Commissioner and his deputies. This arrangement died with the Syrian Federation, and the French found themselves as the mandatory Power supervising the functioning of the predominately Moslem state of Syria with its capital at Damascus, the overwhelmingly Christian republic of the Great Lebanon, the autonomous state of the Alaouites, and the territory of the Djebel Druse, which was to be autonomous under its own feudal chiefs.

These states were to form the basis for a future Syrian Federation on the plan of the Helvetian Republic, the states eventually to have the same relation to the federation as the Swiss cantons. Weygand's personal popularity might have helped to smooth matters over, though it could have brought the Syrian problem little nearer a genuine solution, but he was recalled by the Socialist cabinet in France under Herriot, which had succeeded that of Briand, and his place as High Commissioner was taken by General Sarrail.

Sarrail was a Protestant, some said a freethinker, violently anticlerical and opposed to any form of ecclesiastical hierarchy. In less time than it takes to tell it, he had antagonized the Maronites, the Catholics, the Greek Orthodox, and all the other sects which make up the voters of the Great Lebanon—a serious matter in a state where one's religion is a confession of political faith as well.

Matters finally reached such a pass that the Assembly or Parliament of the Great Lebanon was dissolved by order of General Sarrail, and requests for his removal poured in to the French Ministry from clericals and laymen alike. National sentiment flamed up more strongly than ever and many of the Christian Syrians were even disposed to unite with their Moslem neighbors against the French.

To add to her troubles at this juncture France was faced with the necessity of dealing with a serious revolt among the Druse tribesmen. On the surface the revolt was apparently due entirely to maladministration, and the incident that precipitated it was the most childish imaginable—nothing more or less than a common or garden cat. Here is the story.

In the spring of 1925 a French officer Captain Carbillet was acting governor of Djebel Druse with headquarters at Soueida, the tribesmen not having been able to agree in the choice of their native chief.

Carbillet was one of the officials to whom I have already alluded. He did not in the least understand the manners, customs, or traditions of the people with whom he had to deal and he was constantly offending them. Finally the Captain's wife missed a cat of which she was very fond, and Carbillet ordered that the entire population should be fined if the cat was not returned within a certain time. Pussy was not found, the fine was not paid, and the resignation of Carbillet was demanded by a delegation that went to call on General Sarrail.

The latter very foolishly felt that French prestige demanded that the Druses be forced to accept Carbillet; had they done so, there is every reason to believe that he would have been replaced, but Sarrail failed to take into account the temper of the people or the extent to which they had been infected with the universal fever of unrest which had spread among all subject peoples, from the Riff to the South Sea Islands.

The Druses had always constituted a separate group in no way identified with the other peoples of Syria. For centuries they lived in the mountainous districts south of Damascus and during the Turkish administration they were quite independent under their tribal chiefs, with their own manners and customs, practising an ancient form of worship with secret rites and records which no outsider had ever been permitted to see. When the French first took over Syria, having no love for either the Arab or the Christian element, they voluntarily put themselves under French protection, and reached an agreement by which they were to be allowed complete local autonomy, under a military governor who was to represent them merely in matters outside their own communities. Matters had gone smoothly on the whole until Sarrail's ill-advised action, although the Druses had occasionally been restive. The result of his refusal was to stir up a veritable hornets' nest. A party of Druse tribesmen under their leader Soltan Atrash surprised and surrounded the small French garrison at Soueida. It was not relieved until two months later, and the revolt, which from time to time assumed alarming proportions still simmers, though the country was officially declared "pacified" in the spring of 1927.

I was in Syria in the summer of 1925 and one day I made a trip from Damascus to the base at Deraa from which the French were conducting the operations against the Druses: a point on the railway between Damascus and Medina which had been built by the Sultan Abdul Hamid to transport pilgrims on their way to Mecca.

A few miles south of Damascus the railway enters a desolate

treeless valley known as the Ledja.   Part of it in times past was covered with a tremendous stream of lava from some long extinct volcano.   This lava deposit, many feet in depth, has been worn into ridges and valleys and carved into hollow basins by the action of wind, rain, and sand.   Within these natural hiding places whole regiments could be concealed.   Behind them are the rugged peaks of the Djebel Druse cut into narrow valleys and steep defiles.   It is an ideal country for a guerrilla warfare.   Even the bombing planes, all eyes though they were, could not spot the guerrilla bands who laid in wait for unsuspecting French detachments in the hollow of the Ledja and the passes of the Djebel Druse.

The revolt of the Druses was supported more or less openly by many other elements.   General Sarrail had succeeded in alienating nearly every political or racial group in Syria; even the Christians of the Lebanon were against him, and his tactless actions resulted in a partial understanding at least between the Christian and Arab Nationalists.   Some of the Bedouin Chiefs who had enormous power in the desert region which lay just east of Damascus made common cause with the Druses, and the paralysis of trade from which the city had been suffering for some time owing to unsettled conditions produced much misery and discontent, which made it easy for the malcontents to obtain a foothold in the Moslem quarter by stealth.   Realizing the loss of French life which would ensue if he attempted to dislodge them by street fighting, General Gamelin decided on the bombardment of the Moslem quarter on October 20, 1925.

During this outbreak thousands of persons were killed and wounded.   The railway station, a large part of the famous bazaar along the "Street Called Straight," and the beautiful museum known as the house of "El Adam" were burned.   As a result the Notables of Damascus were forced to pay a fine of 40,000 Egyptian pounds, to deliver 50,000 rifles to the French and submit to the establishment of martial law for fifteen years.   Throughout the country there was disorder.   Convoys on the way to Baghdad by the motor route from Damascus across the Syrian Desert were attacked by Bedouins, forcing its abandonment in favor of the safer route from Amman in Transjordania.   Brigandage was rife.   The Druses kept up their harassing guerrilla warfare.

Reinforcements were rushed to Syria and within a few months the military situation was well in hand, though at a tremendous cost to the French nation in men and money; but the political situation was far from settled. The French had exercised the Mandate for five years under a succession of military governors, and Syria was in just as chaotic a condition as it had been in 1920. None of the plans for a Syrian Federation had proved workable in practice. Public opinion had been stirred by the Damascus bombardment, and there was quite a widespread demand that France should resign the Syrian Mandate, which, so far certainly, had resulted in little advantage to either France or Syria herself, although it was obvious that the military campaign would have to be pushed to a conclusion.

To permit the Druses to get the upper hand would have been to risk a loss of prestige which might have had fatal reactions in Morocco, where the French were engaged in a war with the Riff tribesmen under Abd-el-Krim, and in her Asiatic colonial possessions, where there were a widespread national movement and considerable discontent. But there was no reason why the office of High Commissioner should continue to be filled by a military man, and M. Briand, then Minister of Foreign Affairs, determined to try the effect of a civilian administrator.

M. Henri de Jouvenel, a member of the French Senate who had been a delegate from France to the League of Nations and had had experience in colonial administration, was sent to tackle the problem. During his short stay in Syria, from December, 1925, to May, 1926, he succeeded in patching up many of the differences that had arisen between the French government and the Christians of the Lebanon, and did much towards conciliating the Arabs of Damascus. Whenever it was possible to do so without forfeiting French prestige, he granted amnesties to those who had taken part in rebellions, while energetically pursuing a campaign to establish order and security.

He revived the project of a Syrian Federation, which was further elaborated by his successor M. Ponsot, another civilian, upon the basis of whose recommendations M. Briand announced the adoption of a definite plan in April of this year, for the settlement of the Syrian question. It was France's intention, he declared, to create a Syrian Federation of autonomous cantons, bound together by a security pact and mutual guarantees, whose applications should be submitted to the arbitration of France as mandatory Power. The treaty embodying these provisions would be similar to that concluded between the British government and its ward, the kingdom of Iraq.

In the meantime internal order had been restored, negotiations were in progress between the Druse leaders and the High Commissioner with the object of reaching an understanding, the revolt having been virtually suppressed.

Treaties had been concluded by France (acting as Mandatory in behalf of the Syrian State) with the neighboring countries of Turkey, Palestine, Transjordania, and with Ibn Saoud, the Wahabite ruler of Nejd, who had extended his central Arabian kingdom till it touched the eastern border of Syria. These treaties not only established boundaries, but regulated commercial and other intercourse between Syria and her neighbors. It would seem that conditions are becoming settled in Syria, but stability is not a natural condition in that part of the world, and the arbitrary political frontiers of the present Mandate do not make for permanence.

Syria has been described as a wharf giving access from the hinterland of Western Asia to the sea. The ports of Northern Syria form natural outlets for Northern Mesopotamia and Turkey south of the Taurus Mountains. The Lebanon is the "quay" for the rich oasis of Damascus and the fertile valleys of the Anti-Lebanon. Its precipitous mountain slopes produce the finest grapes in the world, and the most stupendous flocks of goats, which, incidentally prevent attempts at reforestation by eating up all the young trees. Its climate is delightful; it is beautiful beyond description, and filled with what might be described as points of interest to the tourist, as indeed is all Syria. However, the Lebanon cannot be self-supporting, and attempts to maintain it as a separate state in the interest of the Christian population have done inestimable harm to Syria as a whole.

A short stretch of railroad, from Tripoli in Syria to Haifa in Palestine, only about 200 kilometres, is all that is needed to connect London and Paris by rail with Cairo—and here again we come across a fertile source of trouble—the question of Palestine.

Many of the Syrian Nationalists together with the majority of the Arab Nationalists in Palestine have always claimed that Syria and Palestine should be one. They organized the famous Syro-Palestinian Committee with headquarters in Cairo, pledged to work for the independence and unity of a greater Syria which should include Palestine.

The leader of the Committee, the so-called "Emir Lotfallah," a Levantine multimillionaire who bought his title from the Sherif of Mecca in return for loans when the latter was hard up many years ago, has long had a hand in every pie in Syria and aspires to the eventual leadership of a possible Syrian state. However sound may be the grounds for the claim that Syria and Palestine should be considered as one, there is not the slightest probability that either France or England could be made to see the matter in this light, and certain it is, that if France, as has often been suggested, both in the press and in Parliament, should resign her Mandate it would not be in favor of Great Britain, but rather of Italy.

The failure to consider the Syrian littoral as an economic unity has been responsible for many of the conditions that have stimulated Nationalist agitation, and there is as yet no remedy in sight for this situation.

Another cause for concern is the Armenian problem. When the French evacuated Cilicia in 1920, in conformity with their agreements with Turkey, instead of insisting on the protection of the Christian minorities in that territory, they virtually sanctioned their expulsion by the Kemalists. As a result a continual stream of Armenian refugees poured over the Turkish border until practically the entire population of Cilicia and the Aintab-Marash region had overflowed into Syria. As a result there were, when I was in Syria in 1925, approximately 125,000 Armenian refugees living on Syrian soil, and their presence constituted a grave menace to the country.

The French government in dealing with them had displayed the same vacillating policy, or lack of policy, it had displayed in

dealing with the native population. The Armenian refugees
were permitted to settle in large numbers around the edges of the
larger cities. In 1925 there were at least forty-five thousand
near Aleppo, about fifteen thousand near Damascus and nearly
thirty thousand near Beirut. They built themselves hovels of
waste, driftwood, bagging, scraps of canvas, packing-cases, and
any junk they could adapt to their purpose. At Aleppo five
hundred of them were camping out in a half-finished public
building begun under the Ottoman régime. Many of them were
half starved, all were filthy, sources of infection and, what was
still worse, of political agitation. They were loathed by the
Moslems and heartily disliked by the Christians. If they had
been settled in rural communities they might have become useful
citizens, but they refused French offers to supply them with
farm-lands, claiming that they were afraid of being massacred by
the Moslem Arabs.

The truth was that they were naturally traders and artisans,
more industrious, shrewder and keener even than the Jews and they
preferred to follow their natural bent. Everywhere I went in the
refugee quarters I saw tiny shops, sometimes nothing more than
a shelter under a rush mat or a piece of bagging, where some
Armenian, who would in a few years become a rich banker, was
exchanging money; in others a motley assortment of scraps
of-Heaven-knows-what had already laid the foundations for a
prosperous general store. Little by little they were pulling themselves out of the mire of poverty and squalor, at the expense of
the native merchants and artisans, whom they could always under-
bid, adding to the number of native unemployed by taking away
the work which might have been theirs.

They were all, including the more fortunate few who had
already become rich, ardent Nationalists, to the extent of demanding the right to manage, or rather mismanage, what they were
pleased to term their national affairs. The Armenian community
in Aleppo, when I was there, contained to the best of my recol-
lection thirty-six "Benevolent Societies," and the conflicts that
raged among them were excelled only by the Tong wars during
the most troubled period in the history of the Chinatowns of New
York and San Francisco.

Such an element was, and still is, very dangerous in a country like Syria. It is always a delicate matter to criticize the Armenians. They have undoubtedly suffered beyond measure, and yet anyone who has witnessed their treachery and their lack of gratitude, not only in Syria, but elsewhere to those who have been their greatest benefactors, must realize that there was some provocation for the Armenian massacres in Turkey. Another fact always to be borne in mind is that if the Armenian minorities should get the upper hand they would be quite capable of holding up their end in regard to massacres too. It is not a question of Turk or Armenian or Kurd or Arab in the Near East, but of hatred, racial and religious, fanned by propaganda among peoples with pretty much the same standards of conduct and manners. The French have accepted the Armenians as citizens, but it is hard to see how they will ever become assimilated. Unquestionably, so far, they have only served to add to the discontent, poverty, and suffering in Syria.

One of the most serious grievances against the French mandatory administration, according to the Syrians, is the fact that it has brought about the financial ruin of the country. Shortly after the occupation, the French created a Syrian piastre for use as currency, which was to follow the course of the franc, and take the place of Turkish and Egyptian pounds which were formerly legal tender.

Some of the rich men of Syria continued to hoard the old coinage, but the great majority of the merchants were forced in the course of their banking transactions to turn their capital into the new currency; and since the depreciation of the French franc many have been ruined. Unemployment was widespread, trade seriously interfered with, and agriculture paralyzed by the Druse rebellion and general unsettled conditions.

It was not perhaps France's fault, but rather her misfortune that she has been compelled to spend the Syrian budget on an army rather than on the development of the country. In spite of its artificial frontiers, creating a tremendous handicap, the economic resources of Syria could have been greatly increased by judicious expenditure on irrigation in the upper valley of the Euphrates, which could be converted into an immense granary, and where it has been proved the finest qualities of cotton can be grown if an adequate water supply is furnished. The waters of the Euphrates with properly constructed barrages are capable of furnishing light, power, and irrigation to a country much larger than Syria.

Possibly the greatest mistake of all has been made by the French in endeavoring to establish a republican form of government. The success of the British, who have instituted a constitutional monarchy under scarcely more favorable conditions in Iraq, would seem to confirm this opinion. Even Europe in these days is beginning to doubt the political ideal of democracy; the recent successful experiments in government have been along the lines of dictatorships or monarchies. In spite of the fact that it would incur the displeasure of the Christian community of the Lebanon, it would seem that the best chance of creating anything approaching stability in Syria would be by the establishment of a constitutional monarchy with its capital at Damascus, under a treaty agreement with the French.

Another solution might be the transfer of the Mandate by France to Italy. Italy must have an outlet for her surplus population and perhaps on the basis of such a transfer some arrangement could be reached between France and Italy to reconcile their conflicting interests in North Africa; but it is difficult to see how France could possibly afford to surrender her Mandate to Great Britain. Cruel as it may seem, there is apparently no prospect that any of the Powers could be brought to consider the possibility of turning over the Arab Mandates to International control with the definite aim of making them dependent.

The Wilsonian ideology has failed. Nationalism will not give the Arab peoples what they want, until under Western domination they learn the value of teamwork, or until some powerful motive inspired by some leader who can hold them and fuse them as Mustapha Kemal Pasha did the Turks, brings about unity of action. If this comes to pass it will be a miracle. A cause which can unite the Bedouins of the Djebel Shammar, the town-bred Arabs of Syria and Iraq, the Jews of Palestine, and the Christians of the Lebanon to form a solid federation, must indeed lay claim to something more than common Humanity.

THE JEWISH HOMELAND

Owing to its geographical position, it is most natural to take up Palestine after discussing the operation of the Syrian Mandate. In fact as has already been stated, the French have always considered it geographically and politically a part of Syria. Wartime necessities prompted them to acquiesce in the Balfour Declaration of 1917, and in the subsequent dickerings with the British, up to the awarding of the Mandate in April, 1920, Palestine was made an asset by the French in driving the bargain with Great Britain for areas of influence.

Shortly after the San Remo Conference, the military administration of Palestine which had been in force since the occupation of the country by General Allenby's Expeditionary Forces, was replaced by a civil administration. The Mandate for Palestine approved two years later by the League of Nations, differed from the Mandates for Syria and Mesopotamia in that it provided for an Administration within an Administration as necessitated by the Balfour Declaration of 1917. Article 4 of the Mandate states:

An appropriate Jewish Agency shall be recognized as a public body for the purpose of advising and co-operating with the Administration of Palestine in such economic, social, and other matters as may affect the establishment of the Jewish National Home, and the interest of the Jewish population in Palestine.

Again Article 11 :

The Administration may arrange with the Jewish Agency mentioned in Article 4, to construct or operate upon fair and equitable terms any public works services and utilities and to develop any of the natural resources of the country in so far as these matters are not directly undertaken by the Administration. . . .

The Mandate further left it to the discretion of the mandatory Power to extend or withhold the operation of the Mandate in the country east of the river Jordan known as Transjordania and extending on the south to the confines of the Central Arabian Kingdom of Nejd. This territory was at first administered by the British High Commissioner; in 1921, it was made into a small kingdom under British protection having for its sovereign the

Emir Abdullah, one of the sons of Hussein, Sherif of Mecca, who had aided the British in organizing the Arab revolt during the Great War.

Sir Herbert Samuel, the British High Commissioner for Palestine, was a Jew—which might presumably have caused him to entertain a bias towards the Zionists. But this was not the case. Throughout his administration he showed remarkable impartiality in carrying out a difficult and delicate task. He was called on to administer a country with a Moslem population of nearly 600,-000, mostly Arabs, some 73,000 Christians, and approximately 83,000 Jews.

He was pledged not only to control and to supervise all these, but to facilitate and encourage the further immigration of untold numbers of Jews, who under the terms of the Mandate were also to have certain rights and privileges as a group. He was bound to bring this about peacefully, with as little friction as possible, and at the same time he had to protect the rights and privileges of the Arab population.

Before we proceed with an account of recent happenings in Palestine, it may be well to recall the circumstances of the rise of the Zionist Movement which brought about the Balfour Declaration. Zionism as a spiritual movement was born in the dark days when the Jews as a nation were dispersed literally to the four corners of the earth by the Roman Emperor Hadrian. Thereafter at intervals through many centuries there were revivals of interest in Palestine as the lost homeland, and periodical pilgrimages to Jerusalem and the Holy Cities of Israel. Palestine became the focus of the memories and hopes of the Jewish race. It was the magic formula, by virtue of which they maintained their spiritual and national unity.

The idea of Palestine as a practical solution of the problems caused by the growth of Anti-Semitism in Western countries was first mooted after the beginning of what might be called the Pogrom Era in Russia, in the 1880's. At that time little bands of Russian Jewish immigrants began slowly to filter in, but an Austrian Jew, Theodor Herzl, first co-ordinated the impulses of a number of Jews to find, or rather to found, a homeland, where they could satisfy their national and spiritual aspirations, and thus created the modern Zionist Movement. From the first, opinions among the Jews with regard to Zionism were far from unanimous, and to this day the Zionists constitute a minority among the leaders of Jewish thought; but it was a sufficiently strong minority to exert pressure on, and secure from, the British Government during the war, a promise to aid in the establishment of a National Homeland for the Jews.

Palestine was finally settled on as the seat of this Homeland for spiritual and sentimental reasons, although many prominent Jews had favored South Africa or some other more fertile section. Even before the war, the Zionist Organization which officially came into being in 1897, had been tentatively negotiating with the Ottoman Government with a view to securing a charter in Palestine, and quite a flow of immigration had already begun, stimulated by the philanthropy of Baron Edmond de Rothschild.

The National Home was regarded by the Zionists as primarily a focus for Jewish culture and Jewish ideals, the centre of a future Jewish renascence; also, though this was possibly of less importance in their eyes, as a refuge, particularly for the Jews of Eastern Europe who had been so often persecuted and oppressed. To secure the possession of this Homeland they maintained that it was necessary for them to obtain an international guarantee that the cultural centre they hoped to create in Palestine would be safe for all time.

Such were the claims made by the Zionist Executive which led the campaign to secure the Balfour Declaration, and it had its way, although it was opposed by many influential Jews who believed the unity of Israel was purely spiritual, and that in material matters every Jew should seek to assimilate and identify himself with the country of which he was a legal citizen.

Sir Herbert Samuel was assisted in the task of reorganizing the Palestine Administration by an Advisory Council of twenty members, half chosen from among the officials of the Administration, and half nominated by himself as High Commissioner, consisting of four Moslems, three Christians and three Jews. By 1922, a Draft Constitution for Palestine had been adopted by the British Parliament. The British High Commissioner was to be chief executive and final authority in all matters affecting the government of the country. He was to be assisted by an Executive Council and a "Legislative Council" of twenty-two members, of whom twelve were to be elected by the people of Palestine—the other ten to be appointees of the High Commissioner. The Draft Constitution further created a judiciary system, with civil courts whose procedure was based on the Medjelle, the reformed Ottoman Code which had been in operation since the Turkish revolution in 1908, throughout the Empire supplemented by Moslem, Jewish and Christian religious tribunals. Three languages, English, Arabic, and Hebrew, were made official.

Up to the present time, the Constitution has never been put into operation, owing to the refusal of the Arab element to take part in the elections. Consequently the eventual form of government in Palestine is far from settled, and in spite of occasional encouraging signs, there is a continual state of political tension. It is a difficult and delicate matter to get at the rights and wrongs, or indeed even to sum up the net results, of the dual social and economic régime in the Holy Land. It was the outgrowth of an extraordinary combination of circumstances.

After the war Great Britain, as I have said before, felt that control of Palestine was vital to the Empire for strategic reasons. Moreover, she was pledged to further the establishment of a Jewish National Homeland. On the other hand there was no money in the British Treasury for the administration of the Mandate. Palestine was a very poor country. It was very much underpopulated and always had been. Its meagre resources had been utterly exhausted by the Great War. Thousands of acres of arable land had been left uncultivated, thousands more could be made fertile by drainage or irrigation. Lack of good roads hampered communications, there were no harbors for sea-borne commerce except the open roadsteads of Haifa and Jaffa. The Zionist Organization possessed the capital necessary to develop the country, which could not have been obtained in any other manner. Moreover, even between 1918 and 1920, Jewish immigration, interrupted by the war, had begun again and Zionist agencies the world over had already begun to collect huge sums of money for Jewish colonization and industrial and agricultural development.

It was inevitable therefore, in view of Great Britain's pledges, aims, and needs, that the Mandate for Palestine in its final form as approved by the League of Nations should contain provisions for according a special status to the Jews. As a political experiment it was fraught with pitfalls and dangers; but as a practical expedient it was worth the political risk in the eyes of Great Britain, which bargained for and obtained the Mandate from the Supreme Allied Council.

As might have been expected, the economic condition of Palestine showed an improvement as soon as the Zionist Executive under the able local direction of Colonel Kisch began to work out its programme. It was at once made clear that the Jewish immigrants were to constitute no tax on the Administration. The Jews immediately organized their own charities, their own school system, their own sanitary service. A vigorous campaign was made against malaria, the scourge of all Near Eastern countries, and in carrying out this part of their programme the Zionists undertook the draining of vast areas of marsh lands.

Whatever land they purchased from the Arabs was paid for at a fair price, and it was in most instances land which had not been cultivated for many centuries. Many miles of roads were constructed by the Zionist Executive in co-operation with the Palestine Administration to render access to its colonies easier; a colossal scheme for the electrification of all Palestine by obtaining power for light and industry from the waters of the Jordan River known as the Rutenberg scheme, was originated by a group of Jewish capitalists.

As a result largely of Jewish effort and initiative, by 1925, when Sir Herbert Samuel retired as High Commissioner, the Palestine budget showed an excess of receipts over expenditures of more than $1,000,000, and the reserve amounted to more than $2,500,000.

Thanks to this situation it was possible to reduce the taxes of the farmers. More than $35,000,000 had been sent into the country by Jews alone, most of which had been spent on constructive work. Law and order had been established, a local militia and police force created, and the situation was such as to justify the recall of all British troops in the country with the exception of a detachment of 250 Tommies, maintained more as a guard for the High Commissioner and his subordinates than anything else. On the whole, it is quite safe to say that the material and physical well-being of all the inhabitants of Palestine has been greatly increased by the work of the Zionist Organization.

Notwithstanding these undeniable facts there has been, and still is, a tremendous amount of friction between Arabs and Jews in Palestine, with the British Administration as a buffer between them. It had never existed in any marked degree, however, until after the Balfour Declaration. The Orthodox Jews who had been in Palestine since time immemorial, although they were regarded with a certain contempt by their Moslem neighbors, had on the whole lived on good terms with them. Neither they nor the settlers who had come in the early days of the Zionist Movement had ever become rich enough as a community to excite the envy and dislike of the Arabs as they did in Damascus and other places. The Balfour Declaration was a slap in the face to the Arab Nationalists, who had been counting on the creation of some sort of an Arab State.

Soon after the award of the Palestine Mandate to Great Britain, the Syro-Palestinian Committee began its efforts to secure the inclusion of Palestine within the boundaries of Syria, from its headquarters in Cairo. In Palestine itself a joint Moslem-Christian Committee was formed to protest against the establishment of a Jewish Homeland and the desecration of their sacred places in Palestine. As early as 1920, riots broke out in Jerusalem during which Jewish shops were pillaged and some lives lost. In February, 1921, an Arab-Palestinian Congress was held at Haifa to demand representative government exercised only by the Arab population, and a few weeks later anti-Jewish uprisings took place all over the country, but they were particularly serious in Jaffa where over three hundred casualties occurred.

A commission appointed to inquire into the causes leading up to these disturbances brought out an immense amount of testimony on both sides; it was shown beyond question that much of the trouble was to be attributed to ill-advised statements on the part of extremists in the Zionist party, leading the Arabs to believe that the Zionists as a body were aiming at the creation of a purely Jewish political state in Palestine.

Unfortunately this impression was increased by many of the immigrants, who were often inclined to be intolerant and self-assertive, as is frequently the way of enthusiasts. They took possession of Arab towns with an air of proprietorship offending the prejudices, customs, and manners of the Arabs.

Soon jealousy arose over the fact that the Jewish schools and institutions were so much superior to those provided for the Arabs out of their meagre budget eked out by small loans from Great Britain. It was claimed that Arabs were being dispossessed in the interest of Jewish settlers—this last assertion in the majority of cases not being based on any positive evidence.

My own observations in Palestine, while very superficial, would tend to substantiate the claim of the Zionists that most of the land occupied by their "haluzim," or colonists, had been unused and uncultivated for centuries. There was something very fine in the courage with which the Jewish colonists, many of them city-bred, tackled pioneer existence in undeveloped regions. The fundamental mistake made by the British Administration was in giving so much prominence to the Zionist Executive without offering the Arabs an opportunity to form their executive as well. In time this was realized by Sir Herbert Samuel, and on his return from England in 1924, he offered to co-operate with the Arab leaders in creating such a body.

A howl of protest from the Jews greeted the announcement of the formation of the new Executive Committee, with competence and powers equal to those of the Zionist Executive recognized by the Mandate. Lord Balfour, who came to Jerusalem to open the splendid Jewish University there in April, 1925, roused similar indignation among the Arabs by his statement that without Zionism, Palestine could never have developed her agriculture and industries. On his visit to Damascus some time later an anti-Jewish riot broke out, staged for his benefit, and there are still occasional anti-Jewish outbursts in Palestine, and still fears of Jewish political domination.

Sir Herbert Samuel was succeeded by Sir H. C. Plumer, a British Field Marshal, who has so far made no radical changes in the Administration. The material prosperity of Palestine is increasing annually, but after seven years of stormy administration it cannot be said that it has advanced one step further towards local autonomy.

In summing up the causes that have created the present political impasse in Palestine, it must never be forgotten that outside influences have had an important bearing on the situation. There have been many allegations that French interests were working to discredit the British Mandate—the Syro-Palestinian Committee has coquetted with both French and British administrations to the detriment of each. 'An undercurrent of social unrest has furthered the disruptive propaganda of Bolshevism, and no one can predict the outcome of the Palestine experiment.

IRAQ

We now come to Mesopotamia, which in many respects has achieved the status of a real nation, and apparently is on the road to an eventual abolition of the Mandate and recognition by the League of Nations. For some time after the Armistice, Mesopotamia was in the hands of the expeditionary forces which under General Maude had conquered all the territory in the valley of the Tigris and Euphrates to the edge of the mountainous country north of Mosul. Unlike Syria, the greater part of Mesopotamia had been under British control a year or more, and the military authorities had been supplemented by a civil administration under the direction of the India Office.

It had been necessary to call on the Government of India for assistance because practically all the officials in Mesopotamia had been Turks, and they had left with the retreating armies, causing much confusion in consequence.

As the status of Mesopotamia could not be determined until the peace terms had been outlined, a sort of provisional government was evolved, based on the old Turkish system. A special legal code was framed on Indian law and supplemented by the Ottoman Code. It was a makeshift administration, necessitated by the fact that the Arab population of Mesopotamia had never had any part in the government of their country.

Nevertheless, the Arab National Movement had spread to Mesopotamia even before the war, and the Anglo-French Declaration of November, 1918, embodying the promise of self-determination for Arab peoples aroused great hopes in the Nationalist element, which made up in enthusiasm what it lacked in solidarity and trained leadership. Consequently subsequent developments, resulting in the allotment of the Mesopotamian Mandate to Great Britain, were a bitter blow to the Nationalists. In view of the Sykes-Picot and other Anglo-French agreements, the future of Mesopotamia was a foregone conclusion; but it took some time for them to grasp the fact that their hopes of an Arab Federation were not to be realized.

It is difficult to see how they could ever have been carried out in Mesopotamia. This was clearly shown by the results of an inquiry to ascertain the wishes of the inhabitants, conducted by the British government in the winter of 1918-19. In this respect it proved nothing, for the vast majority were quite incapable of forming any opinion. It did show, however, the hopeless chaos existing throughout the country.

The bulk of the population of Mesopotamia was composed of Bedouin tribesmen, shepherds, and marsh-dwellers along the valleys of the Tigris and the Euphrates, and the Kurds in the mountains separating Mesopotamia from Persia and Turkey, to the east and north. They had always been semi-independent, living under the patriarchal tribal organization sanctioned by the Ottoman Sultans, and they had no ideas whatever on the subject of a national government. Even their Sheikhs as a rule were incapable of considering any problems of wider scope than those involved in their relations with neighboring tribes.

The townspeople were hopelessly divided, largely on account of religious differences. The population of Mesopotamia was Mohammedan, but it was divided into two sects, Shiah and Sunni. The members of the latter sect would have liked to have a ruler of the house of the Sherif of Mecca—the former were bitterly opposed to a Sunni ruler, and on the whole favored a British administration. Numerically they formed a small majority but as under the Ottoman Empire they were a fertile source of trouble.

The differences separating Shiahs and Sunni arose as early as the seventh century, when the former favored a hereditary

Khalifate from the descendants of Ali, son-in-law of the Prophet, and the latter demanded that the Khalif should be elected by the Moslem peoples.

The holy cities of Mesopotamia where the martyred Ali and his son Hussein, as well as the last three "Imams," direct descendants of Ali, were buried, are second only to Mecca in the veneration of Shiah Moslems. Nejaf, Kerbela, Samarra, and Kadhimein, the four Shiah shrines, are still visited annually by thousands of pilgrims. Incidentally, under the Ottoman Empire they had always been centres of dissatisfaction and strongly under Persian influence, Persia being officially a Shiah Moslem country.

The Jews and the Christians of various Oriental sects, of whom there are considerable numbers in Mesopotamia, also were in favor of a British administration. At that time, certainly, there was no possibility of finding a native prince who would be acceptable to even a decent minority of the population.

Mesopotamia could not be left to work out its own salvation. As conquerors, the British were morally obligated to give the inhabitants some form of government to replace the Turkish administration which they had destroyed; in any case it would have been necessary for them, in view of the unsettled condition of world-politics, to retain direct control of Basra at the head of the Persian Gulf, which commanded access to Great Britain's chief source of petroleum, the Anglo-Persian oil fields, located in Persia near the Gulf coast. Mesopotamia was also included in Lord Curzon's ambitious plans to create a chain of British protectorates which would serve as buffers for the defense of India. All these facts had been recognized long before the inquiry instituted in Iraq, so it was merely a gesture to regularize an actual situation.

Consequently Great Britain asked for, and was assigned, the Mandate for Mesopotamia by the Supreme Allied Council in April, 1920, and by virtue of the San Remo Convention between the British and the French regarding their respective oil interests the former also took over the provisional administration of the Mosul area, lying north of Baghdad.

The new mandated territory was christened Iraq, the name by which it was known to the majority of its inhabitants, and which had been adopted by the Nationalist organization called the "Ahd el Iraqi," composed of Mesopotamian officers in Emir Feisal's army. Sir Percy Cox was appointed High Commissioner.

When he arrived in Baghdad on October 1st, he found conditions chaotic and far from satisfactory. There had been sporadic revolts among the tribespeople ever since the organization of the occupation—now stimulated by the dislike of direct control of any kind, now by the fanaticism of the Shiah hierarchy in the Holy Cities, now by the agitation of the Nationalists, who wished the immediate establishment of some sort of an Arab state. It had culminated in a series of tribal rebellions which had been suppressed only after five months' fighting, with heavy losses on the part of the British forces. The towns too were seething with discontent and the High Commissioner was faced with an extremely difficult task. He succeeded, however, in forming a provisional Council of State composed of Arabs, each with a British adviser, which, in addition to reorganizing the internal administration, was to choose a ruler for the country.

If the Nationalist intelligentsia of Iraq had been allowed a free choice at this time, they would probably have selected Seyid Talib, the leader of the Baghdad Nationalists; but he was openly anti-British, and besides at this critical juncture Emir Feisal had broken with the French and had been thrown out of his newly formed kingdom of Damascus. Whatever other promises the British government had made or had not made, they had certainly made one which they were in honor bound to fulfil, and that was to provide Feisal, who helped England so materially during the war, with some sort of kingdom. Iraq was the only one at their disposal. Therefore pressure was brought to bear on the provisional council; Seyid Talib was deported to Ceylon, Feisal was invited to Baghdad and duly installed as king of Iraq on August 23, 1921, after a referendum, perhaps manipulated by the British, which gave him the majority of votes over all other candidates.

Dire results were predicted as a result of this alleged high-handed action in Iraq, and it was used by Great Britain's enemies, including the French, who considered Feisal's election as a direct affront, to stir up anti-British feeling throughout the Empire wherever there was discontent.

In Iraq, King Feisal was everywhere received by lukewarm subjects. He was a total stranger in the country; his family, that of the Sherifs of Mecca, had been traditionally opposed to the great Shiah personages of Iraq, and he was regarded as the tool of the British; but his strength lay largely in the fact that there was no unity in the opposition and that the British, who backed him, were in a military sense the masters of the country.

Iraq having been provided with a sovereign, the next step in the organization of the government was the holding of Parliamentary elections, and the new legislative Assembly known as the Medjliss which met in 1922, drafted a Constitution adopted two years later. A treaty with Great Britain, ratified in June, 1924, and a new electoral law were framed and signed by the Medjliss. The treaty, which was to terminate either on the entry of Iraq into the League of Nations, or four years after the ratification of peace with Turkey, whichever was the earlier date, contained the following provisions:

Great Britain was to provide Iraq "with advice and assistance without prejudice to her national sovereignty" and Iraq agreed to follow such advice in all matters "affecting the international and financial obligations and interests of His Britannic Majesty." No part of the territory of Iraq was to be alienated in any way, and the main provisions of the Mandate were safeguarded by a number of clauses dealing with such questions as liberty of conscience, community rights, equality of commercial opportunity, and the status of foreigners. Great Britain agreed to use her good offices to secure the admission of Iraq to the League of Nations at the earliest opportunity. Supplementary agreements provided that she should furnish advisers for fifteen years, make administrative loans to the government, maintain as many of her troops as might be necessary until 1928, and have the right to train and organize the new Iraq army.

There was much opposition in Iraq to the ratification of the treaty and its accompanying agreements, and gossip had it, when I was in Baghdad just after its ratification, that it was passed only after a threat on the part of Sir Henry Dobbs, who had succeeded Sir Percy Cox in September, 1924, to leave the country, bag and baggage, with his entire administrative staff and all the military forces. The real reason why it was passed, however, was probably the fact that even the hotheads among the Nationalists realized that without the co-operation and friendship of Great Britain they could never hope to secure the inclusion of the Mosul area within the boundaries of Iraq.

We have already seen, in connection with post-war happenings in Turkey, how the dispute as to the ownership of Mosul would have caused a rupture of the Lausanne Conference had not the Turks and British alike agreed to submit the matter to arbitration by a joint commission. This commission had failed to reach an agreement in June, 1924, only a few weeks before the ratification of the treaty, and the matter was referred for settlement to the Council of the League of Nations. Since the awarding of the Mandate for Mesopotamia many things had happened to alter the outlook of the British government and the nation, on the subject of Iraq: Curzon's imperialistic schemes had been thrown into the discard; British support of the Greeks against the Turks had led to disaster; England had been compelled to withdraw from Trans-Caucasia and Persia, and had concluded a peace recognizing the entire independence of Afghanistan.

The Iraq Mandate had cost her dearly in men and money and there was a large body of public opinion in England in favor of resigning guardianship of Mesopotamia and taking chances on its falling into the hands of interests inimical to the British. Mosul, it was argued, contained valuable petroleum deposits, but would it not be better for Great Britain to secure her interests in these by driving a profitable bargain with Turkey and letting Iraq go? If the Iraqis had failed to ratify the treaty, public opinion might have forced the British Government to retire from Iraq.

King Feisal at that time was vacillating between the Liberals and the Nationalists. Whatever might have been his personal bias, he would have been in a difficult position. When I met him in Baghdad that summer I found him very charming, but I could well understand why he had failed where men like Mustapha Kemal had succeeded. He could never have become the leader of a great cause—one always felt that he was not quite sure of himself in matters of state, though as regards his personal courage there could be never any question.

The treaty once passed, Great Britain threw herself with enthusiasm into the task of retrieving Mosul for Iraq. The League of Nations Council in the autumn of 1925 assigned Mosul to Iraq upon the condition that she should extend her treaty with Great Britain for a period of twenty-five years. We know how the Turks refused to accept this decision even when it was declared binding by the Hague Tribunal. It was not until Great Britain had pulled a few political strings in the Mediterranean, including a promise from Mussolini that Italy would invade Anatolia in case of conflict, that the Turks began to listen to reason. Finally in June, 1926, the agreement reached between Turkey and Great Britain whereby the former agreed to give up all claims to Mosul and establish the frontier between Turkey and Iraq, practically as it had been fixed by the Commission of the League of Nations, definitely committed both countries to close relations for another quarter-century.

The two years that elapsed before this decision was reached, were trying ones for Iraq. All along the border there had been serious disturbances. Time and again the Turks had threatened the Iraq frontier. On their own side, in addition to making formidable demonstrations against Iraq, they had been engaged part of the time in suppressing the Kurdish revolt, in which the Kurds on the Iraq side of the border had participated to some extent as well. In the course of this campaign Turkish soldiers had attacked and pillaged the villages of the Assyrian Christians who were still left in Kurdistan, and they had poured over the border, often destitute and starving, carrying with them blood-curdling tales of Turkish cruelties.

These Christians joined the colony of several hundred thousand Assyrians who had been in Iraq since shortly after the Armistice, and who had been a continual source of embarrassment and difficulty to the Iraq government owing to their insistent demands for local autonomy during the spread of the contagion of self-determination.

In a previous chapter I have told how the British gave them temporary asylum in Iraq after they had been nearly annihilated while fighting the battles of the Allies. When I was in Mosul in 1924, I met their woman leader Surma Hanum, a charming

person with an English education, who had held them together
during their tragic exodus from their fatherland. It was infinitely pathetic to hear her assert the proud claim of the Assyrian
nation to the heritage of Nineveh—now but a heap of stones and
a little Arab village containing the alleged shrine of the prophet
Jonah.

The award of Mosul to Iraq assured the economic future of the
country, just as the control of the Soudan has guaranteed the
prosperity of Egypt. The Mosul area, with the exception of the
marshy district near the Persian Gulf where dates are the chief
crop, is the only part of Iraq where cereals can be grown without
artificial irrigation. It is the granary of Iraq. Consequently it
has fewer nomads and a larger settled agricultural population than
any other section of the country. In addition it is the source of
part of Iraq's water supply.

The entire valley of Mesopotamia is watered by the Tigris and
Euphrates rivers. The former, which rises in the Zagros Moun-
tains of Turkey just north of the Iraq border, traverses the entire
country until it empties into the Persian Gulf at Basra. The
Euphrates, which also has its source in Turkey, crosses northern
Syria and empties into the Tigris. Together they constitute a
wonderful water supply, and many centuries ago under the great
Sumerian, Chaldean, Assyrian, and Babylonian empires, a remarkable irrigation system made the reputed site of the Garden of
Eden one of the most fertile areas in the known world. It was
not until successive invasions from the east, culminating in the
devastating progress of Tamerlane, had completely destroyed
these irrigation canals, that Iraq became an arid waste.

In recent times the Turkish government awoke to the fact that
a water-supply was all that was needed to make Mesopotamia one
of the garden spots of the earth, and under the Ottoman administration irrigation was begun on a large scale by the building of the
great Hindiya Barrage on the Tigris. It was partly destroyed
during the war, but it was repaired under the British administration and it is now irrigating thousands of acres of land on which
are cultivated cereals, rice, and cotton. The undisputed possession of Mosul by Iraq will mean that other irrigation schemes
will be carried out with British assistance. In addition Iraq has

gained a safe strategic frontier, the Zagros Mountains forming
natural barrier between her and Turkey.

In view of these facts the political problems raised by the
possession of Mosul do not deserve undue importance. Nevertheless, the territory originally claimed by Turkey, extending
south to within sixty miles of Baghdad, is a potential source of
trouble. Mosul, despite the respective contentions of Iraq and
Turkey, is neither principally Turkish nor predominantly Arab.
It is chiefly Kurdish, there being over 450,000 Kurds within
it as compared with approximately 186,000 Arabs and 66,000
Turks. The Christian population in the Mosul district numbered over 60,000 before the arrival of thousands of refugees
from across the Turkish border during the Kurdish revolt.

The increasing prosperity of the country is minimizing the
chances of political disturbances, however, and the development of
the Mosul region is proceeding rapidly, including that of the
famous oil wells, which have been the subject of so much controversy. As yet their value is problematical, and until extensive
exploitation of the area is under way no one can estimate the
future field. Turkey under the new agreement is to receive 10 per
cent of the Baghdad government's share of the output, fixed by
the new treaty between Iraq and Great Britain, extending the
Mandate for twenty-five years as was stipulated in the League
Council's decision awarding the Mosul area to Iraq.

No matter what future developments in the oil-bearing regions
may reveal in the way of potential wealth, the possession of Mosul
by the same government which controls the waterways of Iraq
must contribute greatly towards the prosperity and stability of
that government.

Already in Iraq, the material well-being afforded by the British
administration, which has had the merit of consistency and con-
tinuity so conspicuously lacking in that of the French in Syria,
has done much towards reducing political agitation.

Since the occupation the British have built the railway opening
Baghdad to the Persian Gulf, extending it northward to within
forty-eight miles of Mosul, and eastward almost to the Persian
border, to connect the fertile grain-producing territory of Kerkuk
with the capital. Irrigation of extensive areas has already in-

duced many of the nomad tribespeople to settle, and has enormously increased the cultivable land in the country. Increasing facility of communications and the excellent educational system inaugurated under British auspices and continued almost entirely under local control, are beginning to produce something like political solidarity, and the birth of an Arab Federation was perhaps foreshadowed in the treaty concluded last year by Iraq with the neighboring kingdom of Nejd.

The Iraqis have undoubtedly shown great aptitude for administration. As early as 1924, only three years after the disturbances which had made it unsafe for travellers to venture outside the principal cities, the desert motor route to the Mediterranean was entirely patrolled by a native mounted constabulary under native officers, and the close of 1926 saw the inauguration of the first passenger service by airplane from London to Karachi, India, via Baghdad.

Sir Henry Dobbs, the British Commissioner, who in November made a report on the British administration in Iraq before the Permanent Mandates Commission of the League of Nations, stated that the number of higher British officials in the government had been reduced since 1920, from 473 to 104, subordinates from 530 to 100, and the Hindu functionaries, who six years before had numbered 2,200, had been reduced to 600.

Soon Iraq will claim her share of the world's tourist travel; and in this respect there are few countries more interesting than Mesopotamia, the seat of the earliest civilization of the human race: Ur, Kish, Ctesiphon, Babylon, Nineveh, the Holy Moslem cities—are all within easy reach; even Kerkuk, where, according to tradition, is the fiery furnace of Shadrach, Meshach, and Abednego—a stretch of volcanic ash underneath which to this day are glowing coals. Baghdad and Basra now are modern cities with taxicabs, motion-picture palaces, country clubs, and electric-light systems.

There is, however, one thing which is important to remember in considering Iraq—that it proves nothing for or against the Mandate system. Owing to its compactness, its inclusiveness, its comparative isolation, it presents fewer problems than the other mandated areas. It is interesting to note that its tranquillity and comparative prosperity have been due to the ignoring of the principle of self-determination, for without Mosul and its part Kurdish, part Christian population, the outlook might not have been as promising in Iraq.

Until, or unless, the complexion of world-affairs undergoes a radical change, Great Britain must not only keep a strong hold on Iraq and Palestine, but also retain sufficient influence in the other small countries of the Arabian Peninsula to prevent political combinations inimical to her interests. Recently she has had to reckon with a new force in Arabia—the Wahabite revival under Ibn Saoud, Sultan of Nejd, one of the most remarkable, though one of the least known of the great Dictators who have come into power since the World War.

Chapter Eight

ARABIA DESERTA

UNTIL the outbreak of the Great War, the importance of the southern part of the Arabian peninsula was negligible in international politics. The edges bordering on the Red Sea, the Persian Gulf, and the Indian Ocean, were occupied by a number of small Mohammedan states, of which four, the Hedjaz, Asir, Yemen, and Koweit, recognized the suzerainty of Turkey. Of these the Hedjaz was most important, for it contained the Holy Cities of Mecca and Medina, locally governed by the Emir Hussein-ibn-Ali, Grand Sherif of Mecca, a member of a family claiming direct descent from the Prophet, and a hereditary right to the rulership of Mecca.

Moslems the world over had a direct interest in the Hedjaz, for a fundamental principle of Islam was that control of the Holy Places must always remain in Moslem hands. The Sultan of Turkey, who ruled the Hedjaz and thus indirectly Mecca, was Khalif, the successor of Mohammed and guardian of the temporal as well as spiritual power of Islam. As long as the Ottoman Sultans held their power, there was no question as to their right to the Khalifate.

The small countries of Arabia which did not acknowledge Turkish suzerainty, had come more or less under British control. For nearly a hundred years Great Britain had owned a small territorial concession at Aden at the mouth of the Red Sea. The petty potentates of Oman and Trucial on the Persian Gulf were under British protection and only one, El Hasa, stayed independent.

The interior of the country had remained to most people a sealed book. A few missionaries and travellers had been to Riyadh, the capital of Nejd and the stronghold of the Wahabis, a Moslem sect founded by a certain Mohammed-ibn-Abd-el-Wahab, who converted one of the principal chiefs of the many rival

182

tribes in Nejd in the middle of the eighteenth century. The Wahabis were puritans of the most rigid sort. They scorned as idolatrous most of the ritual which had grown up around the pure unitarianism preached by Mohammed. They took the teachings of the Koran simply and literally, touching neither wine nor tobacco, and refusing to wear gold ornaments; their faith possessed much of the flaming enthusiasm that had spurred the earlier leaders of Islam.

By the beginning of the nineteenth century, they had become so powerful that they were able to take and hold for some time the Holy City of Mecca; subsequently they were driven back into the desert by a Turco-Egyptian force, and until the Great War the outside world heard very little of the Wahabis, who were confined to their inland kingdom.

The plateau of Nejd, which extends from the states bordering on the Persian Gulf to the confines of the Hedjaz, and from the unexplored Southern Arabian desert to the fringe of the desert of Syria, is a more or less fertile area with immense plains that are fine for pasturage, and oases which produce excellent crops. Most of the inhabitants, numbering between five and six millions, are pastoral nomads; it has no cities unless Riyadh may be called a city, and no one knows what natural treasures may be hidden in the mountain ranges that intersect it from north to south.

When the war broke out the Sultan Abdul-Aziz-ibn-Saoud, a very remarkable man, had just begun to centralize his government with a view to the inauguration of a Wahabite revival. He had no reason for taking sides in the conflict as he neither owed allegiance to, nor had any great love for the Sultan of Turkey, but he was keen enough to see that the chaos occasioned by the war would afford him an excellent opportunity to extend his power. The British, who had sent Major St. John Philby to investigate conditions in Central Arabia, found it worth while to pay him a subsidy to remain neutral, and leave their ally, Hussein the Sherif of Mecca, in peace.

Ibn Saoud used the British money to great advantage in strengthening and equipping his army, and while the Great War was in progress he made several private wars of his own which resulted in his obtaining the subjection of the Djebel Shammar tribes and of the rich oases of Hail and Djuf, as well as the fealty of the Sheikh of El Hasa, which assured him access to the Gulf of Persia. True to his engagements to the British, however, he let the Hedjaz alone.

We have seen what developments took place during the War, how the Sherif of Mecca lent his support to the British, how his son Feisal under the tutelage of his mentor the famous Colonel Lawrence organized the Arab revolt, how eventually the Sherifian family was "rewarded," Hussein being made king of the Hedjaz, his son Abdullah king of Transjordania, and Feisal king of Iraq.

The kingdom of the Hedjaz was a very small sphere indeed compared to what Hussein had expected, or had been led by the British to expect. He had dreamed of becoming the overlord of a great Federation, but with the post-war revelation of the aims of France and Great Britain to retain indefinitely their spheres of influence, the allocation of the Mandates, and the collapse of the short-lived kingdom of Damascus, he saw all his hopes vanish.

It must be said in justice to the British that even if they had been willing to keep their promises to Hussein he was not the man to hold together a people as independent, as individualistic, and as impatient of authority as the Bedouin Arabs. He was old, he was vacillating, he was sly and shrewd but without real force of character, overweeningly vain and ambitious. He had to be satisfied perforce with what he got, and it suited the purposes of the British to allow him to assume a certain importance.

When it became evident that Turkey was not going to accept the Sèvres Treaty or the Greek occupation foisted on her by Lloyd George, and the Kemalist movement began to assume serious proportions, there appeared to be a new use for Hussein. In the event of the abolition of the Khalifate, which seemed highly probable in view of the anticlerical policy of the Kemalists, Hussein would be the logical aspirant to the honor. There had long been a progressive element in the Moslem world which favored the reorganization of the Khalifate on a purely spiritual basis: if the Khalif was to be the spiritual head of the Moslem

Faith, what could be more suitable than to invest the Sherif of Mecca, the traditional keeper of the Holy Places, with the office? Hussein himself had long had such an ambition and he received the British proposals with enthusiasm. When the Khalif Abdul Medjid was deposed by the Grand National Assembly of Turkey on March 3, 1924, Hussein was proclaimed Khalif by his own subjects and the Moslems of Hedjaz, Palestine, Syria, Iraq, and Transjordania; that is to say, he was supported by the countries more or less under his influence. At first he was undoubtedly encouraged by the British, but when protests against Hussein's arrogation of the title of Khalif began to pour in from all the other Moslem countries under British rule, they realized that they had made a mistake. It was obvious that Moslems the world over would never accept as Khalif a man who was a protégé of England, and who would not even be able to defend the independence of the Holy Cities. Either there would have to be an entirely new conception of the Khalifate or it would have to be vested in an independent sovereign. Today this question is no nearer solution than it was in 1924, for there is still no Khalif.

Hussein having been in a measure abandoned by the British, and having failed to secure the allegiance of most Moslem communities, should have been exceedingly circumspect. But he was not. Complaints of maladministration and extortion in Mecca and Medina had been pouring in to him for some time from pilgrims who had been fleeced and ill treated in the Holy Cities, but Hussein did nothing to remedy these abuses, and among all the malcontents there were none so vehement as the Wahabis, who had for a long time viewed with horror the corruption and vice, together with the idolatrous practices which had polluted the cradle of Islam.

Ibn Saoud was possibly all the more willing just then to embark on a crusade for the liberation of the Holy Places because Great Britain had ceased to pay him the subsidy he had been receiving for some years. During the summer of 1924, using the abuses in connection with the pilgrimages to Mecca as a pretext, he instituted a campaign against Hussein which resulted in the conquest of the Hedjaz.

Mecca was taken on October 13, 1924. Hussein was forced to

abdicate a few months later and fled to Cyprus on a British warship. He died there in the early part of 1927. His eldest son
Ali, in favor of whom he renounced his throne, held out against
the Wahabis until he was forced to surrender the port of Jeddah
in October, 1925, and to retire to a small strip of territory in the
extreme north adjoining the British-protected kingdom of his
brother Abdullah. He was finally compelled to abdicate and take
a British steamer for Basra.

The Wahabis, having become masters of Mecca and Medina,
instituted a thorough housecleaning in accord with their puritanical principles. They closed all the tobacco shops and many
of the purely commercial enterprises which had waxed rich on the
pilgrims, sold a palace of King Hussein to a merchant for six
hundred dollars, and destroyed many of the Moslem shrines.
Everything that in their opinion savored of idolatry was ruthlessly swept away, and Ibn Saoud became undisputed master of
the Hedjaz. Shortly after his accession he issued a royal proclamation beginning, "People of Hedjaz—recognize me King"!

It might have been expected that Great Britain would take some
action to prevent Ibn Saoud from helping himself to the Hedjaz,
but such was not the case. The Emir Ali received but scant assistance in his efforts to hold out against the Wahabis, and the
Sultan of Nejd on his part showed no haste to subdue Transjordania and Iraq, both ruled over by the sons of his enemy Hussein.

Alleging the necessity for resting his armies and for restoring
order in the Hedjaz so that the pilgrimages to Mecca and Medina
could be resumed, Ibn Saoud remained inactive—it was said,
owing to the fact that the British had once more made overtures
to him. This fact became apparent shortly after when Sir
Gilbert Clayton, Assistant High Commissioner for Palestine, was
sent to negotiate the accords of Hadda and Berra, fixing the
boundaries between the dominions of Ibn Saoud and the adjacent
Kingdoms of Transjordania, and Iraq.

Ibn Saoud's son and heir-apparent, the Emir Feisal, was made
Governor of Mecca, the pilgrimages were resumed, not without
some friction, however, between the fanatical Wahabis and
other Moslems, and last year a Pan-Islamic conference was held in
Mecca for the purpose of drawing up regulations to safeguard

the comfort and health of the pilgrims. In the same year a conference on the Khalifate was held at Mecca as well, but the whole question was referred to a commission; and for many reasons, which will be discussed when we deal with Islam as a force in international politics, it is likely that the Khalifate as an institution will stay in abeyance for some time.

Meanwhile, Ibn Saoud remains politically the most remarkable man Arabia has yet produced. Backed by his crusading tribesmen, he has done more towards the creation of an united Arabia than all the enlightened intelligentsia of Syria, Palestine, and Iraq combined. By virtue of his recent alliances with all these states he has laid the foundations for a possible Arab Confederation. He is actually master of all of Central Arabia, with outlets both to the Red Sea and to the Persian Gulf.

Recently he has still further extended his power by an alliance with the Imam Idrisi of Asir, and while he has an understanding with the British, he is by no means as supine a tool as Hussein. He is not a young man, however, and his power is built almost wholly on his personality, while the Wahabite movement of which he is the champion has yet to stand the test of contact with the enervating influence of money, creature comforts, and higher standards of living.

There are such tremendous differences between the desert Bedouin and his town brother, between the infinitely more advanced mandated Governments and the virtually medieval countries of Central and Southern Arabia, that the series of alliances which Ibn Saoud has concluded cannot be based on anything but political expediency; nor can the mandated States be said to have acted as entirely free agents. For the present Ibn Saoud has made a complete picture from the pieces of the Arabian puzzle with the help of England, which thus, by roundabout means, is still toying with the idea of an Arab Confederation.

No one can predict whether in the future the Arab states will become strong enough to assert themselves as a group. There is considerable propaganda in all Arab countries favoring a rapprochement with Turkey; there is a pan-Semitic movement which would tend towards closer relations with Egypt. Whatever the future holds for the peninsula, one thing is certain: education, improved means of transportation, and some sort of stable economic conditions in all the Arab states must precede any attempt at group political organization—and that is not the work of a year or a day.

Chapter Nine

INDIA IN THE CRUCIBLE

IN 1929, when the present Constitutional Charter must be revised in conformity with the terms of the Government of India Act of 1919, the British Parliament and the people of India will be compelled to consider a readjustment of their mutual relationship. The existing system of government for India will automatically cease and steps must be taken which will lead either to the incorporation of India as one of the self-governing Dominions of the British Empire or her permanent alienation from England. Upon the solution of this problem will depend in large measure the solution of many other questions at issue between East and West.

At the present time there is a conflict of ideals and types of civilization in Asia. In India the conflict is accentuated by the long contact of its intelligentsia with Western culture. If India fails to reach a modus vivendi with England, to which she is attached by ties far closer than those connecting any other Asiatic people with a European nation, it will go far to prove that Western civilization and ethics have failed to provide a vehicle for the reconciliation of Orient and Occident.

For this reason, the trend of events in India since the World War is just as significant as the more spectacular happenings in Turkey, China, and Central Asia. Indeed, it is possible to trace the influence of Indian developments on all the movements that are stirring Asia to its foundations, and in particular in the racial issues that have become of paramount importance in the relations between Europe and Asia.

In India, as in many other countries, the color line was deepened and broadened by the decisions of the Versailles Peace Conference. The Indian delegates, Lord Sinha and the Maharajah of Bikanir, no matter how profoundly they believed that India's salvation lay in co-operation with the British Raj, could not prevent their people from knowing that in spite of her seat in the League of Nations, India did not have the same status as the self-governing Dominions; neither could they gloss over the fact that Indians in Great Britain's African possessions were denied the privileges of citizenship. They saw the Persian delegates refused admission to the deliberations of the Conference; they witnessed the defeat of the resolution introduced by the Japanese to secure recognition of the principle of race-equality. And *this* *after* India had loyally supported Great Britain in the Great War, *after* she had accepted the Wilsonian Gospel in all good faith and proved her sincerity with her blood!

We have seen how the Nationalist leaders in India had begun to lose faith in Mr. Asquith's promises when they had borne no fruit up to 1917, and how the growing political agitation prompted the British government in 1918 to send Mr. Edwin Montagu, Secretary of State for India, to confer on the spot with Lord Chelmsford, then Viceroy, and to draw up a report to serve as a basis for new reforms.

The result of the Montagu-Chelmsford report was the passage by Parliament in 1919 of a new Government of India Act, providing for the drawing up of a Constitutional Charter under a system of administration to remain in force for ten years, which came to be known as "Dyarchy." Before trying to understand the character of this entirely new governmental system which is still on trial we must realize the conditions under which the Dyarchy was inaugurated in India.

The Montagu-Chelmsford reforms had been looked on with deep distrust by the more conservative elements in England and the old-time sun-dried administrative officials in India. Consequently after the Armistice, when the widespread discontent and agitation in India were intensified by her reaction to the revolutionary movements in Russia and Germany and the universal post-war demoralization, these elements insisted on and obtained the maintenance of the emergency war measures for the suppression of treason and criminal conspiracies. They were embodied in two parliamentary bills known as the Rowlatt Acts.

These bills, coming into force at a moment when India was still clinging desperately to her waning faith in the Fourteen

Points and the rights of subject peoples, dealt a mortal blow to Wilsonian idealism among the Indian Nationalists. In February, 1919, the Legislative Council solemnly demanded the repeal of the Rowlatt Acts. The refusal of the government brought about the Non-Co-operation Movement sponsored by Gandhi, which despite its failure in India has had a profound effect the world over, through its appeal to the solidarity of the colored races as against the white.

So completely did Satyagraha (Non-Co-operation, or refusal to obey the government) take hold of the mentality of the Indian Nationalists that for several years the political history of India was largely the history of the Gandhi movement. Swaraj and Swadesh—self-government and boycott—had been the slogan of the pre-war Indian Nationalists. They were given a new interpretation by Gandhi when in the spring of 1919 he proclaimed the 6th of April as Non-Co-operation Day in a protest against the Rowlatt Acts. In order to realize the depth of feeling that prompted him to advocate Non-Co-operation—literally the classification of the government and everything pertaining to it as "untouchable," just as the upper-caste Hindus classified the Pariahs or outcasts of their social system—we must know something of Gandhi's history.

An orthodox Hindu and a member of an old provincial family, Gandhi at first had no aversion to Western institutions, but rather the reverse. He had an English education and as a young man he was a firm believer in the Western civilization which he afterwards repudiated. His first political activities, curiously enough, were in co-operation with the British against the Transvaal Republic during the Boer War. After the opening of South Africa to colonization, large numbers of Indian farmers and laborers had settled in the British portions, gradually spreading to the Boer Republic, where their ill treatment called forth vehement protests from the British and was among the causes leading up to the Boer War in 1900.

During that war Gandhi, who at that time had a considerable personal fortune, equipped and supported an Indian ambulance corps with the British forces in the Transvaal. But when, after peace had been restored, the insidious color-bar made its appearance in South Africa and the British as well as the Dutch colonists began to demand legislation to curtail Indian immigration, and to prevent the Indian settlers from enjoying full citizenship, Gandhi adopted their cause with the greatest enthusiasm. It was in South Africa, hoping to rouse British public opinion to the gross injustice of racial discrimination, that he organized and carried out a programme of passive resistance, in which hunger strikes and mass-demonstrations were the chief weapons. Just before the war his efforts were crowned with partial success, and he returned to India after many years' absence with a profound hatred for Western materialism and a burning sense of racial injustice.

Even then, however, he had not entirely lost faith in British fairness. He saw in German Imperialism the quintessence of materialistic civilization, and he believed that by supporting England against Germany, India was serving her own interests and those of all humanity. While the idea of war was abhorrent to him personally, for he was a Tolstoyan pacifist, he saw that the conflict with Germany would have to be fought to a finish, and until the very end of the war he was steadfast in his loyalty to Great Britain. Like many Indians he believed that India would prove her right to be accepted on a footing of equality with England's other Dominions, and like many other idealists the world over he believed that the war had been fought to do away with the arbitrary authority which was the root of militarism and all its attendant evils.

When in the wake of the Montagu-Chelmsford report on the eve of the promised reforms, the government passed legislation sanctioning the repressive measures he so heartily abhorred, Gandhi rose in revolt! He traversed India from one end to the other preaching Non-Co-operation, exacting vows for its observance from the thousands who flocked to hear him. Local conditions in many parts of India were very bad at the time. There were severe outbreaks of bubonic plague and famines in certain . districts; the Mohammedan population was inflamed against Great Britain on account of her oppression of the Turks, and the time was ripe for a great national movement. Non-Co-operation spread like wild-fire, but unfortunately, as Gandhi might have foreseen had he not been wrapped in his internal vision, it could not be kept free from the violence he personally so abhorred.

The 6th of April, 1919, witnessed riots in Delhi, followed by disturbances in Bombay, and finally by a widespread rebellion in the Punjab. Gandhi protested in vain and the disorders continued. The population of Lahore rose en masse, driving out the British and remaining masters of the city for three days. In Amritsar, the Holy City of the Sikhs, the municipal buildings and railway station were destroyed by a mob which was, however, soon dispersed by the British forces. Unfortunately, General Dyer, who was sent to take charge immediately after the incident, resolved to make an example of Amritsar in order to terrorize and bring all the Punjab to submission. The day after his arrival, having had word that a public meeting was being held in contravention of his orders in an enclosure known as the Julianwalla Bagh, he and a detachment of soldiers surrounded the crowd of more than six thousand persons, all unarmed, and fired point-blank into their midst without warning. Dyer and his men, according to the former's own admission, did not stop firing on the panic-stricken multitude until their ammunition was nearly gone. The scene was one of unparalleled horror; men and women crowded the narrow exits, trampling one another, trying in vain to scale the high walls about the enclosure, all the while subject to rifle-fire at close range. Three hundred and seventy-nine persons were killed, and twelve hundred wounded, for whom General Dyer made no attempt to provide assistance. Subsequently Dyer issued an order to Amritsar compelling all Indians who wished to pass through a certain street where before his arrival an Englishwoman had been mishandled by a mob, to traverse it on all fours. This order, issued by a supposedly superior Anglo-Saxon, was virtually identical with an order, issued by a Japanese commander at Khabarovsk in Siberia a year later!

Incredible as it may seem, General Dyer's action was upheld by his superiors, so an official inquiry by the British government resulting in a severely censorious dispatch to the Government of India did little to appease the flood of indignation which spread far beyond the bounds of India, and even of Asia. Amritsar did more to intensify the bitterness of race-conflict in Asia than any other isolated act of any white Power since the beginning of the present century.

In the face of the universal horror over the happenings at Amritsar, Indian moderates were stunned. "At the moment when the country was awaiting the application of principles proclaimed to all the world by Anglo-Saxon statesmen," says René Grousset, "India found herself treated as Belgium had been treated by Germany. Amritsar was the equivalent of Louvain."

The Council of the National Indian Federation under the liberal Banerjea protested almost as violently as the radicals of the school of Tilak, who had just died. The Indian National Congress which met at Amritsar in December accepted the report of a special investigating commission of its members condemning the massacre in scathing terms. Gandhi himself, while horrified at the lapses of his followers from the doctrine of passive resistance, began to urge Non-Co-operation more enthusiastically than ever. In deference to his teachings whole masses of country people refused obedience in any form to government officers, often with tragic results as when they opposed inoculation, vaccination, and all efforts made by the sanitary service to stamp out the bubonic plague and smallpox. In the cities Non-Co-operation found expression in a succession of strikes, which tied up many industries and frequently held up all municipal departments and public utilities.

Meanwhile the Moslems of India, some seventy million in number, who had always been traditional enemies of the Hindus, were driven by a sense of race-injustice and their indignation over Great Britain's treatment of Turkey, the seat of their spiritual and temporal Overlord the Khalif, to make common cause with the Non-Co-operationists.

At the close of 1919, when all India was seething over Amritsar and the government's belated censure of General Dyer's ill-timed expedient to suppress the rebellion in the Punjab, the new Government of India Act, embodying the Montagu-Chelmsford reforms, became a law. The general elections of the spring of 1920 were the first to be held under the Act and the new Constitution came into full operation with the meeting at Delhi in February, 1921, of the All-Indian legislative bodies consisting of a Chamber of Princes, an Indian Legislative Assembly, and a Council of State.

It was not the first time that representative government had been essayed in India. The Provincial Councils had been put on a partly elective basis by the Morley-Minto reforms before the Great War. The new Government of India Act considerably enlarged the franchise, based on communal representation, the qualification for membership in the various Provincial and the All-Indian Legislative Assemblies varying slightly in different districts. As a rule it was also based on the ownership of real property, illiteracy being no bar. At the first general elections over six million names were registered—representing about one-fortieth of the population of British India, comprising Madras and the United Provinces, Bengal and the Central Provinces—in all only two-thirds of the area of the Indian subcontinent. We are prone to forget this last fact in connection with India: Actually, one-third of the country is still under local native potentates enjoying a greater or lesser degree of autonomy, but all with their own institutions and forms of internal government, often greatly at variance with the principles of British rule.

There have always been certain subjects affecting the interests of all India, however; these are dealt with in the various Native States, over 700 in number, by the Viceroy of India, and the degree of local autonomy enjoyed by the various states is regulated by treaties and agreements. The Indian Princes had their own representatives in the Imperial War Council, at the Versailles Peace Conference, and more recently they have had a representative at the annual meeting of the League of Nations.

By the Constitutional Charter of 1919, they were brought into close association with the Government of India through the creation of the Chamber of Princes which sits at Delhi simultaneously with the All-Indian Legislative Assembly although it constitutes merely a consultative body with regard to matters of common interest to all India.

Consequently the new system of Dyarchy, providing for a greater measure of autonomy in British India does not affect a third of the country. Nationalist agitation and all-Indian political activities in connection with the demand for Home Rule, and other even more revolutionary movements, affect British India alone, although there is the same widespread racial antagonism to Anglo-Saxons among the inhabitants of the native states.

When we speak of the Dyarchy in India, we mean merely the new system of government devised under the Act of 1919 for British India. It is called Dyarchy because of its dual character. Each province has a governor who is responsible to the Viceroy and through him to the British Parliament for his administration. He has an executive council of his own choosing which assists him in dealing with certain governmental subjects classed as "reserved," comprising principally those concerned with the maintenance of law and order, such as justice and the policy system.

The remainder of the subjects affecting the provincial population, such as education, industries, public health, agriculture, local revenues, taxes, and public improvements, have been transferred to a cabinet of native ministers responsible to the Provincial Legislature. The authority of the legislature over all "transferred" subjects and even over certain reserved departments theoretically amounts to control. But—and here is the all-important reservation—the Governor may, subject to the approval of the Viceroy and ultimately of the British Parliament, nullify any action taken by the legislature. The All-India Legislature however has no such powers, for Dyarchy has not been applied to the Viceroy's executive council though it contains a large number of Indian members. Legislation passed by the All-India Legislature is subject to the Viceroy's veto just as the legislation passed by the provincial bodies is subject to that of the provincial governors. The spheres of the All-India and the Provincial Legislatures have in turn been rigidly defined by the classification of all possible subjects for legislation as Central and Provincial.

There have also been certain changes in the British end of government for India. The Secretary of State for India is the intermediary between Parliament and the Viceroy, and he is advised and to a certain extent controlled, by the Council of India in Whitehall. But the Indian Office no longer performs the liaison service between the Native States and the Crown. They have an official representative in a High Commissioner with the same status as the High Commissioners of the Dominions.

Such is the frame within which India must develop a capacity for Constitutional Government sufficiently great to earn for her the status of a Self-Governing Dominion if the principles embodied in the Montagu-Chelmsford Reforms are accepted unqualifiedly by her and Great Britain.

So far, however, neither side has been satisfied with the actual working of the Dyarchy, and small wonder, for it is a system which, without perfect co-operation from all concerned, affords unequalled opportunities for "passing the buck." It is very easy, for example, for a minister who has control of a "transferred" subject, like Agriculture, to claim that the failure to carry out important irrigation projects promised the inhabitants of a certain district is due to a reduction of his appropriation by the Governor in order to provide more money for some unpopular "reserved" subject, such as the creation of a larger police force.

Nevertheless, in spite of these and many other obvious disadvantages, Dyarchy has worked surprisingly well in some places. On the other hand, it broke down entirely in others, notably in Bengal, where it was suspended by the Governor with the Viceroy's approval for more than two years, and was only restored to operation in January, 1927. In any case it is only an experimental system to be radically modified or done away with altogether when the Constitutional Charter is revised in 1929.

Far more important to us are the changes in Indian psychology and Indian politics within the last few years. While they have produced no very startling events they have profoundly modified the situation not only in India but in many parts of Asia. At first sight it is difficult to extract anything very definite from the intricate tangle of internal affairs in India since 1919, but if we look in perspective at recent events they may be divided into several distinct periods:

The first, which we have already reviewed briefly, was the period of ferment and agitation from the publication of the Montagu-Chelmsford report down to the first meeting of the All-Indian Legislative Assembly in 1921; it marked the rise of Gandhism, the organization of Non-Co-operation as a political movement; the ill-advised repressive measures of the harassed Indian Government, still reluctant to modify its pre-war Imperialism in conformity with post-war actualities—in curious juxta-position with a genuine desire on the part of Great Britain to eventually satisfy what were generally regarded as the legitimate demands of India for the same status as that accorded the Dominions.

The second period, which may be included with the three years from 1921 to 1924, marking the life of the first Legislative Assembly under the new constitution, witnessed the decline and the final collapse of Gandhi's political programme.

When the first elections for the All-India and Provincial legis-lative bodies were held, the Non-Co-operationists, in obedience to Gandhi's instructions, abstained from voting and only half of those who had the franchise actually went to the polls. The All-India Legislative Assembly was composed of members of other parties, who, however much they might differ, at least all sup-ported the Constitution. During the three years of its existence it carefully steered a middle course, enacting much valuable legisla-tion on non-controversial and purely constructive lines, in spite of the political storms that raged around and outside it. The Pro-vincial Councils followed about the same line of action, only with this difference—the new system of Dyarchy, which did not apply to the All-India legislature, often hampered their activities, par-ticularly where finances were concerned.

Meanwhile the Central Government was putting into practice a series of reforms provided for under the Government of India Act, which did not come under the provisions of the new con-stitution, but which were none the less vitally important if India was to be made ready in ten years for self-government. They comprised nothing more nor less than a complete reorganization of the Public Services—the vast and cumbersome administrative machinery of the Government. Formerly all the higher branches, including the entire Indian Civil Service, were staffed entirely by British officials, and one of the chief grievances of the Indian Nationalists from the early days of the Indian National Congress had been that Indians were not admitted to the Civil Service.

Despite some partial reforms and many qualified promises, the disabilities of Indians had never been entirely removed up to the passage of the Government of India Act of 1919, although

pledges to this effect were included in Mr. Asquith's war-time
declarations to the Indian people. But under the Act of 1919 the
proportion of Indians to be included in the Civil Service was
fixed at 33 per cent, to be increased to 48 per cent by 1930, and
steps were taken for the eventual Indianization of every branch of
the Administration. Indian ministers presided over all the transferred departments in the provincial governments wherever the
Dyarchy was in operation, and a number of Indian members were
included in the Viceroy's Executive Council. The Indianization
of the army, an exceedingly delicate task, was cautiously begun.

While the Government was introducing all these changes and
the Indian legislative bodies were beginning to function more or
less efficiently, Gandhi and his followers were not idle. Tilak,
aggressive leader of the Nationalist party, died in the spring of
1920, and most of his disciples turned to Gandhi, who was in
many ways a far more redoubtable adversary of the British Raj.
His personality was calculated to make a tremendous appeal to
Hindu mentality. "India is religious, just as Greece was æsthetic,
Rome judicial, and the Anglo-Saxon world utilitarian. Everything, even atheism, takes a mystic form," says M. Grousset. It
was Gandhi's ability to transform Nationalism into Religion and
to identify it with the most hallowed traditions of India, that won
him his following.

When he proclaimed a boycott of British institutions and
British goods in June, 1921, as the means of attaining Swaraj,
promising that if the people of India followed his orders they
would be free within a year, there were thousands that joined the
mobs of students who made huge bonfires of British calicoes,
picketed the bazaars where British goods were sold, and discarded
their British clothes to wear the homemade *khaddur,* cloth woven
by their own hands.

At the same time Gandhi made common cause with the Indian
Moslems, who were up in arms against the Sèvres Treaty and for
a few brief months his preachment of a return to the patriarchal
simplicity of India's "Age of Gold" sung in the Vedas, and the
power of passive inertia against the "Satanic Civilization" of the
West, held a large portion of the people of India under a mystic
spell. But such conditions could not last. Human Nature being

Human Nature, passive resistance meant strikes and other demonstrations that must inevitably lead to violence. Matters were not long in coming to a crisis.

The agitation, which even the Mahatma, the "blessed" Gandhi, could not keep within peaceful bounds, was becoming a great mass movement when Lord Reading, who had followed Lord Chelmsford as Viceroy, succeeded in creating a schism among the Non-Co-operationists. Inviting Gandhi to a Conference at Simla and expressing the greatest sympathy with his pacific doctrines and his political convictions, he persuaded him to issue a statement condemning violence and to induce the Moslem leaders, Mohammed and Shaukat Ali, to do the same.

The immediate result of this course of action was precisely what Lord Reading had doubtless foreseen : it produced a break-up in the National bloc. The alliance of the Moslem Nationalists with Gandhi was merely a matter of political expediency, for pacifism finds no place among the tenets of Islam. Their quarrel with the British Raj was not so much over its Indian administration, as over its attitude with regard to the Khalifate, and the whole tragic problem of racial prejudice which had become so acute since the Great War. They had been hereditary enemies of the Hindus ever since the Mogul conquest. It was this enmity which led them frequently to support the British as against the Hindus in India, despite occasional outbreaks against their rule.

The Indian Moslems were from the first eager to assimilate British culture and British institutions. The Moslem University of Aligarh, founded by the great leader Seyid Ahmed, the first of the Modernists of Islam, was based on English models and it was said at one time that it was worth to the British at least four fighting divisions. There had never been any close sympathy between Turkey and Moslem India until the rise of the Pan-Islamic movement, which nevertheless did not prove strong enough to prevent Indian Moslem troops from serving Great Britain loyally during the war. Their espousal of the cause of the Khalifate was largely due to the burning sense of racial injustice which had grown up as an outcome of the Great Peace.

Soon after Gandhi's parley with Lord Reading had pledged the Non-Co-operation movement to a course of inaction which the

Indian Moslems felt would defeat its ends, the artificial alliance between them and the Hindus was broken. The brothers Ali quickly realized that they had been tricked. The Moslems went their own way, which often led to riots in which Hindu lives and property were endangered no less than British. Finally a rebellion among the Moplahs on the Malabar coast, first directed against the English, resulted in appalling massacres among the Hindu population. The rebellion was eventually put down by British troops.

The two Alis were tried for inciting the Sepoy regiments to rebellion, and sentenced to prison for two years. When they were released conditions in Islam had radically changed. The Lausanne Treaty had automatically righted many of the wrongs of Turkey; the Khalifate question had taken an entirely different turn, and the Angora Government, which they had held up as the defender of the Khalifate, was about to depose the Khalif, while Egypt, where militant Islam had found many adherents to oppose British Imperialism, was being launched on the road to independence.

Their programme perforce had to be greatly modified. Since that time the Moslems and Hindus have never really made common cause in India, though their common hatred of "white" domination sometimes produces the same reactions. Generally speaking, the Indian Moslems are more closely identified with the Pan-Asiatic movement and the universal reaction against the West than with the Nationalist movement in India. The real roots of Non-Co-operation and its successor the Swaraj party are deep in the heart of old India.

The Moplah rebellion called forth repressive measures almost as violent as those that marked the suppression of the revolt in the Punjab, and Gandhi was driven, in spite of his promises to Lord Reading, to proclaim a boycott of the Prince of Wales on his visit to India at the close of 1921. When the Prince landed at Bombay on November 17th, there was a riot in the streets of the city which was suppressed only with considerable loss of life. At Allahabad and Calcutta there were no visible disturbances, but the streets of the native quarters were deserted, the houses closely shuttered, and not a Hindu or a Moslem appeared to greet the future Emperor of India.

The situation was rendered still more serious through the open assistance given by the British to the Greeks who were fighting the Kemalist Turks in Anatolia, particularly when a British squadron was sent to the Dardanelles after the capture of Smyrna. At the same time race hatred was inflamed to still higher pitch among the Hindus by the failure of Mr. Srinavasa Sastri, India's representative at the Imperial Conference, to secure equal civic rights and just treatment for the Indians in South Africa and the colony of Kenya, formerly known as British East Africa.

Gandhi was caught up and carried on the wave of the agitation he had helped to create, far beyond the limits he had set for the activities of the Non-Co-operationists. In vain he prayed and fasted and implored his followers to listen to reason. The "Soul Force" which he invoked to bring about the triumph of Eastern Spiritualism over Western Materialism had been transmuted into an Earth Force over which he had no control. Lord Reading, realizing what the consequences of all the ferment in India might be, telegraphed to Lloyd George, then Premier of England, urging him not to make war on the Khalifate. The telegram, which was made public by Mr. Montagu, Secretary of State for India, lost the secretary his position, but it at least helped to keep the moderates among the Indian Moslems from making common cause with the extremists.

Not even Lord Reading's tact could neutralize the effect of Gandhi's remarkable personality, and the almost worshipful awe with which he was regarded by the Indian masses, and it soon became evident that more stringent measures would be necessary in order to counteract his influence. Gandhi was arrested on March 10, 1922, and condemned to six years in prison. He was released on February 5, 1924, on account of ill-health, and resumed his place as leader of the Non-Co-operationists. But his political leadership was not the same—spiritually he still had an extraordinary hold on India, but the movement he had inaugurated had undergone radical changes during his term of imprisonment. There had been, at his own request, no outbreaks of violence following his arrest and condemnation. The masses, whose personal loyalty to him remained unshaken, nevertheless felt that Non-Co-operation had failed—it had not given them Swaraj, which the Mahatma had promised within a year.

The keener and more practical minds in the party realized the necessity for applying Western methods to combat Western materialism, and Mr. C. R. Das, Gandhi's lieutenant in the important province of Bengal, with the Pundit Motilal Nehru, a well-known Indian barrister who had embraced the Nationalist cause, began to advocate obstruction instead of non-participation as a means of securing the independence of India. For that was what the Nationalists, who only a few years before would have been more than content with Dominion status for India, were beginning to demand. The white man would have to get out of India, said they, as he would eventually have to get out of Asia!

During Gandhi's imprisonment the idea grew apace, and the Indian National Congress which met in January, 1924, confirmed and approved the action of Mr. Das, who, during the previous autumn, had lifted the boycott on the elections to the provincial All-India legislative bodies. The majority of the former Non-Co-operationists, as members of the reorganized Swaraj party, took part in all the elections. They secured a large number of the seats in the Provincial Councils, notably those of Bengal, the Central Provinces, and Bombay. They obtained forty-one out of the ninety seats in the All-Indian Legislative Assembly, and when Gandhi was set at liberty he found that the practical direction of Nationalist policies had passed from his hands. His formal abdication of leadership took place at the meeting of the National Congress at the end of 1924, where he made a long speech confessing to the failure of Non-Co-operation as a political weapon. His subsequent complete retirement from active politics changed the complexion of the Nationalist movement in India. From a religion it developed into an exceedingly able, brilliant, and effective political opposition.

The third period of contemporary history in India, which may be included within the lifetime of the second All-India Parliament from the beginning of 1924 down to the gathering of the third All-India Assembly in January of the present year, 1927, has seen still further changes in the relations between Great Britain and India.

Just as the Non-Co-operation movement overshadowed all other political issues in India during the first three years of constitutional government, Das's Swarajist party held the centre of the stage from 1924 until shortly before the elections in the autumn of 1926; with Gandhism in eclipse, and with the best brains of the Non-Co-operation movement at its disposal, the Swaraj party began its programme of obstruction in the All-India and Provincial Legislatures. Although Das and his followers were agreed that parliamentary tactics were the most effective means of preventing the operation of the Constitution and of forcing Great Britain to accord self-government to India, they nevertheless, indirectly at least, gave encouragement to the extremists, many of whom either belonged to, or were affiliated with, the Indian section of the Communist International.

The Communist School of Propaganda established at Tashkent had been training Hindu agents since 1920, and had established branches in Benares and Delhi. The latter was reported to have secured 91,000 members for the Indian Communist party, paying dues aggregating £120,000 a year, eighteen months after its foundation! The Indian Communists made common cause with the extreme Nationalists in obedience to their instructions from Moscow, and the Swarajist leaders unquestionably profited now and then by their activities.

While India was not "ready" for Communism, as the leaders of the International frankly acknowledged in a secret circular of the "Polit Bureau" sent out at the close of 1922, many of the Indian Nationalists saw a useful ally in Communist agitation. Their attitude was very similar to that of the Turkish Nationalists at the beginning of their struggle for independence.

When I was in Moscow in 1920, I met Djemal Pasha, who had come to "sound out" the Bolshevists with regard to an alliance with Kemalist Turkey. Knowing him to be a conservative of the old autocratic school, I asked him if he were not afraid of Bolshevist propaganda in the event of an alliance with Persia. His answer was most illuminating: "My dear lady," he said, "if your house is on fire, do you ask the politics of the man who comes to help you put it out?"

Whatever may have been the underlying causes, the parliamentary obstruction of the Swarajists was not unaccompanied by violence. In Bengal, where they caused a suspension of the Dyarchy by their refusal to vote the budget, appoint ministers, or pass necessary legislation in the Provincial Council, the local disorder became so serious that the Governor was obliged to secure a special ordinance from the Viceroy authorizing the use of repressive measures similar to those sanctioned by the Rowlatt Acts which had been repealed by Lord Reading.

An inquiry committee appointed by the government in 1924, however, reported that the reforms were working well on the whole in many provinces, despite the Swarajist tactics. The fundamental difficulty was the impossibility of regulating financial questions under the Dyarchy. While the assemblies voted the budgets, and ministers responsible to the assemblies received their share of the revenues for their respective transferred departments, the governors and their executive councils could pare and redistribute the various items, while a certain share of the provincial revenues had to be handed over to the state.

This condition of affairs often resulted in much friction, and gave rise to a widespread demand even among the moderates who did not subscribe to Das's policy of obstruction, for what was called "complete fiscal autonomy," not only in the provinces but in the central government.

The parliamentary history of the last All-India Legislature was largely made up of efforts to block the administration until the government would consent to a revision of the Constitution granting India complete independence with regard to finances.

It cannot be denied that in principle the Indian demand for control over Indian revenue was based on solid grounds. It is undoubtedly true that the Imperial Government has often shown a disposition to make the revenues of India pay for expansion elsewhere, and this is particularly true of the Indian army, which the Swarajist party very cleverly cited as a concrete example of British unfairness. The Indian army was kept up to its actual strength for Imperial rather than for Indian necessities. When there was trouble in the other portions of the Empire, Indian troops were frequently sent to quell the disturbances. The Indian army, supported by the taxpayers of the country, was officered until very recently only by Britishers. There was no school where young Indians of the better classes could be trained for commissions, and the only Indian officers were the "non-coms" and a few junior officers who had risen from the ranks.

This state of affairs was changed by the policy of Indianization introduced by the Government of India Act not only into the army but into the public services, including the Civil Service, in which as we have seen, the proportion of Indians was to be gradually increased. A Royal Military College was founded in India, and its graduates were admitted to Sandhurst. Indian officers received their commissions from the King instead of the Viceroy, and a plan for the creation of a force of Indian Territorials was elaborated and put into execution. The provincial departments under Indian Ministers were soon almost filled with Indian employees.

But there were many difficulties in the way of these changes, not the least of which was that the Swarajists had passed the stage when they were willing to share the government with Englishmen. Nothing would do but the ousting of all English officials. The All-India Legislature, controlled by the Swaraj element, developed a habit of rejecting bills providing appropriations for administrative purposes, whereupon they had to be "certified"— that is to say, put into effect by the declaration of the Viceroy that they were necessary to the machinery of government.

For a year Das directed the parliamentary obstruction of the Swarajists, with considerable immediate success. At the beginning of 1925, Lord Reading went to England to discuss the situation with Lord Birkenhead, the present Secretary of State for India. It was proposed that a Round Table Conference be called at London, to which Das, Gandhi, and Indian leaders of all parties should be invited to discuss a revision of the Constitution. While Lord Reading was trying to convince the home government of the wisdom of such a step the attitude of the Swaraj party underwent one of those sudden changes so characteristic of Indian party politics.

At the opening of the Bengal Provincial Congress Das startled his hearers by proclaiming that India might attain independence "without Swaraj," by which he meant that unless she solved the problem of consolidating her various antagonistic elements, India could not be really self-governing. On the other hand he declared that Swaraj was possible in the heart of the British Empire, citing the example of the Dominions. Then he proceeded to outline the conditions under which the Swarajists would co-operate with the British government. Violence was immoral, and revolution could not bring liberty; but the government must repeal repressive measures, declare a political amnesty, renounce its discretionary powers, recognize the right of India to autonomy, and take steps towards the granting of such autonomy. Upon receiving assurances that these conditions would be fulfilled the Swarajists would cease their obstructive tactics and join hands with the British Raj.

It is difficult to guess what might have resulted if Das and Lord Reading had been able to agree on a policy of conciliation and co-operation, and to induce the Secretary of State for India to concur in their views. Unfortunately these tentative efforts at a rapprochement were brought to an end by the death of Das in June, 1925. At that time he was mayor of Calcutta, and his funeral was as extraordinary a sight as had ever been seen in that city. All parties united in honoring one of the most remarkable leaders India has yet produced. In the funeral procession to the Burning Ghat by the temple of Kali, where his body was cremated according to the ancient Hindu rites, Gandhi was the chief mourner.

The character of Das was singularly contradictory and typical of the effect of Western education on the Oriental mentality. He combated parliamentary institutions but he used parliamentary tactics to defeat the Dyarchy. He combined the most profound idealism with the cheapest demagogy; past master in the art of swaying a political assembly, he could not face hard realities. He wished to revert to the village as the administrative unit and the basis of political organization. Under him India would have become a federation of autonomous village-communities. He ignored the difficulties of breaking with the world-wide economic system and world-wide political combinations, and he counted far too much on the possibility of bringing about internal peace and unity.

Indeed, there had only been a very brief period when India might have been said to have displayed any real solidarity even

against the universally detested "white" supremacy, and that was
in 1921, under the spell of Gandhi and the bond of common suffering. The post-war depression bringing famine and misery, combined with the epidemics of 1919, had found the masses of India
responsive to Gandhi's movement. In the succeeding years material conditions had greatly improved, and the masses had re-
lapsed into apathy; the various antagonistic factions in Indian
politics had all resolved into their original groupings.

We have discussed the break between the Hindu and Mohammedan leaders which was shortly afterwards followed by the failure of the Non-Co-operation movement and the formation of the
Swaraj party: meanwhile there had been other active parties less
in the limelight perhaps, but by no means unanimous in their patriotic endeavors to help India. There was the group known as the
Responsivists, who favored co-operation to the fullest extent with
the British Raj, the Independents, who steered a middle course,
the Orthodox Hindus, who condemned Gandhi and the Swarajists
for wishing to lift the bars of caste, then there were the "Untouchables" themselves, who had their own organization to fight
for political representation.

There was a strong tendency in many groups, headed by the
powerful Moslem party, predominant in the Punjab and embracing
70,000,000 of the 320,000,000 of India, which favored communal
representation in legislative bodies; this naturally was not favored
by the Hindus. Added to these elements were the Native States,
with their enormous population only a little less than one-fourth
of that of all India. Their rulers, feudatories of Great Britain,
with well-defined rights and powers fully protected by treaties,
and with forms of government in general more autocratic than
constitutional, were almost without exception loyal to the British
crown. They did not favor at all the spread of what they regarded as subversive ideas from British India, tending to undermine their institutions. The growth of the Swaraj movement
could not fail to weaken their authority. Moreover, their subjects
were for the most part utterly unready for even partial self-
government, and agitation among them could only produce
political chaos.

Great Britain was pledged to consider their interests as well as those of her own Indian subjects. The above statement is not meant to imply that the Native Princes or their subjects have any particular love for the British or that they too have not felt the universal wave of anti-Western and racial feeling; but they do know on which side their bread is buttered. Consequently a large portion of the Indian sub-continent is politically divorced from the seething parliamentary turmoil of British India.

After the death of Das the confusion in Indian party politics became even greater. The National Congress which met at the close of 1925 was particularly remarkable for the fact that it was presided over by a woman—Sarojini Naidu; and strangely enough it was another woman—English this time—Mrs. Annie Besant, who caused the greatest amount of agitation in Nationalist circles by bringing forward a draft bill for the creation of an Indian Commonwealth which was to supplant the Dyarchy established under the Act of 1919.

There were sporadic disturbances during the period we have been reviewing, but nevertheless the governmental machinery showed no sign of the collapse which both conservative Die-Hards and radical Nationalists had been predicting. On the whole it moved smoothly and in many respects conditions were much improved. Trade, which had suffered greatly in the post-war depression and during the boycott, had become much nearer normal; the institution of a mild protective tariff afforded some aid to Indian industries, though the allegation that the government always had in mind Imperial rather than Indian interests in framing the import and excise duties, was made in Swarajist circles.

A broader system of primary instruction was inaugurated in the provinces, and perhaps the most important of all, a vigorous campaign of popular instruction in modern agricultural methods was instituted all over rural India.

These measures contributed to decrease the prestige of the Swarajists. In the election of 1926, they lost considerable ground, and when the All-India Assembly met in January of 1927 the Swarajists no longer held a majority in the Provincial Councils—not even in Bengal, the stronghold of Swarajism. There was only one province, Madras, where they retained control.

While the Swarajists still continued to adhere to their obstructionist programme, it was obvious that they could no longer really obstruct without the support of one of the other parties.

General conditions at the beginning of 1927 indicated the beginning of a better understanding between the Government and the Nationalists. The Indianization of the army had made great strides—a bill for the creation of an Indian navy similar to the Australian fleet had been introduced in the British Parliament; the budget showed a probable large excess of receipts over expenditures; but perhaps the most important development was the settlement of the long-drawn-out contest between the Government of India and the South African Union, which resulted in a compromise securing civic rights to Indians in South Africa under certain conditions, and providing for the repatriation to India of those who were unable to comply with those conditions.

All things considered, it is improbable that any very startling changes will take place in Indian party politics, or that any legislation of moment will be introduced into any of the Assemblies pending the revision of the Constitution which will take place in 1929. It may be rash to hazard a guess as to what will happen then, but according to present indications it would seem likely that India will be accorded full Dominion status or guarantees of progressive changes which will bring about complete self-government within a definite period.

But even if the various political parties should co-operate sufficiently to administer the government of British India as the governments of Canada, Australia, and New Zealand, are administered, many other elements must be taken into account by those undertaking to rule India. If we attempt to visualize it, the social and political map of India is a veritable "Joseph's coat" with the threads of its many-colored fabric interwoven in inextricable confusion or forming patches that stand out isolated from all the others.

Approximately 73 per cent of India's population of 320,000,000 consists of farmers, large and small. They are distributed all over the Indian subcontinent—in the Native States as well as in British India. Education, even in the most advanced provinces of British India, has so far penetrated but little among them, for the educational policy of Great Britain has hitherto only tended to produce a small class of highly educated Indians qualified for professional life—hence the enormous number of Indian politicians and the scarcity of technicians in all branches. The Indians who have gone from the villages to the cities and who have obtained Western educations, have usually been swallowed up in professional or political life and lost touch with the villages. Among the rural classes, therefore, there is the greatest amount of illiteracy and ignorance, and their agricultural methods are marked by appalling economic waste.

The vast majority of the villagers cherish the old Hindu beliefs, which prevent their harming various animals considered as sacred, such as cows, whose manure may not even be used for fertilizer, and monkeys, who often destroy an entire crop. Caste distinctions, which tend to become less marked in the large cities, are still rigidly observed in the villages, and when we stop to think that there are roughly speaking 2,500 castes in India, we can realize what this may mean even in small communities where but few castes are represented.

Then there is the communal life in the villages, which in the main still exists as it has existed for many centuries. The village social organization and the village government are virtually autonomy within the smallest possible limits—almost the only constant factor in the development of India. In the villages is the nucleus, if it can ever be stimulated to further growth without losing its character, of an Indian nation. The village is essentially the same, whether in the Native States or in British India, and despite wide differences there is even common ground on which Hindus and Mohammedans of the rural masses may meet. Their interests are to a certain extent identical. Every Indian of the peasant class wants two things above all—good roads and low taxes.

That the Indian peasant is potentially a power to be reckoned with was shown a few years ago when Gandhi's doctrine of Non-Co-operation swept through rural India like wild-fire; its eventual failure was due to the fact that the peasants soon perceived that it could not give them what they wanted. However, Gandhi and Das taught a lesson, still further thrown into relief by the shrewd observations and comments of nearly a million of their fellows who served in the Indian forces during the war; namely, that government—not only the British Raj, but any government—can be successfully defied.

The strange new leaven of Bolshevism which has begun to work among them gives them an instrument with which to defy authority so similar to their age-old institutions that they might easily be taught to apply it under powerful stimulus. A Soviet India could perhaps achieve more surface uniformity than any other form of government possible outside the British Empire, but that would not mean independence—only a change of jurisdiction —Russian, instead of British.

The Moslems form a distinct unit, which is intensely democratic within its own borders, but despises the Hindu population. While there are only about seventy million Moslems, they make up in energy what they lack in numbers, and, as I have pointed out before, their activities are perhaps more identified with Pan-Asiatic than Indian National politics. They are concentrated largely in the Punjab.

Among the smaller groups are the Parsees, a small minority, less than 100,000 in all. As is well known, the Parsees are descendants of the Fire Worshippers or Zoroastrians, who were driven out of Persia after her sovereigns had been converted to the Moslem faith. They probably are more nearly related to Europeans than any other inhabitants of India, having to a large extent kept the Aryan strain which was intermixed with other racial elements in India and they are extraordinarily able business men and administrators. Intellectually they have much in common with the educated classes among the Hindus, but politically they are inclined on the whole to fraternize with no particular element.

The Sikhs, who have a religion and a political movement of their own, form a distinct group, as do the small numbers of Indian Buddhists; there are various other elements, each equally unassimilable socially and politically.

Added to all these, within the last decade the industrial workers of India, numbering about 10 per cent of the total population, have become articulate as a class. The war greatly accelerated the process of industrialization. Today the jute and cotton industries of India, largely in Indian hands, have reached enormous proportions. Competition between the British and Indian cotton mills has given rise to one of India's most serious grievances against England. In an effort to protect British cottons, which cannot be produced as cheaply as the Indian textiles made with home-grown cotton, the British government has at various times opposed a protective policy for India or imposed an excise duty on native cottons. Gandhi's boycott and advocacy of homespun *khaddur* were no panacea for the real or fancied wrongs of the Indian mill-owners of Bombay or the 25,000 workmen employed in their spinneries. Nor could a return to the simple life be possible for the workers in Indian industries, who are organized in labor unions similar to those in Western countries, not so efficiently perhaps, but with the same international affiliations, including contacts with the Red unions of the "Profintern," the right arm of the Communist International.

Then there are the Indian Christians, largely made up of the Untouchables or Pariahs, in whose behalf not even Gandhi, Das, and the other Hindu leaders had been able to break down the barriers of caste. In this respect Christianity has accomplished wonders, and to a certain extent the labor unions have achieved a like result.

The groups just enumerated, with many more just as typical, are quite as unassimilable as the various forms of government included in the Native States, the Crown Colonies, and the groups of provinces which make up the Empire of India. In view of all these facts it is next to impossible to picture India, within an appreciable time and under normal circumstances, as either united or closely federated, except under some outside pressure. Her isolated position, her peculiar culture, and her dominant religion, unique among the religious systems of the world, all would seem to militate against her combination with any other Asiatic group, even if she could achieve internal unity. And yet India is far too important to stand alone!

Morally as well as strategically and politically, India may be the determining factor in the future of the Asiatic continent. So far, however, there does not seem to be any pressure or influence sufficiently strong to unify the conflicting impulses among the Indian people.

If the breach between England and India is widened, India will almost inevitably fall under the domination of Russia and her Eurasian culture, unless, as some people think possible, she is absorbed in a Far Eastern Bloc under Japanese domination.

Chapter Ten

THE BULWARKS OF INDIA

BURMA

IN SPITE of the fact that Burma is under the Government of
India, it cannot be included within the orbit of Indian politics.
Strategically it is one of the buffer states that constitute the land
defenses of India; ethnically, politically, and geographically, it is
as different from the adjoining province of Bengal as chalk from
cheese, and it must be treated as a separate entity, included purely
for administrative convenience within the Indian Empire.

Burma is best known in the West through the genius of
Rudyard Kipling, who immortalized the stretches of the Irrawaddy River "from Rangoon to Mandalay." There are thousands
of persons who will never know the history of Burma but will
remember the name of Supi-yaw-lat, the ill-starred "Theebaw's
Queen."

King Theebaw was the last of the sovereigns who misruled
Burma for three hundred and fifty years, maintaining a precarious
independence but eternally menaced by the hill tribes of Assam
and the Tibetan frontiers on the north, and the warlike kings of
Siam whose domains adjoined theirs on the south. British interest in Burma, which is exceedingly rich in natural resources,
began in the eighteenth century and increased, as it became necessary for the East India Company to protect the province of Bengal
from the tribes along the Burman border.

Burma was partly conquered by the middle of the nineteenth
century, and when some thirty years later British Imperialism
began to dream of the Seven Seas, and among them of the Indian
Ocean as a sort of English Mediterranean, its absorption became
inevitable. Theebaw was conquered and deposed in 1885, and
Burma became a British province administered by the government
of India. Its political history, while less turbulent, has to a cer-

tain extent kept pace with that of the Indian provinces. It was
given a Legislative Assembly under the Government of India
Act of 1919, and is progressing rapidly towards local autonomy.
While there is a National party that dreams of independence and
makes common cause with the Indian Nationalists, the vast majority of Burmans care nothing for the Indians. Indeed, as far as
their indolent good-natured tolerance permits, they dislike their
neighbors the Bengalis, with whom they have nothing whatever in
common, neither race nor religion.

The Burmans belong as a whole to the great family of peoples
from which are derived the Chinese, the Tibetans, as well as the
people of Indo-China and Siam, who compose the bulk of the
population of their corner of Asia. Many of their social institutions, particularly their form of village-government, are similar
to the Chinese, and their women are not kept in "purdah" or seclusion as are the Indian women. Their religion is a form of
Buddhism. There is no possible excuse politically, except Imperial necessities, to justify their inclusion within the bounds of
the Indian Empire. If any important territorial regrouping takes
place in that part of Asia, they will unquestionably be attached to
an eastern group. But in the present scheme of things, as a glance
at the map will show, the great importance of Burma is to Great
Britain's commercial expansion, recently so seriously threatened
by the situation in China. Burma is the back door, so to speak,
to the coveted valley of the Yangtze-kiang. Meanwhile its riches
are a great source of wealth to England. The gold and ruby
mines, and the oil fields of Northern Burma, are an important
economic asset.

TIBET

Tibet, the buffer country between India and Chinese Turkestan,
occupies much the same relation towards the British Empire as
Mongolia towards Soviet Imperialism. Both Tibet and Mongolia
were formerly colonial possessions of the Chinese Empire; both
have been separated from it by the inexorable demands of Imperial security and penetration. Mongolia is an outpost of Siberia,
no less than Tibet is a frontier post of India. Between the two
lies Chinese Turkestan—still a No Man's Land, with China exer-

cising nominal control, Russia pulling the strings, and Great Britain cutting a strand or two whenever she gets the chance.

British control over Tibet differs from Russian control in Mongolia only in that it has not brought about any change in the outward form of government. The method which Britain has adopted has been to isolate the Tibetans as far as may be from all outside influences, and to preserve their ancient form of government. Tibet is the only theocracy left in Asia. From the latter part of the seventeenth century until the last years of the Manchu dynasty the Dalai Lama, its spiritual and temporal ruler, was a vassal of the Chinese Empire. Ties of race and religion—for the Tibetans are Mongols and their religion an offshoot of Buddhism —bound them to their powerful neighbor on the east.

A Chinese Resident at Lhasa, the capital of the Dalai Lama, maintained the somewhat loose connection with Peking, and Chinese Governors along the Tibetan Marches adjoining the province of Szechuan kept the central authority in evidence, though in the background.

China was responsible for Tibet's external relations and it was the failure of the Chinese to curb her aggressions on the Indian frontier that first led Great Britain to interfere in Tibetan affairs. Her protest led to a Sino-British Convention for establishing border security and certain trading privileges. Unfortunately, under the circumstances such an agreement was impossible of fulfilment. Chinese and Tibetans alike became suspicious of British commercial penetration, which was blazing trade-routes from India through Tibet into Western China. At the same time Russia, whose rapid expansion in Central Asia had already caused British statesmen many sleepless nights, began to cast a covetous eye on Tibet. The Dalai Lama was strongly pro-Russian and managed with Russian encouragement to successfully defy the British and prevent any intercourse between Tibet and India. At one time, in conformity with orders from the Dalai Lama, a wall was built across the road to Yatung, the trading post which had been opened to Indian merchants, and caravans were turned back by Tibetan guards.

In 1904, the British having failed to adjust these differences, took advantage of Russia's Far Eastern imbroglio with Japan to send a punitive expedition to Tibet under Colonel Younghusband. The Dalai Lama had fled to China, but Colonel Younghusband signed an agreement with the Tibetan parliament at Lhasa, the capital of Outer Tibet, where no Europeans with the exception of a few hardy explorers had ever set foot before. By this agreement, free trade was established between Tibet and India and the principle of the territorial integrity of the Dalai Lama's dominions was asserted. In all these negotiations China was represented, and she later separately ratified the agreement of Lhasa, which received still further sanction through the Anglo-Russian Convention of 1907. By the terms of this Convention Great Britain and Russia agreed to keep hands off, and both recognized the suzerainty of China in Tibet, though England's special interest in that country was conceded.

The adjustment of her relations towards Russia and Great Britain did not bring any internal stability in Tibet, but rather the reverse. There had always been a certain amount of friction between the Chinese and the Tibetans, particularly in the border districts, where the provincial governors were often tyrannical, corrupt, and exacting to the last degree. In Outer Tibet there was considerable rivalry between the Dalai Lama and his powerful vicar the Tashi Lama; as the revolutionary ferment in China began to grow, there was a corresponding agitation in Tibet against the arbitrary power of the Lama priesthood, who constituted a veritable hierarchy.

For the next ten years the country was torn with internal dissensions interlarded with rebellions against Chinese authority. In most of Tibet's disputes with the Chinese government Great Britain took a hand, insisting politely but firmly that China should keep her troops from the neighborhood of the Indian border, and when the Dalai Lama was forced to leave the country as the result of the defeat of his partisans, he found an asylum in British India. Another sudden change in the fortunes of war, however, brought him back into power in 1912, after two years' exile in India, and a year later Tibet proclaimed her independence of China.

This proclamation was received with somewhat mixed feelings at Peking. On the one hand the government had no mind to relinquish Tibet, which was officially classed as one of the five nations of China with its stripe in the flag of the Republic. On the other hand Peking's domestic affairs were too involved, and the problems of reconstruction in China were too pressing, to leave much time for the outlying dominions. A long-drawn-out series of conferences between China and Tibet, in which Great Britain also took a part, ended in an agreement between the representatives of the three Powers, dividing the country into two parts. The eastern section, to be known as Inner Tibet, was to be under direct Chinese control, and the western portion with Lhasa and Shigatse the holy city of the Tashi Lama, chief prelate of Lamaism, was to be autonomous as Outer Tibet. This agreement, which also provided for the resumption of trade relations between Tibet and Great Britain was never signed by China, however, because of a disagreement of Lhasa with Peking over the boundary question.

Up to the present time the relations of China and Tibet have not been satisfactorily adjusted, and a state of chaos has existed on both sides of the frontier. In 1919, the question was very nearly settled thanks to British mediation, but before an agreement could be signed the Chinese government and Chinese public opinion alike had become so inflamed by the unjust treatment of their country by her Allies at the Versailles Conference, particularly with regard to Shantung, that they were in no mood to consent to the alienation of another acre of Chinese territory.

Some four years later, it was reported that Great Britain had pressed for, and obtained from the Chinese government, acquiescence in what were known as the Twelve Demands with regard to Tibet.

Besides demanding joint participation with the Chinese in all mining development, Great Britain claimed exclusive rights to construct railway lines between India and Tibet, to establish a foreign postal service, and to engage in industrial enterprises. All previous treaty obligations between Great Britain and Lhasa were reaffirmed, the Chinese government was not to appoint or dismiss officials on its own responsibility, all loans contracted for administrative purposes were to be negotiated through British agencies, China was to secure the redemption of such loans, she was not to interfere with any actions of the British government in Tibet, and neither country was to send troops into the realm of the Dalai Lama without reason. But the most important clause of all was that no privileges or concessions in that country were to be granted to any other nation than Great Britain.

Naturally, subsequent developments rendered these agreements inoperative as far as China was concerned. Since then, the central government has been too deeply involved in foreign and domestic complications affecting its very existence, to devote much attention to its relations with Tibet. Great Britain has been the only Power acting as intermediary between all Tibet and the outside world, and her influence amounts to a virtual protectorate.

Strictly observing the letter of the agreements she has entered into with regard to the inviolability of Tibetan territory, Great Britain has made it virtually impossible for any foreigners, including those of British nationality, to penetrate the country. Stray travellers who from time to time reach Lhasa from India, are obliged to circumvent not only the Tibetan but the British authorities. The state of anarchy on the Chinese frontier is usually sufficient to keep out intruders from that quarter.

Nevertheless, the British authorities manage to keep their fingers on the political pulse of Tibet and to guide the often tortuous mazes of her politics. For modern ideas regarding society, politics, and religion have managed to reach the Roof of the World. The doctrine of self-determination was preached very glibly by the young Tibetan Nationalists who welcomed England's aid in securing the autonomy of their country. These same young men, who are now going to England to obtain a Western education, constitute a liberal party that is fighting against the influence of the reactionary priesthood.

Relations between Lhasa and the Government of India are conducted through a British Political Officer who is established at Gantok on the Indo-Tibetan border, and has the status of a diplomatic representative. He has an assistant at Gyangtze, where there is also a representative of the Dalai Lama. Recently a telegraph line was built to connect Gyangtze and Lhasa.

The new Tibetan army wears khaki uniforms of British make. It is well groomed, well disciplined, supplied with rifles made from British models in the arsenal at Lhasa, and its units are sent in succession to Gyangtze to be drilled by British officers. Lhasa has a telephone system, a mint where paper money is printed, an electric light and power plant, and a postal service connects the principal Tibetan cities with the outer world. A cabinet of ministers holding portfolios similar to those in Western countries, and a parliament known as the Tsong Du, assist the Dalai Lama in governing the country. The establishment of several secular schools has marked the beginning of a system of popular education; hitherto learning has been confined entirely to the priesthood and a few great families who sent their children to the monasteries (or perhaps in rare instances to China) to acquire a rudimentary education.

In spite of all these innovations Tibet remains an inaccessible country with the elusive charm of the unattainable to all but the fortunate handful who have penetrated its recesses. Physically it is a huge tableland, whose average altitude is over ten thousand feet above sea level, watered by a number of rivers, several of which, like the Irrawaddy, the Yangtze-kiang, and the Brahmaputra, become great inland waterways in their lower reaches.

Barley is the only cereal that can be successfully grown in Tibet; there is much pasturage for the huge flocks of cattle, yaks, and sheep, so wool and hides are the chief articles of export. Its mineral resources are as yet undeveloped though they are known to be very great. There are some gold-mines which up to the present time have been worked only by the most primitive placer methods; iron ore in large quantities is known to exist, and it is suspected that there may be oil in certain districts, though no deposits have been definitely located.

The Tibetans are a vigorous, turbulent people, numbering several millions; possibly half of them are nomadic and banded into tribal organizations, while the remainder live in village communities. Where tribal rule does not prevail, they are dependent either on the feudal nobility or the Lamas, who are opposed to all progress and own virtually all the land—a state of affairs that will probably produce an agrarian problem when the Tibetans have advanced a little further towards the creation of a modern state.

For the present, British influence seems supreme in Tibet, and its political evolution is apparently developing along the lines indicated by British advisers; but it is safe to assume that the Russian propaganda which was so active there in the days of the Czars, is no less on the alert now under the expert guidance of the Commissariat of Foreign Affairs, supplemented by the Communist International. There are strong ties of sympathy between the Tibetans and the Russians, who understand their mentality far better than the British can ever hope to do; these ties extend far back into the mist of history.

In Tibet as in Mongolia, where I myself found it to exist, there is a widespread popular belief in Salvation from the North. The people are convinced that some day a Messiah from the country lying northward will come to lead them, that he will establish a powerful government in Lhasa, convert all China to Lamaism and restore the Empire. Then a new era of peace and prosperity will dawn for both China and Tibet. Doubtless the Bolshevists have been quick to turn this idea to their advantage, and to put the true ring of Messianic faith into their preachment of the Gospel of Lenin.

The contest between Russia and England, but one phase of the clash of civilizations in Asia, is being waged on many battlefields. At present it is centred in China, but we may be sure that it is being carried on none the less along the approaches to India, of which Tibet is one; even were Great Britain eliminated, the Tibetans would still stand at the crossroads between China and Russia. Consequently, in spite of her isolation, in spite of the backward state of her culture and primitive development, Tibet is an important factor in the evolution of Asia.

THE MALAY STATES AND SINGAPORE

Sixteen hundred miles of ocean separate Calcutta from Singapore, and yet Singapore may be said to be almost inseparable from India. With the Malay States under British protection, it is the last link in the long chain of bulwarks defending India to the East, just as the Sinai peninsula and the Hedjaz, dominating the Suez Canal, may be said to be the first link on the west. Singapore, in unfriendly hands, would constitute a constant menace to

India by affording an admirable base for a blockade that would cut her off from the supply of imported rice which is the mainstay of the Indian people, since India does not raise enough to feed herself. Singapore is also important as a stage in the line of communications between Great Britain and her Pacific Dominions; it is the point where the maritime routes between Europe and the Far East converge, and in the eyes of many British at home and in the Dominions, it is a most satisfactory substitute for the Anglo-Japanese Alliance.

For all these reasons, Singapore and its hinterland, the long tonguelike strip of territory known as the Federated Malay States, must be included in any survey of the present-day Asia, though they play merely a passive part in the events on the mainland.

The Malay peninsula, which is joined to Asia only on the north where it touches the little kingdom of Siam, belongs, as its name implies, rather to Malaysia than to Asia. Only the Malacca Straits separate it from Sumatra. It has a population of nearly 3,500,000, including nearly 750,000 Chinese colonists. The natives, known as Malays, are a Mohammedan people closely related to the insular Malaysians. They are lazy, happy-go-lucky, totally without capacity for government or organization, but brave, loyal, and good fighters. In the old days they lived gloriously, if insecurely, by piracy, which fact induced the early traders in the Pacific to pay particular attention to securing control of the Malacca Straits.

The tip of the Malay peninsula was held first by the Portuguese, then by the Dutch, and finally by the British. The last, thanks to the foresight of Sir Stamford Raffles, one of England's Empire builders in the Far East, acquired the site of Singapore by treaty in 1819, from a local potentate, the Sultan of Johore. Five years later Great Britain obtained from Holland the group of colonies comprising Malacca, known as the Straits Settlements, surrendering in return her holdings on the island of Sumatra.

At that time Singapore was most valuable as a base from which to operate against the Malay pirates whose activities imperilled Great Britain's China trade, but it was not long before its importance in the whole scheme of Imperial defense was recognized. With a view to obtaining complete security, Great Britain began in the last quarter of the nineteenth century a gradual process of pacification and absorption, on the Peninsula, which resulted within twenty years in the creation of the Federated Malay States. Each of these States has retained its local Sultan, who acknowledges allegiance to the Governor-General of the Straits Settlements. He is assisted in governing his domains by a Resident-General and a Chief Secretary appointed by the Governor-General. Every state has a local council which may pass purely local legislation, and its own budget, but the administrations of Posts and Telegraphs, Agriculture, Forestry, and the Customs, are all federal.

Besides the Federated States there are still a number of native principalities under British protection, each with its independent form of local government. However, in spite of the slightly different status of the various portions of the peninsula, it is all under British control. From an administrative point of view the English have accomplished wonders, bringing about peace between the native States which had preyed on one another continually for centuries, and creating local order out of chaos, improving sanitary conditions and means of communication. Besides nearly a thousand miles of railways and as many miles of roads, they have installed complete telegraph and postal systems.

In addition British enterprise has developed two enormously valuable industries on the peninsula—the production of rubber, from Brazilian cuttings sent by Queen Victoria from Kew Gardens in 1876, and tin from the mines in the interior, which had scarcely been touched until they were opened by British capital.

Singapore since its foundation has grown to be one of the great ports of the world. An idea of its size can be gained from the fact that its docks can accommodate 200,000 tons of shipping, and it has facilities for coaling at the rate of 5,000 tons a day or for supplying the equivalent in oil fuel.

These data give some idea of its importance to world commerce, but it is not in this connection that we usually think of Singapore, nor is it in this connection that its future is most vital to Asia. It is, with Gibraltar, the Dardanelles, Suez, and Panama, one of the strategic keys to world dominion. The nation that holds

Singapore has a base for operations both in the Indian Ocean and in the Pacific.

It was for this reason that Great Britain in 1923 decided to establish a naval base at Singapore second to none in the world, in contravention, if not in letter at least in spirit, of the agreements of the Washington Conference. A discussion of the Washington Conference and its results naturally falls under a general survey of the relations of Japan and China with other Powers having interests in the Pacific. But it may be well to recall, in connection with Singapore, that the Conference was summoned by President Harding in 1921 to settle Pacific problems that had come up since the Great War, and that one of its objects was the exchange of guarantees among the Powers which would result in general security without the necessity for great naval armaments.

In pursuance of this object Great Britain, Japan, and the United States agreed at Washington not to create any further fortified bases within certain areas in the Pacific. The British port of Hongkong, called the Gibraltar of the Far East, was included within this area, and at the time it was not contemplated by the other participating Powers that Great Britain would establish a naval base outside the restricted zone just as effective, if not more so, than any within. Nevertheless, she will have secured such a base when the defenses of Singapore begun in 1926 are completed after being temporarily shelved during the life-time of the Labor Cabinet in England.

The decision to fortify Singapore is a testimony to the inadequacy of the "conference" plan of dealing with international questions of first magnitude. It is obvious that the only Power that might constitute a serious menace to Great Britain's hold on Singapore by direct action is Japan. After the Anglo-Japanese Treaty had lapsed in 1921, and was not renewed for reasons which we shall discuss later, the parleys of the Pacific Powers at Washington could not forestall the subsequent passage by the British Parliament of its bill for the fortification of Singapore, nor Japan's overtures to Russia and her propaganda in China.

It is interesting to recall the reasons advanced in the British press in favor of the bill at the time when it was being debated in Parliament. They may be summarized as follows: Japan is overpeopled and its population is rapidly increasing; in the Dutch Indies, Borneo, and the British islands of Malaysia, as well as Australia, there are thousands of square miles available for colonization; England is directly obliged to defend her colonies against possible Japanese penetration; she is morally bound by the unwritten law of the Commonwealth to protect Australia, and equally bound to intervene in case of trouble between the Dutch and the Japanese in the East Indies, because of the proximity of the Dutch islands to her own possessions. Unless she holds Singapore she cannot fulfil these obligations, and the Indian masses cannot be sure of their supply of rice from Indo-China and Siam!

An equally convincing array of arguments might be marshalled to prove that Japan, as the leading Asiatic Power in the Pacific, should have control of such an important approach to her Island Empire, but possible aggression by the Japanese for some such end is so highly improbable that it is not worth while to enumerate them.

Meanwhile there are other influences far more insidious undermining British influence on the Malay peninsula. One is Bolshevism, which has obtained a great hold among the peoples of the Dutch East Indies and threatens to infect the Malay States. A successful Communist revolution in Sumatra would compel Great Britain to take drastic steps to protect her interests in Malaysia, which might result in many international complications. The other influence is that of China.

Notwithstanding her internal chaos, China presents a united front in the field of commercial penetration abroad. The Chinese immigration question is one of the most serious administrative problems not only in the Malay peninsula, but in Indo-China as well, as we shall presently see. In Singapore the Chinese form two-thirds of the population of approximately half a million inhabitants. They control nearly all the lighterage and commission business of the port. The bulk of the workers in the tin mines of the Federated States are Chinese; Chinese planters own much of the most valuable land; a large portion of the local banking business is done by Chinese, and thus the Yellow flood pushes on gently but inexorably. When the Chinese achieve some degree of internal stability they will find ready to their hand an instrument more dangerous to Western supremacy than armed force!

Chapter Eleven

THE MONGOL INDIES

GEOGRAPHICALLY as well as ethnically it is difficult to disassociate Indo-China and Siam. Together they form a peninsula hanging like a pendant from the southeastern end of Asia, with the Malay States added like a long pear-shaped drop. The Mekong, a large river flowing between them, serves as a common outlet, and mountain ranges tapering down from Tibet and Western China divide them into longitudinal strips.

The inhabitants of the Indo-Chinese peninsula are all of much the same original racial stock, principally Chinese, or Mongol, mixed with the aboriginal strain of the peoples known as the Dravidians, who are supposed to have been the first inhabitants of India and to have been gradually pushed out of Asia by the great southward Aryan and Mongol migrations. They are predominantly Buddhist in religion, and profoundly influenced by Chinese civilization, which is the basis of their culture. In the past they were generally feudal dependencies of China, though at times they established local dynasties sufficiently powerful to assert their independence, for in spite of their common origin they developed in the course of centuries strong national characteristics which differentiated them from the Chinese. Politically, however, they never developed any sense of solidarity. The three principal kingdoms were those of Annam, Cambodia, and Siam.

SIAM

Siam, which occupies a little more than half of the peninsula, is the only country of the Indo-Chinese group which has kept its independence down to the present day. That it has done so is due partly to the energy and enterprise of the Siamese, who constitute one of the most remarkable of the smaller peoples of Asia, and partly to the position of their country. For Siam is a shock-absorber, neutral ground, between Burma, India's outer line of defense toward the east and French Indo-China.

In the middle of the last century, when the French first established a territorial foothold in Cochin-China, the little kingdom of Cambodia, a feudatory of Siam, separated them from the Siamese. The Cambodians, never very powerful, maintained a perpetual feud with the Siamese in which they usually got the worst of it. Therefore it was quite natural that they should do what many other peoples in their position had done before them—seek the protection of the European Power established near by. They appealed to the French, who, nothing loath, sent a mission to Cambodia which promptly took the country under French protection. The next step by the French was to acquire the mountain territory of Laos, long a bone of contention between Siam and the kingdom of Annam, which had also become a French protectorate. The Siamese were overawed by a French naval demonstration before their capital of Bangkok, and forced to sign a treaty in 1893, renouncing all claims to Laos.

The piecemeal absorption of Siam might have continued indefinitely but for the fact that the French were edging uncomfortably near Burma. Siam became a subject of "conversations" between the French and British governments which led to a series of agreements during the period from 1896 to 1904, by which the independence and territorial integrity of Siam were guaranteed. Notwithstanding the fact that these agreements divided the country into spheres of commercial influence, somewhat as the Russo-British agreement of 1907 had effected the commercial partition of Persia, the Siamese profited by them enormously.

Very wisely they perceived, what the Japanese had found out before them, that it was useless to combat Western Imperialism without using the technical weapons of the West, and they proceeded to Europeanize their methods of administration so effectively that they were able to retain control of their own natural resources. By 1909, they had obtained from Great Britain a renunciation of her jurisdiction in Siam and a partial surrender of her extraterritorial rights, in return for waiving their claims to sovereignty over the Malay States adjoining Siamese territory to the south, which passed under British protection.

In 1917, Siam followed the lead of China in declaring war on Germany and sent a small expeditionary force to France. After the war, the various European Powers concluded treaties with Siam relinquishing extraterritorial rights, for there was no longer any reason to maintain them. The new legal code of Siam, which will be completed in 1928, will afford adequate protection to all foreigners.

Like many well-administered nations these days, Siam is governed under a benevolent despotism. The reforms which have completely modernized the country were due to the vision and foresight of the late king, known as Rama VI, who was educated in England. The creation of a system of popular education, the establishment of a sanitary service providing for quarantine, vaccination, and other safeguards to public health, the installation of a pure water supply in Bangkok, the modernization of law courts and all forms of legal procedure, are some of the many radical changes introduced by King Rama, who died in 1925. His son has adhered to the same policy.

Siam has its own university at Shulalongkorn, founded in 1917, where the Rockefeller Foundation has established laboratories for studying the hookworm disease, which is almost as great a curse to Indo-China as malaria is to Western Asia. The Siamese army, with a war-time strength of 400,000, recruited by compulsory military service, is one of the most up-to-date in the world. Shortly after the war it possessed a most efficient aviation service, which made a particular impression on the late Lord Northcliffe when he was on his tour around the world.

"Siam has," he remarked, "5 aerodromes, 25 landing fields. At Don Muang are 115 planes and a personnel of 650 men." Other equally keen European observers have commented on the fact that the Siamese possess what is known as "flying sense"—a quality lacking in most Orientals. The Siamese also have an Air Postal Service! Communications throughout the country are secured by good roads and a network of railways.

Siam is one of the great rice-producing countries and its cultivable area is being constantly added to by irrigation. In 1919, the Siamese went through the same period of post-war depression as the rest of the world, due to the rise in silver, which was the standard for her monetary system, but of recent years she has become prosperous.

The transformation effected by the Siamese has many points of resemblance to the evolution which took place a quarter of a century earlier in Japan. Without losing their ancient culture or abandoning their religious customs or traditions, they have been able to fit their country into a modern frame. Consequently it is not surprising to find that Japan possesses great influence in Siam. Japanese instructors are employed in the army, Japanese advisers are attached to many departments of the government, and Japan occupies the position of the most favored nation in a commercial treaty which she has recently concluded with the Siamese.

INDO-CHINA

The Annamite Kingdom which forms the backbone of the region now known as Indo-China under a French protectorate, was in early times the most powerful on the peninsula. Its most serious rivals were Siam and Cambodia, both of which possessed a highly individualized form of art and culture. These three Powers were almost continually at war among themselves or with the other peoples of Indo-China, comprising the Tonkinese, the inhabitants of Cochin-China, Laos, and the peoples of the interior, among whom were the Mois, supposed to be descendants of the peninsular aborigines.

During the early centuries of colonial expansion Indo-China escaped the notice of the European empire-builders who lingered on "India's coral strand" or passed eagerly on to tap the fabled wealth of Cathay and to capture the China trade. The French, who had been forced to renounce their pretensions to India during the eighteenth century and had been preoccupied with European affairs during the stormy years of the Revolution and the First Empire, began to perceive the advantages of Indo-China as a commercial base from which to establish further relations in the Far East.

By the middle of the last century they had already established trading posts and Catholic mission stations in Cochin-China, and in 1858, using the ill-treatment of French missionaries as a pretext for intervention, the French government sent a punitive expedition against the Kingdom of Annam. Within three years they were masters of the Annamite port of Saigon in Cochin-China and the surrounding territory. For the next decade French penetration continued steadily; the Annamites, who opposed every forward step made by the French forces, carried on a losing fight until in 1874 they were forced to sign a treaty by which they surrendered control of Cochin-China.

Meanwhile French traders were penetrating the northern province of Tonkin, but their policy during these years was vacillating. As in the eighteenth century they were handicapped by troubles in Europe. The Franco-Prussian War, the disturbances consequent upon France's defeat involving the fall of Napoleon III, the interlude of the Commune and the establishment of the Republic, made it impossible for France to pursue any consistent colonial policy. French influence was pushed by a series of pioneer enterprises part religious, part commercial, led by intrepid priests, explorers, and officers, acting as a rule on their own initiative with little backing financial or military from France.

No matter what we may think of their methods, the fight against overwhelming odds by this handful of Frenchmen who saw the advantage to their country of obtaining a foothold in the Far East is one of the most romantic episodes of the imperialistic era. But it had no Rudyard Kipling to glorify it, and it was not until the beginning of this century that the French really began to appreciate the possibilities of their conquest.

Meanwhile they proceeded, now half-heartedly, now with a sudden burst of energy, to acquire the better part of Indo-China. Attacks on French merchants and missionaries in Tonkin by pirates, known as the Black Flags, led to a long series of incidents culminating in the landing of an expeditionary force in 1884, at Hué the Annamite capital, to force the government to consent to give the French a free hand in dealing with the Tonkinese. The treaty concluded at that time made Annam a French protectorate with a French Resident-General, and turned the administration of Tonkin over to France. Tonkin was not entirely subdued for seven years, but meanwhile the French had secured recognition of their rights there from the Chinese government, which still retained a shadowy claim to sovereignty in that province.

Twenty years before, they had taken over the protectorate for the little kingdom of Cambodia ostensibly to defend it against Siam. But there had been no unified plan for the administration of all these territories and the country was still far from pacified, on account of the continued resistance of the inhabitants of Laos, the high plateau country interspersed with mountain valleys which separates Indo-China from Siam. The agreement with Siam in regard to the frontier, in 1893, established the frontiers between Siam and Laos, thereby furthering the task of pacifying the country. The protectorate of Laos, established in 1899, completed the division of the country for administrative purposes.

The real organization of Indo-China under an orderly colonial administration was begun by M. de Lanessan, who became Governor-General in 1891. He laid the foundations for the prosperity of the country by increasing its revenues through judicious taxation, and by instituting many public improvements such as roads, railways, wharves and docks in the seaport towns, and by taking measures to improve public health and curb epidemics.

He also centralized the Governor-General's administration, by improving the organization of the Superior Council, and gave the native rulers of the Protectorates a definite status more consistent with their self-respect than the old haphazard system under which their prerogatives had not been defined, and which left them at the mercy of the Residents in their respective states. Soon the administration of Indo-China, which had first been under the Admiralty and then under the Ministry of Commerce, was placed under the Colonial Office.

By this time France's expansion had brought her near England's preserves in Burma, and only Siam stood between her and the Bay of Bengal as well as the feeble Malay States that gave access to Singapore and the Malacca Straits. It was the advisability of maintaining a buffer between French and British interests that led the two governments to enter into a pact to guarantee the independence of Siam in 1896, followed by a second agreement eight years later, which still further defined the respective positions of France and England.

Meanwhile France's administration in Indo-China was further elaborated to include native officials. Cochin-China, which is a French colony, has native representatives on its Colonial Council and sends a representative to the Chamber of Deputies in France. Annam and Cambodia, still kingdoms under a French protectorate, have their own local councils and local governing bodies, all subject to French officials. Tonkin is governed by a French Resident assisted by a Council of fifteen with two native Nobles, and Laos is locally administered under the native Mandarins, supervised by French inspectors, who report to a Resident-Superior.

But everywhere, whenever possible in Indo-China, there are native officials. Local forms of native governmental procedure have been preserved throughout in all purely local affairs, and on these is superimposed an elaborate system of federal administration essentially French.

The result has been on the one hand to check national solidarity by perpetuating the local institutions of the different states, and on the other to create a common ground on which all the various elements meet.

Consequently there has grown up a strong movement for the independence of Indo-China, which was stimulated by the pronouncement of the doctrine of self-determination by President Wilson, and fanned to fever-heat by Communist agitation. In Indo-China as in other Eastern countries the spread of Western education has vastly accelerated the growth of nationalism based on race-prejudice, which was a new conception of human relationships to the Oriental. It is not as strong in Indo-China as in other parts of Asia, for the French do not draw the color-bar as rigidly as the Anglo-Saxons—nevertheless it is there, and it can be used to advantage with the masses by skilful agitators.

Indo-China has not escaped the all-pervading propaganda of the Communist International, and the Nationalists, whatever their private concepts of government, are only too glad to make use of Russia. In 1925, when the new Governor-General M. Varenne, a Socialist, arrived in Indo-China, he stirred up a hornets' nest by intimating in public meetings that the mission of the French was to prepare the peninsula for independence—or at least so his words were interpreted by his hearers. A prompt repudiation of any such aim by the French government brought about riots, demonstrations, a students' strike and other disturbances, particularly in Annam. There were many arrests and a number of Nationalists were imprisoned or deported. During one of the strikes an agitator let fall a remark which illustrates the attitude of the Annamite Nationalists: "If the government can at will expel one of our brothers from the Indo-Chinese Union," he declaimed, "where will he go? *I* say to Moscow!"

In spite of these disturbances the material prosperity of Indo-China has steadily increased. The extension of the school system, the establishment of native universities and the policy of placing the administration as far as possible in the hands of natives, is producing a relatively large politically educated class. Modern improvements have transformed all but the most remote parts of the country without destroying the native atmosphere. In 1925, the commerce of Indo-China was valued at 4,236,000,000 francs and its exports exceeded its imports by 676,000,000.

Unfortunately the natives of Indo-China are not the ones who have profited most by this state of affairs. Aside from the commercial interests of the French firms, which are considerable, practically the whole trade of the peninsula is in Chinese hands! There are virtually no Annamite merchants—between the native producer and the foreign buyer there is always the Chinese middleman. The entire rice-crop of Indo-China, the second largest in the world, as well as the output of pepper and the teakwood industry, are monopolized by Chinese merchants. The city of Cholon with approximately 200,000 inhabitants is seven-eighths Chinese. In Tonkin, which adjoins the Chinese province of Yunnan, the natives have become almost completely denationalized from contact with the Chinese genius for assimilation, and all through rural Indo-China, the shrewd Celestials have a powerful influence over the peasants from the fact that they are the money-lenders and bankers.

Japanese propaganda is no less widespread throughout the Indo-Chinese peninsula than the commercial penetration of China or the subversive propaganda of Bolshevism, and it is no less dangerous, though a much more subtle menace than either, to European influence. The famous Kodama plan for Japan's future expansion which became known not long after the Russo-Japanese War, contemplated the inclusion of the Dutch Indies, British Borneo, the Philippine Islands, and the whole of the Indo-Chinese peninsula, Singapore and the Straits Settlements, within the Japanese sphere. At the time it undoubtedly helped to reconcile the Annamite to the French protectorate, for dislike and considerable fear of Japan were widespread among the Indo-Chinese, who had the fate of Korea before their eyes.

But the complexion of Asiatic nationalism was completely changed during the years immediately preceding and following the Great War. The tendency towards the formation of blocs united by bonds of race or religion is the outcome of the racial challenge thrown down by the West. This tendency in the Far East is crystallizing into the conception of a Yellow Bloc under the political leadership of Japan. It has made itself felt in a very different attitude throughout Indo-China, typified by the rapprochement between Japan and Siam, the only free agent among the countries of the peninsula. We shall soon have occasion to trace its progress among the other Yellow peoples.

Even among those who would not admit Japan's qualifications for leadership, there is the idea of a Far Eastern Federation which some of its proponents would extend as far as India, and within the last few years this idea has made great headway. It only needs a leader to transform it from a speculation into a widespread movement. As a Hindu writer has expressed it: "We Orientals form a vast fan with four sticks—Japan, China, Indo-China, and India. When an Oriental arises, the man we all desire, sufficiently powerful to seize the fan and wave it with an imperious hand, let the West beware."

Chapter Twelve

RUSSIA'S RETURN TO ASIA

OF ALL the changes that have taken place in the world since 1914, there is none so momentous or fraught with such possibilities for the future as those brought about by Russia's return to Asia. Reverting to the day of the great Mongol conquests and stirred by the call of her Tartar blood, Russia has turned her back to Europe and her face towards the East. The immediate cause of this reversion which has completely altered the complexion of Russian-Asiatic problems was the Revolution, but it was by no means the only cause.

As we have seen, Russia had taken far deeper root in Asia than any other European Power, long before the Great War. She had colonized and settled the entire northern half of the continent and had developed an aggressive policy in China, due to her imperative need for ice-free ports as outlets for the trade and commerce of the Empire. She had penetrated almost to the gates of India, obeying her race-instinct to push south.

Her efforts at westward expansion had always been more or less artificial. Fundamentally she had much more in common with the peoples of the East, for unlike the Western countries over which the Mongol-Tartar invasions broke and receded, Russia was largely settled by the invaders, who became assimilated with the original Slav population. Indeed, until the days of Peter the Great, "Muscovy" was more an Asiatic than a European country. In the words of the old Russian song it was Peter who "cut through the window" to Europe; and even Peter in his last will and testament enjoined on his people the conquest of India. The efforts which won Russia an outlet on the Baltic were exerted for over three centuries. Her eventual acquisition of Poland was small compensation for all the wars, intrigues, plots, and European entanglements, through which she gained it. Her influence in the Balkans was exerted at the cost of many wars, largely with a view to the ultimate possession of Constantinople, Asia Minor, Arabia, and the Gulf route to India. Her expansion in Europe has resulted only in her dominion over unassimilable and antagonistic elements such as the Poles, the Finns, and the other Baltic peoples, whose territories contained few natural riches compared with those of her Asiatic dependencies. Beyond them expansion was securely blocked by the powerful states of Western Europe.

It was only natural that the doctrines of self-determination enunciated by President Wilson during the World War should have spread rapidly among the subject-peoples living under Russian rule in Europe. The separatist movements in all the border countries which had at first been encouraged by the Germans while Russia was still one of the Allies, were supported more or less by all the European Powers after the Revolution, in an effort to stem the spread of Bolshevism further west.

The Soviet Republic found itself shut in by an iron ring of enemies. Finland, with the Baltic republics of Esthonia and Latvia, closed all access to the Baltic Sea; Lithuania and Poland shut her off from Central Europe; the fertile Black Earth belt comprising the Ukraine and the Black Sea region was still held by monarchists and the region east of the Volga was in the hands of almost as many governments as it possessed provinces. A way out had to be found if the new Russia was to live.

Urged by an instinct of self-preservation, the Bolsheviks first of all had transferred their capital from Petrograd to Moscow. It was symbolical of their future course that they abandoned the European capital of Peter the Great for the seat of the government of Ivan the Terrible, who had paved the way for Russia's Asiatic Empire.

Soon their instinctive move had transformed itself into a definite policy. Siberia and Southern Russia were far more important to them than the lost western provinces. As long as they were in the hands of counter-revolutionaries there could be no stable government in Russia. Moreover, without Siberia, the Ukraine, the Don Basin, and the Caucasus, Russia was deprived of her main sources of raw materials—wheat, sugar, hides, coal, iron, and petroleum. Consequently the Soviet government assumed purely defensive tactics on its western frontiers while it devoted all its energies to reuniting and consolidating Southern Russia and the Siberian provinces.

In the first months of the year 1919, while the Allies were wrangling over the peace terms in Versailles, the Bolsheviks were beginning to put their own house in order. They had repulsed an attempt to overthrow their government directed from the Baltic provinces and largely financed by Western Powers; they defeated the Monarchist forces still holding out in Southeastern Russia, and obtained possession of the Donetz coal mines; they were beginning a successful campaign against the counter-revolutionary armies of General Denikin in the Ukraine. By midsummer they had stemmed the advance of Admiral Kolchak's forces from Siberia, which at one time had penetrated beyond the Volga. The next year, 1920, saw liquidation of the civil war in Russia by the defeat of General Wrangel's forces in the Crimea, the conclusion of treaties with the Soviet government's Baltic neighbors, and a war with Poland which marked the only apparent deviation from the policy of the Bolshevist leaders to refrain from military aggression in Western Europe.

Actually the war with Poland would seem to have been provoked at the instigation of France and Great Britain in a last attempt at intervention in Russia. In a military sense it was inconclusive, for while the Red army under the famous Soviet General Tukachevsky advanced almost to the gates of Warsaw, it had outdistanced its bases and weakened its lines of communication, counting on Communist propaganda to bring about a Soviet revolution in Poland. The failure of the Red agents in Poland, together with the pressure exerted by the labor elements in France and Great Britain, who demanded "hands off" in Russia as far as their governments were concerned, made both Moscow and Warsaw ready to call the war a draw and to conclude a mutually satisfactory peace.

Security having been established along her western frontiers, Russia could safely turn her entire attention to Asia, where she had already made considerable progress. We shall shortly trace this progress from the beginning, but in order to understand the extraordinary growth of Russia's Eurasian Empire we must go back to the early days of the Soviet Republic. One of the first acts of the Soviet government was to issue a manifesto, a sort of proletarian Bill of Rights recognizing the doctrine of self-determination, whose provisions were incorporated in the first constitution of the Russian Socialist Soviet Republic of July, 1918.

The Communist A B C, which has been translated into practically every language in the world, contains the following statements as part of its programme:

"The right of nations to self-determination including the right to complete separation . . . the liberation of colonies and the support of all colonial movements against imperialism. . . . The union of Soviet republics shall be effected first through federation." Besides these points the programme of the Communist International stresses equality of rights for all peoples, and the abolition of all exclusive legislation against any people or nation.

The Soviet leaders were not slow to see the advantages of this programme in Russia and they began to do methodically and thoroughly what the Czarist government had done to a limited extent in the past—to recognize the native languages and the native elements included within the boundaries of the Empire.

From the beginning a Commissariat of Nationalities was one of the sixteen departments that made up the Soviet administration. At first it did not include many national elements. There was a Jewish section, a Polish section, representing the Polish population of Russia's western provinces, a White Russian section and a Ukrainian section, to safeguard the interests of the Slavic peoples of Minsk and of the Ukraine, who spoke kindred but different languages, possessed similar but slightly different cultures from that of the Great Russians. The German colonies near Saratov, which had existed as separate entities since the days of Catherine the Great, had their representatives in the Commissariat of Nationalities as did the Tartars and other Moslem communities on the Volga. Each group was permitted to have its own schools, its own newspapers and was promised some form of local autonomy.

The Revolution had brought on the one hand a disaggregation of all these and many other elements that contributed to make up the old Russian Empire, and on the other hand it was drawing them together in a new bond of mutual sympathy.

The enunciation of the Soviet programme with regard to nationalities came just at the psychological moment to the people of Asia, who began to lose faith in the Wilsonian ideals soon after the Armistice and whose disillusionment was completed with the signing of the Treaty of Sèvres.

It seemed to them, as Chicherin, Russia's Commissar for Foreign Affairs, remarked to me in the summer of 1920, that "Soviet Russia had taken up the doctrine of self-determination where President Wilson laid it down."

Certainly anyone who was in Moscow at that time would have been forced to believe that the subject peoples of the world were of that opinion. Moscow was the most cosmopolitan city on the globe, despite its physical isolation from Europe. The "International of the Malcontents" was centred in the Kremlin, and it was largely composed of Asiatics.

An Afghan delegation was discussing the preliminaries of the treaty concluded a year later which was to bring Great Britain to terms. Djemal Pasha was preparing the way for an alliance between Soviet Russia and Kemalist Turkey. Persian Nationalist leaders were soliciting Russia's help in ousting the British from North Persia. Indian Moslem leaders like the famous Barakatulla, on whose head the British had put a price, and Roy the Hindu Nationalist, were begging Russian aid to bring about a revolution in India. Chinese and Korean revolutionaries in Moscow forgot their mutual antagonism in a common hatred of foreign capitalist imperialism.

Whether they were Communist or not did not matter at that time. Nationalism was fostered and encouraged by the genius of Stalin (who had organized the Commissariat of Nationalities), the skilful statesmanship of Chicherin, and the subtle manœuvres of Vosnesyensky, the director of the Eastern Section of the Soviet Foreign Office.

The offensive of ideas conducted by these men was of prime assistance in the military campaigns by which the boundaries of Soviet Russia were gradually extended until at the present time her Asiatic possessions embrace a greater area than that included in the former Russian Empire. In Europe she has, it is true, lost much territory, but in Asia the only portion of her original dominions unredeemed is the district of Kars in Trans-Caucasia which was ceded to Turkey, and it has been more than compensated in gains elsewhere.

Before the new Red Republic began to feel reasonably secure near home, even before the civil war and attempts at counter-revolution had been stamped out in European Russia, circumstances compelled her to take the offensive in Asia. The energies of the Soviet leaders were diverted into three different channels —Trans-Caucasia, Siberia, and Central Asia—on whose pacification and reconstruction the existence of Soviet Russia depended.

The peoples of Trans-Caucasia were of many nationalities, none of them Slavic, most of them Moslem; all had kept their national characteristics, held to the Empire by the racial democracy of the Russian colonial policy, which was always a source of strength as well as weakness. Naturally, when the Revolution took place they were fired as were all the little peoples of the world, with the idea of self-determination, and they at once declared their independence, forming the three democratic republics of Georgia, Azerbaijan and Armenia.

At the same time innumerable small communities throughout Southern Russia, the Crimea and the Caucasus, including those of the Don and the Kuban Cossacks, all of whom had enjoyed a certain amount of local autonomy under the Imperial government, set up independent governments of their own. One by one they were coerced, coaxed, or conquered until they were incorporated as autonomous districts or republics into the Soviet system, but the Trans-Caucasian republics for some time maintained a separate although precarious existence.

Georgia, with its capital Tiflis and its port Batum on the Black Sea, was the largest and best organized of the three republics. Its people were largely Christian, strongly imbued with Russian culture, and like all mountaineers enterprising, brave, and with a passionate love of personal liberty.

Azerbaijan was economically the complement of Georgia. Occupying the eastern portion of Trans-Caucasia, which forms a bridge to Asia, separating the Caspian from the Black Sea, it contained the enormously rich oil deposits from which Russia drew most of her supply of petroleum and in which foreign interests had a share as well. A pipe line between Baku, the capital of Azerbaijan, and Batum in Georgia carried the oil to the Black Sea. Its people were principally of Tartar origin and it had been at various times, before coming under the dominion of Russia, part of the Persian and Ottoman empires.

The Armenian Republic had a checkered career from the very beginning of its short existence. As originally constituted it comprised the old district known as Russian Armenia, but the Armenian nationalist leaders who appeared before the Peace Conference in its behalf, claimed as part of their patrimony Turkish and Persian Armenia as well. They obtained in April, 1920, though on paper only, the better portion of Turkish Armenia and recognition by the Allies, together with the promise that they would be made wards of the League of Nations under a Mandate administered by one of the Allied Powers. The Supreme Allied Council had recognized the independence of Georgia and Azerbaijan.

But beyond recognition, the Allies did virtually nothing for the struggling Trans-Caucasian republics. After having assumed the responsibility for the existence of Armenia, not one of the Allied Powers was willing to take on an Armenian Mandate. The British, who had sent a small expeditionary force to Baku at the request of the Azerbaijan government, withdrew it at the close of 1919. Georgia's pleas for loans and other assistance went unheeded, and Trans-Caucasia, disillusioned, bitter, forsaken by the Allied Powers that had given her lip service only, became an easy prey to Soviet propaganda. The three infant republics were not yet ready to walk alone, and they had been abandoned by the Powers who had sponsored their christening.

Differences between France and England, which had grown acute by the beginning of 1920, were largely to blame for the abandonment of Trans-Caucasia, and the indifference or preoccupation of the other Allied Powers in their own affairs was also partly responsible. The year 1920 was a period of readjustment, demoralization, and social unrest in all the countries which had taken part in the Great War. The germ of Bolshevism had caught in many places, and the infection had to be rigorously

stamped out. Most of the Powers believed that if left alone it
would run its course in Russia. Otherwise it is hardly possible
to think that Great Britain, which had vital interests in that part
of Asia, would have deliberately backed the Greeks against
the Turks, merely in order to checkmate French designs in the
Near East, or would have abandoned Trans-Caucasia, which was
a most valuable buffer against Soviet penetration to Persia.

It is not unlikely that France's intrigues to attract Great Britain
elsewhere were stimulated by the fear that she might get control
of the Baku oil wells. However that may be, Allied policy, having
encouraged the national aspirations of the little peoples of Trans-
Caucasia, abandoned them to their fate.

Azerbaijan, where there had always been a strong current of
pro-Soviet feeling, was the first to succumb to a Bolshevist coup
d'état. Baku was taken almost without resistance by Soviet
forces who had been called in by the Communist leaders, and a
Red Terror was instituted which effectually wiped out the opposition. The acquisition of Azerbaijan, which cost very little in men
or money, was of immense advantage to the Soviet government,
which was itself desperately in need of oil from Baku. Shortly
before Baku was taken the supply of petroleum in Russia had
dwindled to almost nothing, and in Moscow even the official
automobiles were frequently run and incidentally ruined by kero-
sene, which was carefully hoarded by the government, its public
sale being illegal.

Georgia held its own for another year, and it was not until
March, 1921, that Soviet forces entered Tiflis in response to a
request from the Georgian Communists, who had been supplied
with funds and propaganda material from Moscow to aid in
bringing about a Soviet revolution.

Armenia met an even more tragic fate. She had never enjoyed
possession of the territory promised her by the Sèvres Treaty; on
the contrary she was subjected to pressure from both Russians
and Turks. When the Kemalists in Anatolia revolted against the
Allied peace terms their first act was to seize Turkish Armenia
and advance into Russian Armenian territory. By February,
1921, the Kemalists had made an alliance with the Bolsheviks.
Turkish Armenia was given to the Angora government, while the

Bolsheviks made a superb gesture! Assuming their favorite rôle of defenders of the doctrine of self-determination and the rights of little people, they magnanimously "saved" Russian Armenia, making it into a Soviet Republic with Erivan as its capital.

With a comparatively small expenditure of energy and material, they had recovered in a little over three years all the ground lost in Trans-Caucasia with the exception of the portions of Georgian and Armenian territory ceded to Turkey. The so-called Soviet Republics of Trans-Caucasia became a Soviet Federation, and part of the Alliance of Socialist Soviet Republics approved by the All-Russian Council of Soviets at Moscow in 1923. Since then there have been sporadic revolts in Trans-Caucasia, notably the serious rebellion in Georgia in 1924, but it is as much an integral part of the Soviet Imperial system as it was of the Empire of the Romanovs.

The course of events in Central Asia after the Revolution was rather different from that in Trans-Caucasia, and the problem of its reabsorption as part of Red Russia presented peculiar features. The news of the Revolution had produced no such effects in Central Asia as in the Caucasus, for Nationalist feeling was virtually nonexistent. There were no movements for the formation of small republics.

The vast region of Trans-Caspia comprising the Kirghiz steppes and the territory of the wild Turanian tribes near the Persian border was chiefly inhabited by nomads who had always had a large measure of local autonomy and were quite disassociated from the central government. The changes in Russia affected them but little, except that in the period of chaos immediately following the Bolshevik revolution they were able to pillage now and then, and to pursue their own local feuds undisturbed. The small Russian population of the scattered cities along the railway lines and on the Caspian Sea was at first loyal to the democratic revolution brought about by Kerensky but one part after another was brought under Soviet control by various means —intrigue, propaganda, and terror.

The same general conditions prevailed in the half Siberian, half Central Asian provinces of Semi-Palatinsk and Semi-Rechinsk, where only some Cossack colonies and scattered towns along the principal trade-routes broke the great sweep of steppe, desert, and mountain, inhabited by Mongol-Tartar tribes, nomadic or semi-sedentary.

In Turkestan with its adjoining provinces of Ferghana and Samarkand, the news of the Revolution produced far-reaching consequences. Turkestan was the centre of the cotton-growing industry, which had reached considerable proportions in the years preceding the World War. Tashkent, its capital, was a Russian city, and there were nearly three-quarters of a million of Russian colonists in the country, some of whom were large landed proprietors who had to a certain extent dispossessed the original owners. There were also a number of Russian settlers of the peasant class, and a certain number of industrialized workers in Tashkent and a few other centres. Added to these was the native population of nearly eight millions, mostly Moslems, with the traditions of the ancient Mongol-Tartar culture that reached its highest point in the great civilization centred in Samarkand in the fifteenth century.

The Khanates of Khiva and Bokhara, whose native rulers had been under a Russian protectorate since the latter part of the nineteenth century, made up the remaining portions of Russia's Central Asiatic dominions. Both were immensely fertile, both possessed important native industries, and their people were ethnically and culturally related to the inhabitants of Samarkand. Bokhara and Khiva had kept much of the prosperity and some vestiges of the power of the Empire of Tamerlane, which it was the dream of the Pan-Turanian group in Turkey to reconstitute, and they had never ceased to resent Russian control.

Immediately after the deposition of the Czar in March, 1917, revolutionary committees were formed in Tashkent and other Russian cities of Central Asia, which almost unanimously were in favor of the new democratic régime, but after the Bolshevik revolution in November, they refused to acknowledge the Communist dictatorship. The Soviet government proceeded to act energetically against these Russian counter-revolutionary groups. Detachments of the newly formed Red army were sent at once to Turkestan and Trans-Caspia to deal summarily with them. At the same time very different tactics were adopted with the native population. Soviet propagandists and agents went among the many tribal groups who were still living in a state of society part patriarchal, part feudal, telling them of the new doctrine of self-determination which had replaced the Imperialism of the Czarist era. They were all to be independent and self-governing, keeping their own customs and institutions under the protecting wing of the Soviet government. Each was to have a representative in the Commissariat of Nationalities in Moscow.

To the potentates of Khiva and Bokhara the Soviet government promised full recognition and virtual independence. Everywhere the appeal was to the nascent nationalism of the Central Asiatic peoples. The democratic Russian elements who at first tried to hold out against the Bolsheviks, were gradually eliminated. Tashkent fell completely into Soviet hands after a brief reign of terror —its industries were nationalized and it became an integral part of the Socialist Republic. Bokhara and Khiva were rendered acquiescent to, if not altogether unsuspicious of, Soviet promises. The various tribes were encouraged to form "autonomous republics," under many names baffling to Western tongues.

At the Oriental Institute in Moscow Communist propagandists patiently studied all the tribal dialects, and translated the Communist manifestoes for the enlightenment of Buriats, Kirghiz, Kalmucks, Turcomans, Uzbegs and a host of other small Central Asiatic peoples. Agents trained in its class rooms penetrated the remote mountain valleys, the vast steppes, and the fertile plains of the Heart of Asia preaching the liberation of the subject peoples. Russia had undertaken in earnest the proletarian conquest of Asia —or so it seemed.

Conferences held in Tashkent and Samarkand in 1919 and 1920, under the auspices of the Oriental section of the Commissariat for Foreign Affairs, resulted in the creation of the Union for the Liberation of the East, which has sponsored every anti-imperialistic movement in Asia since that time. It has been behind such apparently disconnected movements as the revolt of Abd-el-Krim in Morocco, the rebellion of the Druse tribesmen in Syria, the troubles in China, and the Communist revolt in the East Indies. Very cleverly indeed, the Bolsheviks managed to turn to their own ends the Pan-Turanian agitation which we should remember had been started by the Young Turks, and sponsored by Germany before the Great War. The Samarkand Congress was only the preliminary to the great Congress of Eastern Peoples held in September, 1920, at Baku.

There were nearly two thousand delegates representing thirty-seven different nationalities, and fifty of the delegates were women. Gregory Zinoviev and Karl Radek, the former then chairman of the Communist International, were plenipotentiaries from Russia. They left Moscow with the other Russian and a few foreign delegates among whom was the American Communist John Reed, in a special train christened appropriately "Krasny Vostok—the Red East." It was painted a flaming red, and on its sides were life-sized figures picturing the various peoples of the East in the act of overthrowing their foreign oppressors and native despots. The departure of that train, like a red torch, was symbolical of the conflagration it was to spread throughout Asia. At the Conference, the Russian envoys who directed the proceedings were extraordinarily astute. The sympathies of the delegates were obtained largely by stressing the idea of self-determination, and not too much emphasis was laid on Communist theories. Soviet Russia was mirrored to all the East as the champion of the persecuted and the oppressed.

It was a marvellous optical delusion, for at the very moment the Communist dictatorship in Russia was ruthlessly crushing all opponents to its policies, even imprisoning the Socialists of other parties who had fought and suffered to bring about the Revolution. Moreover, it was actually taking steps to destroy the independence of Khiva.

In the summer of 1920 the Khan of Khiva, a very splendid person, was invited by the Soviet government to visit Moscow. He arrived just in time for the festivities in connection with a meeting of the Third Communist International.

I shall always remember the brilliant picture he and his suite made as they took their seats in the tribune in the Red Square at Moscow where Lenin and Trotzky, with the rest of the People's Commissars, reviewed a great parade of the Red army and the proletarian workers. Dressed in long brocade caftans, stiff with gold and silver, with curved scimitars and huge turbans topped by jewelled aigrettes, they matched the exotic magnificence of the great church of the Blessed Basil on which, as on them, Soviet aviators were showering Communist leaflets and miniature red flags. A few weeks later the Khan and all his suite were in the Andronovsky internment camp, as a result of an accusation that the Khivan government had fostered Russian plots of counter-revolutionaries on Khivan territory, and a Revolutionary Soviet put in power by a skilfully manipulated coup on the part of Red agents, had proclaimed a Soviet Republic in Khiva. Not long after, the Khan of Bokhara lost his throne through similar intrigues, but, more fortunate than his fellow sovereign, he sought refuge in Afghanistan.

But these moves took place only after Soviet propaganda had succeeded in enlisting widespread sympathy throughout Central Asia. They resulted from a change of policy that was inaugurated after the meeting of the Communist party Congress in the spring of 1921. The report of Stalin, Commissar of Nationalities, read to the Congress showed that of 146,000,000 inhabitants of Russia and her sister Soviet republics 65,000,000 were of non-Russian origin. He opposed the old policy of Russification and advised the encouragement and development of the national culture of each group. More than half of these non-Russian peoples, he explained, were still living under some form of tribal organization, and about ten millions of them had been deprived of their lands by the Russian Kulaks, the large peasant proprietors. By establishing Communist centres among them they could be used to combat the remaining bourgeois elements in the Russian Empire.

Following Stalin's report a Council of Nationalities was created, and from that time the policy of the Bolsheviks towards nationalities underwent a complete change. They no longer emphasized the right to self-determination among the peoples of Central Asia. On the other hand they laid all the emphasis on the statement that there could be no salvation for the little peoples outside of Sovietization.

The inauguration of this idea precipitated a series of small civil wars and coups d'état, resulting in a repetition, though in an infinitesimally short space of time, of the historic process of expansion. Unquestionably the Bolsheviks themselves were actuated by a desire to bring about the Communist evangelization of Asia as a step towards the World Revolution, but the real reason for their amazing success was that they were, although subconsciously, obeying the natural instinct and following the historic vocation of the Russian people in turning towards Asia. We have no time to trace the progress of Sovietization, but there was one episode of the civil war in Central Asia which had rather more than a local significance—the Basmatch revolt.

The Basmatchis were a group of malcontents from Bokhara, Ferghana, and Turkestan, somewhat like the Bulgarian comitadjis, and were organized and led by Enver Pasha, one of the most extraordinary personalities of the present century. Enver was a Turk—one of the Germanophile group which brought about Turkey's participation in the Great War. With two other leaders of the Young Turks, Djemal Pasha, the infamous commander of the Turkish army that opposed General Allenby in Syria, and Talaat Bey, an astute politician, he virtually controlled Turkish politics during the war.

After the Armistice they all had to flee from Constantinople. Talaat went to Berlin, where he was assassinated in 1919, and Djemal and Enver made common cause with Mustapha Kemal Pasha, who had raised the standard of revolt against the Allies in Anatolia. It is supposed in many well-informed circles that at one time Mustapha Kemal Pasha, in contradiction to his later policy, which has been to confine Turkish influence within the physical frontiers of Turkey in Asia, lent his approval to a scheme for the creation of a great Pan-Turanian Empire. It would have included Turkey, Trans-Caucasia, Trans-Caspia, Khiva, Bokhara, and Turkestan, with parts of Persia, and Mesopotamia. Mustapha Kemal was to have been the dictator of the western portion of this vast territory, Djemal was to have had Northern Persia, Mesopotamia, and the Caucasus, and Enver Pasha was to have ruled Central Asia. The assassination of Djemal Pasha in Tiflis eliminated one of the triumvirate, and differences soon arose between Enver and Mustapha Kemal. The latter refused to listen to Enver's picturesque and visionary schemes of conquest in Central Asia and devoted his time to preparing a national army to drive the Greeks out of Anatolia, succeeding so well that the Bolsheviks wisely decided to back him against the Western Powers, and continued with him the negotiations begun with Djemal at Moscow in 1920, resulting in the Russo-Turkish Treaty.

Meanwhile they kept Enver in the background, in case the Turks should play them false and make peace with Europe. In that event they could use Enver to overthrow Mustapha Kemal. Enver, who was a man of boundless ambition, could not wait. He began to organize a plot in the Caucasus against Kemal, but the Bolsheviks found it out and ordered him to come to Moscow. Instead of obeying he escaped and made his way to Afghanistan, where he ingratiated himself with the mother of the Amir, Saradjoul Khivatin, an extraordinary woman who has played a prominent rôle in Central Asiatic politics.

With the backing of Saradjoul Khivatin, the Catherine de' Medici of Afghanistan, Enver, and a little group of Pan-Turanian fanatics put themselves at the head of the Basmatchis, proclaiming the independence of Turkestan. A detachment of the Red army was sent out against Enver. Having failed to bring about a mass uprising as he had hoped, he offered his submission to the Moscow government, but it was refused. After a brilliant campaign, in which he accomplished wonders with his few troops against the Red army, he was defeated near Valdojan in Bokhara, overtaken by the Soviet troops as he was fleeing towards the Afghan border and killed by machine-gun fire which riddled his body with bullets.

With him died the dream of a Pan-Turanian Empire, but the memory of it will linger long in Asia. It is said that his tomb has become a pilgrimage spot, and a cult is growing around his personality. The devout and ignorant Moslems of Bokhara believe that he is under a spell like Barbarossa and that some day he will return to unfurl the victorious standard of Islam.

The Basmatch revolt was the last important counter-revolutionary movement in Central Asia. Meanwhile the Bolsheviks had been pushing steadily eastward in Siberia, until the close of 1922 saw the re-establishment of Russia's historic frontier on the Pacific.

In order to understand how Siberia was lost and subsequently regained for the Revolution within a remarkably short space of time, we must go back a little before the troubled period at the close of the war, when as we have seen, the Allies sent an expeditionary force to Siberia to help to extricate the Czecho-Slovaks and to support Admiral Kolchak's counter-revolutionary armies.

When the Great War broke out in 1914, Siberia was just entering on what promised to be an era of great prosperity. Communications had been greatly improved by the construction of several branch lines connecting with the Trans-Siberian Railway. Freight and passenger steamers were navigating all the large rivers, and there was a flourishing overland trade between European Russia, China, and Manchuria. The main cities like Omsk, Chita, and Vladivostok were growing by leaps and bounds. New mining enterprises were beginning to tap and exploit the vast resources of Northeastern Siberia and the region sloping down to the Arctic. There was even talk of opening a sea-route to Northern Siberia from Europe, around the North Cape and through the Kara Sea. Then came the war, putting a stop to many of these plans for development.

Siberia contributed her quota to the Russian armies, but physically she was isolated from all the fighting fronts. The only result of the great conflict visible to stay-at-home Siberians was the flood of prisoners-of-war. The Germans were kept in internment camps, but prisoners from such countries as Hungary, Austrian Poland and from that part of Austria which is now Czecho-Slovakia, who were known to be disaffected and unfriendly to the cause of the Central Powers for which they had been compelled to fight, were allowed considerable freedom.

Frequently they were permitted to wander virtually at liberty in a restricted area; numbers of them were put to work on the railways, on farms, and in factories, where supplies of shoes and clothing, canned goods and other equipment, were made for the armies in the field. Encouraged by Russian agents, they formed their own organizations, nationalistic and semi-political in character, in the hope that when the time came they might be given their freedom and utilized to fight against the Central Powers, for already President Wilson's enunciation of the doctrine of self-determination had spread and was bearing fruit among the disaffected peoples of Austro-Hungary. Incidentally they helped as well to spread the social unrest which was seething in the countries of Central Europe.

Then came the revolution. The news of the abdication of Nicholas II on March 8, 1917, and the establishment of a provisional government under Kerensky, was received with wild enthusiasm by the political exiles in Siberia. Thousands of expatriates who had been living in out-of-the-way places began to hurry back to the homes they had never expected to see again; thousands of prisoners set free in the penal settlements along the Amur River and in the prisons in the towns, joined the crowds that packed every train going west to Russia, persuaded that the way was paved for the coming of the Millennium.

But the native Siberians took the news more soberly. Like most people living in pioneer countries they had been too busy fighting the forces of nature in order to wrest a living from the soil to pay much attention to politics. The announcement of Kerensky that the land would be partitioned among the peasants did not cause any particular stir, because great landlords were few in Siberia and the settlers had almost invariably received land-grants from the government.

They had always governed themselves very efficiently through their village Dumas, without much interference from the central government. There were few cities, few factories, and consequently almost no industrial class, therefore there was practically none of the element of class war and class bitterness in the sturdy democracy of the Siberian people, who as a whole were genuinely glad to see the dawn of a new era. Except among the officials of the Chinovnik class, one of the bureaucratic institutions of the Imperial régime which throve under the old system of bribery and corruption, the passing of the monarchy was viewed with satisfaction in Siberia. Even the army officers in the garrisons were mostly tinged with democratic ideas and "fed up" with the incapacity and venality of many of their generals.

Until after the Bolshevik coup d'état and the second revolution in November, 1917, the Siberians were proceeding quite tranquilly to organize democratic Zemstvo councils in co-operation with Kerensky's government. Actually in many remote districts they did not even know there had been a revolution until many months afterwards. The first result of the seizure of power by the Bolsheviks was a general exodus of the moderate and democratic elements from Russia to Siberia, where they promptly began to organize centres of counter-Bolshevik activity.

Early in 1918 at Ufa on the skirts of the Urals, a provisional government, consisting of a Directorate of five members elected by the dissentient parties, was formed. Omsk, which was chosen as the capital, soon became the centre for all the democratic elements, and if the Directorate had pursued a firm policy and devoted all its efforts to consolidating its power in Siberia it might have succeeded in establishing an all-Siberian government; but the odds were against it. To begin with, the eyes of its members were turned west. Their main object was to use Siberia as a base for the overthrow of the Bolshevik régime in Russia, and in this they did not have the co-operation of the Siberian people. There were too few large centres to form nuclei of real public opinion, and the issues in Russia seemed too remote to the average Siberian colonist to warrant his making any sacrifice to overthrow the new government in Moscow, thousands of miles away. Long afterwards, when travelling in Siberia in 1922, I found this indifference among the peasants.

"What business of ours is it," they asked, "what sort of government they have in the Centre?"

In addition the vast distances, the slow infiltration of news, and scanty means of communication, the small Russian population interspersed with other racial groups many of which enjoyed local autonomy (there are fifty-nine different nationalities in Siberia) would have made the task a difficult one even if the Directorate had had the support of all the Russian elements. But this was not the case. There were still numbers of former officials, army officers, and monarchist refugees, who constituted an influential reactionary faction. Like the Democrats they wished to use Siberia as a base for action against the Bolsheviks—but their aim was the eventual restoration of the monarchy.

The Directorate at Omsk proceeded to organize a provisional government. The Zemstvo Councils elected by the people, in their turn elected delegates to a Siberian Territorial Duma. The military affairs of the new government were directed by a group of former Imperial officers headed by Admiral Kolchak, who managed to get together a fairly efficient army reinforced by the Czecho-Slovaks, whose story has been told in the chapter dealing with the Great War in Asia.

The first campaign against the Bolsheviks in the spring of 1918, by Admiral Kolchak and General Dieterichs, had as its primary object the rescue of the Imperial family, which had been held captive first at Tobolsk and later in Ekaterinburg. We all remember how the whole world was shocked by the execution in the face of the Czecho-Slovak advance, not only of the Czar and the Czarina but of their four daughters and the little Czarevitch, by order of the panic-stricken Soviet of Ekaterinburg which had been held responsible by Moscow for their safe keeping.

The Siberian forces, who took Ekaterinburg just too late, at one time advanced as far as the Volga River, but they were hampered by internal dissensions and Bolshevist propaganda, as well as by the growing discontent of the Czecho-Slovaks, who after the peace of Brest-Litovsk no longer saw any prospect of hitting at Germany and Austria through Russia. In the summer of 1918, they openly revolted and began their eastward march to join the Allies.

Notwithstanding these and other difficulties which forced Kolchak's troops to retreat in the autumn, the Admiral managed to reorganize his army in the winter of 1918-19, and he soon acquired sufficient power to overthrow the vacillating Directorate and proclaim himself Supreme Ruler of Siberia.

As we have seen, the Allies had intervened in Siberia, first in order to aid the Russians to keep up an offensive against Germany, then to facilitate the exit of the Czecho-Slovaks. They were in control of the Trans-Siberian Railway and its branches as far west as Omsk, but they had recognized no government in Siberia. However, in the spring of 1919, they accorded recognition to Admiral Kolchak, and an Allied Mission was sent to Omsk to assist him in his operations against the Bolsheviks.

Unfortunately there was no unity of plan or action either in the All-Siberian government or among the Allies. Kolchak was able and well-intentioned, but he allowed himself to be dominated by a group of reactionary monarchist officers who alienated from him the sympathies of democratic Siberia. The Allied Mission was torn by jealousies and petty quarrels, and no two representatives of the Great Powers seemed to have identical aims. The British and French were genuinely desirous of assisting Kolchak, but General Knox and General Jenin could never agree as to methods. The Americans were chiefly interested in assisting in the rescue of the Czecho-Slovaks, and the Japanese were pursuing a policy entirely their own, concentrating their attention on the virtual annexation of all of Eastern Siberia. Their object was to take advantage of the Allied occupation and to create such chaos that it would be necessary for them to remain indefinitely in the occupied territory to preserve order.

Consequently while ostensibly supporting Kolchak, they effectually prevented his extending his control east of Lake Baikal, by subsidizing, one after another, various so-called "governments" in the Maritime Province and Trans-Baikalia whose leaders were often merely bandits or adventurers, sometimes Red and sometimes White.

All these intrigues greatly handicapped the new government. Kolchak had acted most unwisely in arresting and imprisoning the members of the Directorate on his accession to power, and he had since antagonized all the liberal elements by arbitrary acts instigated by his monarchist advisers. He had been obliged to formally recognize the reactionary government set up in Trans-Baikalia by the Ataman Semionov, a protégé of the Japanese, and his last campaign in the summer of 1919 was foredoomed to failure.

There was then no unity among the members of his staff with regard to plans for military operations any more than in the Allied Military Mission. Jealousy and corruption were everywhere in evidence; the Japanese were playing a constant game of obstruction, the troops were discontented and their morale undermined by Red propaganda, and the Socialist and Democratic elements in the government were disaffected.

The Bolsheviks had observed the course of events, and when the Red army took the field against the Kolchak forces it had from the first a moral advantage, that of unity of purpose, which contributed not a little to its ultimate victory. Kolchak suffered a series of defeats ending in the capture of Omsk in November by the Red forces.

The remnants of Kolchak's army fled headlong eastward towards Irkutsk and Lake Baikal. The retreat from Omsk was an appalling spectacle. A terrified and demoralized mob of soldiers and civilians stormed the trains and officers shot civilians who refused to yield them places. The railway employees many of whom were in sympathy if not with the Bolsheviks, at least with the Democrats and Socialists whom Kolchak had ousted, refused to run the locomotives, and the trains were operated by half-crazed officers and officials.

At Irkutsk, Kolchak attempted to gather his army and make a last stand, but it was too late. He was overtaken and captured by a detachment of the Red army as he was trying to escape, and summarily shot on a station platform in January, 1920. After that there was no longer any question of the status of western Siberia. Up to Lake Baikal it was in complete possession of the Bolsheviks, who at once proceeded to send able organizers to form temporary revolutionary Soviets under military control, with full power to act until a permanent administration should be established.

The conquest of Siberia had been achieved in a remarkably short space of time, not through the strength of the Bolsheviks but through their ability to profit by the weakness of their adversaries. They began, with remarkable enterprise, considering the depleted state of Soviet finances, to repair the Trans-Siberian Railway and to restore communications with Russia. By the end of April, 1920, trains were running twice a week from Omsk to Moscow, covering the distance of approximately two thousand miles in nine days.

Conditions in Siberia, however, were very bad, particularly in the towns along the line of the Trans-Siberian where the Whites, Reds, and Czecho-Slovaks had all contributed towards destruction; food was scarce and such luxuries as sugar and tea were almost unheard of. Politically, few of the inhabitants were in sympathy with the Soviet government, but there was no organized opposition and the Reds were clever enough not to introduce too many radical changes at once. They even managed to patch up a temporary truce with the other revolutionary parties and within a few weeks they were firmly seated in the saddle. Then they began to look farther east.

It took them only a little over two years to reunite and consolidate all Siberia. On October 25, 1922, when Vladivostok capitulated to the Red army, the Bolsheviks became masters of the entire country from the Urals to the Japan Sea—and this almost without armed opposition.

But before we discuss the means by which the triumph of Red Russia was secured with so little effort, we must realize how the Allies had unwittingly furthered Bolshevist aims in the Far East.

Their dissensions and lack of unity of purpose were largely responsible for the conditions that brought about the disastrous Kolchak adventure. They should have either consistently carried out, or just as consistently abstained from, a policy of intervention—but they did neither. It must be said in fairness to the Allies, however, that their post-war difficulties at home seriously interfered with the execution of their policies in Siberia. England was threatened with serious labor troubles as the result of the demobilization, and the unemployment and confusion accompanying the readjustment of industry on a peace basis. France was experiencing the same sort of process. Italy, worse off financially than either of her Allies, was going through the critical period which culminated in the abortive Revolution of 1920 and the Fascist dictatorship; the United States Government was "through" with all European complications resulting from the war. But whatever the cause, the inefficient meddling of the Allies in Siberia, as in Russia, had the very result it was meant to avert. It hastened the unification of Siberia under Bolshevik rule.

In the spring of 1920, conditions in Western Siberia were approaching something like stability, but east of Lake Baikal the situation beggared all description. The Allied forces except those of the Japanese had withdrawn by the first of the year. The latter had agreed to take over the policing of the Trans-Siberian east of Lake Baikal until all the Czecho-Slovaks had been evacuated, and meanwhile they continued their policy of fomenting disorder in the Far East.

The Japanese Expeditionary Forces had, on one pretext or another, been increased from time to time since the landing of the first contingent in August, 1918, until, instead of the 8,000 troops agreed upon, there was an army of more than 80,000 in Siberia. Several detachments were utilized along the Trans-Siberian, but their presence hampered rather than hastened the evacuation of the Czecho-Slovaks. There was constant friction resulting in many bloody encounters between Czecho-Slovak units and the Japanese, or their tools the partisan leaders Red and White, who harassed them on the long journey.

Trans-Baikalia was under the despotic rule of Semionov, who was subsidized by Nipponese gold. The rest of Eastern Siberia, comprising the Amur region and the Maritime Province with its capital of Vladivostok, was occupied by Japanese forces which supported now one, now another, of the various "paper" governments, mostly reactionary, that appeared and disappeared with amazing rapidity. None of them had any real popular backing. Such political sentiment as there was in Eastern Siberia was revolutionary rather than reactionary.

In 1918 the inhabitants, who had welcomed the Revolution and organized Zemstvo Councils like the rest of Siberia, were in hearty sympathy with the All-Russian Directorate. But the Directorate had been overthrown, and Kolchak after his coup d'état had been much too occupied with the campaign against the Reds to give any thought to the organization of popular government in the far-off Amur and Baikal provinces.

It would have been doubtful, in any case if any government could have succeeded in restoring order and civil liberty under the watchful supervision of the Japanese, who were determined to bring about a state of chaos, but Kolchak's action in delegating authority to local leaders, all counter-revolutionary and nearly all in the pay of Japan, resulted in a continual state of civil war. The people, thoroughly fed up, equally with the Kolchak government and with foreign intervention, started what was known as the Partisan movement—a spontaneous revolt against the foreign-controlled reactionary leaders.

After the fall of Kolchak many of these partisan groups received substantial aid from the Bolsheviks, who had at once begun penetration of the territory east of Lake Baikal by means of intrigue and propaganda. The Bolshevist agents were welcomed in many places as the saviors of the country. There was a growing feeling that only reintegration within the boundaries of Soviet Russia could protect Eastern Siberia from the menace of Japanese annexation.

In March, 1920, the population of western Trans-Baikalia, encouraged by powerful support from the Bolsheviks, revolted against their tyrant, the Ataman Semionov. The Japanese, realizing that their intervention would mean a war with Russia, abandoned Semionov to his fate and he was forced to flee to Mongolia in an airplane. The revolt was prevented from spreading by the Japanese occupation of all important places in the Amur and Maritime provinces, where they resorted to the most brutal repressive measures to maintain their authority. It would take much too long to describe their methods, but I will cite one instance because it led to important international complications which we will have to deal with later.

Taking advantage of the presence of partisan bands of Red insurrectionists in the neighborhood of Nikolaievsk in the spring of 1920, the Japanese, it is commonly believed, deliberately provoked the massacre by the Reds of several hundred of their own citizens who had settled there many years previously, and of the small garrison sent for their protection in 1918. This gave them an excuse not only for occupying Nikolaievsk, an important fishery centre, and the reaches of the Amur River providing access to rich gold deposits and timberlands of great value, but also of the northern half of the island of Sakhalin, which they had coveted since obtaining the southern part from Russia by the Treaty of Portsmouth.

Thereupon they announced that pending the settlement of their claims for a large indemnity from a future Russian government, they would hold both Nikolaievsk and Sakhalin. Actually, however, as I shall endeavor to show later, they had no intention of abandoning Sakhalin, while the military party even contemplated the annexation of the Maritime provinces and part of the Amur region.

Meanwhile at Chita, Semionov's former capital in Trans-Baikalia, a democratic government had been organized under the name of the Far Eastern Republic. While nominally quite independent of Soviet Russia and actually representing the political complexion of the greater part of Siberia, the new democratic republic was, from the first, merely an instrument for the further-ance of Bolshevist aims.

At that time it seemed unlikely that any of the great Powers would soon recognize Soviet Russia. A buffer state professedly democratic, on its eastern frontier, would probably obtain early recognition; it could be used as a sort of open door for the importation and exportation of merchandise and for intercourse with the outside world from which Russia was shut off by the blockade of her European frontiers. The Soviet government saw to it that there was at least one Communist agent on every local executive body, and created the machinery by which a Bolshevist coup d'état could be brought about whenever it was desirable.

Gradually the steady infiltration of Soviet propaganda in the Amur and Maritime provinces began to make itself felt. The Japanese experienced more and more difficulties in keeping their hold on those regions. None of the reactionary governments of their creation lasted very long.

At Khabarovsk there were sharp clashes between the Partisans and the Japanese troops in which numbers of women and children were wantonly killed. During the Nipponese occupation Russian civilians were forced, under threat of death, to go down on their knees whenever they passed a Jap soldier. On abandoning Khabarovsk after the defeat of the Cossack leader Kalmykov in whose behalf they had reduced it to subjection, the Japanese army systematically wrecked the railway between Khabarovsk and Vladivostok, destroying every station and bridge, burning and sacking the villages, raping and murdering the noncombatants.

All this while an Eastern Red army was being quietly organized in the Far Eastern Republic, and Soviet Russia bided her time. The Chita government had brought about order in most of Trans-

Baikalia and was gradually extending its power eastward towards the Amur and the Maritime provinces. It had been recognized, de facto, by several Powers including the United States, partly because they regarded the existence of the Far Eastern Republic as a check on Japan. For by this time the World Powers, who had for the most part been too busy partitioning the spoils of the Great War, competing in conflicting spheres of interest, and settling their own domestic affairs, had begun to realize that something must be done to check the overweening ambitions of Japan in the Pacific.

As we know, the growing tension culminated in the calling of a conference of all the Powers interested in problems of the Pacific, by President Harding on behalf of the United States.

The agenda of the Conference, which met at Washington in the latter part of 1921, did not include the question of the occupation of Siberia; nevertheless public opinion had been so thoroughly aroused in the United States and elsewhere by the reports of Nipponese high-handed proceedings that an assurance was sought and obtained from Japan by the other Powers that she would evacuate Eastern Siberia at the earliest possible moment, and that she would withdraw the guards she had maintained on the Chinese Eastern railway, the Manchurian branch of the Trans-Siberian, long after necessity for military control had ceased.

As it happened, the Japanese were willing to accede to these demands for the evacuation of Siberia because a considerable amount of opposition to the continuance of the occupation had grown up in Japan itself. It was realized that the annexation of Eastern Siberia was impossible, and that it was equally impossible for Japan to maintain at her own expense a series of unstable and unpopular counter-revolutionary governments. It was only a question of time when Russia would become strong enough to throw off the mask and go to war to recover her lost provinces. Besides, sooner or later there was sure to be opposition among the other Powers to any annexation on the Siberian mainland.

In September, 1922, all the Japanese troops were withdrawn from the Amur region, which was turned over to the Far Eastern Republic, with the exception of Northern Sakhalin where an expeditionary force was retained pending the settlement of the indemnity claimed by the Japanese for the massacres at Nikolaievsk. A few weeks later the Maritime provinces and Vladivostok were abandoned to what proved to be the last of the reactionary governments—the military dictatorship of General Dieterichs. Dieterichs, who had managed to escape from the débâcle of Kolchak's army, had drifted to Vladivostok after many vicissitudes, where he had collected the remnants of various counterrevolutionary forces that had operated from time to time in Eastern Siberia, and had seized the power by a military coup d'état. The story of his short-lived attempt to lead a White Crusade is one of the most picturesque episodes of the Revolution in Siberia.

I was one of the few foreigners in Vladivostok during his brief tenure of power. His army, composed largely of the riff-raff of the Far East, full of swashbuckling adventurers and desperate men who had burned all bridges behind them, was about as rotten as an army could be. His ministers and administrative officials belonged mostly to the old corrupt Chinovnik class riddled with bribery and corruption. Dieterichs himself, a strange mixture of idealist, fanatic, and man of action, walked among them all unseeingly, unbelievingly. To him Holy Russia was a sacred thing to be redeemed from the hands of the Red barbarians who had overthrown the monarchy and slain its divinely appointed head. He believed firmly that he had but to get a small force together and proclaim a Holy War in order to start a tremendous wave of religious enthusiasm among the peasants and to induce them to follow him to Moscow.

"If the people would only have faith," as he once said to me, "God would perform a miracle!"

A few weeks after the departure of the Japanese, Dieterichs and a handful of devoted and visionary priests started to preach the White Crusade, backed by their rowdy army of adventurers. Needless to say they received no support from the peasants of the Maritime provinces, who were beginning to long for the Bolsheviks to come and put an end to the continual changes.

The army of the Far Eastern Republic, backed by several units of the Red army, was sent against the Dieterichs forces, which melted away after a series of skirmishes lasting less than two weeks, and Dieterichs was forced to abandon Vladivostok, which surrendered without resistance. He escaped to Japan, and the Red troops entered the city.

A few days later, the time being ripe for such a step, the Far Eastern Republic was peacefully legislated out of existence by the controlling Communist faction in its National Assembly and this part of Siberia became an integral part of the Russian Socialist Soviet Republic.

Shortly afterwards all of Siberia was reorganized, and divided into administrative districts based on the old provincial divisions, with local soviets, which in turn elected delegates to the All Russian Council of Soviets. Novo-Nikolaievsk was made the administrative centre for the country. In accordance with the well-established policy with regard to nationalities which had been adopted from the beginning of the Revolution, a number of the non-Russian communities in Siberia were made into autonomous republics or autonomous districts, all incorporated within the Soviet Union. Siberia, without having ever been seriously Socialist, or even rabidly revolutionary, became solidly Soviet.

The success of the Bolsheviks in this vast region was due not so much to their skilful tactics, their propaganda, or their military prowess, as to the weakness and dissensions of the Allies and the imperialistic greed of Japan, which created a solidarity that otherwise would never have existed. It was foreign pressure that drove Siberia into the arms of the Soviets, just as it was foreign pressure that consolidated the power of the Bolsheviks in Russia.

Resentment against the Allies for what they considered their abandonment of Russia made supporters of the Soviet régime out of many counter-revolutionaries. Below the surface there was a still deeper impulse than any of these—the call of Asia. Behind the Communist mask there have always been the features of the Slav—more Asiatic than European.

Having regained the historic frontiers of Russia in Asia, the Bolsheviks gradually modified the Constitution of the Soviet Republic with a view to closer reorganization.

In December, 1922, the first congress of Soviet nationalities met at Moscow to draw up a new constitution for a confederation of Soviet Republics. This constitution was ratified by the

Central Executive Committee and became operative on July 6, 1923. The Union of Socialist Soviet Republics constituted a single state in so far as diplomatic relations, national defense, industry, commerce, and transportation were concerned. The individual interests of the Federated States as well as their language, customs, and culture were safeguarded by complete local autonomy.

The legislative power was vested in the Assembly of Soviets of the Republics composing the Union, which was to meet once a year, its function in the interim being vested in the Central Executive Committee of the Union with 371 members, elected from the delegates to the Assembly, and a Council of Nationalities with 99 members. We should recall in this connection that the Central Executive Committee is like the apex of a huge pyramid and the real governing body for 146,000,000 people. For according to the Soviet system of representation, having as its base the innumerable district Soviets elected by vocational franchise, each group of Soviets elects a smaller number of delegates to other groups who represent a greater extent of territory. The Central Executive Committee actually frames and passes most of the laws, appoints the sixteen Commissars who constitute the Cabinet of the Soviet Union, and elects the President of the Council of Commissars, who is the real president of the Soviet state.

From the Central Executive Committee are drawn the judges of the Supreme Court and the heads of the "G. P. U."—the Government Political Department, so called—in reality the secret service and counter-espionage organization of the Union, the successor of the notorious Extraordinary Commission known as the Cheka.

As originally constituted, the Union of Soviet Socialist Republics consisted of four federated republics with fifteen autonomous republics, and fifteen autonomous provinces representing various small national groups. In 1924, its organization was slightly modified. Six federated republics of which three, Trans-Caucasia, Uzbegistan, and Turkmenistan, are in Asiatic Russia, now compose the Soviet Union together with the autonomous republics and provinces scattered over Siberia and Central Asia.

The Uzbeg and Turkmen republics in Central Asia have been

created from a division of Trans-Caspia, with the old states of Khiva and Bokhara, along ethnographic lines. There, as elsewhere Bolshevik tactics have been extremely subtle. Soviet propaganda has concentrated largely on education. In Uzbegistan there are 868 educational establishments with 64,363 pupils. Everywhere Red tea-houses have been established to serve as centres for the dissemination of Communist propaganda. There is a government printing office in Tashkent which prints Communist A B C's in every dialect of Central Asia. I saw one of these, destined for Uzbegistan, in which by some amusing mistake, the printer had used a French tricolor to illustrate the word "flag"!

In spite of all this propaganda, however, Communist doctrines as such have made little headway. On the other hand Bolshevism seems to be undergoing a process of Asiatization; the mystic internationalism of the Russian Communist is giving way to a new national feeling based on community of interests. After having decentralized the Empire by proclamation of the right to self-determination, the Bolsheviks are drawing it together again by calling the various peoples composing it to defend it against outside imperialism, and by so doing they have contributed towards consolidating Asiatic and European Russia to form a united "Eurasia." Indeed it is not too much to say that the new Soviet Union is more closely knit than the old Russian Empire ever was. The passing phenomenon of Bolshevism is only a stage in this evolution.

Having reviewed the steps by which Russia has regained her Asiatic Empire we must not neglect her progress towards her historic goal in the Far East—a warm-weather outlet on the China Sea and control of the China trade.

As early as 1921, Soviet penetration began in Mongolia. The virtual protectorate which had existed since the establishment of Mongolian autonomy, thanks to Russian assistance, had lapsed during the World War and the demoralization of the entire foreign policy of Russia following the Revolution. Possibly the attention of the Bolshevist leaders, occupied as they were with the reintegration of Russia proper, would not have been drawn to it except for the fact that it served as a base for counter-revolutionary activities, after the fall of Kolchak had driven all the monarchist elements out of Western Siberia.

When the Chita government of the Ataman Semionov was overthrown in the spring of 1920, the remnants of his army were reorganized by a former Czarist officer, Baron Ungern-Sternburg. He offered its services to the Mongolians to drive out the Chinese, who had reoccupied Outer Mongolia in 1919, taken Urga the capital, and imprisoned the Living Buddha, High Priest of the Mongol theocracy.

Having retaken Urga and sent the Chinese southward in a headlong retreat during which ten thousand men were killed or perished in the Great Gobi Desert, Ungern-Sternburg, who was known as the Mad Baron, instituted a White Terror much more horrible than the Yellow! He put to death all Russians, Mongolians, or Chinese, suspected of Red tendencies, often with the most horrible tortures. Jews were murdered without exception, and Ungern's chief executioner, a man named Zipailov who strangled his victims, boasted that he had killed over two hundred men with his own hands. It was commonly said of him in Urga when I was there a year later, that he practiced on dogs to keep in training.

During his occupation Sternburg was not in the least concerned about the Mongolians or their future, and when he had sufficiently strengthened his forces, using Urga as a base, he advanced towards the Siberian border to attack the Bolsheviks, leaving the terrified Mongolians to pull themselves together as best they could, and set some sort of governmental apparatus going. He was defeated and captured in the summer of 1921, and executed by order of a military court-martial at Novo-Nikolaievsk. It is said that the Bolsheviks, who admired his military genius, offered him a commission in the Red army or death. That he chose the latter, remaining loyal to his convictions, whatever they were, should at least be recorded to his credit. Meanwhile a punitive expedition of the Red army had been sent across the Mongolian border to disperse the remainder of Sternburg's forces, a small detachment going as far as Urga.

The Red commander assisted the Mongolians in restoring order and in establishing a People's Revolutionary Government nominally under their Living Buddha, but really under Russian control. Soon a consular representative was sent to Urga, where he acted as adviser to the government. He was the real power behind the throne. Gradually Soviet instructors and advisers were put into every department, and finally when the Living Buddha died in the spring of 1924, the republican and socialist elements combined to block the election of his successor.

The next step was easy. In the early part of 1925, Mongolia became a Soviet Republic united by the closest possible alliance with Russia. The next step in its evolution is likely to be its legal incorporation with the Soviet Union.

The name of Urga was changed to "Ulan Bator" or Red Hercules; the aristocratic parliament composed of hereditary princes, spiritual and temporal, and high government officials, became a Red Soviet. Soviet officers were employed to train the Mongolian Red army. Most of the foreign interests with investments in Mongolia were forced to leave and the economic development of the country passed entirely into Soviet hands. This, in spite of the fact that Outer Mongolia was recognized as part of the Chinese Republic by the Russo-Chinese Treaty signed in 1924, to which we shall often have occasion to refer in discussing developments in the Far East.

The establishment of the Mongolian Soviet Republic has attached Outer Mongolia far more firmly than ever to the present Russian state, and it marks the realization, like many of the Bolshevik accomplishments, of part of the Imperial Russian scheme of expansion in Asia. The possession of Mongolia is of vital importance to her as an Asiatic Power. At present the Bolsheviks have extensive plans for economic development, in-. cluding the building of a railway across Mongolia, from Kalgan in North China to the Siberian border.

They have seized and incorporated in the Russian Soviet Union certain outlying districts such as Urian-Hai on the fringe of the Altai Mountains. They are also conducting widespread propaganda in Chinese Turkestan, which adjoins Siberia, Mongolia, and their own federated Republic of Uzbegistan.

If they succeed in detaching Chinese Turkestan from the Chinese Empire by some such process as they have employed in

Mongolia, the way will be open for a project just as ambitious and as far-reaching in its consequences as the Berlin-to-Baghdad railway. A railway across Mongolia protected by a friendly state in Chinese Turkestan to the west would pave the way for land access to the valley of the Yangtze-kiang and enable Russia to tap the riches of Western China at the source.

In Manchuria, Russian penetration has followed a rather different course. The three provinces composing Manchuria have so far constituted a solid barrier against the political spread of Bolshevism. That this is so is partly due to the remarkable personality of Chang Tso-lin, the dictator of Manchuria; but even more to Japanese influence. Nevertheless, the present Russian government has important interests there, and in spite of many obstacles it may be said to have recovered practically all the ground lost by the Revolution.

That Manchuria is inevitably destined to play a great rôle in the future of Eastern Asia no one will deny. In the first place a glance at the map reveals the fact that Manchuria logically belongs to Eastern Siberia. Actually it is part of the vast stretch of territory composing the Amur and Maritime provinces which was ceded to Russia by China in 1860. It was never included among the provinces composing China proper, from which it is separated by the Great Wall. Originally it was the home of the Manchu dynasty which conquered China, and its three provinces are governed by a Viceroy appointed from Peking.

We already know how in the first decade of the present century it was the principal bone of dissension between Russia and Japan, and one of the chief causes for the pronouncements of the great Powers with regard to the open door, equality of opportunity, and for all the fine phrases invented to protect the competitors for the trade of China. We have traced the steps by which Japan and Russia obtained territorial footholds, but before we go any further perhaps it may be as well to recall the position of both at the close of the Great War.

Russia was apparently out of the running with regard to Manchuria in 1918. The Bolshevik government, in a burst of socialistic idealism, had declared, after its accession to power at the close of 1917, that it renounced in principle all the old Czarist concessions as well as the privilege of extraterritoriality. This meant theoretically that they had turned over to China the Chinese Eastern Railway, passing through Manchurian territory to Vladivostok, with all the concessions along the right of way, including the headquarters of the administration at Harbin, which constituted a miniature Russian city. It also comprised the extension of the Chinese Eastern to Changchun, where it joined the South Manchurian Railway controlled by the Japanese.

At the time, however, Russia was not in control of the Chinese Eastern or any of the territory in question. The railway, owned by the Russo-Asiatic Bank, which had borrowed the money for its construction originally from the Russian government was being administered by the old board of directors, half Russian, half Chinese, with the assistance of an Allied Technical Commission at the head of which was an American, Colonel Stevens, and Japanese military guards were keeping order along its lines. The Japanese showed no signs of giving up control until pressure from the Allied governments including strong representations from America brought about their withdrawal.

Russia was not in a position to take a hand in Manchuria until after her acquisition of Vladivostok; then she began to turn to China. The status of the Chinese Eastern Railway remained uncertain for several years but it was finally settled by the Russo-Chinese Treaty concluded at Peking in the spring of 1924, and a subsequent agreement at Mukden. These accords established the principle that the railway should be regarded not as an instrument of domination but as a purely commercial enterprise. Nevertheless, they re-established the old Russian leasehold for the remaining sixty years of the ninety-nine-year period agreed on as the term of the lease, and virtually placed the railway under Russian control. At the same time, however, the Bolsheviks were careful to do everything possible to prevent the Chinese from "losing face." Theoretically, the civil, fiscal, and military administration of the Railway Zone was to be in Chinese hands. Three of the seven administrative committees were to have Chinese chairmen—the financial committee was to be presided over alternately by a Chinese and a Russian.

One of the first results of the new administration was the cancellation by the new Russian director-general of a contract with the Japanese-controlled South Manchurian Railway for the shipment of all goods designed for export from Northern Manchuria to the Japanese port of Dalny, and the substitution of Vladivostok; transport rates on the Trans-Siberian were lowered 50 per cent and every effort was made to stimulate Russo-Chinese overland trade. During 1926, under the auspices of the Soviet Commissariat for Foreign Trade a great commercial propaganda demonstration was staged in Harbin, the headquarters of the Chinese Eastern, with the name of the "Russo-Oriental Exposition."

A glance at the map will show the importance of this move to Japan. Unless she wishes to renounce a large part of her commercial and political influence in Manchuria she must either cooperate in a friendly manner with Russia or engage in active competition by building railway lines of her own to tap the resources of the Manchurian Hinterland.

By the terms of the Peking Treaty, Russia also acknowledged theoretically the independence of Mongolia; she denounced all the old Czarist treaties embracing extraterritorial privileges and all claims to territorial footholds in China; she consecrated her share of the Boxer indemnity to educational work, as the United States had done many years previously, and transferred all the former property of the Russian Orthodox Church in China to the Chinese government, which was to use it for social betterment or educational purposes. The treaty further provided for resumption of full diplomatic relations between the two countries.

The resumption of relations and the signing of the treaty with the Central Chinese government, represented a diplomatic triumph for Russia which was gained only after protracted negotiations, for there were many factors against such an alliance. Even in 1924, it was a well-known fact that Soviet agitators were supporting Sun Yat-sen and the South Chinese government against Peking; moreover, no matter what promises might be made regarding the independence of Mongolia, the Sovietization of the Mongols was an accomplished fact, and the Chinese were much too shrewd not to see that the advantages they would gain by the treaty were largely those resulting from satisfied amour propre.

In addition, while we cannot know all that went on in the Legation Quarter at Peking during the negotiations, we may be sure that certain Powers, particularly France, whose citizens were stockholders in the Russo-Asiatic Bank which held the majority control of the Chinese Eastern, and Great Britain, which foresaw only too clearly the growing Red menace to her interests on the Yangtze-kiang, were exerting pressure on the Chinese Foreign Office against the treaty. While less directly interested, the United States could not have been more satisfied than the other Powers with a Russo-Chinese accord.

It would have seemed to the casual observer that Japan would have been no better pleased with the Russo-Chinese rapprochement, which was bound to be prejudicial to her interests in Manchuria. Nevertheless, in view of subsequent developments there is room for interesting speculations as to whether she did not secretly encourage the conclusion of the Peking Treaty. In spite of many setbacks and differences, in spite of the possible significance to Japan of Russia's legalized interests in Manchuria, in spite of the loss to Japanese commercial interests through the labor troubles fomented by Soviet agitators in her industrial and mining enterprises in China, Japan herself concluded a treaty with Russia less than a year later, on January 20, 1925.

The terms of this treaty did not affect Russia's expansion beyond securing her the territorial ownership of Northern Sakhalin, so we will not discuss them at length here, but they resulted in a complete understanding on many points at issue between the two Powers.

One of the results of this rapprochement was the formation of a Japanese company with a capital of 30,000,000 yen, controlled by Baron Goto and Viscount Inouye, to develop Eastern Siberia and to cultivate rice there. The company in its prospectus frankly asserted that its object was to secure close cooperation between Russia and Japan, and the Soviet government participated in the monopoly accorded it. It was planned to send 90,000 Japanese laborers into the country to exploit the forests, mines, fisheries, and rice farms.

Recent events in China, which have seemed to indicate loss of Soviet prestige among the Chinese national and revolutionary elements, and to foreshadow a complete rupture with Peking, have as yet produced no such results, nor have they caused a break with Tokyo. Out of these apparent contradictions it seems possible to deduce only one conclusion. Japan and Russia, with quite different methods, are working together with a common object—to oust Great Britain from Asia—and so far the opposing forces are stalemate.

China's rôle in the conflict is not easy to define—perhaps even to the Chinese; but out of all the chaos in the Far East is emerging the idea, nebulous and faint, but visible nevertheless, of a solid bloc of Yellow Peoples as part of an Asiatic Confederation, in which the Eurasian Empire created by Russia would play a vital if not a dominant part. This idea alone can avert the otherwise inevitable clash between Russia and Japan on the shores of the Pacific.

Chapter Thirteen

THE FAR EASTERN TRIANGLE

SINCE the Great War the attention of the world at large has been focussed frequently on the Far East. Nowhere have the disastrous results of the Wilsonian policies been more evident—nowhere have the indirect consequences of the great upheavals in Europe since 1914 been more momentous.

Amid the welter of conflicting ideals, forces, and movements let loose by Armageddon, the East is undergoing a transformation which M. Grousset the eminent French historian compares to that of Europe during the nineteenth century—"the transformation of age-old countries into young nations." He might even have gone a step further. There are signs that these same young nations are being drawn together in racial groups, and nowhere is this tendency more apparent to the careful observer than in the Far East—where China, Japan, and little Korea, despite their differences and antagonisms, form, so to speak, an irregular political triangle. A sense of race unity has brought about the three-cornered contacts which may later lead to the formation of a Mongol Bloc.

China is at present undergoing one of the periods of apparent disintegration that have recurred at intervals throughout her history extending back over thousands of years. There is not the slightest doubt that it is the travail preceding a rebirth, or that it was precipitated by the tremendous growth of race-consciousness, during and after the Great War. Nevertheless, for the moment the internal chaos in China precludes the possibility of her active participation in a Pan-Mongol movement.

Japan goes through all the motions of outward conformity with Europe. Her statesmen sit demurely in the Councils of the League of Nations and discuss world-peace and naval disarmament. They express the greatest willingness to aid the European Powers in restoring "order" in China. There is apparently no love lost between her and the Chinese, yet once in a while an incident, often trivial, indicates a disposition on the part of Japan to make common cause with China against the West. Korea is inarticulate politically, but those who have watched the development of the new Japanese policy there are well aware that a great change for the better has recently come about in the relations between Korea and Nippon.

Unquestionably Japan, because of her superior technical organization, is best fitted at the present time to become the international spokesman for the Mongol peoples. With England and the United States she controls the Pacific. Moreover, she and Russia are in a fair way either to dispute or to divide in the near future the hegemony of Eastern Asia. For all these reasons the trend of recent events in Japan and the developments in her foreign policies are no less significant, though less spectacular, than the happenings of the last few years in China. Consequently we should begin our study of the Far Eastern Triangle from the angle of Japan.

JAPAN

When the Japanese delegates to the Peace Conference at Versailles returned to Tokyo in 1919, they must have been in a most curious frame of mind. They had been admitted to the Allied Councils, they had debated as equals, sometimes even as arbiters, the fate of this or that portion of the conquered countries of Central Europe. Allies of the British, they had figured as the pampered pets of Mr. Lloyd George; they had had Shantung handed them on a silver platter, so to speak; they had acquired all Germany's possessions in the Pacific north of the Equator, and they had been signers of the Covenant for the creation of the League of Nations.

At the same time the Japanese, together with the Chinese whom they had wronged so deeply, had been classed as inferiors by the failure of the Supreme Council to pass a resolution establishing the principle of race-equality—in spite of Wilson's Fourteen Points and Lloyd George's adroit flatteries, they still found themselves excluded from the United States and Australia.

Their representatives came back to a country, small, compact, united, and mobilized to the highest point of efficiency, with a large gold reserve, a tremendous foreign trade, a navy ranking third among the navies of the world and an army whose manpower had not been impaired or weakened on the battlefields of Europe. Under such circumstances it could not have surprised them to find the military party in the ascendancy, and Japan seething with the ferment of imperialism. They brought no arguments from Europe which might have served to calm the universal chauvinism and it would have been impossible for them to explain to the Japanese people the anomalies of their position in the Conference.

The fact that the ministry was in the hand of the democratic Count Takahashi did not materially influence the all-pervading belief in the vital necessity for expansion—a belief substantiated by the course of events since the beginning of the Great War. Simultaneously with the evolution of her foreign policies, vast changes had been taking place in Japan since 1914.

The war had come just two years after the death of the great Emperor Meiji who had achieved the modernization of Japan in a little over twenty-five years. The establishment of industries on a large scale during the latter years of Meiji's reign had temporarily relieved a situation which was assuming serious proportions by absorbing in the industrial population of the cities the large number of individuals who could not longer find a living on the land. It had become apparent soon after the opening of Nippon to the outside world in the middle of the nineteenth century, that the growth of her population, encouraged by modern conditions of living, would soon crowd her peasants off the land and make it necessary for her to develop an industrial system at home, and to import raw materials and foodstuffs from abroad.

It was the need for raw materials and markets that drove Japan in the first place to establish herself in Manchuria, whose mines and natural resources were vital for her industries. The acquisition of Korea afforded her an outlet on the Chinese mainland, as well as additional acreage for cultivation, but it must be remembered that Korea, like Japan, where only one-fifth of the total area is cultivable, is a mountainous country and already thickly populated and not particularly rich in minerals or raw materials.

It was not long before Japan began to covet the inexhaustible supply of rice, the enormous deposits of coal so necessary for her iron and steel industry, the reputed deposits of petroleum, and the wonderful market for cotton goods in China. The prospect of obtaining control of the collieries of Shantung was one of the determining factors of Japan's participation in the World War. We have seen that her first act was to seize the German holdings in Kiaochow. During the four years of the war Japanese industry made gigantic strides and her merchant shipping kept pace with her industrial growth.

Japanese manufactured goods took the place of European products in the Asiatic, Pacific, and South American markets. In the Japanese textile industry alone the number of spindles was increased from 2,500,000 to 3,500,000 between 1914 and 1919. The production of silk increased over 100 per cent. The orders placed by England alone for cotton underclothing to supply the Tommies in the army amounted to more than $1,000,000. Wages had doubled and trebled during the war period, factories had worked overtime, production had been kept up at fever heat, and despite the enormous expense entailed in keeping her army and navy at war-time strength, Japan had accumulated a huge surplus amounting to over $700,000,000 between 1914 and 1918. She also dominated many of the markets formerly supplied by Great Britain, Germany, and the United States.

It was obvious to Japanese financiers and manufacturers that in the nature of things they could not expect to hold all these markets after the war was over. Whether the Central Powers or the Allies were the victors, a large portion of the trade Japan had usurped would inevitably revert to Europeans. Consequently, long before the Armistice, they were looking for markets and sources of supply which they could reasonably hope to retain after the war. They lost no time in making their position perfectly clear with regard to Shantung, and we have seen how pressure, skilfully exerted by Japan at a time when the Allies had need of her co-operation, secured the acquiescence of England

and the United States in the Twenty-one Demands forced on the Chinese people.

Japan had secured a firm financial hold on the Chinese government through her war-time loans, and large textile mills had been established in China with Japanese capital, while the exploitation of the Manchurian mines had kept pace with the development of the cultivation of the soy bean, the great source of agricultural wealth in Northern China. All through the war, in spite of the boycott against Japanese goods instituted after the forced acceptance by the Peking government of the Twenty-one Demands, China had no other source of supply in many classes of manufactured articles. At that time the Japanese government was in the hands of the military party headed by the Premier Terauchi and backed by the only surviving members of the Council of Elder Statesmen, Matsukata and Saionji.

It may be well to explain here just what is meant by the military party, for it did not figure as a political division. Party-politics in Japan were undergoing a process of evolution. Just as the constitution itself represented in many ways a compromise between the ancient feudal system and the modern order, with its Parliament and Notables elected by their own class or appointed by the Emperor, and its House of Representatives elected by limited suffrage, the political parties reflected the transition. In feudal days the power passed from one to another of the great Clans. Parties had sprung up, but they were still infused with something of the Clan spirit. The Elder Statesmen known as the Genro, who so long directed the internal and external policies of controlling the appointments made by the Emperor and keeping a firm hand even on the Diet itself, were drawn from the Clans. When this or that political leader is mentioned in Japan even to the present day, it is no uncommon thing to hear the remark, "Oh, yes, So and So is a ———— man," naming one of the great Clans: Satsuma, Choshu, Tokugawa, or Hizen.

The officers of the navy, the army, and most important government officials were clansmen of the old Samurai class of fighting-men in whom the military spirit had existed for countless generations. It was not to be wondered at that they combined, forming a military oligarchy which exerted a powerful influence on the politically immature Japanese people. The gradual growth of democracy and the dawning comprehension of the power of popular government eventually undermined their influence, but even down to the present time there are traces of the Clan influence.

The militarists were convinced that force and force alone would enable Japan to keep the markets she had won. They also felt that the pressing needs of the country could be satisfied only by territorial expansion on the mainland of Asia.

The Allied occupation of Eastern Siberia during the last months of the World War gave them an opportunity to obtain a foothold in that vast country. The fact that it was not suitable for colonization was of small consequence to them compared with the importance of securing control of its natural resources. There were huge deposits of coal in the Ussuri region. The reaches of the Amur River and its branches were rich in minerals, lead, silver, gold, not to mention valuable fisheries. The forests of the Maritime Province alone contained an immense amount of excellent timber: the Island of Sakhalin, half of which has been in Japanese hands since the Treaty of Portsmouth in 1905, contained in the portion still belonging to Russia, deposits of petroleum said to be fabulously rich, and there was nothing that Japan needed more than this very petroleum. With oil rapidly supplanting coal as fuel for naval vessels, Japan was greatly handicapped by the fact that she controlled only about 2 per cent of the world's available supply of petroleum.

We have seen that the Japanese Expeditionary Force was increased in Siberia on every possible pretext, that it remained long after the other Allied countries had withdrawn their troops, that Japanese intrigue prolonged the state of chaos in Eastern Siberia in order to find an excuse for remaining, until domestic and foreign pressure forced the military party to concede defeat and assent, however grudgingly, a reversal of its policy in Siberia. We shall have occasion to discuss later Japan's change of heart with regard to China as well.

But in 1919, undoubtedly the great mass of Japanese public opinion supported the military party. Imperialistic aggression seemed to be the only means of assuring a supply of raw materials and markets for the colossal industries that had grown up mushroom-like during the war. Siberia, Manchuria, and Shantung were the bases for a systematic economic penetration of the whole of Eastern Asia.

The need of an outlet for the growing population of Japan constituted another, less powerful, motive for expansion, although as a matter of fact there were few regions among those picked for commercial exploitation that were suitable for Japanese colonization.

The Japanese are poor colonizers except in regions where the climate is suited to their needs; they cannot be persuaded to remain in countries where rice cannot be grown or can be grown only with difficulty. Therefore Siberia was almost out of the question. Shantung was already thickly settled and the rigors of the winter climate in Manchuria did not appeal to them. All things considered they preferred to stay at home as long as possible, for British insularity is mild, as compared with the Japanese.

Industrialization had already taken over two million people from the land and could take many more if Japan can be assured of raw materials, markets, and the food she cannot raise herself, to support her urban population and her masses of industrial workers. The emigration question, for the time being, was far less pressing than the economic problems of markets and materials.

Realization of Japan's needs in this respect, and unwillingness to precipitate a crisis that would strengthen the hands of militarists in Tokyo, who even in 1919 were beginning to talk openly about military penetration in Siberia and Mongolia, doubtless influenced the Allies in their decision to permit Japan to retain the Shantung peninsula until she settled the time and manner of its restoration to China. It will be remembered that this decision caused the Chinese delegates to withdraw from the Peace Conference, and that it still further widened the breach between Japan and China created by the Twenty-one Demands; but *if* the United States and Great Britain had not refused to admit the principle of race-equality by declining to discuss the question of

Japanese immigration in Australia and the United States, there would never have been any Far Eastern Triangle.

Racial discrimination relegating the Japanese to the position of inferiors, had the moral effect of creating a barrier between Japan and the West, appearing at the very moment when Japan and Europe seemed to be drawn closer together than ever before in history. It was like closing a window which, though transparent, cut off communication. Then and there was laid the foundation for Japan's new policy towards the other Mongol peoples, which is now beginning to make itself felt.

In the spring of 1919, however, Japan's first reaction from the disillusionment of Versailles was to support the militarists. Bills were passed in the Japanese Diet providing for the execution of a formidable naval programme. At the same time the militarists continued their schemes for the penetration and eventual absorption of Siberia by encouraging a state of chaos which would, they hoped, eventually afford an excuse for annexation. To all these schemes both government and people lent willing support. Even the liberal Count Takahashi who had succeeded to the Ministry allowed himself to be carried away by the patriotic fervor of the moment. Plans for further penetration and colonization were pushed in Manchuria, where the Japanese secured the support of the powerful dictator Chang Tso-lin. Japanese influence in China was exerted through control of the powerful Anfu party until its downfall in 1920, and later in more subtle ways.

The first and most important result of the racial imbroglio at Versailles was the growth of public sentiment against the United States, which was heartily reciprocated by the States on the Pacific Coast backed up by the people of Australia and the western provinces of Canada, among whom there was an almost hysterical fear of the "Yellow Peril."

Friction between Japan and the United States had resulted in such a tense situation that it seemed as if both countries were drifting towards an inevitable war. At this juncture Great Britain was induced by pressure exerted by the Dominions in the Imperial Conference to promise not to renew her alliance with Japan, which would automatically expire in 1921. As a substitute Mr. Lloyd George, who was at that time Premier, proposed that Great Britain and Japan should accept an invitation to a general conference to discuss officially the limitation of naval armaments, which had been issued by President Harding at the suggestion of Charles E. Hughes, then American Secretary of State, in the hope of catching up some of the loose ends left by the Versailles Peace and averting the menace of a war with Japan.

The invitation to the Conference came at an opportune moment to the Japanese, for notwithstanding the antagonism against the United States the military party had lost much of its influence. Military penetration in Siberia had not been a success. The conduct of the occupationary forces there had not helped to overcome the hereditary hatred of the Russians for the Japanese and the political confusion was not conducive to commercial penetration or exploitation of Siberia's natural resources. No extensive development could be undertaken without some definite settlement of the status of ·the occupied territory. It was realized that America would never give her consent to the alienation of any portion of Russian territory pending the establishment of a stable government in Russia—in fact the American Department of State had officially gone on record on the subject. Soviet Russia was gradually growing stronger and pushing farther East. Why—the Liberals began to ask—should the Japanese people be saddled with the expense of maintaining such enormous forces in Siberia with such small prospects of any returns? Gradually the Japanese people, despite their intense patriotism and their habit of unquestioning obedience to authority, began to think so too.

Further, the war-time bubble of prosperity had burst. As had been foreseen, the former European belligerents who had been obliged to let their foreign trade go during the war, were coming back into their former markets. Japanese trade with South America, the East Indies, and India began to fall off. The failure of the rice crop in 1919 had caused a scarcity of rice, accompanied by a rise in price, which brought about serious riots and demonstrations; there was considerable unemployment and a reflection of the universal post-war depression was evident in business circles. The war surplus had began to shrink, taxes were high, and so was the cost of living. Any prospect of reaching a settlement of Pacific problems which would enable Japan to safely reduce her military budget and to withdraw with dignity from the Siberian situation, was welcome to the government harassed by these domestic difficulties.

Consequently America's invitation was accepted and Japan was represented at the Conference which opened at Washington on November 12, 1921, and closed on February 6, 1922. Despite the avowed purpose of the Conference, which was to reach an agreement on the relative naval strength of the great Powers, it was generally understood that one of its main objects would be to thresh out all vital questions affecting the Powers with interest in the Pacific.

The question of naval armaments was disposed of by an agreement signed by Great Britain, the United States, Japan, France, and Italy, limiting the number of capital ships for each country, and fixing the relative strength of the three first-named at a ratio of 5-5-3. Further, each of these three Powers guaranteed the integrity of the territorial possessions of the others, in the Pacific—an agreement to which France also was a party. The United States and Great Britain, as evidences of good faith, agreed not to construct any fortified bases west of Hawaii or north of Hongkong respectively.

This treaty, known as the Four Power Pact, was a poor crust for Japan compared to the generous loaf of bread afforded her by the Anglo-Japanese Alliance. To Great Britain as well it could not have been as satisfactory as the close alliance which had helped to curb the designs of Russia in Manchuria without involving England, had relieved her from all anxiety about her Pacific possessions during the Great War, and might still prove invaluable to her in dealing with the new Russia and with China.

But the Mother Country was no longer a free agent in Imperial matters. The Dominions had to be handled with gloves, particularly after the war, which had developed a sturdy local patriotism and a whole class of "Dominion" policies not always identified with those of Great Britain. Although the Four Power Pact served to remove the fear of war in the Far East, it was not happy in its readjustments of Pacific problems. In fact it was remarkable not so much for the questions it discussed, as for the questions left untouched and unanswered.

From the first, the participating Powers, including, besides the Big Four (Great Britain, America, France and Japan), China, Italy, Belgium, and Portugal put aside all questions involving Siberia and Russia, merely reiterating vaguely the principle of the integrity of Russian territory. They also succeeded in eliminating from the agenda all discussion of Tibet, where Great Britain had predominant interests; Mongolia, torn between China and Russia; and Manchuria, where Japan insisted on hands off.

Instead they devoted particular attention to China. Japan readily agreed to evacuate Shantung as soon as possible, stipulating only for the protection of her rights to the operation of the Kiaochow-Tsinan railway pending its purchase by China through the gradual redemption of treasury notes.

The retrocession of Shantung made little impression on China, which regarded it as a tardy act of justice on the part of the great Powers. Events had moved rapidly in the Celestial Kingdom since 1919. Local political confusion had not obliterated a general political conviction that China had been very poorly rewarded for her participation in the Great War, and the tremendous spread of European education had only intensified the sense of racial injustice. The Chinese delegates to Washington, duly mindful of the fact that the Peking government was hopelessly mortgaged to the Treaty Powers, went as far as possible in pushing its demands for the abolition of extraterritoriality and restoration of tariff autonomy, control of the postal service, and the return of leased territories. To most of these demands they obtained evasive answers though they did succeed in obtaining a definite pledge of an upward revision of the Maritime Customs and the promise to call conferences to discuss the tariff and extraterritoriality, which were embodied in the agreement known as the Nine Power Treaty.

Japan, on her own initiative gave assurances that she would evacuate Siberia, with the exception of the northern half of the island of Sakhalin, as soon as possible; partly in deference to public opinion at home and abroad, partly because her statesmen had begun to perceive that Siberia was unprofitable as an invest-

ment, and lastly because she had already opened negotiations with
Russia through the Soviet-created buffer state, the Far Eastern
Republic. It may be noted here that these negotiations, taken up
and broken off at intervals for a period of four years, culminating in the conclusion of the Russo-Japanese Alliance in January,
1925, mark important stages in the evolution of Japan's foreign
policies, and the fact that they had actually begun when Japan
"magnanimously" consented to evacuate Eastern Siberia, is
significant!

No one in Japan was particularly impressed with the Washington Conference. To be sure it had the immediate result of reducing Japan's financial burdens, but on the other hand the stopping
of work in many shipyards due to the agreement to limit naval
armament increased the unemployment and distress among the
industrial workers. Admiral Kato, who headed the Japanese
delegation at Washington, was considered by many people to
have sold out Japan's interests to the Western Powers by his
concessions on the subject of armament.

Notwithstanding this feeling he was made Prime Minister on
his return from Washington, for Japan, always extraordinarily
sensitive to the cross currents of international politics, had begun
to realize that military imperialism was out of date. Her statesmen set themselves the task of completing the economic readjustments of the post-war period, and of remodelling the foreign
policy of the country with a view to expansion through economic
and commercial channels.

In the summer of 1922, when I was in Japan, economy was the
watchword in internal politics. The government had instituted a
crusade against wastefulness in government expenditure; the Diet
had pared the budget to the lowest possible figures. A systematic
propaganda campaign was being waged against extravagant living
and high prices. Production had been cut down in many industries, but prices were kept high by the refusal of most manufacturers to sell their stocks, accumulated at war-time prices under
the impression that the war might last much longer. This state
of affairs, coupled with unemployment, caused much suffering,
particularly among the poorer classes, including the tenant farmers

who constituted the majority of the agricultural population of
Japan.

It was estimated at that time that the average net income of the
small Japanese peasant-farmer after paying his rents and taxes,
was about 125 yen, roughly $65 a year, which was all he and his
family could count on for clothes and manufactured articles. Of
course he got his food and lodging off the land, but even so $65
seemed a pitifully small amount especially in view of the fact
that the peasants in Japan were practically all literates, and there
was such an appalling difference between their living standards
and their mental development. Whenever I saw, as I often did,
a group of these poor peasants in some country village sitting
under the electric lights supplied by the municipality, reading a
newspaper passed from hand to hand, after ten or twelve hours'
work in the rice-fields knee-deep in water, I used to wonder at
the social discipline of the Japanese. It is this social discipline, a
heritage of the clan feudal system combined with the passionate
nationalism which was part of the same system, that has enabled
them to go through the tremendous evolution since 1869, without
a popular revolution.

In 1922, however, there was a great deal of unrest though it
did not develop into any widespread disturbances. The labor
movement had been introduced from the West and had grown
with the industrial developments of the war period, but it was
still weak in comparison with the number of workers. By the end
of 1922 there were 389 trade unions with a membership of only
130,000 among over 2,000,000 workers, the small union membership partly accounted for by the large number of children employed in Japanese factories. Also there were only about 3,000,-
000 voters in a country of nearly 60,000,000 inhabitants. The
agitation for a manhood suffrage bill giving the vote to every
Japanese citizen over twenty-five years of age, which was not
passed until three years later, was almost universal, and it found
an outlet in a few rather wild demonstrations. Socialism had
taken root, as well as Communism, but the radical movement was
rigorously suppressed and even the Japanese Socialists, however
much they might decry the form and methods of the government,

THE FAR EASTERN TRIANGLE

were convinced that Japan must present a united front on any matters of external policy.

Commercial penetration, instead of militarism, was the slogan of Admiral Kato's Cabinet, which opened negotiations with the Soviet government shortly after the date had been fixed for the evacuation of Siberia. The Japanese troops began to leave Vladivostok early in September, and almost simultaneously, Yoffe, the representative of Soviet Russia, and Mr. Matsudaira, the representative of the Japanese Foreign Office, met at Changchun in Manchuria to discuss the bases for a possible Russo-Japanese accord. Naturally the military clique had had no hand in bringing about these negotiations, and remained as intransigent as ever. The navy faction, which was on the whole liberal, and Japanese big business, represented by such names as those of the Mitsuis, the Rothschilds of Japan, Baron Iwasaki and Viscount Inouye, the Mitsubishi interests, despite their conservatism, were urging on the government a rapprochement with Russia.

An ardent partisan of a Russo-Japanese accord was Baron Goto, the powerful Mayor of Tokyo and one of the most astute of Japanese politicians, who had pressed the government in 1918 to take part in the Allied Expedition to Siberia. After Japan had been compelled to relinquish her territorial hold on Eastern Siberia he felt that peaceful penetration might still retrieve what armed force had failed to win.

The negotiations at Changchun fell through, as those with the Far Eastern Republic at Dairen in 1921 had done, because of the firm attitude of the Japanese government with regard to Sakhalin. In following the reconquest of the historic frontiers of the Russian Empire by the Bolshevists we saw how the massacre of seven hundred Japanese at Nikolaievsk by Red Russian partisans in 1920—a massacre provoked in furtherance of the imperialistic aims of the military clans in Japan—resulted in the occupation of the entire Amur province in which Nikolaievsk is situated and of the northern half of Sakhalin, the southern half of which had been in Japanese hands since the Treaty of Portsmouth.

The Japanese government had been quite willing to evacuate the Siberian mainland after the Washington Conference, in furtherance of its new policies and in response to general dissatisfaction with the Siberian adventure, but it had refused to budge from Sakhalin, claiming the northern half of the island as security for an indemnity to be exacted at some future date from Russia. Actually it had no intention of surrendering Northern Sakhalin, which was rich in natural resources, particularly coal and petroleum, either to the Bolshevists or to any other Russian government, and it was supported by the great mass of public opinion, which, divided on the subject of peace with Russia, was almost unanimous on this point.

There were few foreigners who visited Sakhalin during the occupation between 1920 and 1922, but I chanced to be one of the number. In August, 1922, I was the guest of General Machida, commander-in-chief of the Japanese forces at Alexandrovsk, the principal town on the island. There, I saw indisputable evidences that the Japanese were preparing to stay. They were building substantial quarters for married army officers, something they would never have done unless they had contemplated establishing a permanent garrison, constructing a long mole and a jetty which would make an important port of the primitive harbor, advancing their railway line in Southern Sakhalin towards the occupied northern half of the island, bringing Korean immigrants by thousands to settle near Alexandrovsk, and they were cutting roads and prospecting over every foot of the interior. They had made preliminary tests to determine the extent of the oil-deposits on the island the concession for which had already been awarded to the Sinclair Oil Company of America, subject to the recognition of the Soviet government by the United States. Representatives of the Sinclair interests were refused permission to land there by the Japanese authorities!

At Changchun the Japanese remained adamant on the subject of Sakhalin, refusing to consider evacuation without the payment of an indemnity for Nikolaievsk, to which Russia would obviously never consent in view not only of the palpably provocative character of the massacre, but also of the fact that at the time it took place Moscow had no jurisdiction in the territory in question.

Even when Mr. Yoffe went informally to Tokyo in 1923, at Goto's invitation after the breakdown of the Changchun Conference, to discuss the possible establishment of commercial relations with Russia, the Sakhalin question obtruded itself on every occasion. It was not until two years later that developments in the international situation made it advisable for Mongol and Moscovite to come together.

The truth was that Japan, after the Washington Conference, lingered for a while at the crossroads. She was virtually isolated from Europe, diplomatically, by the breakdown of the Anglo-Japanese Alliance, for which the Four Power Pact and a membership in the League of Nations made a very poor substitute. At the moment she was not quite sure of herself—the time was scarcely ripe for her to be identified with a Pan-Asiatic policy or to attempt the upbuilding of a Mongol Federation.

Besides, there were many thoughtful men in Japan who sincerely desired to see her throw in her lot with the West in world-politics. After the Washington Conference there was a distinctly better feeling towards the United States and a relaxation of the tension that had become almost unbearable. The same attitude was evident with regard to Australia, whose "All-White" policy had aroused such bitterness among the Asiatics. The question of racial discrimination was not allowed to creep into official intercourse at least.

The frightful earthquake of 1923, which partly destroyed both Yokohama and Tokyo with appalling loss of life, roused the sympathy of the whole world. If it had not been for the fact that only a few weeks before their generous assistance to the earthquake sufferers both Great Britain and the United States had announced plans for the construction of formidable naval bases at Pearl Harbor in the Hawaiian Islands, and at Singapore, the gratitude of the Japanese nation would have been deeper and its foreign policy might have been considerably modified.

The reaction to these measures, however, was the creation of a cabinet headed by Admiral Yamamoto, who was a militarist very different from the pacific Admiral Kato. Yamamoto, who took office during the great earthquake, although he remained in power but a few months, gave a decisive turn to Japan's foreign policies. He was supported by Baron Goto, the mayor of Tokyo, and a rapprochement with Russia was on the boards, when the attempted assassination of the Prince Regent by a Communist temporarily discredited the Bolshevists and the pro-Russian Japanese faction. Goto was obliged to resign his office simultaneously with the Yamamoto cabinet.

In the meantime Japan had made overtures of friendship to China. The bitterness created by the Twenty-one Demands could not be wiped out all at once. There had been intense feeling with regard to Shantung, and the boycott of all things Japanese had been widespread, but when the Japanese took up negotiations directly with the Chinese concerning the ways and means for the evacuation of Kiaochow there were evidences of a distinct improvement in the relations between the two countries. In fact there were not a few influential Chinese whose attitude in the Shantung question was more a protest against the action of the European Powers in conceding Japan's right to hold Kiaochow, than a protest against the presence of Japanese troops in Shantung.

When the time came for the evacuation of the province, the Chinese were not ready to take over the port of Tsingtao and actually requested the Japanese not to leave at once. According to a Frenchman long resident in China whose account of the evacuation was published in a Paris newspaper, there were no Chinese soldiers to garrison the port of Tsingtao, and when soldiers were finally found they had no arms, so the commander begged the Japanese to leave some rifles. He was told that no Japanese soldier ever parted with his arms, but was promised a supply of rifles and cartridges in the near future. True to his promise, the Japanese commander after his return to Japan, sent a shipload of munitions for the Chinese garrison!

Almost simultaneously with the withdrawal from Shantung the Japanese Diet passed a bill authorizing the establishment of technical schools in China with the proceeds of Japan's share of the Boxer indemnity and a system of exchange professorships was created between Chinese and Japanese universities. Shortly afterwards when some Shantung bandits had held up a train between Peking and Shanghai and captured thirty foreigners, holding them for ransom, the other Treaty Powers headed by Great Britain were virtually unanimous in support of a plan for international control of Chinese railways. If it had not been for Japan's sturdy opposition to this plan Chinese railways would have gone the way of the Maritime Customs and the Salt Tax administration, falling under foreign management.

This action by Tokyo went far to wipe out the memories of the Twenty-one Demands, though the antagonism to Japan did not by any means disappear. In Manchuria, where the Japanese already had their established position, the closest relations existed between them and the Manchurian dictator Chang Tso-lin, who was, at the moment, sulking in his tent, metaphorically speaking, after an unsuccessful attempt to seize the central government at Peking.

Efforts at conciliation were also being made at this time in Korea. In Siam too a Japanese mission and Japanese advisers were helping to create closer relations between the two countries; feelers regarding the trade agreements with Indo-China were put out by the Foreign Office, and a strong current of Pan-Mongol sentiment began to appear among the students in the "Yellow" countries. They were all straws showing which way the wind blew. Japan while not yet isolated from the West was obviously seeking new ties in the Orient.

"Asia for Asiatics" was not a new slogan in Japan; it had been raised during the Great War by the militarists, who had favored deserting the Allies for Germany, and it was soon to be taken up again. Only a final touch was needed to complete the Asiatization of Japan's foreign policy. That touch was given by a bill restricting immigration to the United States, which threw down the gauntlet to racialism.

This bill, which became a law on July 1, 1924, as the Alien Immigration Act, put an end to the Gentleman's Agreement of 1908, by which the government of the United States had promised to oppose the passage of discriminatory laws against the Japanese in her various states, while Japan restricted the emigration of her nationals to laborers whose wives and children were already domiciled in America. It had been loyally kept on both sides, and had served to focus Japanese antagonism against America on the Western states which, in spite of pressure exerted from Washington, had enacted much anti-Japanese legislation.

The Pacific seaboard states, particularly California, the states along the Mexican border, and a few others, had their Alien Land Laws to prevent the Japanese from further aquisition of real property and placing various restrictions on the sale of their holdings. But after the Great War, when it was universally recognized that drastic legislation would be necessary to prevent the United States from being deluged by a flood of emigration from the war-exhausted countries of Europe, the anti-Japanese elements in America began a propaganda campaign for the exclusion of the Nipponese specifically and by statute. They succeeded in having inserted into the Alien Immigration Act a clause forbidding the entry into the United States of persons not eligible for naturalization, except as non-quota immigrants. As the Japanese were not eligible, the only persons permitted to come from Japan to America were those who had been previously admitted and were returning from a temporary stay abroad, students, and a limited number of professional men.

The clause was based on decisions of the Supreme Court in test cases brought by a Japanese resident of Hawaii and a Hindu respectively, which denied their right to citizenship, and interpreted the law on the statute-books of the United States forbidding the naturalization of any but "white" persons, as applicable to all peoples except those belonging to the Caucasian branch of the parent Aryan stock to which many Asiatic peoples owe their origin. Therefore the Alien Immigration Act was directed not only against the "Yellow Races"—it meant the exclusion and implied inferiority of all Asiatics.

Moreover, it was quite unnecessary. The general provisions of the act limited the number of emigrants from any country to the United States within a fixed quota amounting to 3 per cent of the emigrants from that country in 1900. The quota was to be reduced after 1926, to 2 per cent to be figured on the basis of 1890. As the number of all Asiatics in the United States, with the exception of Chinese and Japanese was negligible, the application of the quota would have practically eliminated any possibility of immigration from other Asiatic countries. One hundred Chinese and one hundred and forty-six Japanese only, could have been admitted yearly without the Exclusion Clause! Pernicious agitation on both sides was partly responsible for this step, the consequences of which none can foresee, but which are bound to be far-reaching in the history of civilization.

The rapid modernization of Japan had produced a group of ardent Imperialists with all the egotism of sudden success touched by the "folie de grandeur." They had visions of vast territorial expansion; stirred by the parallel between the position of Japan and that of Great Britain, they visualized a Yellow Empire on which the sun would never set. It did not obscure the dream of a vast Far Eastern Federation. It was merely part of their ambition to make the Pacific a Mongol sea. Australia and the East Indies called them, the South Sea Islands beckoned, but above all, the Americas. They wrote and talked a lot of high-sounding phrases about a Mongol America.

This attitude was bad, for it did not represent the views of the majority of the Japanese any more than it did those of the government. The natural trend of Japanese expansion is on the Asiatic mainland and along the coast towards the Philippines and the East Indies. There, for those who chose to regard it as such, lies the "Yellow Peril." Only a comparatively small part of the United States is suitable for Japanese colonization. From the beginnings of history the Japanese have been a rice-eating people. They will become acclimatized only where there is rice in abundance, and in general the climate of the United States is not favorable for rice culture. Besides these fundamental facts all the developments in Japan's foreign policies since the war have pointed towards Pan-Mongolism.

But in the Western states, particularly California, where there were about 70,000 of the 110,000 Japanese settled in the United States, the ideas of the Japanese chauvinists found ready credence. Japanese frugality and low living standards had made Yellow labor a formidable competitor to White. The increasing prosperity of the Japanese farmers inspired both fear and dislike. Irresponsible agitators began to talk wildly about the Japanese "menace." The new doctrine of racialism and of Nordic supremacy was invoked to demand a "lily-white" America. People began to discuss the possibility of a Japanese invasion on the Pacific Coast.

After the war there was the added argument, pushed by the American Legion, that Japanese aliens were keeping American-born demobilized soldiers out of their jobs. Fantastic stories were circulated about the high birth rate of the Japanese in the United States, of their dual citizenship, no different from the status of the nationals of many other countries! Australia and Canada, also haunted by the bugbear of yellow Imperialism, passed legislation against Asiatic immigration. Anglo-Saxon and Mongol formed distinct antagonistic groups in the Pacific.

When the Supreme Council of the Allies of which Japan, China, India, and Siam formed a part, refused to admit race-equality at the Versailles Conference, it marked a turning point in the relations between Europe and Asia. For a time Japan stood between the two civilizations to which she owed her origin and her development; with her exclusion from America she turned her back to the West. The rupture of the Anglo-Japanese Alliance in 1921, Singapore and Pearl Harbor in 1923, and the Alien Immigration Act in 1924, were so many steps towards the unification of Asia.

The storm that burst in Japan after the passage of the American exclusion act shook the country to its foundations. A coalition cabinet with Viscount Kato at its head, was swept into office; the entire press of Japan was vitriolic. Meetings of protest were held everywhere. The Christian communities of Japan took steps to unite with the Shinto and Buddhist sects to combat race hatred and race prejudice. Japanese public opinion sympathized passionately with the war for racial equality and political recognition being waged by the Indians in South Africa, and in many circles the same sympathy was openly expressed for the anti-foreign movement which was beginning to assume serious proportions in China.

Only a few months previously the Chinese revolutionary leader Sun Yat-sen had visited Japan, where speaking under the auspices of the Union of the Asiatic Peoples he had forecast an alliance of Russia, China, and Japan against the United States and Great Britain, and he had urged an immediate coalition between China and Japan as the first step towards this end. The idea was taken up and preached from one end of Nippon to the other by many ardent Pan-Mongol enthusiasts.

Viscount Kato and his cabinet let the storm rage. Baron Shidehara, the Japanese foreign minister, said little. But within a few months Japan had sent an important financial mission to Turkey, had arranged for a Japanese commercial fair in Constantinople, opened negotiations for the commercial treaty recently concluded with Turkey, as well as for a treaty with Persia, and had reopened negotiations with Russia, which this time resulted in the signing of a Russo-Japanese treaty in which Sakhalin was no longer a stumbling block.

The terms of the Russo-Japanese accord were drawn up by M. Yoshizawa, Japanese Ambassador at Peking, and M. Karakhan, the representative of Soviet Russia in China. The treaty provided for the resumption of normal relations between the two countries and stipulated for the future revision of all accords, treaties, and conventions concluded before the Russian Revolution of November, 1917, with the exception of the Portsmouth Treaty. The conclusion of a commercial accord, a convention with regard to fishing rights granted to Japanese citizens in Russian waters, and the question of the settlement of Japanese loans to the Imperial Russian government and of mutual claims, were to be made the subjects of future negotiations. Finally Soviet Russia expressed regret for the massacres at Nikolaievsk.

There was no mention of an indemnity for these massacres, however, in the two protocols attached to the treaty itself; the Japanese obtained something far more important than any indemnity—a first call on the natural resources of Sakhalin. The claims of the American company which had first obtained the right to exploit 50 per cent of the oil-deposits already located on the island were made over to Japan, and the exclusive right to prospect for further wells during a period of from five to ten years. Half of any new deposits discovered by the Japanese were to be conceded to them, and they were to have equal opportunities with other foreigners to lease the remaining fields, title to which was held by the Russian government. Japan also received the exclusive right to the development of the valuable coal-mines on the west coast of Sakhalin. In return the Soviet government was to receive a percentage of the yield from both oil-fields and coal-mines. Japan was to have the right to cut timber, build roads, import machinery, and install all the necessary technical equipment for the development of her concessions. The military evacuation of Sakhalin was to be effected by May 15, 1925, five months after the signing of the treaty.

While this agreement did not entirely satisfy the extreme Nationalists in Japan, it was on the whole most satisfactory, for it secured for her a priority amounting almost to exclusive rights on the resources of Sakhalin. As to the political control of the territory in question, Northern Sakhalin could easily be seized and held in the event of a rupture with Russia.

There is little doubt that eventually, by peaceful means or otherwise, Sakhalin will be absorbed as part of the Japanese State. Its strategic position no less than its oil deposits and its natural resources, make its possession most vital to Japan. Northern Sakhalin in Russian hands, is a broken link in the chain of the Japanese Archipelago which extends from Formosa to the tip of Kamchatka. It seems just as obvious that Japan must covet Sakhalin and scheme till she gets it, as that Russia, under whatever government, can never rest until she has filled out the southern line of her Siberian frontier by taking in Northern Manchuria, cutting off the nasty salient that bites into her territory and obtaining control of the Chinese Eastern Railway.

In any case the Russo-Japanese treaty accomplished one of the immediate objects of the new Japanese foreign policy—it struck a direct blow at England! With the Asiatic mainland as her objective and her back resolutely turned to Europe, Japan's next move must obviously be to usurp Great Britain's place, as far as may be, in China. The fact that Russia's aims were identical did not at all disturb Japanese statesmen. They knew perfectly well that while Karakhan was negotiating the Russo-Japanese treaty he was supporting the extreme Chinese Nationalist elements in the perennial civil war which was bound to have its usual summer effervescence. But it happened that Nationalist aims were centred about the Valley of the Yangtze-kiang, where British interests were the greatest.

Notwithstanding the losses she must incur, for there were many investments of Japanese capital in South China, Japan watched the course of events with great composure. Gauging the extent of Bolshevist influence in the Kuomintang far more accurately than the European Powers, she was not altogether averse to letting Communist propaganda get the odium of having inspired Chinese Nationalism morally and materially, in its combat against the Western Powers and particularly Great Britain. She had no fear of permanent Russian dominance in any government which might be eventually established on the Yangtze-kiang, and with such a government she might perhaps very profitably negotiate.

The Peking government was too hopelessly bound by its debts to the European Treaty Powers to free itself within a reasonable time, and the Southern movement held more promise for the future as far as Japanese interests were concerned. However, Japan's policy was to seem to co-operate with the other Powers in any measure they might take to support the central government. Consequently she was represented in the Customs Conference and on the Extraterritoriality Commission which met in Peking in 1925, in conformity with promises made to China three years before at the Washington Conference.

At the former she came out openly in favor of tariff autonomy for China. The fact that the increasing internal confusion made it impossible to accomplish anything at the conference did not prevent Japan's gesture from having a profound effect upon the Chinese people, although they could not quite forget that Viscount Kato, as Minister of Foreign Affairs in 1915, had drawn up the Twenty-one Demands.

In the meantime Japan took good care to strengthen her position in Manchuria, which was a most valuable asset politically as well as economically. As long as her hold on Manchuria was secure, Russia's propaganda in the South could only further her plans to create conditions which would result in loosening Europe's hold in China and its possible division into several separate states which might be united as part of a Mongol Federation under Japanese leadership. While the Russians were engaged in penetrating towards the Yangtze they would not care to risk antagonizing the Japanese, who could attack them in their most vulnerable spot in the Far East—the Manchurian salient that penetrated Eastern Siberia, and could block the shortest route between Moscow and Vladivostok. The Japanese, moreover, were aware that Siberia was potentially a valuable market and a friendly Power in their rear on the Asiatic mainland would be invaluable in the event of the remote contingency of war with the Anglo-Saxon Bloc, Great Britain and her colonies.

For all these reasons the Russian Alliance was highly desirable to Japan, its many advantages fully compensating her for the possible disadvantages from contact with the contagion of Bolshevism. Nevertheless it is one of those Machiavellian combinations based on expediency and running against the grain, racially, geographically, and politically. It is hard to foresee a reconciliation of Russia's historic claims—warm-water outlets on the Pacific, penetration to the Yangtze, a flank approach to India, with Japan's imperative needs for markets and outlets in China and Manchuria, unless we assume the feasibility of a Pan-Asiatic League of Nations.

Doubtless all these ideas and many more were in the minds of Viscount Kato and the members of his cabinet when they concluded the treaty with Russia; at the same time they took care to adopt a uniformly friendly though strictly neutral policy towards the warring elements in China while making it perfectly clear that they would tolerate no interference in Manchuria.

The conclusion of the treaty drew forth much comment in the European press, and there were sensational reports regarding clauses whose contents had been rigidly guarded from the public. The Japanese Ambassador to London was obliged to formally deny the truth of an article published in a German newspaper which declared that Russia and Japan had agreed to put at the disposal of China 200,000 Russian troops equipped with Japanese munitions in case of armed intervention by Great Britain, America, or France. French opinion inclined to the belief that the Russo-Japanese alliance foreshadowed a Russo-Asiatic Bloc backed by Germany.

But the Kato cabinet, having solved the most immediate of Japan's foreign problems—that of relations with Russia—and having outlined the bases of a future Asiatic policy, turned to domestic matters even more urgent which demanded their attention. Foremost among these was the extension of the franchise to which the coalition government composed of the representatives of the three principal parties known as the Kenseikai, the Seiyukai, and the Kakushin Club were pledged. Actually the differences in principle between these factions were very small. Roughly the Kenseikai represented the more conservative elements, the Seiyukai with its affiliated faction the Seiyuhonto was liberal and expressed the views of Japanese business interests, and the Kakushin favored the views of the growing Pan-Mongol group, friendly to the South Chinese and all anti-European movements.

It had been easier to get the coalition to agree on foreign policies than on internal questions, but notwithstanding many differences the Kato cabinet secured the passage of the Suffrage Bill which gave the vote to eleven million electors, including the industrial workers who had hitherto not had a voice in the government. Only the military were excluded from the franchise, which was given to every male Japanese over twenty-five years of age.

The carrying out of the other reforms necessitated by post-war conditions in Japan was a difficult task. The favorable commercial balance of 1919 had shifted. Imports had steadily increased, and after the earthquake, when the need of reconstruction demanded the importation of materials and manufactured articles, the value of goods brought into the country exceeded the value of those exported to foreign markets by many millions. A duty of 100 per cent on luxuries was imposed, and the budgets were cut until a saving of $25,000,000 was realized on military and $60,000,000 on civil expenditure. Steps were taken to extend Japan's markets. An intensive commercial propaganda was undertaken in Indo-China and the East Indies and the unfavorable ratio of exports to imports was reduced by two-thirds, the embargo on the export of gold which had existed since the war was lifted, and the yen which had sunk extremely low during the acute commercial depression of the post-war period, came within a few points of its normal value, forty-nine cents.

Nevertheless conditions were far from satisfactory. In spite of an increase in the rice crop justifying the reimposition of the tax which had been lifted several years previously, Japan was still compelled to import over 1,500,000 tons of rice. Unemployment continued, and the efforts of the government to revise the system of taxation and to stabilize the cost of living were hampered by political intrigues, while the enormous cost of the reconstruction work necessitated by the earthquake was a constant drain on the treasury.

The Coalition Government, notwithstanding many difficulties and much internal disunion, had a long life, continuing in power after the death of Viscount Kato in January, 1926. The first elections which took place under the Universal Suffrage law in the spring of 1926, caused the blossoming-forth of any number of new parties shading from pink to red. Foremost among them were a Social Democratic Party, and an Agricultural Bloc constituted with the idea of waging war on the absentee landlords and large landholders.

The formation of all these factions, no one of which was large enough to be a serious competitor to the established parties, was nevertheless an evidence of the profound unrest created in Japan, as elsewhere, by social and political movements since the war. It had been made articulate by the extension of the suffrage. There were some riots and disturbances created by the radical parties but they were caused by discontent with low wages, long hours in factories, unemployment, and the high cost of living in the towns, and by the eternal differences in the country between the landlords and tenant farmers, rather than by any revolutionary political activity.

Japan's foreign relations continued to follow the lines laid down by Kato's ministry. Conditions in China had grown more and more chaotic and the serious riots in Shanghai in the summer of 1925, were only the beginnings of a series of anti-foreign outbreaks. Through all these disturbances Japan acted with the greatest moderation, only interfering in the war between North and South when it became absolutely necessary to protect Japanese lives and property. Time and again the Japanese Foreign Minister, Baron Shidehara, intimated in speeches and otherwise that he would be quite willing to negotiate with any government or governments formed in China which would recognize Japan's rights in Manchuria.

Public opinion in Japan was strongly against any intervention in China and felt that no plans for reconstruction imposed on her by any foreign nations could be successful. Russo-Japanese relations continued to improve after the signing of the treaty; the first important step towards the long desired commercial penetration of Siberia was taken when Viscount Goto and other Japanese financiers secured the concession already mentioned to exploit the resources of the Maritime and Amur provinces permitting 90,000 Japanese laborers to be sent into the country. Concerning this concession a French newspaper remarked pertinently: "The Japanese hope to obtain from Siberia many materials which they have hitherto been obliged to get from abroad, principally in America. Many steamship lines will cross the Japan Sea, which will become a real Nipponese Mediterranean."

The exportation of Japanese and Chinese goods to Europe by way of Russia was encouraged by the Soviet government, which reduced rates on the Trans-Siberian Railway by 50 per cent, but perhaps the most significant indication of the political expediency of the Russo-Japanese accord was that apparently no friction existed between Tokyo and Moscow on the burning subject of propaganda. Even when a Communist uprising took place in Korea, instigated by the Japanese Communist Katayama who had been living in Moscow for several years, the Japanese government took no official cognizance of Russia's hand in the matter, and in China it skilfully avoided any conflict with the Russians.

The European Powers, their protégé Chang Tso-lin in Manchuria, or the central government at Peking, always bore the brunt of any unpleasantness affecting Japanese interests. In the spring of 1927, negotiations were opened for the drawing up of a commercial treaty between Japan and Russia, and negotiations for a similar treaty with the Peking government had made considerable headway.

Meanwhile the United States had protested in vain to Peking against the virtual Japanese monopoly of the wireless service, notwithstanding the existence of a consortium by which America, Great Britain, and Japan were to operate the radio in China; and when there was a dispute between the British and the Peking authorities over the administration of the Maritime Customs, the Chinese government intimated that it might replace the British Inspector General with a Japanese.

In January, 1927, there was an important though unofficial conference at Tokyo between an envoy of the Chinese Nationalist government and officials of the Japanese Foreign Office. The Japanese press at the time stated that economic concessions in the Valley of the Yangtze-kiang had been offered to Japan including the rights for railway construction. Japan's game in China was to play all combinations, turning the tide of Nationalist sentiment against the Western Powers—a game requiring considerable skill, which she used most admirably during the troubles at Hankow when it was necessary for her to protect her nationals and not seem to desert the other Treaty Powers without antagonizing the Chinese too much.

During 1926, the economic condition of Japan had not materially improved. The coalition government, united on external policies, was still unable to accomplish vital reforms in the administration and in financial matters, and the burden of the earthquake was very heavy on the government—$110,000,000, for reconstruction constituted one of the largest items on the budget of 1926-27. The unfavorable trade balance continued. In an effort to combat it a widespread thrift campaign was inaugurated by the women of Japan who combined to save a sen, or half a cent a day to help to pay the foreign debt of the Empire. The rise of the yen, beneficial in some respects, and the drop in the price of silk, one of Japan's chief articles of export, presaged the financial crisis which came in the spring of 1927 when a number of large banks went to the wall because of the delay of the government in securing the passage of a bill providing payment for emergency paper notes issued at the time of the earthquake in 1923. It was later passed but not soon enough to prevent the downfall of the coalition ministry, which was succeeded by a Seiyukai cabinet under Baron Tanaka.

One of the first acts of the new cabinet was to declare a moratorium of several weeks and to guarantee a loan to the Bank of Japan, which restored credit, kept up the exchange, and averted the danger of a disastrous panic. By early summer the country had apparently weathered the crisis.

With regard to relations with China, the tendency of the Tanaka government as evinced in a speech made by the Prime Minister, seemed to be towards the maintenance of harmonious relations with the other Powers in China, but it is extremely doubtful if the groundwork of Japan's Asiatic policy based on reconciliation with China has suffered any modifications. Under all the surface differences the three peoples of the Triangle in the Far East are being drawn together by the ties of race and a common antagonism to the West.

In spite of the economic difficulties and all the social readjustments precipitated in Japan as a result of her forced industrialization and the Great War, the stability of Japanese institutions and the strength of her national sentiment were strikingly demonstrated after the death of the Emperor Yoshihito, which occurred on December 24, 1926. There are few Japanese, even among the radicals, who are not proud of the fact that their government is the oldest on earth. The new Emperor of Japan, Hirohito, who has also taken the name of Showa—"The Enlightened Peace"— is the 124th of his line, which extends far back into the shadowy regions where history and mythology merge into one.

Through all the vicissitudes of Nippon's past, the "Heaven-Born" emperor, even when deprived of temporal power during the age of the feudal barons, was the spiritual leader of the nation, the link between every Japanese and his past—his ancestors, who were part and parcel of his daily life. The family, the clan, and the nation, all were personified in him. When the Emperor came out of his seclusion after the nearly bloodless revolution of 1869 that overthrew the feudal system, he none the less continued the tradition. Meiji, the Great Emperor, the father of modern Japan, in his own person did much to harmonize the new institutions with old beliefs and to make the imperial office the symbol of the unity of the state.

The funeral of Yoshihito, which took place on February 8, 1927, afforded a striking illustration of the loyalty and reverence of the Japanese people for this symbol. The ceremonies, the same as those which had existed in Japan for sixteen centuries, brought thousands of people to Tokyo, who in spite of the bitter cold camped out on the pavements to see the cortège pass in the early morning, for the funeral ceremonies lasted all night. At every door in Tokyo on the eve of the funeral hung a memorial lantern, and the smart guard of khaki-clad soldiers which accompanied the funeral procession marched with the Shinto priests, who sang weird chants in a tongue so old that it was unintelligible to most Japanese. At eleven at night, trains and automobiles stopped, telegraph and telephone were still, all the machinery of modern life was hushed for three minutes to do honor to the mortal remains of the Heaven-Born passing through Tokyo in an ancient palanquin with wooden wheels, while his people knelt in the streets.

While the Emperor Hirohito, who was regent for six years before his accession to the throne, has modern ways and extremely liberal views, he is still the spiritual heir of Japan's past and the symbol of its present greatness to the vast majority of Japanese, in spite of the religious scepticism and the new social and political ideals that are so widespread. The tradition of the Empire and the discipline inherited from the feudal government of the Clans, have so merged the individuality of the Japanese in that of the state that the interests of the nation come before those of any group or faction. This fact accounts for their having weathered so far all the political storms and economic upheavals of the post-war period.

National interests impelled the Japanese in the beginning to seek expansion on the mainland of Asia at the expense of other Asiatic peoples. Their national pride, roused by their relegation to a position of racial inferiority in Europe, is urging them to combine with the exceedingly practical aspirations for markets and materials the ideal of a Pan-Mongol Federation in which Japan would take the leadership. If the Mongol people should eventually form such a union, Japan would probably find herself of far less importance to the vast continental population of the "Yellow countries" than insular Britain is today to her Dominions, but for the present she is the one constant factor in the flux and confusion of Far Eastern policies.

KOREA

Were it not for the strongly individual character of the Koreans themselves, Korea, so small in comparison with the vastness of China and the widely dispersed Island Empire of Japan, could scarcely be considered to form a side of the Mongol triangle. Chosen, as its inhabitants call it, is a long peninsula, a prolongation of Manchuria, separating the Japan Sea from the Yellow Sea. Geographically it forms a natural stepping stone between the Asiatic mainland and the Japanese Archipelago. The Korean Straits, less than a hundred miles in width, separate Chosen from the Japanese island of Kiushu.

Politically, Korea would normally seem to fall within the sphere of Manchuria, but from the earliest times the Koreans possessed a distinct civilization and national characteristics that differentiated them not only from the inhabitants of near-by Manchuria, but also from the Chinese and the Japanese who at various periods overran their country. The fact that Korea was a poor country was probably responsible for the failure hitherto of either China or Japan to take steps to assimilate the Koreans. The Korean Empire, now acknowledging the suzerainty of China, now that of Japan, remained intact under its weak and decadent rulers until, as we have seen, Japanese and Russian penetration running afoul of each other in the Far East precipitated a struggle which began with the elimination of China as a factor in the rivalry of the two Powers for the economic control of Manchuria and ended with the annexation of Korea by Japan in 1910.

Under a beneficent and liberal administration, Japanese control of Korea would have been the best possible thing for the country. Even if their government had not been so hopelessly backward and inefficient, the Koreans did not have within their own boundaries the economic makings of a modern state. Their natural resources were very limited; the cultivable area of their territory was insignificant compared with the vast ranges of barren mountains from which it was impossible even to eke a bare living. The majority of the 17,000,000 population lived under conditions little better than those in which they kept their live stock. They were densely ignorant, learning among them being confined to a class of dry-as-dust scholars versed in little but Buddhist lore.

Oppressed by a despotic and utterly rotten bureaucracy which dissipated the public revenues and did nothing for their well-being, they nevertheless had the passive resignation and endurance that go with Buddhism and a very profound attachment to their rulers and the ancient Korean culture, of which little was left but the tradition. The small progressive groups, who had come into contact with European ideas largely through the missionaries, would have been powerless without outside assistance to raise their country to the status of an independent modern state.

Ethnically, morally, and socially, Japan and Korea were akin. Despite the dislike of Japan which was part and parcel of the innate Korean conservatism and contempt of everything foreign, if the Japanese had pursued a different course with regard to Chosen they might have laid the foundations at least a decade earlier for their present Pan-Mongol policy.

But the Nipponese statesmen of the pre-war period were too shortsighted to grasp the possibilities of friendship with Korea; they were going through a process of evolution in Imperialism, the first stage of which is Militarism. The Koreans were to be treated like a conquered people and forcibly assimilated. A few farseeing Japanese like Marquis Ito, realizing the strong national individuality of the Koreans, tried to convince their government that it would be wiser to make friends than slaves of them, but they were powerless to stop the ruthless colonization, the heartless exploitation of Chosen, and the cruel assumption that the Koreans must surrender their identity and become Japanese.

During nine years between the annexation and the close of the Great War, Korea became materially prosperous under Japanese rule, but morally she was a nation in arms. It would take much too long to describe in detail the policy that made the Koreans a nation of conscientious objectors to all things Japanese, until finally a national movement was born. It had its headquarters in Shanghai, and was directed by a group of young political exiles, most of whom had been educated in Europe. They were very much under the influence of Western ideals, and when the Great War broke out they took quite literally the declaration of President Wilson that it was to make the world safe for democracy. Nowhere did Mr. Wilson have more passionately loyal followers than among the Korean Nationalist leaders, who organized the "Bloodless Revolution" and prepared the Korean declaration of independence in 1919, fully convinced that the benevolent Powers assembled at Versailles to punish Germany for her grasping imperialism, would see that justice was done to Korea. They had no concrete programme, they had formed no plan of revolutionary action. It had not occurred to them that such a thing was necessary. They took quite simply and literally the statements regarding the rights of little peoples to self-determination that were flooding the press and resounding in the assemblies of Western countries.

Their tragic disillusionment when they found that not only Japan but all the Allied Powers ignored the principles for which ostensibly they had fought the war, can better be imagined than described. The wholesale arrests, tortures, and executions that followed the peaceful mass-demonstrations of the poor Koreans roused the indignation of the whole world, as well as that of the liberal elements in Japan, but the Koreans never forgot that not one of the Western Powers which had prated so smugly of self-determination was willing to take official action to restore what they felt were the inalienable rights of the Korean people. To complete this disillusionment they witnessed the relegation of the Yellow peoples to a position of inferiority at the Versailles Conference and they began to realize that there was no hope of salvation from the West.

Almost at the same time Japan had come to this same conclusion, and the government was beginning to perceive the advantages of reaching a better understanding with the other Mongol peoples.

In August, 1919, Admiral Baron Saito, who was noted for his liberal views, was appointed Governor-General and he at once inaugurated a more liberal policy with regard to Korea. Three years later, when the Washington Conference had been instrumental in forcing out the old military party, Saito was left free to carry out his ideas, and he inaugurated further reforms. The present policy of the Japanese government tends towards the development of organs of local government which may ultimately place Korea on a footing similar to that of Great Britain's overseas Dominions.

The Governor-General of Korea is a civil, not a military, official. He is assisted in his administration by a number of bureaus, composed of department heads forming a sort of rudimentary cabinet. In each of the thirteen provinces into which the country is divided there is an advisory council to handle financial matters as well as taxation, with a majority membership of Koreans. There are also local school councils. Koreans are eligible for all public offices, they receive the same salaries as the Japanese and there is no apparent discrimination against them. There is a uniform school system, and the study of both Korean and Japanese is compulsory in the common schools.

Korea has her own budget and a considerable degree of fiscal autonomy. Steps have been taken to stop the iniquitous system under which Koreans were forcibly transplanted to Manchuria and elsewhere to make room for Japanese colonists. Freedom of the press and speech have been granted in large measure and the abominable system of espionage and police supervision which prevailed under the old military régime has been virtually wiped out. The Japanese school teachers no longer wear swords; they have Korean colleagues with whom they are on excellent terms! There are Korean policemen, and even Korean judges who sit on the bench to judge their fellow countrymen.

Anyone who travels in Chosen will inevitably have an opportunity of comparing conditions in the old days with the improvement brought about by the Japanese. Excellent roads, comfortable railways, good hotels, magnificent schools and public buildings, evidences of an efficient public health service, new factories, model farms and experiment stations, all created by the Japanese, make a favorable impression, while even the most casual observer may still see here and there one of the miserable poverty-stricken mud-villages of the old days when there was such a vast gulf between the governors and the governed.

The patronizing attitude of the Japanese towards the Koreans which was so galling to their national pride has almost entirely disappeared; the people, better off physically and materially than they have been for many generations, are beginning to assert their native intelligence and to develop initiative and real ability along many lines. It is still claimed that there is some commercial discrimination against Koreans by the Japanese, but on the whole there is much better feeling.

The Nationalist movement has undergone a considerable modification. Broadly speaking it is divided into two factions—a moderate group which believes that Korea can earn her right to independence within the fold of a Mongol Federation, and the extremists who profess, either sincerely or as a means to an end, adherence to Communist doctrines. There is a representative of the "Provisional Korean Republic," which has never existed on Korean soil, who lives in Moscow. Once in a while the officers of this Republic start disturbances in Korea, usually taking advantage of some circumstance that recalls to people the glories of their past. Thus the last outbreak, in June, 1926, was an abortive revolution with the object of declaring a Communist régime in Korea, which took place during the funeral of the late Emperor, Prince Yi, who became a puppet ruler with the inauguration of the Japanese protectorate and was forced to abdicate in 1910.

While there is still some distrust of Japan among the more intelligent Koreans, and the lower classes can still be stirred to unreasoning loyalty to the vanished empire, the majority of such public opinion as exists in the country is in favor of making common cause with Nippon. There is no doubt that the old struggle for the control of Manchuria is on; the Soviet camouflage cannot entirely conceal the Russian Bear or the purpose of his movement south. Korea is unable to stand alone between Russia and Japan, because she is not strong enough to play one against the other. If she wins her independence it must be within a Mongol bloc.

CHINA

Events have moved so rapidly in China during the last eight years that it has been next to impossible for most of us to follow them. Indeed the complexities of the current dispatches are such as to make them the despair of anyone who was not born and bred in familiarity with the Chinese nomenclature, so unintelligible to

Western ears. We often miss the real significance of movements and happenings in our efforts to remember which one of half a dozen "Changs" won or lost this or that battle, or to recall the relative positions of Hankow and Hangchow. They help to make it more difficult to trace the ebb and flow of the apparently endless civil war which is but one of the many disruptive forces in China today, or the conflicting currents in her internal and external policies. We become involved in a mass of bewildering details and kaleidoscopic changes punctuated with puzzling names until we are likely to lose sight of the real issues.

Before we attempt to review contemporary happenings in China, we must above all remember that in the tangled web of Chinese politics since the world peace there is one unbroken thread —a newly awakened race consciousness. We call it nationalism, but it is stronger than mere nationalism. Its existence has changed the whole trend of Far Eastern politics. As we have seen, it is not confined to China; it must be considered apart from Chinese domestic problems, which are many and complex. Among the latter, however, we may pick out several that may be considered to be of prime importance.

First and foremost is the question of the establishment of a system of government that will effectively take the place of the Empire, for the Republic has been a failure! With the abdication of the Emperor, the symbol of the unity of the Chinese state, China ceased to exist except as a geographical entity. The struggle between North and South and the groupings and regroupings of the provinces around or against the two chief combatants are the result of efforts, conscious or unconscious, to find a satisfactory substitute for the vanished Empire.

On general lines the issue which the opposing factions must decide is whether China is to have a centralized government or to form a federation of autonomous states. In this connection, it is interesting to remember that even in America where the people may be said to have been politically ripe for representative government, it took a war lasting four years to determine whether the United States constituted a Union or a Federation.

Secondly, China must kill the hydra of militarism—no easy task when there is not, as at present, a central authority strong enough to curb the power of the Tuchuns, or War Lords, whose maintenance of separate armies in the various provinces contributes to the existing chaos. The War Lords themselves are a product of the Republic. When the Constitution was proclaimed there was so little understanding of the real nature of a republican government throughout the country, that one of the first acts of the President was to send into the provinces, some of them nearly a month's journey away from Peking, officers of the newly created national army to act as military governors and to keep an eye on the conservative and often recalcitrant civil authorities. These military governors, called Tuchuns (meaning literally heads of army corps), recruited their local armies ostensibly for the purpose of keeping order and were therefore permitted to apply a portion of the provincial revenues to their maintenance. Their power was very great, so that any one of them could easily, if he had the mind, defy the central government. When such a situation arose the President was obliged to call on the Tuchuns of adjoining provinces to compel him to submit to the central authority.

Soon the waning prestige of Peking made the control of the War Ministry over the provincial War Lords merely nominal. The Tuchuns increased their forces at will, becoming absolute dictators in their own provinces; soon the control of the central government itself was vested in the hands of the Tuchun in command of the metropolitan army area. The Tuchuns are ubiquitous. Their groupings and regroupings, due to the fact that many of them with their armies can be bought and sold, frequently account for the baffling changes of allegiance recorded in news dispatches from China. When we hear that General So-and-So, who has been fighting with this or that faction has gone over to the other side, we may be sure that the new combination has been formed either for pecuniary reasons or because one War Lord has become so powerful that his former allies combine with his opponents to drag him down.

The existence of these provincial armies, said to number about two million men, is an unmitigated evil for China. Until they are abolished the civilian population can never be secure from the depredations of the War Lords and civil war will be endemic in China. Improvement in communications, the extension of roads, railways, and telegraph lines, will help to undermine the power of the Tuchuns in the outlying provinces by creating a community of interests between various sections. The steady growth of an industrial population in the large cities, forming a more or less enlightened proletariat, and popular education, which is making great headway despite political conditions, are helping to weaken the authority of the Tuchuns, but at present China is still in the grip of this pernicious form of military despotism.

Thirdly, China must attune her economic, social, and cultural life to the tempo of the modern world of which she is becoming a part—a step necessary for the realization of her racial aims and ambitions. Japan has made this readjustment. Turkey and other countries are taking steps to bring it about today under far more stable internal conditions. China must undertake it in the midst of a political upheaval and of an attempt to restore her racial prestige lost during the era of foreign aggression.

Economically, China is in a state of transition. Within a relatively short space of time the coast cities have become industrialized; machines and factories have largely replaced home industries, but there has been no proper legislation for the protection of industrial workers. She must take steps in the interest of these workers or face the possibility of serious labor disturbances. She must tackle the problem of the redistribution of her population. It is a far cry between the densely populated areas of Canton, with 875 inhabitants to the square mile, and the far western provinces, where in many districts there are less than 40 in a corresponding area. She must improve communications, develop her enormous resources, and mobilize her great national wealth.

China must pay her debts, for the sake of her own credit, without regard to the manner in which they were incurred. She must eliminate illiteracy, for unless this is done there is no hope of establishing any form of representative government to take the place of the old communal village life which is doomed to disappear; and her people must adapt their old culture, ethics, and social habits to the new ideals and habits of living that are part of the new world order.

Lastly—and this is perhaps the most vital problem of all for the Chinese—they must readjust their international relations. To do this they must cement their relations with the other members of the great Mongol family; but they must also find a modus vivendi with the West.

The crux of this matter is the problem of the "unequal" treaties concluded with various European Powers since 1842. That these treaties, granting rights to foreigners in China without securing any corresponding privileges or advantages to the Chinese, must eventually be abrogated or modified is unquestioned. Today all factions and all parties are agreed on this point. Consular jurisdiction by the Treaty-Powers over their own nationals, foreign control of the customs, leased territories which constitute so many foreign colonies on Chinese soil, and the most favored nation clauses applicable only in one direction, must go!

But the question is the means by which China is to free herself from the incubus of the treaties. The South Chinese have taken the stand that they must all be abrogated at the same time; the Peking government has held that they should be abrogated as they terminate. No thinking Chinese would like to see matters reach a pass where any or all of the Powers might employ military intervention to protect European vested rights amounting to more than $2,500,000,000. Even the South Chinese, antagonistic though they may be with regard to foreigners, cannot afford to isolate themselves, as Soviet Russia has done, from the world economic system.

In their relations with the Treaty Powers the Chinese must find a nice mean which will satisfy their newly roused race-consciousness, restore their loss of prestige, or "face," as we have learned to call it, and still enable them to profit by European co-operation in the creation of a modern state.

They are handicapped in their efforts not only by their own internal problems, but also by the fact that China is the battle ground in the struggle between Russia and Great Britain for the control of the Yangtze valley and the strategic approaches to India. The end of this contest, of which the Bolshevist agitation in China is only a passing phase, is not in sight. It must long be a disturbing factor, although it may help to further the formation of the Mongol Bloc. Certainly the only nation that can hope to gain any advantage from it is Japan, to which China is already more or less consciously turning.

If we keep in mind the problems just outlined, contemporary happenings in China appear important or unimportant only as they denote progress or lack of progress towards their ultimate solution, and we can afford to forget the names of warring Tuchuns and changing cabinets. Therefore, if the appelations of certain personalities sufficiently important to figure prominently in recent events do not appear in these pages, they have been deliberately omitted. We are more interested in China's reactions to the Versailles Conference than in the delegates who refused to sign the Treaty because they felt that they had been betrayed by the European Powers which had awarded Shantung to Japan, and had at the same time proclaimed by inference the essential inferiority of their Yellow Allies.

The Shantung award put the finishing touch to the lessons in international politics that the Chinese had learned during the Great War. In the first place, they had seen the Treaty Powers which had always presented a united front, split into two camps by the great conflict itself. They had seen in the cases of Germany and Austria, how easy it was to abolish extraterritoriality. No one insisted on the restoration of former treaty rights to the defeated Central Powers. Then they had seen revolutionary Russia voluntarily relinquish these same treaty rights. They had listened to all the bickerings and disputes at Versailles and they had come to perceive that the European Concert was not so formidable after all. Just as the Russo-Japanese War had destroyed the myth of European invincibility, so the Great War destroyed the fiction of Western moral solidarity.

The indignation over Shantung found its expression in the Japanese boycott and the downfall of the pro-Japanese Anfu Club, but the disillusionment with Versailles also found vent in a growing national movement directed against all foreign influence. It was not confined to any particular section of the country though it was most in evidence among the students, particularly in Peking, where there were no less than 20,000 in the various higher schools and colleges.

All through the sessions of the Peace Conference mass student demonstrations were held in various Chinese cities. The student movement which had been identified with the "New Tide"—a movement to stimulate a national renascence—became political as well as cultural. Its inspiration, however, was drawn not so much from the old placid philosophical China of the Confucian Sages as from the turbulent Western world that had at last invaded the Celestial calm of the Chinese Intellectuals. Modern education in China had come exclusively through Western channels. The unequal treaties so bitterly denounced had been responsible for providing Young China with the weapons she was beginning to turn against Europe. The schools and colleges established in China by the Christian missionaries, thanks to these unequal treaties, had disseminated European social and political ideals.

The students who "went to see England, the first Western nation that invaded her, soon after 1842," as a Chinese writer in a recent periodical naïvely remarked, were the first of many who emigrated to foreign countries, where they came in touch with all the currents of modern thought. They soon began to perceive the vast difference between the Christian ethics professed by Western nations and their application of these ethics in their relations with China. Their sense of humiliation gradually crystallized into a deep resentment that found its outlet in political action.

The great masses of the Chinese people were quite untouched by the new movement. It was only among the industrial population of the coast cities and a few manufacturing centres on the Yangtze that it found an outlet in strikes and labor agitation. The seeds of class war and industrial discontent had begun to sprout, but the agitation was focused on the foreign mill-owners.

If at this juncture the Allies had recognized the signs of the impending storm and had satisfied the national pride which was about the only sentiment common to all the parties and factions, much that has since happened might have been averted and China would not have called in her Eurasian neighbor Russia to help her combat Europe. Definite assurances that the Treaty Powers would take steps towards the gradual relinquishment of extraterritoriality, and the establishment of tariff autonomy, the retrocession of Shantung, and the assertion of the principle of racial equality would have saved China's face and would have trans-

formed a national crusade into a diplomatic problem. But the
rivalries and differences between the Powers themselves, coupled
with the pernicious racialism of the post-war era, precluded any
such action.

Meanwhile the internal divisions in the country became more
marked than ever. The wave of national feeling had not been
strong enough to bridge over the differences between North and
South. The Canton government comprising the five southern
provinces under Sun Yat-sen, with its rump parliament, representing the old revolutionary party, the Kuomintang, still claimed
to be the legal government of China. In the spring of 1919, a
conference was held between the representatives of Peking and
Canton at Shanghai, but they could reach no agreement. For the
next few years, however, there was an armed truce between the
two governments, chiefly because both were occupied with sectional differences.

These differences were actually only accentuations of conditions
that had always existed in China. There had never been any real
union of the eighteen provinces that made up the Middle Kingdom. Family life had been the basis of the old Chinese order—
after that the various guilds, forerunners of the Soviet system,
played a leading part in the communal life that had flowed on unbroken for more than four thousand years. Each community
formed a complete unit; the feudal lords of the provinces who
held authority from Peking represented the Emperor, to whom,
with far more truth, might have been applied the famous saying
of a French monarch: "L'État c'est moi!" Except for their
common Overlord there was nothing that the provinces shared in
common. Some of these provinces had as many as 50,000,000
inhabitants, none had less than 8,000,000 or 10,000,000, and even
the smallest were larger than the smallest countries of Europe.

Mountainous Kiangsu on the confines of Tibet had no points
of contact politically, geographically, or economically, with the
industrialized provinces of the lower Yangtze or the broad plains
of Manchuria. Communications have always been poor, and at
present the railways and water-routes in China are utterly insufficient for the most elementary needs of the country. There was
not even a community of the spoken word in China. The dia-

lects of the various sections were so different as to constitute different languages. The average man from Canton cannot understand the man from Peking any more than a Frenchman can converse fluently with an Italian. The only language used all over China, the Mandarin dialect, was confined to the small intellectual class and the officials, and it was an alien tongue introduced three hundred years ago by the Manchu conquerors of China.

Under such circumstances it was small wonder that when the Empire disappeared, there was no tie which bound the Chinese to Peking or to the Parliament. The small body of men who sincerely believed in a representative form of government could not impose respect for its authority on the distant provinces. The Tuchuns became the symbols of local power. They themselves had little or no respect for the government they were supposed to represent, and their control of the provincial revenues gave them an immense advantage. Had it not been for the revenues accruing to Peking from the Maritime Customs and the Salt Tax (called Salt Gabelle), the administration of which was in foreign hands, the Peking government would have fallen under the control of the War Lords even earlier. Until 1920, however, it still preserved a show of independence; in that year the military party in Chihli, the province in which Peking is situated, obtained control of the central government by a military coup d'état. To accomplish this the Tuchun of Chihli had sought the help of the two most powerful War Lords of the North, General Wu Pei-fu, Tuchun of the rich central province of Honan, and Marshal Chang Tso-lin, dictator of Manchuria.

It soon became evident that they were rivals for the control of Peking. Wu Pei-fu had the first innings, and when he began to assert his authority too peremptorily the President—his name does not matter : there have been no presidents whose names are worth remembering since Yuan Shih-kai—sent for Chang Tso-lin to help him. Chang was nothing loath; he had been waiting for this opportunity! He was backed by the Japanese, who would have liked nothing better than to see him in control of Peking, for the Washington Conference had come and gone, depriving them of their alliance with Great Britain and leaving them isolated in the Far East. They had consolidated their position in Manchuria by

making friends with Chang Tso-lin. Their next move naturally
was to cast about to find a substitute for the Anfu Club in Peking.
Japanese munitions and Japanese advice fortified Chang, who advanced to the Great Wall in an attempt to invade Chihli, while
Wu Pei-fu brought his forces from Honan to oppose his adversary.

At this juncture the South Chinese government became involved in the fight between the two Northern Tuchuns. Sun Yat-
sen, who was always opportunistic, was persuaded by Chang
Tso-lin that he would recognize the Canton government, and in an
attempt to come to the aid of the Manchurian War Lord from the
South, he was defeated by the opposing faction in his own five
provinces and was obliged to flee to Shanghai on a British warship. Thus began what has been called "the military vaudeville"
in China, with Chang Tso-lin and Wu Pei-fu as principals, which
has furnished the most spectacular features of the situation in
China for the past five years.

The sensational turn performed by the two super-Tuchuns
was not the only important development in the internal situation
in China during the year 1922. By that time the general confusion had still further increased the isolation of the provinces,
which had been little affected by the happenings in and around
Peking. In many of them there had arisen a very real and spontaneous movement for local autonomy. Five of the great central
and western provinces had already elaborated constitutions. The
regularly elected Provincial Assembly of Hunan which met in the
summer of 1922 declared itself unanimously in favor of a federal
system for China. Almost at the same time the Manchurian
Assembly denounced the attempts of the military chiefs to unite
the country by force. At Shanghai a number of officers of the
Chinese fleet, all from the eastern province of Fukien, issued a
manifesto declaring the independence of their province based "on
the principle of Federal autonomy and on the fact that Fukien
could be governed by its own people." Similar manifestoes were
issued in several other provinces.

But these federal tendencies were combated by men like Wu
Pei-fu and Sun Yat-sen, both of whom believed in centralization,
with the difference that Sun wished to see the central authority

vested in the Canton Republic and Wu sought to place it in the
hands of Peking. Chang Tso-lin undoubtedly at that time
was inclined to favor decentralization, certainly as far as Manchuria was concerned. With due allowance for the presence of
200,000 Japanese in Manchuria and for their preponderant economic and commercial interests, all of which have tended to
stabilize local conditions, Manchuria enjoying what amounts to
unquestioned autonomy, has been prosperous and peaceful during
the last five turbulent years in China. Her example is a very
good argument for the federal system.

The issue between the Centralists and De-centralists was soon
lost, like most issues involving principles in Eastern countries, in
the quarrels and rivalries of the various leaders, but it was not a
dead issue by any means, as we shall see.

Although the Peking government had ceased to have any real
authority in many parts of China, nevertheless it was still the
medium of intercourse between China and the other Powers.
Ministries succeeded each other with bewildering rapidity—even
Presidents came and went, but the framework of a cabinet and
parliament remained. China was represented by a delegation
from Peking at the Washington Conference, which signed the
Nine Power Pact guaranteeing the integrity of China, reiterating
the principle of the open door in international commercial relations with China which had been previously established by the
United States, and pledging the contracting Powers to "provide
the fullest and most unembarrassed opportunity to China to
develop and maintain for herself an effective and stable government." Moreover, it was agreed that the customs duties under
British administration, the better part of which went towards
meeting China's financial obligations towards the Treaty Powers,
should be increased and all foreign post offices should be closed,
and that commissions should be appointed to study ways and
means for a more radical tariff revision, marking a step towards
tariff autonomy, and to formulate a plan for the abolition of
extraterritoriality when China had reformed her antiquated
judiciary system.

The restoration of Shantung was guaranteed by a treaty with
Japan also signed at Washington, and Great Britain and France

likewise agreed to relinquish the territory leased by them for naval bases at Weihaiwei and Kwangchow respectively, when an agreement should be reached between China and the Powers for the return of all leased territories, providing the necessary safeguard for foreign properties and vested interests.

Two years previously, in 1920, France, Great Britain, and Japan, on the initiative of the United States, had attempted to arrest the disintegration of the Peking administration by forming a Consortium, an association of international bankers which was to pool all loans and give financial assistance to China under a unified plan and for certain specific objects, principally for railway construction and public improvements. But from the first there was widespread antagonism to the Consortium in China. It did not suit the War Lords because there was no possible way by which loans made under it could be diverted to the maintenance of their armies. It was most unwelcome to the Cantonese because it could not fail to strengthen the hand of Peking. It was opposed openly by Japan, who had acquired a tremendous hold financially on the Peking government through her war-time loans, though finally she was induced to withdraw her opposition on being assured that the Consortium would not affect any existing financial agreements. Generally speaking it offended all Chinese in whom there was as much as a spark of nationalism, as they felt that it was an attempt to keep China in leading-strings, and it was asserted, rightly or wrongly, in many quarters that the whole scheme was a clever device to counteract the growing influence of Japan in financial matters.

Partly for these reasons and partly because of the impossibility of financial reconstruction under the weak Peking government, the Consortium was never tried as a panacea for China's ills, and the lack of a unified policy among the Treaty Powers delayed the appointment of the tariff and extraterritoriality commissions until the internal confusion made it hopeless for them to accomplish any definite results.

Indeed, it is doubtful if any political or financial nostrums could have averted China's major troubles consequent upon the destruction of the old order. Those who know Chinese history are aware of the fact that after the fall of every dynasty China has gone through a more or less lengthy period of political chaos. Twice in her history she was conquered, once by the Mongols and again by the Manchus, who more or less revolutionized her social fabric. In each instance, after a period of anarchy lasting for several decades, the Chinese Empire arose Phœnix-like and reasserted its own culture, having absorbed and transmuted all alien influence. The process that began with the overthrow of the Manchu dynasty was in many respects a repetition of the past.

When Marshal Chang Tso-lin retired beyond the Great Wall to his capital of Mukden in Manchuria and Wu Pei-fu remained in power at Peking, everyone in China recognized the fact that it was merely a lull in the battle between the super-Tuchuns. There were still plenty of small wars to keep the vaudeville running. The Canton government was going through a crisis almost as stirring as those in the North.

Sun Yat-sen had been driven from Canton for the moment, but the control of the Cantonese government was being disputed violently by several other rival Tuchuns south of the Yangtze, which then as now formed the broad line of division separating North and South.

Certain provinces held completely aloof from both governments and each provincial War Lord collected the local revenues, including the vicious interprovincial customs called "likin." Small armies of parasites throve on the provincial administration under the system known as "squeeze."

While squeeze is not by any means confined to Eastern countries, it is more widespread and more in evidence in Asia than in the West, and is particularly evident in China. Squeeze is a system by which any participant in any transaction gets a percentage of the amount disbursed.

In the mind of the Oriental there is nothing unethical in squeezing one's neighbor or one's government. It is not an infringement of the immutable laws centring around the preservation of the family and family life, and it still plays a vital part in internal developments in China.

Something worse than squeeze brought about the next important change in the Peking government after the war between

Chang and Wu. The presidency was purchased by Tsao Kün, the Tuchun of Chihli through whom Wu Pei-fu ran the central government. It is said that his election by Parliament cost $5,-000 per member, and the new administration proceeded to amass wealth to meet these and other expenses by certain obscure transactions around Shanghai. It was more than suspected that these concerned the illicit opium trade, which is a mine of wealth. However that may be, Chang Tso-lin, who had spent a year and a half accumulating military supplies, many of which had been purchased from the Japanese, accused the Peking government of interfering with shipments of goods destined for Manchuria, and a second war between the super-Tuchuns began in the late summer of 1924. At first the forces of Wu Pei-fu so far outnumbered those of his rival that it looked as if nothing could stop the invasion of Manchuria.

But Wu Pei-fu was hampered by the doubtful loyalty of his chief lieutenant, the "Christian" General Feng Yu-hsiang, who commanded the Peking troops. It was suspected that he might profit by the situation to seize the power in Peking, and for this reason he was relegated to the extreme western flank of Wu's forces high up in the mountains north of the capital. Chang and Wu sparred along the Manchurian border without either side gaining a decisive advantage, until affairs were given a very different complexion by the active co-operation of the Japanese, who stopped at nothing short of actual intervention to prevent the advance of Wu's troops beyond the Great Wall.

Dissatisfaction began to appear in the army; there were many desertions and the morale of Wu's men was badly shattered, when like a bombshell the news came from Peking of a coup d'état executed by General Feng, who had quietly marched in and taken possession of the city while Wu was on the Manchurian front. Caught between the upper and nether millstones, Wu Pei-fu could do nothing but retire from the scene. He did, by the only road left open; taking a steamer down the coast with a few faithful followers, he made his way to the mouth of the Yangtze and thence to his own province of Honan, where he remained in seclusion.

It might have been expected that Feng's dictatorship would

have resulted in a genuine revolutionary upheaval in North China. Feng was a friend of Sun Yat-sen, who had recovered his position in South China and professed the same democratic ideals, tinctured with socialism. He was known, moreover, to have the support of Soviet Russia, with which the Peking government had a few months previously concluded an alliance. The Soviet Ambassador Karakhan and Sun Yat-sen were his chief advisers. The President was in jail, and the government apparently quite helpless, and there were many people who anticipated the establishment of a Red regime in Peking. One of Feng's first moves seemed to justify this expectation. The last representative of the Manchu dynasty, the seventeen-year-old Boy-Emperor, so called, who had been allowed to live in the Forbidden City in the heart of Peking ever since he had been deprived of his throne by the Revolution, was driven out by Feng's orders. The treasures of the imperial palaces were mostly turned into the revolutionary coffers, and the Boy-Emperor took refuge in the international concession at Tientsin, where he now lives as a private citizen.

Feng's army, called "The People's Army"—a truly revolutionary appellation—swaggered about Peking and talked of revolution. Chang Tso-lin remained curiously inactive, taking no part whatever in the events going on in Chihli, but Feng took no steps to overthrow the administration.

To tell the truth the central government had reached a point where it was so weak that it was almost as impossible to overthrow it as it is to dismember a jellyfish. Peking during those days seethed with rumors and contradictory statements! It was noised about now that Feng and Chang Tso-lin had reached an understanding, now that the old war was about to break out afresh between Peking and Manchuria, but finally it became evident that the two rivals had declared at least a temporary truce.

When is was announced at the close of the year that Sun Yat-sen would shortly visit Peking it was predicted in many circles that he would seize the power and install a Red government.

But when the Southern leader arrived at the capital a few weeks later it was as a sick man, stricken with the mortal disease that caused his death on March 11, 1925. His funeral was at the expense of the State and all China paid him posthumous honors, for no matter how much the various factions and leaders disagreed with him, they all recognized him as the author of the Revolution that had overthrown the Manchu dynasty and reasserted the rights of the Chinese in the face of all domination—Manchu or alien.

Sun Yat-sen's tactics were opportunistic—he might have been described as the Lloyd George of Canton. His political ideals were not always clear. He believed in a central government for China, democratic in form, but there is reason to believe that his profession of Socialism towards the close of his career was actuated more by expediency than by any genuine conviction. The reason for his rapprochement with the Bolsheviks was clearly shown in his political testament, which stated: "For forty years I have given my time to a national revolution with the end in view of assuring the liberty and equality of China. After my experience I know that to attain these ends we must engage the Chinese masses to collaborate with the other races of the world which treat us on a footing of equality." There is no doubt as to what Sun meant when he wrote these words—he was referring to Russia, Japan, and perhaps in a lesser degree to Germany. His views in this respect were shared with remarkable unanimity by most politically minded Chinese of all parties.

That this was true was shown by the developments in China's foreign relations between 1922 and 1925, in which the feeble Peking government nevertheless continued to act as spokesman for the country. The most important of these developments concerned Russia.

After the Revolution of 1917 had automatically destroyed all ties between China and Russia, the Chinese concerned themselves very little with the fortunes of the Bolsheviks. They received the high-sounding pronouncements of Moscow concerning Russia's voluntary renunciation of all the rights and privileges of the old Imperial government with polite indifference. They had been automatically abolished with the Revolution. Russia in chaos afforded no opportunity for the quiet commercial expansion so dear to the pacific Chinese genius and it was not until 1920, when the Soviet government was beginning to reach out once more towards Russia's historic frontiers on the Pacific, that Chinese statesmen began to take an interest in the doings of the Bear in the North.

A Chinese commission was sent to investigate conditions in the Soviet Republic and the Bolsheviks began to hold out to Peking the alluring bait of a new treaty, based on absolute equality. Meanwhile their aggressions in Mongolia, which the Chinese were powerless to oppose with military forces on account of the confused state of internal politics, brought home the strength of the new Soviet Republic, and the Chinese commercial instinct began to sense possibilities in the Russian trade.

When I was in Peking in the autumn of 1922, there was apparently little love lost between the Russian Commercial Mission that had been allowed to establish itself on sufferance, and the Chinese Foreign Office. The principal Western Powers, none of which had yet recognized the Soviet government, were exerting much pressure through the amiable Dr. Wellington Koo, then Foreign Minister, to prevent a Russo-Chinese conference. But I had just come from Siberia, where a steady infiltration of Chinese was taking place. I had seen Chinese merchants established everywhere in Soviet Russia's buffer state, the Far Eastern Republic which everyone knew was doomed to disappear when Moscow gave the word. I had had an inkling of unofficial conversations between representatives of Peking and the Russian delegation then negotiating with the Japanese in Manchuria.

Certain questions like the status of the Chinese Eastern Railway and the Mongolian situation pressed for settlement, and it did not seem that an understanding with Russia could be far distant. Consequently few people were surprised when Yoffe, the Soviet spellbinder who had conducted the negotiations with Japan, received permission to come to Peking for informal discussions. In spite of the fact that it fell to the lot of his successor Karakhan to conclude the treaty of peace with China, Yoffe deserves most of the credit for the Russo-Chinese rapprochement. It was his subtle logic that paved the way for Karakhan's more direct tactics. Before he left the Far East Yoffe had also met Sun Yat-sen in Shanghai and had persuaded him that the Soviet system of government was thoroughly consistent with the aim of the Kuomin-

tang, which was primarily to crush the remains of the Manchu
oligarchy in the North, and that the Bolsheviks were ardent supporters of the doctrine of "Asia for Asiatics."

Karakhan was spectacular. He alternately bullied and cajoled
the Peking government; he intrigued and plotted, skating on the
thin edge of diplomatic proprieties. He dispensed the Soviets'
funds lavishly and lost no opportunity to stimulate the new racial
consciousness of the Chinese. Following his arrival there was a
marked growth of anti-foreign feeling in Peking, particularly
among the students, and student strikes and other demonstrations
began to take on a distinctly Red tinge. In opening negotiations
with the central government, however, Karakhan's position was
strengthened by the fact that the British Labor government had
accorded recognition to Moscow, and that several European countries had done the same. The Russo-Chinese treaty signed on
May 31, 1924, had a tremendous significance for China.

Briefly, it provided for the resumption of full diplomatic and
consular relations between the two countries; recognized, on
paper, Chinese suzerainty over Mongolia; formally confirmed
Russia's renunciation of extraterritoriality and all special rights
and privileges conferred on her by treaties under the Imperial
regime. It settled, temporarily at least, the vexed question of the
Chinese Eastern Railway, by restoring the old status of the management which was formerly divided between Russian and Chinese officials. It also reaffirmed the old agreement under which
the Chinese had the right to buy out the Russian interest after a
certain period, recognized Soviet Russia's responsibility for all
claims of shareholders, bondholders and creditors prior to the
Revolution of 1917 and accepted the Russo-Asiatic Bank as the
legitimate proprietor of the railroad. Another clause provided
that what remained of Russia's share of the Boxer indemnity
should be devoted to educational purposes in China.

The treaty was acclaimed everywhere in China as the first equal
pact ever concluded with any foreign Power. But Nationalist
sentiment failed to take into account that the "inequality" in the
treaties had been first established by the old Manchu Emperors,
superbly arrogant in the consciousness of China's self-sufficiency,
blind and deaf to the economic evolution in the West that had

created an imperative need for world markets. European aggression developing into imperialism was provoked by China's refusal to accord equal treatment with her *own* citizens, to the European "barbarians."

It had only been a century and half since the Emperor Chien-Lung had written to King George III of England: "You, King, live beyond the confines of many seas; nevertheless, impelled by your humble desire to partake of the benefits of our civilization, you have dispatched a mission respectfully bearing your memorial." The Emperor's letter, quoted in a study of China's foreign relations recently issued by the Oxford University Press, ends with the statement that "China wanted nothing from the West." But much water has flowed under the bridge since then!

If there were thoughtful statesmen who discerned a nascent imperialism behind the altruism of Soviet Russia, their opinions were disregarded in the universal satisfaction over the Russo-Chinese treaty. Even Chang Tso-lin, a confirmed reactionary, reached an understanding with the Soviets on the subject of Manchuria; it was not until the Northern government found out to its cost months later that Karakhan was actively promoting the efforts of the Cantonese to overthrow it, that the spell originally cast by Yoffe was broken.

In the meantime Japanese diplomacy had pursued almost equally successful though tortuous tactics. While the Japanese had supported Marshal Chang Tso-lin against Wu Pei-fu, they had also taken a hand in the coup d'état at Peking that had placed the Christian General in power. During 1924 and 1925, while the administrative chaos in China was growing worse and worse, they lost no occasion to befriend her. When the Treaty Powers suggested international control of the Chinese railways, after the bandit outrages in Shantung province in 1924, as we have seen, the Japanese fought the proposition tooth and nail and saved the government this last humiliation.

The forbearance of the Japanese was extraordinary in many other incidents provoked by the widespread lawlessness which the government was powerless to control. They had no wish, however, to see Feng effect a reconciliation with the South, so they kept political intrigues boiling in Chihli and finally helped to bring about a new civil war in the North at the close of 1925, between the Manchurian War Lord and the Christian General, the dénouement of which was the retreat of Feng to Kalgan on the Mongolian border in the spring of 1926. Thence he disappeared into the regions under the Red flag of the Soviets, and a few months later he was fêted in Moscow.

Chang Tso-lin became master of Chihli and consequently virtually of Peking, after a breathless interval during which his old rival Wu Pei-fu came to life, mobilized his forces, and created considerable suspense by leaving everyone in the dark as to whether he intended to make common cause with one of the two combatants, or go it alone. Finally they met and patched up an anti-Red alliance, while Peking breathed a sigh of relief. In addition to the excitement of civil war there had been another coup d'état. A President who had been locked up for eighteen months by Feng was released so that he could sign his resignation and make legal the position of his successor, who had been Provisional President. In all these changes in North China the Japanese had unobtrusively pulled the strings. The political leaders in Peking since 1924, had for the most part belonged either to the old Anfu party or to the Manchurian faction, both of which were pro-Japanese.

While these events were taking place the Treaty Powers continued to keep up the polite fiction of the existence of a central government at Peking. The foreign Ambassadors continued to make representations to the Foreign Office with regard to the increasing lawlessness throughout China, which was focused more and more on outrages against Europeans. The diplomatic representatives of Peking abroad endeavored to uphold the dignity of the moribund government.

In the autumn of 1925, the international commission on extraterritoriality and the Customs Conference, which according to the provisions of the Nine Power Treaty should have begun their deliberations three years before, met in Peking. Various causes contributed to delay the calling together of these conferences—the chief of which was the unwillingness of France to sign the Nine Power Pact until she had settled the terms for China's payment of the arrears due on her share of the Boxer indemnity.

An agreement was reached in the spring of 1925. As might have been expected the results accomplished by the extraterritoriality commission were practically nil. Their report, issued in 1926, was confined largely to an analysis of existing conditions with mild intimations that extraterritorial rights might be gradually abolished province by province, when the necessary reforms had been carried out and the necessary guarantees for the protection of foreigners had been furnished by the authorities.

While the Extraterritoriality Report was anything but acceptable to the Nationalists, conservative Chinese sentiment concurred in its findings. In this connection a most interesting statement was made by General Sun Chuang-fang, Tuchun of the Five Provinces along the eastern seaboard.

"When I enter one of the treaty ports," he said, "I am profoundly humiliated, not so much on account of our loss of sovereignty as for the following reason . . . I feel that I am going into another world . . . Nothing in Chinese territory, roads, buildings, hygiene, can be compared to the concessions. That is the greatest of our national humiliations, incomparably greater than the loss of our sovereignty. If the Powers gave us back the concessions we would not be ready to receive them."

The net results achieved by the Tariff Conference were almost equally inconclusive with those of the Extraterritoriality Commission. The original purpose of the Conference as defined in the Washington agreements was to take measures for the abolition of the likin taxes on goods passing from province to province and to compensate the provincial administrations for their loss by the assignment of a certain proportion of the increased Maritime Custom revenues over and above the regular tariff known as the Washington surtaxes. The discussion, however, soon drifted into a general argument as to the future tariff policy of China—a subject on which agreement was next to impossible because of the conflicting interests of the interested Powers.

China demanded the right to fix her own surtaxes and to settle all matters relative to her tariff policies. Japan, who felt that her commercial interests would be seriously menaced by a tariff wall in China, insisted that any new tariff should be subject to commercial accords. The United States took the view, shared to a great extent by Great Britain, that China should have tariff autonomy after January, 1929, provided that the likin taxes were abolished by that date. This view was finally adopted by the Conference, which then set about the more difficult task of organizing a provisional tariff régime for the application of the Washington surtaxes and their possible increase; but it was finally forced to abandon the work by the internal disorders and the weakness of the central government, which rendered all efforts to reach a further understanding useless.

Developments from day to day made it more and more apparent that there was no authority in China capable of guaranteeing the fulfilment of any agreements. The civil government was paralyzed! In addition to the war between North and South and the universal anti-foreign movement fostered by Russian intrigue, with which we shall presently have to deal, the Northern factions were fighting among themselves in Honan, Shantung, and Chihli. Banditism was widespread. The railways were either out of commission or under the control of military chiefs who pocketed the receipts, and the stations were littered with millions of tons of goods that could not be moved. Producers and merchants were helpless. The financial situation of the phantom government at Peking was becoming more and more hopeless. All income from the Customs and the Salt Gabelle was hypothecated long in advance. The coupons on the external loans due at the Chinese New Year on February 13, 1926, were paid by an internal loan negotiated only with much difficulty through native banks. The pay of officials was in arrears and the Ministry of the Interior was obliged to sell government property to obtain $7,000 to pay part of the salaries of its employees.

Chang Tso-lin's advance against General Feng had produced fighting around Tientsin which endangered the concessions, calling forth sharp protests from the Powers, and so the Dictator of Manchuria had his own domestic problems to deal with. During his struggle to wrest the control of Peking from the Moscow-subsidized forces of the Christian General, Chang had run afoul of the Bolsheviks in Manchuria. Charging that the Director appointed by the Soviet government to manage the Chinese Eastern Railway after the Russo-Chinese accord had endeavored to hold

up troop-trains carrying reinforcements for the armies opposing
the Christian General, Chang had arrested the Soviet representative. He was not released until the Japanese had exerted considerable pressure on the Dictator. The Manchurian provincial
assembly had proclaimed its complete independence of Peking
pending the establishment of a local government in the capital and
had taken steps to draw up a constitution.

Meanwhile the Russians began to revert to the old Imperial
policy in Manchuria. It became apparent that the joint control
of the Chinese Eastern was just as much a farce as it had been
in the heyday of Russian Imperialism. With a managing board
of five Russians and five Chinese and a quorum of seven the
Russians could prevent any action that was not in their interests.
When the tension between the Soviet government's representatives and Chang Tso-lin was at the worst, Moscow even hinted
that extraterritoriality might be revived in Russian interests. But
for the presence of the Japanese in Manchuria the feeling on both
sides would have undoubtedly led to an open break and perhaps
a Soviet invasion of Manchuria from the Siberian border, where
troops were massed in anticipation of a crisis. After one of
Chang's own generals had rebelled against him there was a moment when things looked very critical.

But the Japanese plainly intimated that they would suffer no
interference in Manchuria. They took steps to lessen the importance of the Chinese Eastern Railway by commencing the construction of a line of their own connecting South Manchuria
with the region served by the Chinese Eastern. Russia had no
wish to quarrel with Japan, with whom she was just beginning
to establish profitable commercial relations; neither country could
be oblivious of the fact that it was to their mutual advantage to
preserve the peace until they could usurp Great Britain's place in
China. Identity of interests no less than misfortune makes
strange bedfellows. Thus Manchuria was preserved from a
Soviet invasion thanks to the virtual protectorate of Japan.

The undermining influences of Red propaganda had made little
or no headway in Chang Tso-lin's dominions partly because of
Japanese vigilance and partly because of the lively recollections
which the Manchurians still retained of the Russian attempts at

domination in Manchuria a quarter of a century earlier. Else-where, however, it had been a different story.

In Peking Karakhan and Chang Tso-lin were at daggers drawn over the Soviet Ambassador's open espousal of the cause of the Christian General and his recall was demanded by the Manchurian dictator. Karakhan had furnished munitions to the Red Kuomin-tang, he had incited the students of the Red university founded in Peking with Russia's share of the Boxer indemnity against the Manchurian faction. He had fanned the flames of anti-for eign and anti-Christian feeling which were gaining headway in every part of China, and he had been a thorn in the flesh of the Peking diplomatic corps.

When China was beginning to chafe at the delay in the appoint ment of the Extraterritoriality Commission Karakhan remarke at a public function: "I was very glad to see the declaration of th Chinese Minister of Foreign Affairs that the revision of th treaties with the Powers was the order of the day. Would h permit me to say in a more definite manner that these treatie should not only be revised but be torn up and disregarded?"

In Canton, Michael Borodin, ostensibly the head of a Sovie Commercial Mission, had been established since the close of 192; acting as adviser to the Southern government. Under his guic ance a school for military cadets established at Whampoa turne out officers for the Southern Nationalist forces, and Communi agents worked indefatigably securing members for the Chine: Communist party, which had been admitted by Sun Yat-sen to tl Nationalist organization, the Kuomintang. Acting under Bor din's tutelage the Kuomintang leaders in Canton organized Political Bureau similar to the organization of the same nan existing in Russia. It is a department devised to exercise politic control and see to the political orthodoxy of every section of tl National government, particularly the army, where its agents a attached to every unit in the large industrial cities, and among t' students.

Borodin's assistance at this stage of its development was i valuable to the Kuomintang. He and his aides supplied the c ganization and discipline in which the Chinese were conspicuous lacking. They gave an impetus to the movement for the co solidation of the Southern forces under a really competent leader —the only general of the Kuomintang to be compared with the War Lords of the North—General Chiang Kai-shek, but there were other factors apart from the unremitting Soviet propaganda that helped the cause of the Kuomintang in the South after the Christian General's defeat had scotched it north of the Yangtze.

Foremost among these was the feeling roused by an incident at Shanghai on May 30, 1925, when a mob of student demonstrators was fired on by the foreign police of the International Settlement, who killed several and wounded many more of the manifestants. In the opinion of many people it was this incident that definitely infused a new spirit into the many-sided struggle taking place in China.

Up to that time anti-foreign feeling and a sense of racial injustice had been kept more or less in the background by the innumerable civil wars and internal disturbances, but from that time on they became paramount. The antagonism roused by Japan's Twenty-one Demands in 1915 was a summer breeze compared to the hurricane of indignation created by the Shanghai incident. Its repercussions were felt even among the North Chinese and were reflected in the decided attitude of the representatives of the Peking's puppet government at the extraterritoriality and tariff conferences.

While all foreigners were objects more or less of the universal xenophobia, Great Britain was the one country singled out for the particular hatred of the Chinese Nationalists; notwithstanding Japan's equally serious encroachments on Chinese sovereignty the reprisal of the Kuomintang against the British was prompt and deadly, taking the form of a boycott of all British goods in Canton. The Peking government was quite powerless even if it had been inclined, as seems to have been the case, to temporize in view of the lack of unity among the Treaty Powers. For the happenings at Shanghai revealed to the world serious differences among the principal Powers which made it impossible for them to adopt any common course of action. These differences finally resulted in separate declarations of policy which did not contribute towards the maintenance of foreign prestige.

The Canton boycott, which produced riots and serious local

disorders, inspired strikes and student demonstrations in all the treaty ports, besides many attacks and outrages on missionary settlements and individual foreigners. Anti-foreign and anti-Christian feeling spread like fire in dry prairie grass. China in spite of her Tuchuns and her civil wars, of which there were no less than half a dozen in progress, besides the struggle for power of the two great factions, was more united morally than she had been since the destruction of the Empire.

But there was a subtle difference between her attitude towards the White races and that which she displayed towards Japan. When the future history of China is written it may be that some of the disturbances laid to Russia's door may be attributable to her island neighbor.

However, by the middle of 1926, there could no longer be any doubt as to the seriousness of the anti-foreign movement.

In August the Cantonese forces under Chiang Kai-chek began to exhibit signs of great military activity, their objective being the Yangtze valley with its populous industrialized areas so favorable to Red propaganda, its rich cities and its unrivalled route of communication with the western provinces. Opposing them were the forces of Wu Pei-fu in Honan. Marshal Chang Tso-lin was still busy in the North, settling the revolt in Manchuria and pushing the remains of the Christian General's army back into Mongolia. Between his forces and those of the Southern Nationalists in the east was the powerful Sung Chuang-fan, the War Lord of the Five Provinces whose "armed neutrality" doubtless caused many a bad quarter of an hour to the Northern leader. When the Southern armies began their northward march Sun remained inactive and the victorious troops of Chiang Kai-chek swept everything before them; he finally made a half-hearted stand, but it was too late to prevent the capture of the great cities of the lower Yangtze including Shanghai.

Wu Pei-fu, with poorly disciplined troops whose morale was undermined by Red propaganda, was unable to withstand the advance of the Southern forces and was obliged to abandon Hankow. By April, 1927, practically every city on both sides of the Yangtze from Shanghai to Hankow was in the hands of the

Nationalists, and it looked as if nothing could stop the victorious march of Chiang Kai-chek to Peking.

Then one of those curious pauses so characteristic of China's civil wars occurred, and rumors flew all over China. It was said that Chang Tso-lin was preparing a great combination against the Christian General, who had come back from Moscow and was beginning to show signs of activity in the Western provinces. Almost simultaneously it was noised abroad that the dictator of Manchuria and the Southern generalissimo might become reconciled. This news was disseminated by the Japanese press. Then came definite confirmation of reports that there was discord in the Nationalist government.

For some months the radical wing of the Kuomintang had been, metaphorically speaking, eating out of the hand of Borodin. After the capture of Hankow the Cantonese government accompanied by its Soviet advisers had moved there bag and baggage and declared that city the capital of the Nationalist Republic, which was to be modelled along Soviet lines. Borodin and his lieutenants were behind every move. Soon the majority in the Nationalist party, which was nationalistic and democratic but not in the least inclined to Communism, led by Chiang Kai-chek himself, rebelled against Bolshevik dictatorship. His answer to orders from Hankow directing him to resign his command was to establish himself at Nanking while one of his generals secured Canton, and to announce that he proposed shortly to advance against Hankow.

He was supported, most unexpectedly, by the Christian General, who began to threaten Hankow from the west. Suddenly a round-up of the Communists began. Chiang Kai-chek and General Feng arrested all they could lay their hands on; hundreds were executed and the tide of popular sentiment everywhere turned against the radicals.

Borodin suddenly awoke to the fact that Hankow might not be a healthy place a little later, and like the Greeks he struck his tents and departed silently and unobtrusively on board a German merchant steamer without intimating his intentions to his Chinese associates. The next development on the cards apparently was a pact between Chiang Kai-chek and the Northern War Lords, by which they agreed to respect the Yangtze as the boundary between the Southern and Northern governments.

Meanwhile Chang Tso-lin had come perilously near to war with Russia. He had sent his minions to conduct a raid in the Russian Embassy at Peking, and the Northern forces in Shantung had arrested Madame Borodin and several companions on charges of espionage and subversive propaganda, and he was once more in hot water over the Russian administration of the Chinese Eastern Railway; but in spite of a dozen incidents, any one of which was sufficient to have caused a diplomatic rupture if not war, relations of a sort were maintained with Moscow, though the Soviet newspapers quite openly wrote of help sent to the Southern forces.

Only time can elucidate the meaning of the apparent contradictions in Russo-Chinese relations but they would seem to be a bit more involved than is apparent on the surface. My own opinion, right or wrong, is that Russian propaganda was never quite as serious as it seemed to be. Certainly the Southern Nationalists had little difficulty when the time came in getting rid of their Soviet advisers. Nor do I think the wisest heads in Moscow ever had any hopes of Sovietizing China. Moscow wants Chinese Turkestan. She wants eventually to tap the Yangtze region through a railroad already projected to extend across Mongolia. She wants to weaken Great Britain's commercial hold on the Yangtze region as part of her plan to drive the British from Asia. Soviet penetration in China is merely a particularly aggressive and rather crude expression of the racial urge that has always driven the Slav race south.

Some of the extremists in the Russian Communist party may have dreamed of a Red China, but when Stalin began to feel that their propaganda was overstepping the bounds of Russia's interests it is probable that Soviet funds did not flow so freely into the coffers of the Kuomintang and this may have had something to do with Borodin's unpopularity. On the other hand the Chinese Nationalists had gotten all they needed out of Soviet Russia. It is also not improbable that Soviet propaganda was admirable camouflage for the animus of the North Chinese against the foreign Powers, which they were obliged to conceal for the obvious reason that they could not break with the Powers without being swept out of existence by the South.

We should do well to remember that even Chang Tso-lin warned the British government after its concession at Hankow had been taken by the Nationalists that if an attempt was made to recover it by force he would send his soldiers to resist the British forces. Lastly, it is by no means certain that the Japanese have viewed with entire disfavor a propaganda which could only temporarily injure their interests, while seriously harming those of the foreign Powers, particularly Great Britain, and fostering an anti-Western, anti-Christian sentiment calculated to further their aims in China.

Certainly, from the beginning of the anti-foreign disturbances in China the Japanese exercised the utmost moderation and forbearance. Both government and people in Japan were unanimous in supporting the policy of strict neutrality and non-intervention adopted by their Foreign Minister Baron Shidehara.

Indeed it became apparent soon after the Shanghai riots that there were differences among the Powers which rendered it impossible for them to agree on any plan of action to protect their interests in China or unite on any common policy with regard to the internal situation. These divergencies of opinion were brought out by a British memorandum on Chinese policy on December 18, 1926, which was sent to the Peking representatives of all the Powers that had participated in the Washington Conference. It advocated virtual recognition of the Southern government together with an implied admission of the possibility of a divided China, and boldly asserted the advisability of treaty revision, elimination of extraterritoriality and the immediate legalization and application of the Washington surtaxes, which had already been made on its own initiative by Canton.

This was the logical outcome of the tactics which had been pursued by Great Britain for some time. She had negotiated directly with the Southern government on the subject of the Hongkong boycott of British goods, while the other Powers with grievances had only negotiated officially with Peking.

The British note called forth a vast amount of comment in the international press and statements of policy from several of the

Treaty Powers. The American statement, while expressing a desire to deal with China in the most liberal spirit, made clear that the United States still upheld the principle of a united China, and favored the making of new treaties rather than the abrogation of existing pacts between China and the Powers. The Japanese government reiterated its previous statements regarding strict neutrality and let it be known during the discussion of the terms of a commercial treaty with China at Peking, that Japan would be disposed to take steps towards the almost immediate abolishment of extraterritoriality in the event of a coalition of North and South. None of these declarations had much effect in China except to emphasize the lack of solidarity among the Treaty Powers. The Kuomintang government at Canton was disposed, to paraphrase the words of the Trojans of old "to fear the British bearing gifts."

The attitude of the French was one of watchful and hostile waiting as far as Canton was concerned, on account of its nearness to their own colony of Indo-China. Even the feeble government at Peking took good care to make it plain that the old pacts must go, seizing the opportunity afforded by the lapse of the Sino-Belgian treaty to refuse to renew it except on equal terms.

The result of all these conflicting currents was that each of the Powers adopted what measures it deemed fit for the protection of its concessions and its nationals. From the first the Kuomintang, spurred on by Russia, singled out Great Britain as an object of particular hatred. Outrages against British subjects, the destruction of British capital and interference with British trade continued, in spite of representations to the Canton government and conferences between Sir Miles Lampson, the British Ambassador to China, and Eugene Chen, Foreign Minister of the Kuomintang. Consequently Great Britain took the lead in sending troops to China. The Japanese and French displayed extreme caution, as well as the Americans.

In many quarters of Europe American influence was held to be largely to blame for the spread of Nationalist agitation and even for the anti-foreign and anti-religious feeling. It was asserted that the Americans, having no concessions at stake, were less interested than the other Treaty Powers in maintaining the status quo, and that American education and methods had encouraged democratic ideas for which China was not ripe, thus paving the way for revolution and anarchy.

In March, 1927, occurred an event which galvanized Great Britain, the United States, and Japan into something like cooperation. On March 24, the day after the occupation of Nanking by the Nationalist forces, the American, British, and Japanese citizens in Nanking were attacked by armed mobs and Nationalist soldiers who pillaged the consulates and destroyed all the foreign property on which they could lay their hands. Seven foreigners were killed and much greater loss of life was averted only by the fact that British and American gunboats in the Yangtze opposite the city began a bombardment under cover of which a party of Americans besieged in the compound of the Standard Oil Company overlooking the river managed to escape. Even the Japanese, though they did not take part in the bombardment, landed a detachment of sailors to rescue their fellow countrymen.

Identical notes of protest by all the great Powers led to the appointment of a commission to fix the responsibility of the Nationalist troops—and after this brief interlude the Powers continued to pursue their various ways with regard to China. Great Britain made arrangements to turn over her concession at Tientsin to the Peking government, while continuing to parley with the Nationalists, America temporized, Japan kept as inconspicuous as possible, although by that time all three Powers landed considerable numbers of troops in China to protect their nationals. So had the other Treaty Powers, and the situation was growing so acute that another incident might have made the rôle of the foreign troops that of intervention instead of protection, when suddenly, as we have seen, the extreme wing of the Nationalists with its Russian advisers was put out of power, and the persistent reports of an understanding between North and South began to circulate. There was an immediate relaxation of the tension, and the anti-foreign feeling seemed to be less bitter. But events since 1922 have shown beyond peradventure that when it is possible for the Powers to have dealings with the Chinese, whether they constitute a united, a divided, or a federated nation, the abolition of extraterritoriality will have to be accepted as an actuality. To enter into the aspects of such a complicated question would require too much space, but there are two rather interesting points in connection with the controversy, which are not usually emphasized.

The fact that the foreign concessions in China have frequently been used as "funk holes"—refuges—by various warring factions, who have in times of stress transferred themselves and their fortunes to the shelter of the concessions, can be adduced to prove that they encourage factional strife in China, as well as to illustrate the superiority of foreign law and order.

Secondly, although the Austrians and Germans do not enjoy extraterritoriality in China there have been no outcries with regard to the treatment of their nationals. In fact the Germans, despite their loss of Kiaochow and all their previous rights and privileges, are in a very strong position today in China. They have come back with a vengeance, as a few figures will show.

During and after the war Germans were excluded from the East. It was not until August 31, 1922, that the prohibition against German trade in Hongkong was lifted—the next day German commercial houses were open for business. Before the war there were 4,000 Germans in Shanghai, at its close virtually none; at the end of 1922, there were 1,000. Among their non-commercial activities are several newspapers including the German-Chinese News, a German-Chinese Association, and a branch of the "Verein für das Deutschthum im Auslande" which had a membership of over a quarter of a million in 1922. During the recent anti-foreign disturbances Germans went everywhere unmolested wearing armbands indicating that they were citizens of a country which had abolished extraterritoriality, and within the last few years many Germans living permanently in China have applied for naturalization.

The developments in China's foreign relations, the many turns of the military vaudeville, the struggles of her political factions, and the perennial state of collapse of the Peking government have absorbed the attention of the outside world to the exclusion of almost everything else in China. In view of their importance we are to forget the fact that there are hundreds of millions of people in the Celestial Kingdom who have not taken an active part in any of the sensational happenings of the last few years. They are the village Chinese, who compose the vast majority, and the small but prosperous and influential class of merchants and bankers, the capitalists of China.

In China as in Russia the peasants are the backbone of the nation; they constitute more than three-fourths of all the inhabitants, and most of them still till the land as their ancestors did before them for countless generations. They live in their villages much as they have done for thousands of years; the advent of oil lamps, sewing machines, factory-made tools and cotton goods, the infiltration of new ideas brought by missionaries, the spread of the mass-education movement have only just begun to make inroads into the self-contained social and economic life of these village communities. Most of the inhabitants are abjectly poor—it has been estimated that the average per-capita income in China is only $60 a year, and fully 95 per cent are illiterates. Like the Russian peasants they live in a country of vast distances with utterly inadequate means of transportation; in all of China today there are hardly 7,000 miles of railways, and 25,000 miles of navigable waterways. Nearly 4,500 miles, most of which must be covered in carts, separate the coast cities from the farthest towns of Chinese Turkestan; telegraph communication is almost equally undeveloped and the total mileage of roads suitable for motor traffic is ridiculously small although within the last few years more than 10,000 miles of roads have been improved to permit the circulation of motor busses.

Nevertheless, the isolation of many parts of China is so complete that the outside world knows next to nothing of what is happening in those far-away districts. As I write this the European papers are carrying the first accounts of a terrible earthquake in Kiangsu, one of the western provinces, in which thousands of lives were lost—and it happened two months ago! Within the last few years there have been similar catastrophes in China—earthquakes, floods, and famines—all of which have become known only after a certain length of time.

It is impossible that the world should ever know what has been going on in the minds of millions of patient Chinese peasants to whom the endless civil wars have brought untold misery and suffering. There have been as many as fifteen different armies of rival Tuchuns on Chinese soil simultaneously at various times during the last few years; invariably they have been sectional armies recruited within a comparatively limited area, so that the continual mobilizations have not helped to create national solidarity as was the case during the Great War in Russia, where mass mobilizations against Germany and the creation of a large standing army by the Bolsheviks brought together in the same regiments men from opposite corners of the Empire, and gave birth to a genuine Nationalism. In China the civil wars have tended to create intense sectional feeling within a Nationalism born of the hatred of foreigners, and the sense of humiliation. This sectionalism will not disappear until roads, railways, and the intercourse they bring, have created a community of interests.

But sectionalism is one of the least of the evils brought about by the civil wars. The people have felt the yoke of militarism in a thousand ways. The recruits collected by the warring Tuchuns, and the taxes levied for the maintenance of their armies are only part of the price they must pay. The actual casualties on the field of battle are not appalling. Warfare in China consists largely of watchful waiting, skirmishes, retreats; positions occupied or surrendered after negotiations, battles decided by mass desertions or mutual agreements dictated by the Chinese love of compromise and settlement, pecuniary or otherwise. The tragic side of the civil wars is the suffering they entail on the mass of noncombatants, of whom the vast majority are peasants; we can only vaguely speculate as to the number of villages sacked and burned, the property and live stock destroyed, the fields laid waste, the peasants tortured and slain by the scores of armies, the hundreds of bands of outlaws like the infamous Hung Hutze, the red beards of Manchuria, and the thousands of marauding stragglers or bodies of unpaid soldiers that simply helped themselves off the peasantry. Here and there the peasants have organized to resist the military hordes that swarm like locusts all over the provinces. Occasionally peasant organizations similar to the Siberian partisan bands make their appearance, such as the organization known as the "Red Spears" of Honan; but they are soon taken over by the lawless elements.

Yet, in spite of the battle, murder, sudden death, famine, floods, and earthquakes, and in the midst of local chaos the peasants swarm like human ants extraordinarily vital and vigorous in much-tried China. They constitute the raw material for the new China, without which the college-bred intellectuals of Peking and Canton can only theorize. The relatively small but constantly increasing number of industrialized Chinese have contributed in many ways to make life more difficult for the village workers. The competition of the machine is forcing out the hand-worker and producing rivalry between city and village which is disastrous to the latter. It was the realization of this disadvantage that made the Chinese government many years ago buy the first railway ever built in China at Shanghai, tear up the rails, and dump the engines in the Yangtze.

The industrial workers today form the only class-conscious proletariat. Among them the social and political ferment of the hosts of young students trained in European methods of thought and action has found expression in labor movements similar to those in Western countries. They are fallow soil for the Bolshevist propaganda which has been such a valuable ally to the Nationalist movement. It has been easy to focus industrial discontent against the foreigner and foreign domination, because the vast majority of industrial enterprises in China are owned and managed by foreigners.

The Chinese capitalists have in great measure contrived to escape the opprobrium attached to foreign capitalists. They constitute the one fixed quantity in the ever-shifting elements that make up present-day China. Individually and as a class they are solidly, comfortably rich! It has often been stated that if all the bankers combined to form their own consortium they could with little difficulty take over all the external obligations of the Chinese Republic, which amount to a little less than $3,000,000,000. The great merchants have continued to do business through all the vicissitudes of politics and civil war, to such effect that China, though officially bankrupt, has seen her import and export trade steadily increase until today it represents an amount over 100 per cent greater than her pre-war trade.

Even the unparalleled currency confusion and the fact that there are more different sorts of bank notes than there are provinces, does not interfere with mercantile transactions. Moreover, these Chinese merchants and bankers do not by any means confine their interests to China. A large part of the commerce of the East Indies is in their hands. The Chinese are a political as well as a commercial power in Indo-China, Java, and Borneo. They are scattered all over Asia; they are established throughout Siberia. Few important cities in Europe or the two Americas are without a group of rich Chinese merchants.

In their commercial relations the Chinese display a remarkable aptitude for assimilating modern business methods. In finance they display far more acumen and far more imagination than any other Asiatic people. The day is not far distant when they will be thoroughly equipped to develop their own national resources. Politically, however, the merchants as a class have so far held aloof from the Nationalist and anti-foreign movements. For this reason they have often been accused of lack of patriotism and esprit de corps. But when China emerges from her present political chaos she will possess a marvellous instrument of power in the ramifications of her economic system.

Meanwhile it is not unnatural that they should have little sense of loyalty to a government that does not exist. Just as the merchants and bankers who play little part in politics are laying the economic foundations for a greater China, mass education through the Kuo-Yu, the National dialect with thirty-nine phonetic letters, is beginning to prepare the Chinese people for some form of self-government. Speculations as to what that form of government may be are futile. Personally, I am inclined to believe that the next development will be along federal lines. A similar view was expressed nearly thirty years ago by that great authority on Pacific questions, Admiral Mahan:

"It may perhaps be for the welfare of humanity," he wrote, "that the Chinese should undergo a period of political division like that of Germany anterior to the French Revolution, before achieving the race patriotism which in our epoch is tending to bind peoples into larger groups than the existing nationalities."

The race patriotism to which Mahan alludes has since the World War begun to play a vital rôle in Asiatic affairs. It is finding an expression in the growing Pan-Mongol solidarity which may foreshadow the creation of a Mongol bloc under the leadership of Japan.

If this comes to pass it will bring about a radical change in the relations of the Powers bordering on the Pacific. However, for the present we can only guess at the possibilities of a Far Eastern Federation.

Chapter Fourteen

THE SPRINGS OF THE ASIATIC RENASCENCE

IN THE foregoing chapters we have traced the course of events in Asiatic countries since the World War. We have seen what tremendous changes have been brought about in the map of Asia within the last decade. We have followed the national movements and the international developments that have given birth to new countries, leaders, alliances, and, alas! new wars and new dissensions. We have tried to gauge the strength of the revolt against the West and the extent of the racial antagonism to Europe among Asiatic peoples.

But if we stop there we shall not have even an approximately clear picture of what, for want of a better term, we call the Asiatic Renascence. We must try to get at the source of the ferment in Asia. The regeneration of the East is being brought about by internal forces, but the inspiration has come from without.

The seeds of this Renascence were planted by Europe—commercial and economic penetration, colonial imperialism, and Western domination created the contacts that brought about the Europeanization of Asia, and with it there came not only the vast political and social changes we have been studying, but also impulses towards the re-appraisal of old ideals and revision of old social and ethical standards. In the process of readjustment which is still going on in the ancient systems of religion and philosophy, the former concepts of the social order are being weighed against the new ideals that have come from Europe. The East, far more spiritual than the West, is perhaps unconsciously trying to find a synthesis—a common basis for international intercourse in a world that is fast becoming an economic unit.

This is the subjective side of the Renascence, but it is bound up with the objective side, which concerns the political and social changes in Asia.

It is obviously impossible for us to fathom all the springs of this Renascence, but there are three factors that we cannot ignore —the influence of the Gospel of Christ, the revival of the faith of Mohammed, and the force of the ethics of Lenin. Let us begin with the Christ, through whose ministers the Europeanization of Asia has largely come to pass.

CHRIST

What is the reason for the bitter antagonism to Christianity which is so widespread at the present time in many parts of Asia? Why has it become identified, as in China, with anti-foreign feeling? Why, since it has helped to bring about the great awakening among Asiatic peoples, have they turned against the Gospel of Jesus?

These questions are naturally uppermost in the minds of most intelligent folk, from the Christian countries of the West, for whether they are individually Christians or not, the great majority of them accept Christianity as the ethical basis for human relationships. But if they are absolutely fair and unbiased before they attempt to seek the answers they must admit that Christianity has failed in part of its mission.

"Christ for the world we sing—the world to Christ we bring," is a soothing and pleasant axiom to the stay-at-home Christians, but if the missionary has genuine fitness for his calling, he knows it is not so! He knows that there are only about 650,000,000 persons officially classed as Christians in a world with a population of more than 1,700,000,000. He knows that among the professed converts he has made, there are many actuated only by self-interest. He knows that the new world of Asia is not being brought to Christ—certainly not in the accepted sense. We too must realize that this is so.

To understand why it is thus, we must recall the circumstances under which Christian missions developed in Asia. Christianity, like all great religions, came from the East! The conception of a single God, and the teachings of Jesus of Nazareth, are the products of Semitic genius. There are many who do not like to be reminded of this fact, as for instance the lady with whom a friend once remonstrated on her anti-Semitic proclivities.

"My dear," she exclaimed, "you forget that Jesus Christ was a Jew!"

The woman thus rebuked was at loss for a reply for the moment. She hesitated; then, struck by a bright idea, she answered: "Oh, well—I wasn't speaking of converted Jews!"

There was nothing in the fundamental teachings of Christ that was unacceptable to the Oriental mentality, and their spread westward instead of eastward was due to historical conditions. In the time of Christ, Rome was the centre of culture for the countries bordering on the Mediterranean. The Roman Empire extended from the borders of Persia, which formed a solid bulwark against further conquest in the Orient, across Asia Minor and along both sides of the Mediterranean basin to the Pillars of Hercules. Sea communications with the Far East were virtually nonexistent and it was quite natural that Christianity should expand westward rather than eastward. After a few centuries it was centred in Rome itself, while its Eastern branches, the Churches of Asia Minor, the Orthodox Church of the Byzantine Empire, and the Coptic Church of Egypt, had become distinct and separate bodies.

Nestorian missionaries from Syria who took the long and hazardous journey across the plateau of Central Asia to China, were the first evangelists to reach that country. At the time Buddhism was at its height; it had already become the predominant religion in China, though it did not replace entirely the more philosophical ethical system of Confucius. In this period the Celestial Empire was the greatest, the most cultured, and the most civilized in the world. Literature and the arts flourished among the Chinese while Western Europe was immersed in barbarism after the fall of the Roman Empire, and the Arab Empire of the Near East was still in the making.

With the tolerance for which they were noted and the philosophic impartiality of real scholars, the Chinese welcomed the advent of the Christian missionaries. It would be intensely interesting to have records of the debates of these simple-minded, earnest evangelists from the West, with the subtle and highly analytical Chinese scholars. Nestorian monuments found in China bear witness to the fact that they met with considerable success. There ensued, however, a long period of barbarian invasions, which, coupled with the rise of Islam in the Near East, practically destroyed all communications between East and West. Thereafter a few intrepid Catholic Fathers and occasional travellers like Marco Polo reached Cathay, and while they were received with great courtesy and tolerance by the Mongol potentates, their mission seems to have been more diplomatic than evangelical and no effort was made to convert the Far East until many centuries later.

In the Near East the rapid spread of the doctrines of Mohammed threatened the very existence of Christianity along the shores of the Mediterranean. Even the Crusades failed to shake the foundations of Islam and the decadent Byzantine Empire at Constantinople finally succumbed to the Turks in 1453. With it perished all hopes of the extension of Christianity in Western Asia for many centuries.

The little Christian nations like the Armenians and Assyrians in Turkey and Persia, and the various sects of Syria and Asia Minor were pushed into the mountains or concentrated in certain localities by the Turkish invasion. The Holy Sepulchre at Jerusalem became the subject of negotiations between the Ottoman Sultans and the Christian Powers, which secured the right to maintain religious communities in Palestine. Here and there other similar communities were established, always by special treaty with the Sultan and the French, whose sovereigns had been the leading spirits in the Crusades, got privileges in Syria which gave them a definite status as protectors of the Christian Minnorities.

Down to our own time missionary effort among the people of Western Asia has been negligible. Even today, evangelical work among Moslems is relatively small compared to that in Buddhist countries or among the Hindus in India. Islam, like Christianity, is a militant faith and it presents a much more active resistance to Christian doctrines than Buddhism or Confucianism.

It is a lamentable fact that missionary work has usually been the precursor or companion of commercial penetration or colonization. As the Near East did not offer a promising field for either, Christian missions in Turkey and Arabia grew very slowly and their labor was chiefly among the Christian Minorities in Syria and Asia Minor. Because they were exempt from military service these Minorities possessed almost a monopoly of the trade, commerce, and industry among the Turks, their only serious competitors being the Jews. Sometimes persecuted, often treated with indifferent tolerance, they developed a strong sense of social and religious solidarity which soon became identical with political discontent and agitation.

From the beginning of the nineteenth century the discontent among the Armenians was used to foster the political aims of Russian Imperialism. At various times the other Christian communities were utilized by European Powers to create dissensions and to weaken the Ottoman Empire. In our own day came the débâcle of politico-religious hatred culminating in the expulsion of virtually all the Christian Minorities from Turkish territory by the Kemalists, and the assertion of the separate claims to independence or autonomy of practically every Christian people in the Near East, stirred to life by the Wilsonian doctrine of self-determination.

In many instances missionaries had openly encouraged what was virtually treason in Turkey, meanwhile enjoying immunity from arrest through the Capitulations signed by the Sultan in times past, which placed them under the jurisdiction of their own Consuls. Even when they refrained from taking sides in political and religious questions, they rarely made any sincere effort to gain the confidence of the Moslems. Before the war, mission centres in Asia Minor were in districts where the bulk of the population was Greek or Armenian; the schools were crowded with Christian pupils and most missionaries after a lifetime spent in the Turkish field knew little or nothing of the Turks.

Several years ago when I was in a provincial city in Asia Minor I found a well-equipped mission hospital half empty although the Turkish hospitals were filled to overflowing. The American doctor said it was "local jealousy," but when I found that he could hardly speak any Turkish, having been in that country twenty-five years, and had never had a Turkish servant in his house, only Armenians, I thought I understood the real reason! In Syria there was also a disastrous confusion of religion and politics, to which was added, particularly in Palestine, the unedifying spectacle of intrigues and rivalries between Christian sects centring around the guardianship of the Holy Sepulchre and the Sacred Places of Christendom. In Arabia the few missionaries who obtained a footing were regarded with deep suspicion as the forerunners of Western imperialism, for in the small principalities along the Persian Gulf which eventually came under British control, they had been first!

The Moslems themselves have always combined religion with political imperialism; this fact is evident to anyone who is familiar with the past history of the Islamic Conquest which swept to the gates of Vienna in the east, and to the valley of the Loire in the west, bearing the faith of Mohammed on the tide of military imperialism. All their instincts of political self-preservation bade them beware of Christianity, which seemed to be pursuing a course of proselytism not unlike their own, and their suspicions were not decreased by the attitude of the missionaries.

Lately, however, since the Moslem nations have adopted the policy of Westernization, their prejudices have not prevented them from crowding the Mission schools with their young people and protection for missionary workers, teachers, and doctors has been extended by Persia, Turkey, and even far Afghanistan.

The missionaries have of late begun to see the wisdom of disassociating themselves from politics and imperialism; it is good to be able to record that among the most ardent supporters of a treaty between the Turkish Republic and the United States based on the abolition of the Capitulations, are the heads of several Christian institutions in Turkey. Religious antagonism is gradually growing less, except perhaps among the fanatical sects of Arabia, but the Christian dogma is making no more headway than before in Western Asia. Two factors are militating against it—the Islamic revival and the spread of agnosticism, even atheism. We shall discuss these influences later. Let us try to analyze the effect of Christianity among the peoples of the Extreme Orient and in India.

The first missionaries to the Far East after the period of the Mongol domination were the Catholic Fathers who accompanied the Spaniards and Portuguese soon after Vasco da Gama had discovered the sea route to India.

Foremost among them were the Jesuits, and their greatest leader St. Francis Xavier, who with his companion Father Hernandez landed in Japan in 1549, and remained there for two years. They made a large number of converts and over 250,000 embraced Christianity during the first fifty years of Jesuit propaganda. Later, when the Fathers had begun to incite their converts not only to attack Buddhist priests and temples, but also to rebel against the despotic rule of the all-powerful Shoguns, Christianity was abolished by edict, all Europeans were driven out of the country and Japan was closed to the outside world for two hundred years. Most of the converts were massacred and the remainder soon died out.

Christianity made little more headway in China. The Friars Minor who established an archbishopric in Peking in Marco Polo's time had no successors until the Jesuits began to penetrate the Celestial Kingdom in the early seventeenth century. It is interesting to observe that the first Jesuit missionaries obtained a foothold not through their evangelical work, but by their scientific attainments. The training for the order is most thorough and membership is accorded only after years of study. Today there are few universities which can equal or surpass the Jesuit colleges in many branches.

The ideal of a World Empire founded in the Church was the inspiration of the Jesuit Fathers and they did not seek to promote the interests of any special country. In this respect they differed from many of the Catholic missionaries who came after them. If these had exhibited the same esprit de corps, they might have furthered the cause of all Christendom, but when the Orientals were treated to the unedifying spectacle of various orders competing with one another, the foundation was laid for a profound distrust of Christianity which was not decreased when the Protestant missionaries entered the field. With the exception of the earliest evangelists and the Jesuits, inspired by the genius of St. Francis Xavier, all subsequent missionaries, no matter how sincere, began to be identified in the eyes of Orientals with the efforts of various European Powers to obtain the trade and secure the fabulous wealth of China and the Indies.

After the Treaty of Nanking in 1842, ending the Opium War between Britain and China, Protestant missions obtained their first foothold. This treaty opened five ports to European trade, gave Hongkong to the British and established extraterritoriality. The Catholics all this time had been working steadily and had built up splendid missions in China without waiting for special privileges to be extracted by force from the Peking government on their behalf.

What a curious experience for the Chinese when they first began to observe the bitter antagonism between Catholic and Protestant, far different from the rivalry among the Catholic orders! It must have been incomprehensible to them that two groups of followers of the same Teacher could be so opposed as to be mutually convinced that those of the opposite group were past salvation, and their bewilderment must have still further increased when they witnessed the competition among the various denominations of the Protestant faith.

Notwithstanding these differences, Christian missions in the Far East made great headway during the nineteenth century, borne on the tide of Western Imperialism and often backed by Western bayonets! In Japan missions began again, after the lapse of several centuries, with the opening of the country to foreign trade by the American Commodore Perry, who broke down the barriers between Japan and the outside world by negotiating the first treaty with her in 1854. In 1873, all opposition to Christianity was withdrawn and at the present time there are nearly 300,000 converts in the Japanese Archipelago.

The China Inland Mission, founded in 1865, grew more rapidly than any other Protestant organization in that country. It is estimated that there are about 3,000,000 converts to Christianity out of 322,000,000 inhabitants in China today; half a million are Protestants and the remainder Catholics. In India, with a population of 320,000,000 about 5,000,000 are Christians, and of these over 3,000,000 are Catholics. In Korea there are approxi-

mately 17,000,000 inhabitants, of whom nearly 90,000 are Protestant converts and three times as many are Catholics.

The number of converts in any Asiatic country is by no means
indicative of the number of Christians, however. In Japan, for
example, missions were taken advantage of by thousands of
wide-awake Japanese to acquire a Western education; it is safe
to say that more of them have become baptized from a desire to
learn English and to write on the typewriter than from love of
Jesus Christ!

The Koreans bitterly opposed Christianity when it was introduced among them in the eighteenth century by Catholic fathers.
As Korea was not coveted by any of the great Western Powers,
and they were thus without protection, the noble pioneers of
Christ in that land had a long record of heroic martyrdom; even
as late as 1866, there was a massacre of native Christians in which
8,000 were executed, many by means of a frightful guillotine
which chopped off twenty-four heads at once! The opposition
to Christianity disappeared when the Koreans became subject to
the Japanese, and the converts increased rapidly. Later the missionaries played an active and frequently ill-advised part in the
native uprisings against the Japanese.

In China the majority of the converts were among the Southern
Chinese, who had for generations been oppressed by the ruling
Manchus, while in India the Hindus of the lower castes, who
suffered from a sense of social injustice, constituted the great
majority of those who embraced the Christian faith. Among
high-caste Hindus, and the Indians who subscribe to the democratic teachings of Mohammed, the Christian doctrine made no
headway at all.

Thus even in its evangelical aspects, Christianity took on a
political tinge from the moment of its introduction in many
Eastern countries; it was inevitable that it should be so. Since
the essentially democratic creed of Jesus recognized neither class
nor caste, it was in definite opposition to despotism and autocracy
and it appealed to the submerged masses, making their first reaction to Christianity a response to its advocacy of social justice.
Among the upper classes there was definite distrust of a religion
that came hand in hand with Imperialism and economic penetra-

tion; nevertheless in Japan and China as well as in India and Korea, there were thousands of young men during the last quarter of the nineteenth century, who began to appreciate the value of the educational, medical, and industrial work which supplemented that of the evangelical missionaries.

Protestant missions in India were, from the first, definitely associated with the growth of Imperialism. The clergy who accompanied the Dutch and British on expeditions to the Indies were usually sent out more as chaplains than as evangelists, for they were maintained by the British and Dutch East India companies to hold services for their employees. It was not until the nineteenth century that a wave of true evangelism began to sweep the Protestant communities of Europe and the United States. The first to do this work among the natives of India were the Danes and Moravians; they were followed by the Church of England under the famous Dr. Middleton, who became the Bishop of Calcutta in 1814.

Hindus and Moslems of the better class, always mentally alert, flocked by thousands to the missionary schools and colleges established in India. It was certainly through a comparison of the democratic ideals taught in these institutions, with the methods of the British administration, that many young Indians were won to the Nationalist cause and in the reaction numbers turned to Gandhism with its advocacy of a return to the primitive village life and the old Hindu gods.

Through the Christian missionaries they also learned the bitter lesson that religious and social equality do not mean race equality! Most of the churches which taught that the Brahman and the Pariah, or outcast, were equal in the sight of God, and should be held equal by all Indians, made it plain nevertheless that neither was equal in the sight of the Anglo-Saxon, by holding separate services for British and Indians.

European culture and education in India were not disseminated exclusively through missions; the system of instruction established by the British government was largely responsible for the spread of Western civilization. The growth of nationalism and anti-foreign feeling among the Indians was stimulated by the errors of the British administration and by the reactions of the politically minded minority to world-happenings, but a religion which preached the equality of all men in the sight of God, and practised the opposite, was condemned by all thinking natives.

Japan soon became strong enough to emancipate herself from all foreign political influence and in Nippon the adoption of Christianity was a matter either of sincere conviction or of practical expediency. Japanese antagonism to its teachings is therefore not very deep-rooted, nor has it any particular connection with anti-foreign feeling produced by racial discrimination against her citizens in certain countries.

It is in China, where Christian institutions have played so vital a part in stimulating the renascence, that we find the most intense opposition to Christianity. There are in that country today more than fifty colleges under missionary direction. Tsing-Hwa University, north of Peking, was founded with a fund of $10,000,000 remitted by the United States from its share of the Boxer indemnity; the institution known as Yale-in-China, Canton Christian College, and many others, have trained thousands of Chinese lads. Justly or unjustly, the Young Men's Christian Associations established through much of China, have been accused of open sympathy with the Nationalists and even with Communism.

The knowledge of practical politics and organization which they had gained by study of Western systems of government in Christian educational institutions, enabled the newly formed Kuomintang to overthrow the Manchu Dynasty and establish the Chinese Republic in 1911. The student movement, or "New Tide," which has done so much to transform native mentality, as well as the movement for mass education, owes its origin largely to the infiltration of European ideas through Christian teachings.

In spite of these patent facts there is a general tendency among Chinese leaders, radical and conservative alike, to resent the influence or interference of Christian workers in Chinese affairs. This point of view was expressed very clearly in a recent speech made in Peking by Chang Tso-lin, the dictator of Manchuria and head of the group least antagonistic to foreigners, whose son and heir is a Christian:

"Missionaries in China," he said, "would render a greater

service to their cause as well as to their converts, if they would continue their activities in religious teachings only, or that which would be still better, to humanitarian work. When the missionaries mix themselves in Chinese politics they leave their proper sphere, and if in consequence they find themselves in difficult situations they have but themselves to blame. Mission workers who are in my territories depending upon my jurisdiction, have nothing to fear in regard to my attitude to them; I have always assured them my protection; but they must not forget that religion, in my opinion, is a question of personal conviction in some cases, and of tradition in others."

Here we should note that the work of medical missionaries in all Eastern countries cannot be too much praised; as individuals they have been among the most heroic and the most disinterested of all mission workers. The Catholics were the pioneers in medical as well as evangelical services and teachings in Asia, but they were followed by medical workers, both men and women, of all denominations, who not infrequently gave their lives to stem some terrible epidemic.

In 1925, the medical staff maintained by British and American Protestant missions in the Far East, native and foreign, including nurses as well as doctors, numbered 4,165. There were 640 hospitals having a capacity of 25,601 beds. The Evangelical staff for Asia had 16,524 workers and 1,978 stations. There were 299 Bible training schools, and 19 medical schools. When we realize that trachoma, malaria, hookworm, social disease, plague, and leprosy are still prevalent in the Far East, we can appreciate, as do the Chinese, the immense value of medical missions and of such institutions as the great college and hospital established in Peking by the Rockefeller Foundation for the training of medical men in combating Oriental diseases.

Evangelical work also made considerable progress in the twentieth century. The forward-looking Chinese with their usual reasonableness were beginning to wonder if Christian ethics might not prove a sound basis for the new social structure they hoped to build in China; such men as Sun Yat-sen and General Feng were Christians.

We have seen that the Chinese were at first inclined to think their own culture superior to that of the West, and that they at first imposed unequal terms on the "barbarians" who sought to trade with them. But these same barbarians kept up their efforts at penetration until they had reversed their relationship with China, and then it was they who dictated unequal conditions! It was not, however, until the missionaries who came with the foreigners as bearers of a spiritual message began to impress on the Chinese the essential superiority of Western culture, of Western Christian civilization, that their resentment crystallized into an anti-foreign movement which was moral as well as political, and which reached its climax in the Boxer Rebellion.

Just before the Great War the leaders of Chinese thought began to see the necessity for remodelling their own political and social system. Many of them looked to Christianity for material and moral assistance in their efforts to find a common denominator for intercourse with the West. But the war swept all such ideas into the discard.

The mere fact that the Western nations who claimed to have superior ethical systems were obliged to resort to wholesale slaughter to settle their differences offended Chinese reasonableness and love of compromise. Impressions of European morals and customs received by Chinese soldiers and labor corps with the Allied armies not unnaturally conflicted with the teachings of the missionaries! Finally the Peace of Versailles, which failed to bring about what seemed to the Chinese an equitable readjustment of such burning questions as Treaty Revision and a recognition of racial equality, completed the disillusionment of the intellectuals who had welcomed Christian culture. In their eyes the Allies, who represented all that was best in Christendom, had failed to live up to the principles of Christ.

Though there were other contributing factors, the identification of Nationalism with anti-Christian feeling by the students who play such a conspicuous part in contemporary Chinese politics was partly due to this disillusionment. The students and the intellectuals are full of the scepticism which is part and parcel of the revolutionary doctrines that have spread among all the peoples of the earth since the upheavals in Europe. Anti-Christian propaganda is one of the weapons of revolution; there is nothing new about it. The Jacobins used it in France in 1789, and the Communists are employing it today.

We have elsewhere discussed the political side of Russian Bolshevist propaganda, and we shall later describe its force as an ethical movement, so it need only be mentioned here as one of the counter-irritants to Christianity. The moral and political influence in China of the doctrines of Lenin have been greatly overestimated.

When the political readjustment of the relations between China and the great Powers is made—for economic factors more powerful than any moral or racial antagonism press for its solution—it will be possible to gauge the influence of Christianity in China. The fact that recently missionaries have been forced to abandon their charges and leave the country, may mean much or nothing. This seems clear, however—Christian ethics, much less Christian dogma, will never become really assimilated in China until missionaries and politics and self-interest are definitely disassociated and their work and the dissemination of the culture of Christianity are virtually in Chinese hands.

It would be difficult to estimate how deeply doctrinal Christianity has struck its roots into the masses of the people; nor can we foretell what transformation may be wrought on its ethics and dogma by contact with Buddhist and Confucian teachings.

In India there has been a movement to establish an autonomous Anglican Church which resulted in presenting an Indian Church Bill to the British Parliament; many people claim that such a measure would tend to create an Oriental church far removed from Western conceptions of Christianity. This attitude towards the church question, clearly reveals one of the most important, perhaps the most fundamental causes of anti-Christian feeling, not only in India but in many parts of Asia. The following passages from an article on the subject of the Indian Church Bill, which appeared in the London *Weekly Times* of the spring of 1927, contain an excellent exposition of this very point of view:

The Anglican communion is in many ways parallel to the British Empire. . . . It is natural enough that India should desire a freedom like that which obtains in Canada and South Africa: and the

growing spirit of Nationalism makes the demand all the more urgent
to those who spend their lives in an endeavour to persuade the
inhabitants of that country that the Christian religion is universal
in character and equally suitable for men of all races and colours.
But there are special circumstances that impose caution and of
these the chief is that revealed by the census of 1921, which shows
that 108,759 members of the church in India are British, while
there are no fewer than 387,160 Indian Christians of that church.

In these circumstances some anxiety on the part of the British
that they might presently find themselves compelled to submit to
an unwelcome transformation of religious traditions and customs,
is not entirely groundless. The proposed rules [safeguarding
Anglican orthodoxy among the British congregations in India]
are designed to set at rest that anxiety. . . . It is by no means
clear, however, that they will form a permanent security. . . . There
are in short certain peculiarities of Indian religion that cannot be
overlooked when efforts are made to forecast the consequences of
autonomy. Syncretism in religion is inherent in the Indian mind.
Sikhism is largely colored by Moslem ethics, and Mohammedanism
in India bears many traces of Hindu influence. It is true that
Hinduism has been profoundly modified during the last fifty years
by Christian influences. But there are many Englishmen in India
who watch with anxiety the whole movement for autonomy . . .
they cannot conceal their fear that a church entirely dominated by
Indians might move far away from Christian fundamentals. The
criticisms that the new proposals will have to meet will not only
come from those who desire to preserve for themselves accustomed
forms of worship—they will be formulated by those who know
how many delusions are propagated in the East today under the
misapprehension that they are Christian.

The rigidity of the sectarian point of view so prevalent among
evangelical missionaries, particularly those of the Protestant denominations, as expressed in the above quotation, creates intense
antagonism. Not only does it force the Asiatic mentality to
accept the European conception of Christ and His teachings, but
it prevents the genuine assimilation of Christianity. Will it
matter if Hindu, Moslem, or Confucian influence creep into the
Eastern interpretation of the Christian dogma? Have not pagan
festivals and even pagan beliefs become interwoven with Christianity in Western countries?

This attitude has also deepened the racial gulf between the White and the Colored races. If we add to it the comparison by Orientals of Christ's teachings with their application by Western Powers in their relations with the East, we shall understand the bitter antagonism to Christianity and its association with Nationalism.

At the same time we must never forget that Europeanization, which has come through the medium of Christian culture, is tinged with the ethics of Christianity. They have, perhaps insensibly, profoundly modified the mentality and the outlook of the Oriental.

MOHAMMED

Among the sights of modern Paris there is nothing more beautiful or more impressive than the great Mosque recently completed. Within its walls five thousand of the followers of Mohammed can gather at the same time in prayer. From its minaret, five times a day, the muezzin reminds all within earshot that there is but one God, and Mohammed is his prophet. The casual visitor who goes to see the Mosque is likely to wonder why so much money was spent on a Moslem place of worship in an overwhelmingly Christian country and he cannot understand why such a huge mosque should have been necessary in Paris, unless it was meant as a subtle tribute to the amour-propre of France's Moslem subjects. He would probably not believe that the number of Mohammedans who go to Paris in a year is greater than the total of the Islamic pilgrims to Mecca. But such is the case!

The fact is symbolic of the change that has come over the Moslem world. It is shaking off the spiritual lethargy of centuries and something very analogous to the Reformation which swept Europe in the sixteenth century is taking place in Islam. Just as the Reformation was part of Europe's revolt against Medievalism, this Islamic revival represents a phase of the Asiatic Renascence.

The present ferment is very different from the pan-Islamic movement of a quarter of a century ago, which was based on the old ideal of the temporal ascendancy of Islam. It is purely spiritual and intellectual. The progressive Moslem no longer believes in a temporal leader of the faith. He is a Nationalist. He does not accept the old traditions and customs that have grown up around the doctrines of Mohammed; he challenges the ancient dogma and ritual, and the old social concepts that have become identified with Islam. He even applies what was known a generation ago in Christian circles, as the higher criticism, to the teachings of the Koran.

This wide-awake Moslem of today is beginning to realize the defects in his own religious system which have helped to keep his co-religionists behind the Western world in social and material development, and he is remedying those defects. The result of his effort is already noticeable; Islam is a force to be reckoned with in the new Asia, notwithstanding that it no longer possesses a temporal head and that the number of Asiatic countries acknowledging Mohammedanism as the state religion has decreased within the last few years.

In tracing the course of events in Asia during the last decade we have learned how the Ottoman Empire, whose sovereign was the Khalif, the temporal and spiritual head of Islam, was occupied and partitioned by the Allies after the Great War. From its ruins have sprung the Republic of Turkey, a purely secular state, and the mandated territories in Mesopotamia, Syria, and Palestine, in which full religious liberty exists. The Moslems of India, China, and Central Asia, who constitute possibly one-half of the 235,000,000 followers of the Prophet, no longer have a common head who is a symbol of the political and spiritual unity of Islam. Persia, Afghanistan, Turkey and the Arabian Kingdom of Nejd, are the only independent Asiatic countries with Moslem rulers, and even these are reconciling the traditional concepts of Islam with Westernization and modern ideals of social and economic progress.

The spiritual transformation of Moslem countries is necessarily bound up with political changes, most of which we have dealt with elsewhere; but there are phases of this transformation which are not necessarily political. Among the more important are the attitude of the Moslem world towards the Khalifate, the new reform movements, the radical changes in educational methods and social standards in Mohammedan countries, and the influence of Islam on the race question.

The problem of the Khalifate is new in its present form, but it is not new in Islam. The first disputes with regard to it arose soon after the death of Mohammed, who was the temporal as well as the spiritual ruler of his people. Naturally it devolved on them to choose his successor, who was known as the Khalifa—literally in Arabic, "substitute," for no one in their estimation could replace the Prophet of the Almighty. If Mohammed had left a son, the succession would have been a simple matter, but as he had no male heirs various members of his family quarrelled among themselves over the leadership.

The first schism in the faith was caused by the followers of Ali, his son-in-law, who was murdered by a rival claimant. These followers founded the great sect of the Shiah Moslems, who compose the overwhelming majority of the Faithful in Persia. It was not long before wars broke out between rival Khalifs, in which the most powerful vindicated his claim and imposed his authority on the vanquished faction. As the Arab Empire grew and extended its boundaries, the authority of the Khalif grew correspondingly, and the Khalifate came to have more and more political, and less and less spiritual, significance, until after the fall of the Baghdad Khalifate it shifted from one to another of the various sovereigns of Islamic peoples.

At one time the title of All-Moslem Khalif was claimed by the Khalif of Damascus, at others by the Sultans of Egypt. With the conquest of this country by the Ottoman ruler Selim the Magnificent, in 1517, the title together with the sword and mantle of the Prophet, became the property of the Ottoman Dynasty, and the Sultan became the Supreme Khalif, Commander of the Faithful. There were before and have been since then, many other Khalifs: the Mogul Conquerors of India, the Sultans of Morocco, the Moslem rulers of Spain, and other Moslem sovereigns from time to time have assumed the title, on the ground of descent from the family of Mohammed. But in general the rulers recognized as Khalifs by the Islamic world at large have been those who have fulfilled two conditions—they must be entirely independent of any foreign Power and they must have political

ASIA REBORN

control of Medina and Mecca, the birthplace and sepulchre respectively, of Mohammed.

For more than three hundred years the Ottoman Sultans fulfilled these conditions, but the dissolution of the Empire and the
growing conviction in Turkey that the existence of the Khalifate
precluded any real reforms, led to its arbitrary abolition by the
Turkish Parliament March 3, 1924. This created a situation
not without parallel in history but which marked a turning point
in the development of Islam.

Only twenty years previously, Abdul Hamid II, the Sultan-
Khalif of the Ottoman Empire, had sought to bring about a great
Pan-Islamic federation based on the spiritual and political unity
of Islam. This scheme had failed largely because of the nationalism which began to take its place in Moslem countries in
the years preceding the war. It received its death-blow with the
refusal of the Moslem peoples to declare a Jehad, or Holy War,
against the imperialistic Allied Powers for the benefit of Germany, at the beginning of the Great War.

Nationalism was immensely stimulated by the war and post-
war happenings: when the Khalifate was abolished, national
feeling had grown so strong in the various Mohammedan countries that the idea of a Khalif with temporal powers had become
distasteful to liberal Moslems, while the remainder could not
agree on the choice of any one of the few independent Islamic
sovereigns. Two All-Moslem conferences, one held at Cairo and
another last year at Mecca, to discuss the situation, failed to reach
a solution.

Meanwhile Hussein, king of the Hedjaz, had attempted to arro-
gate the title of Khalif after the abolition of the Turkish Khalifate
without any support other than that of his own subjects and
those of the adjacent kingdoms of Iraq and Transjordania, ruled
over by his two sons under British protection. He had received
no approval from other Moslems, and he soon lost control of the
Holy Cities to Ibn Saoud, ruler of the central Arabian kingdom
of Nejd and leader of the puritan sect of Wahabis.

Ibn Saoud was, and still is, a possible candidate for the Khalifate, as are Amanullah, King of Afghanistan, and the Sultan of
Egypt. But neither they nor any other candidate has succeeded

in winning recognition from the rest of the Moslem world. This is due to the fact that the old pan-Islamic ideal is being supplanted by a new spiritual ideal which has not yet found its personification in any Islamic leader. The new trends in Islam indicate an extraordinary vitality. They can truly be said to foreshadow the Moslem Reformation.

In Turkey a transformation has already been brought about in the church by a political movement. With the establishment of the Republic under the dictatorship of Mustapha Kemal—one of the great autocrats produced by the war for "democracy"—Church and State were separated, the government completely secularized, the old Moslem code abolished, the functions of the clergy regulated and defined, principles of religious liberty established, and the burden of maintaining its spiritual influence was placed squarely on the shoulders of the Church.

The immediate result has been to cause profound bewilderment, even consternation among devout Moslems. Prayer in the mosques for the shadowy abstraction of the Turkish Republic could not take the place of prayer for the Khalif, who was the Prophet's substitute on earth, and the many innovations in social customs brought from the West were directly contrary to the dictates of the Sunna, the ecclesiastical interpretations of the Koran.

Among the young Turkish intellectuals there is a tendency towards disbelief in all religion. Freedom of the press with regard to religious matters has brought about a wave of destructive criticism, so that the rôle of Turkey as far as reformation within the Church is concerned, is not constructive, but rather the reverse.

The three centres of genuine reform in Islam are in Arabia, where the Wahabite movement is making tremendous progress, in India, where the Ahmadiya sect and the Aligarh movement exert a profound influence, and El Azhar University in Cairo, where the apologists of the traditional faith are employing subtle arguments to prove that it is not incompatible with modern ideals. As we are not concerned with Islam in Africa, we cannot follow the spread of the new movements which are winning many adherents in Algeria, Tunis, and Morocco, or the revival of missionary fervor which has won thousands of converts in Equatorial Africa.

The Wahabi schism is not new; we have elsewhere discussed its political aspects and the personality of its present leader, Ibn Saoud. It is spreading rapidly in Arabia, although it is bitterly opposed by Orthodox Moslems. The Ahmadiya movement, founded nearly a century ago by one Mirza Ghulam Ahmad of Quadian who proclaimed himself a new Messiah, borrowed much from Christianity. It has many followers not only in India, but also in the West. Woking, near London, is the centre of Ahmadiya activities in Europe. The *Islamic Review,* one of the best Moslem periodicals, published in English, is the principal organ of the followers of the prophet of Quadian. They have also, under the auspices of Lord Headley, an English Moslem Peer, produced The Woking Koran in parallel English and Arabic texts, with commentaries, similar to the Oxford Bible.

The Aligarh School, which owes its origin to Sir Synd Ahmed Khan, founder of Aligarh University, is a rationalist movement within Islam, that seeks to interpret the Koran in the light of modern science. Within recent years some Moslem leaders have conceived the idea of adapting Christian missionary methods to spreading the faith of Mohammed. In Lahore there is a Moslem Book and Tract Depot, and an English convert has produced an Islamic prayer-book and catechism.

All these movements, while significant as showing the renewed vitality of Islam, have not stirred the masses of Moslems in Asia as have the radical changes in manners and customs and educational methods, brought about by contacts with Europe. These changes have nearly all come about within the last few years, and they have been so rapid in some countries as to be revolutionary.

The Moslem peoples of Asia were slow to establish contacts with the West. After they had ceased to expand westward they remained very much shut up within themselves. In the countries where they formed a small minority, such as China, they clung all the more to their traditions, and for a long time they remained impervious to Western ideas and European culture. Although their isolation had been broken before the beginning of the Great War by the impact of European imperialism and commercial penetration, it was not until the world conflict forced them into intimate contact with the West that they began their social and cultural transformation.

The tremendous improvement in methods of transportation stimulated by war necessities was responsible more than any other single factor for the intellectual awakening in Western Asia. Of late years the various countries in that part of the world have been overrun by military forces of the Western Powers, and invaded by European travellers. Automobiles have taken the place of horses, mules, and camels; roads have been built on ancient caravan trails, railways have been constructed along old trade-routes.

Nationalism is largely the outcome of the increased facilities of communication which have transformed tribal loyalty and local patriotism into race patriotism. They have enabled the inhabitants of Moslem countries to travel and to draw comparisons, which have opened their eyes to the defects and weaknesses of traditional Islam.

Since the close of the war there has been a tremendous change of attitude on the part of Moslems towards European education. In Turkey, Westernization has been made compulsory by Kemal Pasha, but in other countries, where no such coercion has been exercised on the people, there are spontaneous movements towards the abolition or modification of reactionary customs, and a genuine thirst for the mechanical and technical knowledge, the education, of the West.

In Arabia Deserta, Sheikhs move their tents and their households in automobiles; and they send their sons to the American University at Beirut or the new Moslem University in Baghdad. Ibn Saoud has founded a modern college in his desert capital of Riyadh, and has established a public health service in his dominions. At Mecca he uses a telephone to communicate with his various ministers.

In this connection a story is told of him which bears repeating: One day he received a visit from an old Bedouin Sheikh and while his visitor was present he had occasion to use the telephone. Noticing from the expression on the Bedouin's face that he disapproved vehemently of such inventions of Satan, Ibn Saoud took up the receiver, but before beginning his conversation he repeated a verse of the Koran. When he had finished he turned to the old Arab. "See," he exclaimed, "how a good Moslem can turn the devices of the infidels to his advantage. No harm can come to him who uses them in the name of Allah, the Compassionate, the Merciful!"

The disposition on the part of many Moslem leaders to do away with traditional superstitions in the name of religion itself, is aiding the abolishment of most reactionary customs and giving new vitality to the Faith. It is undermining the strongholds of Moslem conservatism even in such countries as Persia and Afghanistan. Popular education, the position of women, the legal and judiciary procedure, are all being radically transformed within the frame of Islam.

We now come to its most vital principle—the one which more than any other tends to preserve its unity in spite of the uncertainty and the problems caused by the Khalifate dilemma and the impact of modern disbelief. It is the attitude of Islam to the race question.

Mohammed, who undoubtedly aimed at the establishment of a religious system under which the Arab tribes should unite for mutual protection and forget their feuds, perhaps even more than at their conversion to belief in a single God, emphasized the principle of racial equality. The only dividing line between Moslems and other members of the human family was the line of the Faith. All men were brothers in Islam. Thus we find in the Koran:

The Faithful are brethren. Therefore make peace between your brothers and fear God. . . . O Believers, let not men laugh men to scorn who haply may be better than themselves . . . the noblest of you in the sight of God is the most God-fearing.

The spread of Islam went hand in hand with the growth of the Arab Empire by war and conquest; but, once conquered and converted, the vanquished peoples were assimilated on an equal basis. While the methods of government that grew up in Moslem lands were almost invariably despotic, the Moslem social system was the most democratic in the whole world, and it still is. Nowhere except in Mohammedan countries have there been so many instances of the humblest persons aspiring to the highest rank.

In Islam there is absolutely no distinction of race or color—Negroes, Mongols, Turks, Persians, Arabs, Berbers, Indians, Chinese, Malays—all are equal. All have an equal chance of social and political advancement. Consequently many Moslem peoples have been considerably modified ethnically by the mixture of several racial strains. It was no uncommon thing in Arabia or Turkey for the head of a ruling family to acknowledge as his heir a child born of a Negro slave. Among the tribal population the race-strain has been kept much purer; this, however, is not so much from pride of race as from a desire to increase the wealth and influence of the tribal clan by concentration.

The Turks, in common with other Moslem peoples, have not possessed any hereditary nobility. There were never any princes in Turkey except those of the ruling dynasty. There were no surnames except in a few families of foreign origin. Therefore today, when race prejudice plays such an important part in the revolt of the more backward peoples of the East against European imperialism, Moslem propaganda is tremendously reinforced by the racial democracy of Islam. This is the explanation of the success of Moslem missionaries in the colonies and possessions of the great Powers in which the race issue has become acute, as among Negroes under British, French, or Italian rule in Africa.

Islam serves as a bond to hold together many widely different peoples and cultures, and it has made Nationalism in various Moslem countries part of a great common movement for race equality which has supplanted or rather absorbed and given new life to the old ideal of religious unity. Today the leaders of the New Islam are claiming, and not without some justice, that they are nearer in spirit to the ideal of a League of Nations, than the European Powers, who while accepting in principle the idea of an association of nations on an equal footing, are tolerating within their own boundaries or colonial possessions, conditions that make such an association impossible.

The attitude of Americans towards the Negroes and the Filipinos and of the average Englishman to the Yellow, Black and Brown subjects of the British Empire; the color-line drawn by the West in religion and politics; the self-conscious assumption of essential superiority of the Nordic races; and the refusal by most Western peoples to admit that intellectual equality presupposes a corresponding social equality, have created a tremendous current of sympathy in favor of the religion which condemns these injustices. They have helped to cement the bond uniting Moslem peoples, which is sufficiently powerful to level all differences of culture and, to a great extent, of politics. It is the bond of democracy deep-rooted in the Faith.

LENIN

To many people, doubtless, the inclusion of Lenin with Christ and Mohammed to form a Messianic triumvirate whose teachings have helped to stir the hidden springs of the Asiatic Renascence, will seem monstrous, even blasphemous! In the minds of millions the name of Lenin is synonymous with the social and political principles of Bolshevism, which are irrevocably opposed to Western civilization and tradition.

Lenin is the antithesis of all their preconceived ideas of society and government. His application of the academic materialism of Karl Marx to the ends of a bloody and terrible revolution has even created sturdy opposition among Western socialists who believe in the class war, the abolition of private property, and the rule of the proletariat. To those steeped in "bourgeois" ideals and religious dogmas, Lenin is the Antichrist.

The political expansion of the new Soviet Empire in Asia, the anti-foreign propaganda, the ceaseless warfare against the capitalist Powers of the West waged through their Asiatic possessions, are commonly attributed to the desire of the Communist oligarchy, which now rules Russia, to weaken these same Powers by destroying their economic bases in Asia and thus pave the way for world revolution.

Personally, as I have tried to demonstrate in writing of Russia's return to Asia, I regard Soviet Imperialism in the Orient as a natural consequence of the influence of climate, geography, race instinct, and economic needs. The impulse to regain the old frontiers, to press south to Constantinople, India, and the Yangtze valley and the ice-free ports of the Pacific, is as natural to Russia, as the instinctive control of sea communications is to Great Britain, or the urge to seek new markets and raw material is to Japan. No change in the form of government in any country appreciably alters the fundamental needs of its people.

If the spread of Bolshevism in Asia were entirely due to anti-capitalist fervor or Soviet Imperialism, it would have to be considered as a political or a revolutionary social movement; but its roots go far deeper!

Bolshevism, which in its more spiritual or ethical aspects might better be termed Leninism, is essentially an achievement of the Asiatic Renascence. It has brought about the Asiatization of Russia, one of the historic breaks in the organization of human society. Today there is a widespread movement not only among the Communists, but among Russians who profess profound abhorrence of Marxist doctrines, to regard the Revolution as Russia's revolt against Europe!

These men, who belong to every class from prince to peasant, and who profess every political creed from Monarchism to Anarchism, have inherited the ideals of the Slavophiles, of whom the best-known to Westerners is Dostoievsky. The Slavophiles always maintained that Russia did not belong to Europe, and that her real destiny was in Asia. More than half a century ago, Danilevsky wrote: "Russian genius is the antithesis of that of Europe. Europeanization has proved a pitfall for the Slav." According to Slavophile scholars, Russia was an Asiatic country until the days of Peter the Great, when she was subjected to an unnatural process of Westernization. They never ceased to preach the return to Asia, which Lenin accomplished.

The present-day Slavophiles, who call themselves Eurasians, while abjuring the political system of Lenin, find many of their ideals realized in the actual program of the Bolsheviks. Their point of view has been well expressed in a recent magazine article by a well-known Russian writer, M. Nikitin:

According to the Eurasians [he says], a Germano-Latin civilization cannot lay claim to universality. Russia is a world apart, a

Eurasian system: a mixture of races and beliefs. She is the centre
of the ocean-continent of Asia of which Europe is but a promontory,
one of the regions in the periphery of the Old World which it is
convenient to treat as an entity. The rationalism, the juridicalism,
the machinism of the West, are incompatible with the Russian
mentality. Never since the days of Peter the Great, who deflected
the march of Russian destiny, was the opportunity so favorable
as now for a national revival. It is worthy of note that Trotzky
in his "October" seeks to prove that Lenin, for the first time since
Peter, represented the real orientation of the Russian people. This
is not the only point of contact between the Eurasians, the Emigrés,
and the Bolsheviks. They all declare that nothing is to be expected
from the West, which wishes to exploit the weakness of convalescent
Russia—that Russia should place herself at the head of the exploited peoples, beside the Asiatics. Nevertheless [he concludes],
the Eurasians declare that they will have nothing to do with the
Bolsheviks.

The above statement is worthy of consideration, for it indicates the profound sympathy of the most anti-Bolshevik elements
among the Russians with certain aspects of Lenin's ideology,
which was Asiatic in its inspiration. By comparison of the ideals
of the Eurasians in Russia with those of the Nationalist groups
and the pan-Asiatic enthusiasts in Asia, we can understand the
fundamental appeal of Bolshevism to Asiatics and its influence on
the Renascence. A political and social ideology which sponsors
such readjustments as those above outlined, between East and
West, is a powerful stimulus to the new movements that are
transforming the old Asia.

We need only recall the political history of almost any Oriental
country during the last ten years to appreciate the moral force
of Lenin's alignment of Russia with the exploited peoples of
Asia. The virtual boycott of Russia after the establishment of
the Soviet Republic was a physical demonstration of the break
between Slav and European; it produced a sense of kinship with
Russians among the Asiatic peoples, who also felt themselves
barred from a place in the Western family of nations.

Something deeper than political expediency prompted the alliance of the Kemalist Turks with the Bolsheviks in 1920, and the Entente of Russia with Turkey, Persia, and Afghanistan in 1926.

To Moslems, who are more positivists than other Orientals, the appeal of Leninism is twofold: it is a practical aid to the national aspirations of Moslem peoples, and it professes the principle of racial equality which, as we have seen, is one of the fundamental teachings of Mohammed.

The Japanese, who embody intense materialism in many of their social relationships with a passionate idealism where the future of their race is concerned, have also found much in common with Russia in spite of the wide political differences between the systems of government in Moscow and Tokyo. The Russo-Japanese treaty was the outcome of Japan's isolation from Europe following the rupture of her alliance with England, and her exclusion from America, which was, perhaps, the most momentous international blunder since the Treaty of Versailles.

Economic and commercial considerations played an important part in the declaration of this truce between Slav and Mongol, but the Pan-Asiatic aspirations of both countries helped to bring it about.

The influence of Bolshevist propaganda in China, divested of its "Realpolitik" has stimulated the Asiatization of the ideas absorbed by the young Chinese educated in European institutions. They find little that is essentially new in the doctrines of Lenin, but much that can be traced to the fountain-head of Chinese civilization. "Communism," they say, "was practised in our villages thousands of years ago," which is quite true.

The peasants of rural India and many nomad tribes of Central Asia are not at all unfamiliar with the idea of land and property held in common or with the principles of vocational representation, but there are other tenets of Communism which they are less likely to understand. The materialistic political economy of the Marxist is utterly incomprehensible to the great mass of Asiatics: Lenin was fully aware of this fact, and he sought to win the East not through political propaganda, but through the revival of all the racial, moral, and spiritual ties between Russia and Asia.

Nationalism, although directly contrary to the fundamental

principles of the internationalist creed of Marx, is the usual medium for the propagation of Bolshevist ideals. The new Russia is guide, teacher, and prophet, to the new East. There is something of pentecostal fervor in this aspect of Bolshevism. It is stirring Asia with the force of a political evangel, particularly in India and the Far East, where the existing religious systems have little influence on social or political life. The doctrines of Buddha teach a passive individualism; the worshippers of the old Hindu gods are prisoners of their mystic idealism; the pacific philosophy of Confucius preaches moral force.

All these ideals are negative in so far as their influence on collective action is concerned. We have seen how Gandhi's India could not bring Swaraj—self-government: how Confucian China was unable to resist the impact of the West against her civilization until she had to a certain degree assimilated the more positive ethics of Christianity and Leninism.

The direct effect of Communist propaganda in Asia is not so easy to determine as the influence of the Eurasian ideals of Lenin and his disciples. Political Communism in its modern form is possible only where there are industrialism, capitalism, and all the elements of the class struggle. They exist in very few localities in Asia.

Japan has an industrial proletariat; there is a comparatively small industrial population in India and China. Even in the manufacturing centres of the last two countries class-consciousness has not developed to any great extent, though perhaps it is found in Japan. Nationalism as an issue in all of them, temporarily at least, overshadows other political movements. Even Communist agitation is largely focused on the stimulation of anti- . Western feeling.

In the remaining countries of Asia, Bolshevist doctrines *per se* have made little headway. Among tribespeople where Communism exists in its primitive forms, the political current of the moment is towards a democratic organization, and the establishment of the principle of private property. The inexorable march of material progress has created new needs and new desires foreshadowing the development of capitalism. The destruction of the ancient feudal systems in Central Asiatic countries and the inauguration of constitutional government, have tended to produce the same result.

In the Soviet Republics of Middle Asia there is great dissatisfaction over the rule of the Bolshevist oligarchy, which with its despotic assumption of dictatorship seems to them not radical, but reactionary. Something of the same feeling was doubtless in the minds of the Kuomintang leaders in China who rebelled against the arbitrary control of their party by Bolshevik "advisers."

If the Asiatics accept Bolshevism as a political system, they will transmute the principles laid down by Marx into something more suited to the Asiatic mentality, but the mystic faith of Lenin and the Messianic rôle of the new Eurasia which points the way towards the fulfilment of what Asia believes to be her destiny, is deep-rooted in the minds of all Orientals.

It has nothing to do with the Machiavellian designs of the Communist faction. Unless we grasp its significance, we can never hope to understand the Asiatic Renascence.

Chapter Fifteen

THE RIGHT TO GROW

IN THE explanatory statement at the beginning of this book
I was rash enough to promise to give my readers an account
of happenings in Asia since the Armistice. This I have endeavored to do. But I have an uneasy remembrance of certain questions which constitute the first paragraph. They are the stock in
trade of the racialists, whose views I do not share; nevertheless,
as I am well aware that there are some people who may expect me
to answer them in my own fashion, I shall do so.

It is certain that we shall never see a united East against a
united West, nor will those who come after us!

Since the Armistice we have begun to observe the fruition of
Nationalism and its bastard offspring, Self Determination, in
Asia. In some countries it has been bitter fruit, in others nationalism has produced vigorous young nations on the ruins of old
civilizations. There is a tendency towards the federation or alliance of peoples related by blood or common interests and antagonisms, which has given rise to current speculations as to the
possibility of an Asiatic League of Nations or even a United
States of Asia.

Scattered over the Asiatic continent are small groups of idealists who believe in Asiatic unity. Some years ago they organized
a Greater Asia Association, under whose auspices the Pan-Asiatic
Congress, which met in Nagasaki in the summer of 1926, attempted to launch a genuine political movement for united action
by Asiatic peoples—against Europe! Nevertheless, the differences
which developed even among the small number of intellectuals who
composed the conference proved that the slogan of "Asia for the
Asiatics" has just about as much significance as "Europe for
the Europeans!" There are wider divergencies in civilization, culture, and ideals between various Asiatic countries than between
the States of Europe.

A future Asiatic League of Nations is not an impossibility, but for the present most Oriental peoples are absorbed in the many phases of their own national and racial revivals. Many of them have not yet stabilized their own institutions nor co-ordinated their own national impulses. They are only just beginning to form political ententes and alliances with their immediate neighbors, or countries belonging to their own racial groups. Even these groups present a solid front largely because of their common antagonism to Europe's encroachments on their growth.

Moreover, the amazing progress of modern science, which is breaking down all barriers of distance and inaccessibility, is tending more and more to create surface uniformity the world over, and to establish economic ties which cannot be broken without bringing about a cataclysm which would involve all humanity. The various parts of the globe are becoming economically interdependent. There are certain basic raw materials which all nations now in process of modernization will require in common with those which have apparently reached the apex of material and technical development. No country which possesses its share of raw materials and still lacks the ability to exploit them, can escape Economic Imperialism.

Japan in the Pacific, and Great Britain at the other extremity of the ocean-continent, comprising Asia and Europe, cannot feed their own people! They are inevitably committed to Economic Imperialism in their respective spheres, until some form of international co-operation counteracts the instinctive race-movements and supplants the present world-competition. It matters little whether such Imperialism is right or wrong in principle—it will exist as long as it is necessary to ensure the normal growth of peoples.

If we could look far enough into the future we should probably be able to foresee the establishment of a World Federation based on economic needs. Before this comes to pass there will doubtless be many alignments and re-alignments in Asia. The countries now under European control will gradually assert their independence, as they develop national solidarity and become better equipped materially. There are many ways of bringing about such independence without resorting to war with Western countries infinitely superior to the East in technical knowledge and resources.

This the West is beginning to learn since China is emancipating herself from unequal treaties, through creating economic difficulties for the Treaty Powers by maintaining a state of political chaos; and since Turkey turned defeat into victory by playing the European Powers against one another at Lausanne. Battleships, machine-guns and air-fleets are not the only weapons in the struggle for Racial Equality and the right to National Existence!

The race-problem, involving the often debated question as to the future of European civilization, has been too much stressed; or so it seems to me. I lay no claim to scientific knowledge of such matters, but as the whole story of the human race is the story of the slow assimilation or differentiation of races to form new types and new divisions in the human family, I do not see how we can hope to arrest or divert whatever process of evolution may be going on in the world today.

There is no such thing as essential inferiority or superiority in the race question. The domination of any one group or type is due to the operation of natural laws. I believe that race instinct will take care of that question, and that our anxiety as to the future of the White races is rather puerile. Certainly it should never have been allowed to become a vital issue in world-politics. As for European civilization, it is being assimilated and Asiatized by the peoples of the Orient—a fact which in itself holds the promise of something better than humanity has ever known.

All history is the record of the rise and fall of various civilizations, each of which has assimilated and carried forward something of the vanished culture. Today we seem to have reached a state in human progress which has no parallel in history. Modern Science has created contacts that open the way for the development of a world-civilization to which every race may contribute something of its own peculiar genius.

I have defined the present ferment in Asia in my account of the movements and events in each country since the World War. It is not such as to put fear of any sort into the minds of people who will take the trouble to analyze it. The Asian ferment is the result of exercising what Admiral Mahan, more than a quarter of a century ago, termed, "the right to grow," of the world in general.

The tendency of the West has been to overlook the fact that Asia is included in this world; but we shall have nothing to fear from her if we admit her right to development. Only I must insist on the importance of our application to her of the "live and let live" axiom we are so fond of applying to our own problems.

Common fairness, common humanity, and common sense counsel us to concede Asia's right to grow.

THE END

INDEX

INDEX

385

INDEX

296, 297, 302, 313, 315, 316, 322, 333, 334, 336, 317
Yellow bloc, 236
"Yellow Peril," 281, 293
Yi, Prince, 309
Yoffe, Mr., 287, 288, 325
Yoshihito, Emperor, 303
Yoshizawa, M., 295
Younghusband, Sir Francis, 32, 218

Young Men's Christian Association, 356
Young Turks, 36, 46, 66, 70, 92, 112, 250
Yuan Shih-kai, 39, 62, 63, 317
Yugoslavia, 99

Zinoviev, Gregory, 248
Zionist Movement, 165, 166

Printed in the USA
CPSIA information can be obtained
at www.ICGtesting.com
LVHW031927060823
754442LV00007B/169